WHAT EVERY VETERAN SHOULD KNOW

89th EDITION

BOOK PRICE - $30.00 – INCLUDES SHIPPING

This is the 89th Edition of the book "WHAT EVERY VETERAN SHOULD KNOW," a service officer's guide since 1937.

Monthly supplements are available from the publisher, which provide updates to the information contained in this book. A one-year subscription to the supplement service is $38.00.

The material herein covers veterans' benefits, rights, privileges, and services over which the Department of Veterans Affairs has jurisdiction. All references to "VA" pertain to the Department of Veterans Affairs. Revised and new laws passed by the 119th Congress as of December 31, 2024, are incorporated in this text.

This guide was prepared solely for convenient reference purposes, and does not have the effect of law. Although diligent effort has been made to ensure its accuracy, in the event of any conflict between this book and any regulation, the latter is, of course, controlling.

Veterans and the dependents of deceased veterans are advised to contact their local veterans organization service officers, or the nearest Veterans Administration Office, for help in completing any valid claim.

VETERANS INFORMATION
P.O. Box 111
East Moline, Illinois 612
Telephone: (309) 75
Fax: (309) 278-53
Email: help@vetsinfoser
www.vetsinfoservice.com

T0407131

ASK FOR YOUR **FREE** SAMPLE COPY OF THE
MONTHLY SUPPLEMENT,
DESIGNED TO KEEP THIS BOOK UP-TO-DATE.
ONE-YEAR SUPPLEMENT SERVICE: $38.00

WHAT EVERY VETERAN SHOULD KNOW

VETERANS INFORMATION SERVICE
P.O. Box 111
East Moline, Illinois 61244-0111

Phone: (309) 757-7760
Fax: (309) 278-5304
E-mail: help@vetsinfoservice.com
www.vetsinfoservice.com

═══════════════════════════════════

A NOTE TO THE READER:

Revised and new laws passed by the 119th Congress as of December 31, 2024, are incorporated in the text of this book. The first section of the book contains a brief summary of some of the important legislative changes affecting veterans' benefits during 2024.

You will find a Table of Contents, listing the main subject headings. For your convenience there is also a complete index in the back of the book, as well as an Edge Index on the back cover.

We hope you enjoy this edition of **WHAT EVERY VETERAN SHOULD KNOW**. Any comments or suggestions for future improvements are welcome.

═══════════════════════════════════

© 2025
What Every Veteran Should Know
Library of Congress Cataloging in Serials
ISSN 1532-8112
ISBN 978-0-960087-6-8

Publisher:
Veterans Information Service
P.O. Box 111
East Moline, IL 61244-0111

TABLE OF CONTENTS

VA PHONE NUMBERS

Main VA Phone Numbers

Where to Call	Toll-Free Number
MyVA411 (main information line for VA)	800-698-2411
Telecommunications Relay Service Using TTY	744

VA Health Care

Where to Call	Toll-Free Number
PACT Act Questions	800-698-2411
Health Care Benefits	877-222-8387
My HealtheVet Help Desk	877-327-0022
Civilian Health and Medical Program of the Department of Veterans Affairs (CHAMPA)	800-733-8387
CHAMPVA Meds by Mail	888-385-0235 or 866-229-7389
Foreign Medical Program (FMP)	877-345-8179
Quit Vet (Get Help from a Counselor to Quit Smoking)	855-784-8838
MISSION Act	800-698-2311, Option 1
Spina Bifida Health Care Benefits Program	888-820-1756
Caregiver Support Line	855-260-3274

VA Benefits

Where to Call	Toll-Free Number
VA Benefits Hotline	800-827-1000
GI Bill Hotline	888-442-4551
Students Outside the U.S.	+1-918-781-5678
National Pension Call Center	877-294-6380
Support for SGLI or VGLI	800-419-1473
All Other VA Life Insurance Programs	800-669-8477
Special Issue Hotline (Blue Water Navy Act, Gulf War, Agent Orange, and Other Information)	800-749-8387

Burials and Memorials

Where to Call	Toll-Free Number
National Cemetery Scheduling Office	800-535-1117
Headstones and Markers	800-697-6947

Other VA Support

Where to Call	Toll-Free Number
Women Veterans Hotline	855-829-6636
eBenefits Technical Support	800-983-0937
Debt Management Center (Collection of Nonmedical Debt)	800-827-0648
Vets Center Call Center	877-927-8387
White House VA Hotline	855-948-2311
Veterans Crisis Line	988

Quick References

This chapter provides an in-depth guide to applying for the most commonly accessed VA benefits and services. It includes step-by-step instructions, required documentation, and eligibility criteria to help veterans and their families navigate the process with ease.

2024 Update: Filing Supplemental Claims Online

As part of the VA's ongoing modernization efforts, veterans now have the option to file supplemental claims online through VA.gov. Supplemental claims are designed for veterans who disagree with a previous decision regarding their VA disability compensation or pension benefits.

Benefits of Filing Online:

- **Reduced Wait Times**: Filing online eliminates delays associated with mailing paperwork and ensures faster processing.
- **Secure Information Handling**: Online submissions are encrypted and transmitted through a secure network, protecting veterans' personal information.

To file online:

1. Log in to your VA.gov account.
2. Navigate to the **Supplemental Claims** section under disability benefits.
3. Upload new and relevant evidence that supports your claim.
4. Submit the form and receive a confirmation email with tracking information.

If you prefer, you can still file by mail using VA Form 20-0995 or visit a local VA regional office for assistance.

Applying for Benefits Under The PACT Act

The **Sergeant First Class (SFC) Heath Robinson Honoring Our Promise to Address Comprehensive Toxics (PACT) Act** is a landmark expansion of VA benefits and health care. It provides comprehensive support for veterans exposed to toxic substances during their military service.

Key Features of the PACT Act:

1. **Expanded VA Health Care Eligibility:**
   - **Who Qualifies**: Gulf War and Post-9/11 veterans can receive free VA health care for service-related conditions for up to 10 years post-discharge.
   - **How to Enroll**: Apply for VA health care online, in person, or via mail using VA Form 10-10EZ.
2. **Presumptive Conditions:**
   - Veterans with conditions now classified as presumptive can file a new disability claim.
   - If a previous claim was denied, veterans can file a supplemental claim to have their case reconsidered.
3. **Retroactive Benefits:**
   - Claims approved within the first year after the PACT Act's enactment may receive backdated benefits to August 10, 2022.

Application Steps:

- For health care: Collect required documents (DD214, tax returns, dependents' Social Security numbers) and submit VA Form 10-10EZ online, by mail, or in person.
- For disability claims: Submit VA Form 21-526EZ, ensuring all medical evidence and service records are included.

For assistance, work with an accredited representative or Veterans Service Officer (VSO).

How to Apply for VA Health Care

VA health care is available to eligible veterans and offers a range of services, including primary care, mental health, and specialized treatments.

Eligibility Criteria:

You may qualify for VA health care if:

- You have a service-connected disability.
- You are a former POW or received a Purple Heart.
- You are a combat veteran within five years of separation.
- You served in designated areas (Vietnam, Gulf War, Camp Lejeune during qualifying periods).
- Your income meets VA thresholds.

Steps to Apply:

1. **Gather Documentation:**
    a. DD214 (discharge papers).
    b. Tax returns and insurance information.
    c. Social Security numbers for dependents.
2. **Choose Your Application Method:**
    a. **Online:** Use VA.gov and log in with your DS Logon or ID.me account for pre-filled forms and progress tracking.
    b. **Phone:** Call 877-222-8387 (press 1 for assistance).
    c. **In-Person:** Visit your nearest VA medical center or clinic.
    d. **Mail:** Send VA Form 10-10EZ to the Health Eligibility Center in Atlanta, GA.

3. **Next Steps After Approval:**
    a. Review your benefits and priority group assignment in the personalized handbook sent by the VA.
    b. Schedule an initial appointment at a VA Medical Center.
    c. Obtain your Veterans Health Identification Card (VHIC) to access services.

How to Apply for Disability Compensation

Disability compensation is a tax-free monthly payment provided to veterans with service-connected injuries or illnesses.

Eligibility:

You must prove that your condition is connected to your military service. This includes injuries, illnesses, or conditions that occurred or were aggravated during service.

Steps to Apply:

1. **Prepare Evidence:**
    a. Discharge papers (DD214).
    b. Medical records from military and civilian providers.
    c. Supporting statements from witnesses (e.g., fellow servicemembers).

2. **Submit Your Claim:**
    a. **Online:** Create an account on VA.gov and complete VA Form 21-526EZ.
    b. **By Mail:** Send the completed form to your regional VA office.

3. **Respond to VA Requests**:
    a. Provide any additional documentation requested.
    b. Attend a VA medical exam, if scheduled.
4. **Track Your Status**: Monitor your claim progress through VA.gov.
5. **Review the Decision**: If approved, the VA will send an award letter outlining your rating and benefits. If denied, consider filing a supplemental claim with new evidence.

How to Apply for VA Pension

The VA Pension Program offers financial assistance to wartime veterans who meet age, disability, and income criteria.

Steps to Apply:
1. **Collect Information**:
    a. Social Security numbers.
    b. Financial and medical records.
    c. Military service history.

2. **File Your Application**:
    a. Online: Submit VA Form 21P-527EZ through VA.gov.
    b. Mail: Send the form to the Pension Intake Center in Janesville, WI.
3. **Intent to File**: If you need time to gather documents, submit an Intent to File form (VA Form 21-0966) to preserve your claim's effective date.

Using VA Community Care

Veterans may qualify for care from community providers if certain conditions are met.

Eligibility Criteria:
1. Services unavailable at VA facilities.
2. Excessive travel time (over 30 minutes for primary care, 60 minutes for specialty care).
3. Long wait times (over 20 days for primary care, 28 days for specialty care).
4. Use the VA Facility Locator to find eligible providers.

Accessing Urgent Care

Eligible veterans can access minor injury and illness treatment at network urgent care providers.

Eligibility:
- Enrolled in VA health care.
- Received VA care in the past 24 months.

To use this benefit:
- Confirm the provider is in-network.
- Present your VA ID and verify eligibility.

Getting Started with Mental Health Services

Emergency mental health care is available to all former service members, regardless of discharge status.
- **Veterans Crisis Line**: Call **1-800-273-8255**, text **838255**, or chat at veteranscrisisline.net.
- **VA Medical Centers**: Provide walk-in emergency care.

For non-urgent mental health services, apply through VA health care channels.

Periods of War

The current VA periods of war for eligibility to benefits such as VA disability, pension, and health care are as follows:
1. **World War II**
   - December 7, 1941 – December 31, 1946
2. **Korean War**
   - June 27, 1950 – January 31, 1955
3. **Vietnam War**
   - August 5, 1964 – May 7, 1975
   - (For veterans who served in-country, the period is extended to March 28, 1973)
4. **Gulf War**
   - August 2, 1990 – Present (includes both Operation Desert Storm and the continuing conflict in the Middle East)
5. **Afghanistan War**
   - October 7, 2001 – Present
6. **Iraq War**
   - March 20, 2003 – December 15, 2011 (the VA still recognizes

the period of service in Iraq as part of the ongoing Gulf War era)

For veterans who served in these wars, they may be eligible for special benefits and presumptive service connection for certain diseases or conditions related to their service.

Commonly Used Forms

Category	Form Name	Form Number
Health Care Enrollment	Application for Health Care Benefits	VA Form 10-10EZ
Disability Compensation	Application for Disability Compensation and Related Benefits	VA Form 21-526EZ
Disability Compensation	Disability Benefits Questionnaires (DBQs)	VA Form 21-0960
Pension	Application for Veterans Pension	VA Form 21P-527EZ
Pension	Application for Dependency and Indemnity Compensation (DIC)	VA Form 21P-534EZ
Education	Application for VA Education Benefits	VA Form 22-1990
Education	Request for Change of Program or Place of Training	VA Form 22-1995
Burial Benefits	Application for Burial Benefits	VA Form 21P-530EZ
Home Loan Guaranty	Request for a Certificate of Eligibility for Home Loan	VA Form 26-1880
Survivor Benefits	Claim for DIC, Death Pension, and/or Accrued Benefits	VA Form 21P-534EZ
Appeal	Notice of Disagreement	VA Form 21-0958
Appeal	VA Form 9, Appeal to Board of Veterans' Appeals	VA Form 10182
Income	Financial Status Report	VA Form 5655
Insurance	Application for Veterans' Group Life Insurance	SGLV 8714
Insurance	Claim for Death Benefits	VA Form 29-4125e
Insurance	Life Insurance Waiver Request	VA Form 29-357
Insurance	Application for Refund of Premiums	VA Form 29-1546
Discharge Forms	Request for a Copy of Discharge	SF 180

	Documents (DD Form 214)	
Discharge Forms	Request for Replacement of Discharge Certificate	SF 180
Records Request	Request for Military Records (Military Service Records, including DD Form 214)	SF 180
Records Request	Request for Veterans' Service Records	SF 180
DIC	Application for Dependency and Indemnity Compensation (DIC)	VA Form 21P-534EZ
DIC	Application for Death Pension and/or DIC Benefits	VA Form 21-534EZ

2024 UPDATES

Following is a summary of some of the important legislative changes and VA policy changes affecting veterans' benefits during 2024.

DOD Expands Online Renewal Program for USID Cards

The U.S. Department of Defense has expanded its pilot program for renewing Uniformed Services Identification (USID) cards online, making it more convenient for retirees, family members, and other non-CAC (Common Access Card) holders to renew their cards without visiting an ID card office.

This program, launched in February 2023, now allows eligible individuals to renew their USID cards online through the ID Card Office Online (IDCO) website and receive the renewed cards by mail.

However, this service is currently only available for renewals within the United States, with plans to extend it to non-U.S. addresses in the future.

The initiative aims to streamline processes, reduce the burden on ID card offices, and free up appointments for active-duty personnel and civilian government employees requiring CACs.

Mike Zarlenga from the Defense Manpower Data Center highlighted the program's goal of simplifying card renewal for about one million eligible individuals annually while improving service for mission-critical personnel.

VA Proposes Expansion of Agent Orange Exposure Presumptions

The Department of Veterans Affairs (VA) has proposed a new rule to expand the list of locations and time frames where exposure to Agent Orange and other herbicides is presumed.

This change would simplify access to health care and disability benefits for veterans who served in areas outside Vietnam, including new locations in the U.S., Canada, and India.

Presumptive exposure means the VA assumes eligible veterans were exposed to herbicides, reducing the burden of proof needed to claim benefits for related health conditions, such as certain cancers and chronic illnesses. To qualify, veterans must have served in the designated locations during specific time periods and have conditions linked to herbicide exposure.

This expansion aligns with President Biden's Unity Agenda and the PACT Act, which significantly broadened access to care for toxic-exposed veterans. VA Secretary Denis McDonough emphasized the importance of making benefits more accessible for all veterans.

For more information or to file a claim, veterans can visit the VA website, use VA Form 21-526EZ, or contact a VA-recognized Veterans Service Organization. Survivors of affected veterans may also be eligible for benefits.

VA Updates Disability Rating Schedule for Digestive Conditions

The Department of Veterans Affairs (VA) has revised the VA Schedule for Rating Disabilities (VASRD) for digestive system conditions, incorporating modern medical knowledge and advancements in treatment.

These updates, effective May 19, 2024, include changes to the rating criteria for 55 medical conditions. Key updates include:

- **Celiac Disease:** Previously rated by analogy, this condition now has its own diagnostic code, with evaluations ranging from 0% to 80%, reflecting its disabling effects more accurately.
- **Irritable Bowel Syndrome (IBS):** New criteria offer evaluations of 10%, 20%, or 30% based on symptom frequency, ensuring all cases receive compensable ratings.
- **Hemorrhoids:** Mild or moderate cases, previously rated at 0%, will now qualify for a 10% evaluation.

These updates aim to better align the rating criteria with the average impairment of earning capacity for veterans.

Current ratings will not change unless there is significant improvement under the former criteria. Claims pending as of May 19, 2024, will be evaluated under both old and new criteria, with the more favorable applied.

VA Expands Access to Care for Former Service Members with Other Than Honorable Discharges

The Department of Veterans Affairs (VA) has finalized a new rule to expand access to care and benefits for some former service members discharged under other than honorable conditions or by special court-martial.

The rule introduces updates to the character of discharge determination process, enabling more individuals to receive VA benefits.

Key changes include:

- **Elimination of Specific Regulatory Bars**: VA will no longer bar benefits based on discharges related to "homosexual acts involving aggravating circumstances," furthering the commitment to reduce disparities for individuals discharged due to sexual orientation, gender identity, or HIV status.
- **Compelling Circumstances Exception**: For certain discharges, such as "willful and persistent misconduct" or "offenses involving moral turpitude," VA will consider exceptions based on factors like service length, mental health, combat hardship, and experiences of discrimination or assault.
- **Reapplication Opportunities**: Former service members previously denied benefits may reapply under the updated guidelines.

The rule does not change military discharge status but determines eligibility for VA benefits. Discharges characterized as dishonorable or resulting from desertion, mutiny, or espionage remain ineligible, barring special circumstances.

VA encourages former service members with other than honorable discharges to apply for care and benefits, emphasizing that many are eligible despite misconceptions about discharge status.

Over the past decade, VA has granted eligibility determinations to 75% of applicants with these discharges.

VA Updates Home Loan Policies to Support Veterans in a Changing Market

The VA recently updated its home loan guaranty program to help veterans remain competitive in the changing housing market.

Beginning August 10, 2024, veterans, active-duty service members, and surviving spouses using VA home loan benefits have been allowed to pay certain buyer-broker fees. This update follows a settlement by the National Association of Realtors® (NAR), which requires buyers to cover some of these fees, a departure from the past practice where sellers often paid them. To ensure veterans are not disadvantaged, the VA adjusted its policies to maintain access to homeownership opportunities.

This change allows veterans to negotiate buyer-broker fees with their real estate professionals while ensuring the fees remain reasonable and customary within local markets. The VA has emphasized its commitment to monitoring how the settlement impacts the real estate market and will continue adapting policies to support veterans in navigating the homebuying process.

VA Expands Presumptive Disability Benefits to Include Three New Cancers

The Department of Veterans Affairs (VA) has expanded its list of presumed service-connected disabilities to include three new cancer types—male breast cancer, urethral cancer, and cancer of the paraurethral glands—under the PACT Act. This decision demonstrates the VA's commitment to supporting veterans exposed to environmental hazards during service.

The change applies to Gulf War and post-9/11 veterans who served in locations such as Afghanistan, Iraq, and other areas within the Southwest Asia theater of operations. By presuming these conditions are service connected, the VA aims to streamline the process for eligible veterans to receive healthcare and benefits.

Veterans diagnosed with these cancers during or after military service may be entitled to retroactive disability compensation dating back to August 10, 2022, when the PACT Act was enacted. Additionally, the VA will review previously denied claims for these conditions to determine if benefits can now be granted.

VA Expands Burn Pit Registry to Enhance Research for Toxic-Exposed Veterans

The Department of Veterans Affairs (VA) has unveiled an updated version of the Airborne Hazards and Open Burn Pit Registry, marking a significant step toward improving research and treatment for veterans exposed to toxic hazards during their service.

This redesigned registry, now referred to as the Burn Pit Research Registry, integrates data from over 4.7 million veterans and servicemembers identified through Department of Defense records. By streamlining participation requirements and expanding eligibility, the registry aims to drive advancements in understanding and addressing the long-term health impacts faced by toxic-exposed veterans.

While participation in the registry does not directly influence individual healthcare or benefits, it serves as a critical resource for researchers and policymakers. The data collected will support studies into presumptive conditions, predictive medicine, and proactive veteran care, ultimately shaping future VA policies and treatments.

Eligible veterans, including those who served in various military campaigns and theaters of operation from 1990 to 2021, are automatically included in the registry.

VA Expands Benefits for K2 Veterans and Survivors

The Department of Veterans Affairs (VA) has announced significant measures to extend access to benefits for veterans who served at Karshi-Khanabad (K2) base in Uzbekistan after September 11, 2001, and their survivors.

Among the changes, chronic multi-symptom illness is now a presumptive condition for K2 veterans, allowing them to receive benefits for Gulf War Illness with less burden of proof. Additionally, the VA has recognized exposures at K2 as toxic exposure risk activities, acknowledging contaminants such as jet fuel, asbestos, and particulate matter, which impacted the health of those who served there. Claims processors will now incorporate this exposure data into their decisions, ensuring comprehensive reviews for all relevant claims.

K2 veterans are also eligible to enroll in VA healthcare and receive benefits for over 300 presumptive conditions under the PACT Act without needing to prove service connection.

The VA is actively reaching out to K2 veterans and survivors to raise awareness of these expanded benefits. Currently, over 13,000 K2 veterans are enrolled in VA healthcare, with nearly 12,000 already service-connected for at least one condition.

Veterans and survivors are encouraged to apply for benefits through VA.gov or by calling 1-800-MYVA411. This initiative underscores the VA's commitment to addressing the needs of K2 veterans and ensuring they receive the care and support they deserve.

VA Expands Nationwide Access to Tele-Emergency Care for Veterans

The Department of Veterans Affairs has announced the nationwide availability of tele-emergency care, a virtual healthcare service designed to provide veterans with timely access to emergency care without the need to travel.

This service, part of the VA Health Connect initiative, allows veterans to connect with clinical triage nurses and tele-emergency care providers through phone or video calls. These providers can evaluate symptoms, recommend treatment or follow-ups, and, if necessary, arrange in-person care. In cases of life-threatening emergencies, the service ensures immediate coordination with 911.

Tele-emergency care offers significant advantages, especially for veterans in rural areas or those facing mobility challenges. During its pilot phase, the service successfully resolved nearly 60% of cases without requiring veterans to visit an urgent care center or emergency department.

This expansion reflects the VA's commitment to enhancing access to care and leveraging innovative solutions to meet veterans' healthcare needs. Veterans enrolled in VA health care can access this service by calling VA Health Connect or using the VA Health Chat app.

Disabled Veterans and Retirees to Receive 2.5% COLA Increase in 2025

Disabled veterans and military retirees can look forward to a 2.5% cost-of-living adjustment (COLA) in their benefits starting in 2025, thanks to the Veterans' Compensation Cost-of-Living Adjustment Act of 2024.

Signed into law by President Biden on November 25, the increase aligns with the Social Security Administration's annual COLA adjustment, reflecting inflation rates measured by the Department of Labor's Consumer Price Index. This ensures that government disability and retirement payments keep pace with rising consumer costs.

The adjustment will benefit veterans receiving VA disability compensation, clothing allowances, and survivors receiving dependency indemnity compensation.

For instance, a veteran rated at 100% disability without dependents will see an increase of approximately $93.45 per month, while those with a 10% rating can expect around $4.28 more each month. This adjustment underscores the government's commitment to supporting veterans and their families in maintaining financial stability amid inflation.

Impact of the Rudisill Supreme Court Decision on Veterans' Education Benefits

The Rudisill Supreme Court decision, effective April 16, 2024, changes how veterans can use their Montgomery GI Bill (MGIB) and Post-9/11 GI Bill (PGIB) benefits. Veterans who served in two periods, one qualifying for MGIB and another for PGIB, are now eligible for additional benefits.

Key Changes:
- Previously, veterans had to waive MGIB benefits to use PGIB. Now, MGIB eligibility can be retained while using PGIB.
- PGIB entitlement is no longer limited to the amount of remaining MGIB benefits.
- Veterans can now revoke their previous decision to waive MGIB benefits for PGIB use.

Eligibility for Additional Benefits: To qualify for additional benefits, you must meet two conditions:
1. You have completed more than one period of eligible service.
2. You waived MGIB benefits to use PGIB.

What You Need to Do:
- If your last education claim decision was after August 15, 2018: No action is required. VA will review your claim and notify you of eligibility.

- If your last education claim decision was before August 15, 2018: Submit a claim using VA Form 22-1995 and select the "Rudisill review" option. VA will evaluate your eligibility and notify you of the decision.

Important Deadlines:
- The deadline to submit claims for recalculating your delimiting date is October 1, 2030. After this date, the standard delimiting date rules will apply.

Note: PGIB and MGIB eligibility combined is limited to 48 months, and benefits cannot be used simultaneously.

CHAPTER 1

HEALTHCARE BENEFITS

If you qualify for VA health care, you'll receive coverage for the services required to stay healthy. Every veteran will have a unique benefits package. All veterans receive coverage for most care and services, but some qualify for added benefits like dental care. The full list of covered benefits depends on a veteran's priority group, the advice of their VA primary care provider, and the medical standards for treating any condition a veteran has.

Being signed up for VA health care meets the Affordable Care Act (ACA) health coverage requirement of having minimum essential health coverage.

All World War II veterans are now eligible for no-cost VA inpatient and outpatient health care. Under the expansion, all WWII veterans who served between December 7, 1941, and December 31, 1946, are eligible for VA health care regardless of financial status or length of service.

These veterans don't have to pay outpatient copays, monthly premiums or enrollment fees. These veterans may still have to pay small copays for medication, urgent care or long-term care in some cases, depending on service connection and eligibility.

Eligibility

You may be eligible for VA health care benefits if you served in the active military, naval or air service and didn't receive a dishonorable discharge.

If you enlisted after September 7, 1980, or entered active duty after October 16, 1981:
You must have served 24 continuous months or the full period for which you were called to active duty unless any of the below descriptions are true for you:

- You were discharged for a disability that was caused or made worse by your active-duty service or
- You were discharged for a hardship or early out, or
- You served prior to September 7, 1980.

If you're a current or former member of the Reserves or National Guard:

You must have been called to active duty by a federal order and completed the full period for which you were called or ordered to active duty. If you had or have active-duty status for training purposes only, you don't qualify for VA health care.

If you served in certain locations and time periods during the Vietnam War era:

You're eligible for VA health care.

You may qualify for enhanced eligibility status if you meet at least one of the following requirements. Enhanced eligibility means you're in a higher priority group, making you more likely to get benefits.

At least one must be true:

- You receive financial compensation from VA for a service-connected disability
- You were discharged for a disability resulting from something that happened to you in the line of duty
- You were discharged for a disability that got worse in the line of duty
- You're a combat veteran discharged or released on or after September 11, 2001
- You get a VA pension
- You're a former prisoner of war
- You have received a Purple Heart
- You have received a Medal of Honor
- You receive or qualify for Medicaid benefits
- You served in Southwest Asia during the Gulf War between August 2, 1990, and November 11, 1998
- You served at least 30 days at Camp Lejeune between August 1, 1953, and December 31, 1987

Or you must have served in any of these locations during the Vietnam War era:

- Any U.S. or Royal Thai military base in Thailand from January 9, 1962, through June 30, 1976
- Laos from December 1, 1965, through September 30, 1969
- Cambodia at Mimot or Krek, Kampong Cham Province from April 16, 1969, through April 30, 1969
- Guam or American Samoa or in the territorial waters off Guam or American Samoa from January 9, 1962, through July 31, 1980
- Johnston Atoll or on a ship that was called Johnston Atoll from January 1, 1972, through September 30, 1977
- Republic of Vietnam from January 9, 1962, through May 7, 1975

If none of these descriptions apply to you, you may still qualify for care based on your income.

VA Priority Groups

When a veteran applies for VA health care, they assign you to 1 of 8 priority groups. The system is meant to make sure veterans who need care get signed up immediately. The priority group a veteran is assigned can affect how soon they receive health care benefits and how much, if anything, they pay toward the cost of their care.

Priority groups are based on:
- Military service history and
- Disability rating, and
- Income level, and
- Qualification for Medicaid and
- Other benefits being received, like a pension from the VA

VA assigns veterans with service-connected disabilities the highest priority. Veterans who earn a higher income and don't have any service-connected disabilities are assigned a lower priority. If a veteran qualifies for more than one group, they're assigned to the higher one.

Priority Group 1

You may be assigned to this Priority Group if any of the following are true:
- You have a service-connected disability rated as 50% or more disabling or
- You have a service-connected disability the VA concludes makes you unable to work (you're considered unemployable) or
- You received the Medal of Honor (MOH)

Priority Group 2

You may be assigned to Priority Group 2 if you have a service-connected disability the VA has rated as 30% or 40% disabling.

Priority Group 3
You may be assigned to Priority Group 3 if any of the following are true:
- You're a former prisoner of war (POW), or
- You received the Purple Heart medal, or
- You were discharged for a disability that was caused by or got worse because of your active-duty service or
- You have a service-connected disability the VA has rated as 10% or 20% disabling or
- You were awarded special eligibility classification under Title 38, USC 1151.

Priority Group 4

You may be assigned to Priority Group 4 if either of the following is true:
- You receive VA aid and attendance or housebound benefits, or
- You've received a VA determination of being catastrophically disabled

Priority Group 5

You may be assigned to Priority Group 5 if any of the following are true:
- You don't have a service-connected disability, or you have a non-compensable service-connected disability the VA has rated as 0% disabling, and you have an annual income level that's below the VA's adjusted income limits based on your zip code or
- You're receiving VA pension benefits, or
- You're eligible for Medicaid programs

Priority Group 6

VA may assign you to Priority Group 6 if any of the following are true:
- You have a compensable service-connected disability that VA rated as 0% disabling or
- You were exposed to ionizing radiation during atmospheric testing or during the occupation of Hiroshima and Nagasaki, or
- You participated in Project 112/SHAD or
- You served in the Republic of Vietnam between January 9, 1962, and May 7, 1975, or
- You served in the Persian Gulf War between August 2, 1990, and November 11, 1998, or
- You served on active duty at Camp Lejeune for at least 30 days between August 1, 1953, and December 31, 1987

VA may also assign you to Priority Group 6 if you meet all of these requirements:
- You're currently or newly enrolled in VA health care, and
- You served in a theater of combat operations after November 11, 1998, and
- You were discharged less than ten years ago

Note: As a returning combat veteran, you're eligible for these enhanced benefits for ten years after your discharge. At the end of your enhanced enrollment period, VA will assign you to the highest priority group you qualify for at that time.

Priority Group 7

You may be assigned to Priority Group 7 if both are true for you:
- Your gross household income is below the geographically adjusted income limits for where you live, and
- You agree to pay copays.

Priority Group 8

You may be assigned to Priority Group 8 if both are true for you:
- Your gross household income is above VA income limits and geographically adjusted income limits for where you live and
- You agree to pay copays.

If you're assigned to Priority Group 8, your eligibility for VA health care benefits will depend on the subpriority group you're placed in.

You may be eligible for VA health care benefits if the VA places you in one of these subpriority groups:

Subpriority group a

All of these must be true:
- You have a non-compensable service-connected condition that VA rated as 0% disabling, and
- You enrolled in the VA health care program before January 16, 2003, and
- You have remained enrolled since that date and/or were placed in this subpriority group because your eligibility status changed.

Subpriority group b

All of these must be true:
- You have a non-compensable service-connected condition that VA rated as 0% disabling, and
- You enrolled in the VA health care program on or after June 15, 2009, and
- You have income that exceeds current VA or geographical limits by 10% or less

Subpriority group c

All of these must be true:
- You don't have a service-connected condition, and
- You enrolled in the VA health care program as of January 16, 2003, and
- You have remained enrolled since that date and/or were placed in this subpriority group because your eligibility status changed.

Subpriority group d

All of these must be true:
- You don't have a service-connected condition, and
- You enrolled in the VA health care program on or after June 15, 2009,

and
- You have income that exceeds current VA or geographical limits by 10% or less

You're not eligible for VA health care benefits if the VA places you in one of these subpriority groups:

Subpriority group e

All of these must be true:
- You have a non-compensable service-connected condition that VA rated as 0% disabling, and
- You don't meet the criteria for subpriority group A or b above

Note: You're eligible for care for your service-connected condition only.

Subpriority group g

All of these must be true:
- You don't have a service-connected condition, and
- You don't meet the criteria for subpriority group c or d

Once you enroll in VA health care, your priority group may change if your income changes or your service-connected disability gets worse, and the VA gives you a higher disability rating.

Note: If you're currently enrolled or newly enrolled in VA health care, and you served in a theater of combat operations after November 11, 1998, and were discharged from active duty on or after September 11, 2001, you're eligible for enhanced benefits for ten years after discharge. During this time, VA assigns you to priority group 6.

Priority Group	Description
Group 1	Veterans with service-connected disabilities rated 50% or more or deemed unemployable due to service-connected conditions or you received the Medal of Honor (MOH).
Group 2	Veterans with service-connected disabilities rated 30% or 40%.
Group 3	Veterans who are former POWs, were awarded the Purple Heart, or have service-connected disabilities rated 10% or 20%.
Group 4	Veterans receiving aid and attendance or housebound benefits, or those who are catastrophically disabled.
Group 5	Veterans with a non-service-connected disability and Income below the national threshold, or those receiving VA pension benefits. Also included are those eligible

	for Medicaid programs.
Group 6	Veterans exposed to environmental hazards (e.g., Agent Orange, Gulf War exposures, radiation), or those who served in combat post-1998.
Group 7	Veterans with a gross household income below the geographically adjusted threshold and who agree to co-pays.
Group 8	Veterans with a gross household income above VA income limits who agree to co-pays. Eligibility may be limited by VA's enrollment policies.

How to Apply for VA Health Care

You'll gather the information below to fill out an Application for Health Benefits (VA Form 10-10EZ). The information you need includes:

- Social Security numbers for you, your spouse, and your qualified dependents
- Your military discharge papers (DD214 or other separation documents)
- Insurance card information for all insurance companies that cover you, including any coverage provided through a spouse or significant other. This includes Medicare, private insurance, or insurance from your employer.
- Gross household income from the previous calendar year for you, your spouse, and your dependents. This includes income from a job and any other sources. Gross household income is your income before taxes and any other deductions.
- Your deductible expenses for the past year. These include certain health care and education costs.

Note: You don't have to tell the VA about your income and expenses when you apply, but if you aren't eligible based on other factors, the VA will need this information to make a decision.

After you apply for VA health care, you'll get a letter that will tell you if your application has been approved. If more than a week has passed since you sent your application, and the VA hasn't contacted you, you don't apply again. Instead, call 877-222-8387.

Basic Health Care Services VA Covers

VA will cover preventative services, including:

- Health exams, including gender-specific exams
- Health education, including nutrition education
- Immunization against infectious diseases
- Counseling on genetic diseases that run in families

Inpatient hospital services like the following may be covered:

- Surgeries
- Medical treatments
- Kidney dialysis
- Acute care, which is a short-term treatment for severe injuries or illnesses or after surgery
- Specialized care includes organ transplants, care for traumatic injuries, and intensive care for mental and physical conditions.

Urgent and emergency care services may be covered. To use VA urgent care services, you'll need to have been receiving care from the VA within the past 24 months.

Health Care Costs

You can get free VA health care for any injury or illness that's service-connected. VA also provides certain other services for free, including readjustment counseling and related mental health services, care for issues related to military sexual trauma, and a registry health exam to determine if you're at risk of health problems related to your military service.

You may qualify for additional free VA health care depending on your income, disability rating or other eligibility factors.

You may need to pay a fixed amount for some types of care, tests and medications from a VA care provider or approved community health provider. This is a copayment. Whether or not you have a copay and how much depends on your disability rating, income level, military service record and your priority group.

Services that don't require a copay, no matter your disability rating or priority group, are:

- Readjustment counseling and related mental health services.
- Counseling and care for issues related to military sexual trauma.
- Exams to determine the risk of health problems linked to military service.
- Care that may be related to combat service for veterans who served in a theater of combat operations after November 11, 1998.
- VA claims exams.
- Care related to a VA-rated service-connected disability.
- Care for cancer of the head or neck caused by nose or throat radium treatments received while in the military.
- Individual or group programs to help quit smoking or lose weight.
- Care that's part of a VA research project like the Million Veteran Program.
- Lab tests.
- EKGs or ECGs to check for heart disease or other health problems.
- VA health initiatives that are open to the public.

VA Health Care and Other Insurance

If you have other forms of health care coverage, such as Medicare, Medicaid, TRICARE or private insurance, you can use your VA health care benefits with these plans. You provide information to the VA about your health insurance coverage, including coverage under a spouse's plan. The VA will have to bill your private health insurance provider for care, supplies or medicine provided to treat illnesses or injuries not related to service. VA doesn't bill Medicare or Medicaid but may bill Medicare supplemental health insurance for covered services.

If your health insurance provider doesn't cover all the non-service-connected care the VA bills them for you don't have to pay your unpaid balance. Depending on your assigned priority group, you may have a copay for non-service-connected care.

Whether or not you have insurance doesn't affect the VA health care benefits you're eligible for.

Community Care

VA provides health care for veterans from other providers in the local community outside of VA. Veterans may be eligible to receive care from a community provider when the VA can't provide the needed care. The care is provided on behalf of and paid for by VA. Community care has to be authorized by the VA before the veteran can receive care.

Veterans are charged a copay for nonservice-connected care. Eligibility requirements include meeting both of the following:

- You're enrolled in or eligible for VA health care, and
- You have approval from your VA health care team before you get care from an emergency provider, except in certain cases like emergency or urgent care.

At least one of these requirements must also be true:
- You need a service that's not provided at a VA health facility or
- You live in a state or territory that doesn't have a full-service VA health facility or
- You qualified under the 40-mile distance requirement on June 6, 2018, and live in a location that would still make you eligible under these requirements or
- The VA can't provide the care you need within its standards for drive or wait time, or
- You and your VA provider agree getting care from an in-network community provider is in your best medical interest or
- The VA can't provide the service you need in a way that meets its quality standards.

Step	Description
1. Eligibility	Determine if you are eligible for community care by meeting specific criteria such as wait times, travel distance, or availability of VA services.
2. Referral	Obtain a referral from your VA provider. The referral must confirm that community care is clinically appropriate.
3. Scheduling	Work with your local VA staff or a VA-authorized third-party administrator to schedule an appointment with a community provider.
4. Pre-Authorization	Ensure that the VA pre-authorizes your care. This is necessary for the VA to cover the cost of services from a community provider.
5. Receive Care	Attend your appointment with the community provider. The provider should send all medical records to the VA after the visit.
6. Billing	The VA will handle payment directly with the community provider. You should not be billed for authorized care.
7. Follow-Up	Follow up with your VA provider to coordinate ongoing care and ensure continuity of treatment.

Family Health Benefits

If someone is a spouse, surviving spouse, dependent child, or family caregiver of a veteran or service member, they may qualify for health care benefits. They might also qualify for health care benefits due to a disability related to their veteran's service.

Healthcare programs that might be available to family members include:

- **TRICARE**: This program provides comprehensive health coverage, including health plans, prescription medicine, dental plans and more, to families of active duty, retired or deceased servicemembers, as well as National Guard soldiers, Reservists, and Medical of Honor Recipients.
- **CHAMPVA**: The CHAMPVA program is available to current or surviving spouses or children of veterans with disabilities or servicemembers who died in the line of duty. If someone doesn't qualify for TRICARE, they may be eligible for insurance through CHAMPVA.
- **The Program of Comprehensive Assistance for Family Caregivers**: Under the PCAFC program, support and services for family caregivers for eligible veterans are available. Services include access to health insurance, respite care, and mental health counseling.
- **The Camp Lejeune Family Member Program**: This program is available to people who lived at Camp Lejeune or Marine Corps Air Station with an active-duty veteran who was their spouse or parent. It's available to people who lived there for at least 30 cumulative days from August 1953 through December 1987. Eligible family members may qualify for health care benefits through VA.
- **Spina Bifida Health Care Benefits Program**: If someone is the biological child of a Korean or Vietnam War veteran and they've been diagnosed with

spina bifida, they may qualify for disability benefits, including health care benefits.

- **The Children of Women Vietnam Veterans Health Care Benefits Program**: People who are biological children of women Vietnam War veterans diagnosed with certain birth defects may qualify for VA health care benefits.
- **Pharmacy Benefits:** If someone qualifies for CHAMPVA, Spina Bifida or Children of Women Vietnam Veterans programs, they can get prescription benefits from their local pharmacy or through the VA's Meds by Mail program.

VA Travel Pay Reimbursement

VA will pay reimbursement for mileage and other travel expenses to and from approved healthcare appointments. Health care travel reimbursement covers regular transportation and approved meals and lodging expenses.

A claim can be filed online through the Beneficiary Travel Self-Service System, which is accessible in the Access VA travel claim portal.

As a veteran, you may be eligible for reimbursement if you meet the following requirements:

- You're traveling for care at a VA health facility or for VA-approved care at a non-VA health facility in your community

At least one of these things must also be true:
- You have a disability rating of 30% or higher, or
- You're traveling for treatment of a service-connected condition, even if your VA disability rating is less than 30% or
- You receive a VA pension, or
- You have an income that's below the maximum annual VA pension rate or
- You can't afford to pay for your travel, as defined by VA guidelines, or
- You're traveling for one of these reasons: A scheduled VA claim exam, also known as a compensation and pension exam, to get a service dog or for VA-approved transplant care.

The VA may pay for transportation and related lodging and meals for non-veterans if the person meets any one of these requirements:
- The person is a family caregiver under the National Caregiver Program traveling to receive caregiving training or to support the veteran's care or
- The person is a veteran's medically required attendant traveling to support the care of the veteran or
- The person is the veteran's transplant care donor or support person

The VA may also pay for care for an allied beneficiary when the appropriate foreign government agency authorizes their care or for the beneficiary of another federal agency when that agency has approved their care.

Before filing a claim, keep all receipts for transportation and approved meals and lodging, and track mileage to and from appointments. The claim must be filed within 30 days of the appointment or within 30 days of when the veteran becomes eligible for reimbursement. A new claim needs to be filed for every appointment.

Veteran Health Identification Card (VHIC)

A Veteran Health Identification Card or VHIC is a photo ID card that is used to check in at VA health care appointments.

You'll have to be enrolled to get a VHIC. You can contact your nearest VA medical Center and ask to speak to an enrollment coordinator, who will help you arrange to get your picture taken for your card. You can also use AccessVA to request a VHIC.

Copayment Rates – Current as of January 2025

2025 Update—New Policy on Mental Health Copay Exemptions

Eligible veterans may not have to pay an outpatient care copay for their first their first three visits in a calendar year with a qualified mental health care provider at a VA facility or in the VA community care network. The visits must be between June 27, 2023, and December 29, 2027. The VA will review copays received on or after June 27, 2023, and reimburse for any eligible copays that have already been paid.

Urgent Care Copay Rates—Care for Minor Illnesses and Injuries

There's no limit to how many times you can use urgent care. To be eligible for urgent care benefits, including through the VA network of approved community providers, you must be enrolled in the VA health care system and have received care from VA within the past 24 months. You won't have any copay for a visit when you're only getting a flu shot, no matter your priority group.

2025 Urgent Care Copay Rates

Priority Group	Copay amount for the first three visits in each calendar year	The copay amount for each additional visit in the same year
1 to 5	$0 (no copay)	$30
6	If related to a condition that's covered by a special authority: $0 If not related to a condition covered by a special authority, $30 for each visit	$30

7 to 8	$30	$30

* Special authorities include conditions related to combat service and exposures (like Agent Orange, active duty at Camp Lejeune, ionizing radiation, Project Shipboard Hazard and Defense (SHAD/Project 112), Southwest Asia Conditions) as well as military sexual trauma, and presumptions applicable to certain veterans with psychosis and other mental illness.

Outpatient Care Copay Rates—Primary or Specialty Care That Doesn't Require an Overnight Stay

If you have a service-connected disability rating of 10% or higher, you won't need to pay a copay for outpatient care. If you don't have a service-connected disability rating of 10% or higher, you may need to pay a copay for outpatient care for conditions not related to your military service at the rates listed below.

2025 Outpatient Care Copay Rates

Type of Outpatient Care	Copay amount for each visit or test
Primary care services (like a visit to your primary care doctor)	$15
Specialty care services (like a visit to a hearing specialist, eye doctor, surgeon, or cardiologist)	$50
Specialty tests (like an MRI or CT scan)	$50

Note: You won't need to pay any copays for X-rays, lab tests, or preventive tests and services like health screenings or immunizations.

Inpatient care copay rates—Care that requires you to stay one or more days in a hospital

If you have a service-connected disability rating of 10% or higher, you won't need to pay a copay for inpatient care. If you're in priority group 6 and the inpatient care isn't for a service-connected condition or special-authority care, you may need to pay a inpatient care copay based on priority group 7 or 8 income limits.

If you're in priority group 7 or 8, you'll either pay the full copay rate or a reduced copay rate. If you live in a high-cost area, you may qualify for a reduced inpatient copay rate no matter what priority group you're in. You can find out if you're eligible for a reduced inpatient copay rate by calling 877-222-8387.

2025 Reduced Inpatient Care Copay Rates for Priority Group 7

Length of Stay	Copay Amount
First 90 days of care during a 365-day period	$335.20 copay + $2 charge per day
Each additional 90 days of care during a 365-day period	$167.60 copay + $2 charge per day

Note: You may be in priority group 7 and qualify for these rates if you don't meet eligibility requirements for priority groups 1 through 6, but you have a gross household income below our income limits for where you live, and you agree to pay copays.

2025 Full Inpatient Care Copay Rates for Priority Group 8

Length of Stay	Copay Amount
First 90 days of care during a 365-day period	$1,676 copay + $10 charge per day
Each additional 90 days of care during a 365-day period	$838 copay + $10 charge per day

Note: You may be in priority group 8 and qualify for these rates if you don't meet eligibility requirements for priority groups 1 through 6, and you have a gross household income above our income limits for where you live, agree to pay copays and meet other specific enrollment and service-connected eligibility criteria.

Medication Copay Rates

If you're in priority group 1, you won't pay a copay for any medications. You may be in priority group 1 if VA rated your service-connected disability at 50% or more disabling, if VA determined you can't work because of your service-connected disability (called unemployable), or if you've received the Medal of Honor.

If you're in priority groups 2 through 8 you'll pay a copay for medications your health care provider prescribes to treat non-service-connected conditions and over-the-counter medications, you get from a VA pharmacy. The cost for any medications you receive while staying in a VA or other approved hospital or health care facility are covered by the inpatient care copay.

The amount you'll pay for the medicines depends on the tier and the amount of medication you get. Once you've been charged $700 in medication copays within a calendar year you won't have to pay any more that year, even if you get more medication.

2025 Outpatient Medication Copay Amounts

Outpatient Medication Tier	1–30-day supply	31–60-day supply	61–90-day supply
Tier 0 Prescription and over-the-counter medicines with no copay	$0	$0	$0
Tier 1 Preferred generic prescription medications	$5	$10	$15
Tier 2 Non-preferred generic prescription medicines and some over-the-counter medicines	$8	$16	$24
Tier 3 Brand-name prescription medicines	$11	$22	$33

Geriatric and extended copay rates

You won't need to make a copay for geriatric care or extended care for the first 21 days of care in a 12-month period. Starting on the 22nd day of care, the VA will base copay on two factors. The first is the level of care and the second is the financial information provided on the Application for Extended Care Services (VA Form 10-10EC).

2025 Note: The 2025 community spouse resource allowance (SRA) is **$157,920**. If you have a spouse who is still living in the community and isn't also receiving extended care services, CSRA reduces the value of liquid assets the VA uses to determine the extended care copay amount.

2025 Geriatric and Extended Care Copay Amounts by Level of Care

Level of Care	Type of Care Included	Copay amount for each day of care
Inpatient care	Short-term or long-term stays in a community living center (formerly called nursing homes) Overnight respite care (in- home or onsite care designed to give family caregivers a break, available up to 30 days each calendar year) Overnight geriatric evaluations (evaluations by a team of health care providers to help you and your family decide on a care plan)	Up to $97
Outpatient care	Adult day health care (care in your home or at a facility that provides daytime social activities, companionship, recreation, care and support) Daily respite care Geriatric evaluations that don't require an overnight stay	Up to $15
Domiciliary care for homeless veterans	Short-term rehabilitation Long-term maintenance Care Daily respite care Geriatric evaluations that don't require an overnight stay	Up to $5

VA Copay Financial Hardship Assistance

If you're struggling to pay your VA copay bills due to job loss, decreased income, or rising healthcare expenses, there are options available to help you manage your debt.

Financial Assistance Options

- **Debt Relief Request**: If you're unable to pay your copay bills, you can request financial assistance.
- **Waiver**: Request a full or partial waiver of your debt, stopping collection efforts and forgiving the debt.
- **Compromise Offer**: Make a one-time, smaller payment to settle the debt.

To apply online, visit the VA website to submit your request. Alternatively, you can apply by mail or in person by filling out a **Financial Status Report (VA Form 5655)** and sending it to the nearest VA medical center.

Repayment Plan: If you're unable to pay the entire bill upfront, you can set up a monthly repayment plan. The VA will review your proposed payment schedule and assess your ability to pay within a reasonable period, typically requiring full repayment within 3 years. Use **VA Form 1100** to submit your proposed plan.
Once approved, you can begin making monthly payments. If you receive a new bill, submit an updated **VA Form 1100**.

Copay Exemption for Decreased Income

If your income has significantly decreased, you may qualify for a hardship exemption, which could eliminate your copay obligations for the rest of the calendar year. To request this, complete **VA Form 10-10HS**, and write a letter explaining your financial hardship. Please note that this exemption does not apply to pharmacy copays.

Additional Support

- **Disputing Charges**: If you believe your copay charges are incorrect, you can dispute them through the VA's process.
- **Copay Rates**: For information on current rates for different services and medications, consult the VA's website.
- **Updating Your Information**: If you need to update your financial or insurance details, you can do so by completing **VA Form 10-10EZR**.

For assistance or more information, call the VA at 866-400-1238 (TTY: 711) Monday through Friday from 8:00 AM to 8:00 PM ET.

Medicare Prescription Benefits

Veterans Affairs (VA) benefits provide comprehensive drug coverage, which allows you to delay enrolling in Medicare Part D without facing a late enrollment penalty (LEP). It's important to weigh the costs and benefits of both Part D and your VA drug coverage to determine which option best fits your needs. VA drug coverage typically has no premiums and minimal or no copayments for prescriptions, but it requires you to use VA pharmacies and facilities.

However, you may want to consider Medicare Part D if:

- You live far from a VA pharmacy or facility, or prefer not to use a VA provider for prescriptions
- You need the flexibility to fill prescriptions at retail pharmacies, or find the VA formulary too limiting
- You reside in a non-VA nursing home and want to use the pharmacy affiliated with your facility
- You qualify for full Extra Help, which offers lower copayments than VA coverage

If you're thinking about having both VA drug coverage and Part D, keep in mind that they don't work together. Your VA benefits will only cover prescriptions at VA pharmacies and facilities, while Part D will only cover prescriptions at pharmacies within your plan's network.

For more information about VA benefits and coverage, contact the Department of Veterans Affairs at 1-800-827-1000 or visit their website.

Covered Services—Standard Benefits

VA's medical benefits package provides the following health care services to all enrolled veterans:

Preventative Care Services
- Immunizations
- Physical Examinations (including eye and hearing examinations)
- Health Care Assessments
- Screening Tests
- Health Education Programs

Ambulatory (Outpatient) Diagnostic and Treatment Services
- Emergency outpatient care in VA facilities
- Medical
- Surgical (including reconstructive/plastic surgery as a result of disease or trauma)
- Chiropractic Care
- Bereavement Counseling
- Mental Health
- Substance Abuse

Hospital (Inpatient) Diagnostic and Treatment
- Emergency inpatient care in VA facilities
- Medical
- Surgical (including reconstructive/plastic surgery as a result of disease or trauma)
- Mental Health
- Substance Abuse

Limited Benefits
The following is a partial listing of acute care services which may have limitations

and special eligibility criteria:

- Ambulance Services
- Dental Care
- Durable Medical Equipment
- Eyeglasses (see footnote below)
- Hearing Aids (see footnote below)
- Home Health Care
- Homeless Programs
- Maternity and Parturition Services—usually provided in non-VA contracted hospitals at VA expense, care is limited to the mother (costs associated with the care of newborn are not covered)

Non-VA Healthcare Services

- Orthopedic, Prosthetic, and Rehabilitative Devices
- Rehabilitative Services
- Readjustment Counseling
- Sexual Trauma Counseling

Footnote: To qualify for hearing aids or eyeglasses, the individual must have a VA service- connected disability rating of 10% or more. An individual may also qualify if he or she is a former prisoner of war, Purple Heart recipient, require this benefit for treatment of a 0% service-connected condition, or are receiving increased pension based on the need for regular aid and attendance or being permanently housebound.

General Exclusions

The following is a partial listing of general exclusions:

- Abortions and abortion counseling
- Cosmetic surgery except where determined by VA to be medically necessary for reconstructive or psychiatric care
- Gender alteration
- Health club or spa membership, even for rehabilitation
- Drugs, biological, and medical devices not approved by the Food and Drug Administration unless part of formal clinical trial under an approved research program or when prescribed under compassionate use exemption.
- Medical care for a veteran who is either a patient or inmate in an institution of another government agency if that agency has a duty to provide the care or services.
- Services not ordered and provided by licensed/accredited professional staff
- Special private duty nursing

Emergency Care at Non-VA Facilities

If you're facing a medical emergency, your primary concern should be getting the help you need. Whether you're at home or traveling, knowing how to navigate emergency care at non-VA facilities is essential. If you're a veteran and need emergency care outside of the VA system, there are some guidelines you must follow to ensure that the costs are covered.

Emergency Care Eligibility and Requirements

When seeking emergency care at a non-VA facility, it's important to remember that the facility must be an emergency department. This includes hospitals or free-standing emergency departments equipped with the staff and tools necessary for providing emergency care. Urgent care centers, however, do not qualify. If you're unsure about whether your situation warrants a visit to an emergency department or urgent care, VA is available to help guide your decision.

Notifying the VA within 72 Hours

For VA to cover the costs of your emergency care, the facility must notify the VA within 72 hours of your treatment. Ideally, the provider will make this notification through the VA emergency care reporting portal. If they fail to do so, you or someone on your behalf must notify VA within this time frame. If you're not able to reach out immediately, VA can still process your claim, but this may impact the coverage.

Understanding Your Eligibility

Eligibility for emergency care depends on specific criteria. If you're seeking emergency mental health care, the VA can cover your treatment even if you're not enrolled in the VA health care system. This includes services provided for conditions like immediate risk of self-harm, sexual assault, or conditions related to your service in the Armed Forces. If you were in active service for more than 24 months or served over 100 days in support of a contingency operation, you may also be eligible.

For general emergency care, you must meet several criteria: you need to be enrolled in VA health care or qualify for an exemption, the needed care must not be accessible at a VA or other federal facility in a reasonable time, and a "prudent layperson" would determine that your health was at risk due to the delay in care.

Special Considerations for Service-Connected Conditions

If you experience an emergency related to a service-connected condition, the VA may cover your costs, even if it is outside of a VA facility. In certain cases, such as when you are permanently and totally disabled, or the care is related to your participation in a VA program, coverage may be provided. VA also help with reimbursements if you've already paid for your emergency care.

Emergency Care for Non-Service-Connected Conditions

In cases of emergency care related to non-service-connected conditions, coverage can still be available, but you must meet specific requirements. These include getting care at a facility that provides emergency services to the public, having been treated at a VA or in-network community facility within the last 24 months, and the care being related to an injury or accident. If necessary, you may be reimbursed for any out-of-pocket costs.

The Role of Other Health Insurance

If you have other health insurance, the VA's coverage is limited. If your other insurance doesn't cover the full costs of emergency care, VA may assist with the remaining expenses. However, if your insurance provider denies coverage because of failure to follow their specific guidelines (such as not submitting a bill on time), the VA cannot cover these charges.

Emergency Care Outside the U.S.

If you're outside the U.S. and need emergency care, the VA will only cover the costs if the care is related to a service-connected condition. For further assistance in these cases, you can reach out to the Foreign Medical Care program.

What to Do if You're Charged for Emergency Care

If you're charged for emergency care at a non-VA facility and believe that the VA should cover the costs, you can contact them for assistance. They'll review your case and help resolve any billing issues. You can reach the VA support team during business hours to discuss the charges and initiate reimbursement for any eligible medical expenses.

By understanding the requirements and steps for emergency care, you can ensure that you receive the treatment you need while minimizing your out-of-pocket costs.

Ambulance Transport

The Department of Veterans Affairs may provide or reimburse for land or air ambulance transport of certain eligible veterans in relation to VA care or VA-authorized community care.

VA pays for ambulance transport when the transport has been preauthorized and in certain emergency situations without preauthorization. Two criteria must be met for the VA to pay for ambulance transport.

First, the claimant must meet appropriate administrative eligibility, and a VA provider must determine medical need for ambulance transport. VA must be providing medical care or paying a community care provider for medical care in order to pay for the transport in relation to that care.

2025 Update on Special Modes of Transportation Rates

The VA is adjusting the rates it pays for special transportation services, including air ambulance transportation, to better align with industry standards while continuing to deliver high-quality and affordable care.

A 2018 report from the Inspector General revealed that the VA had been paying approximately 60% more than the standard rates set by the Centers for Medicare & Medicaid Services (CMS) for air ambulance services. In response, the VA is updating its rates to reflect these industry standards and ensure responsible use of taxpayer funds.

Under the new regulation, the VA will pay the lesser of the actual charges for air ambulance services or the CMS standard rate for those services. Exceptions may apply if a local VA medical center has established separate rates through local contracts with air ambulance providers.

These contracts will include provisions to protect veteran care, ensuring that Veterans will not be billed for these services.

Originally scheduled to take effect on February 16, 2024, these changes are now expected to be delayed until February 2025. The rule delaying the effective date will be published before February 16, 2024.

Preauthorized Ambulance Transport

Transport is arranged for eligible veterans before inpatient or outpatient care. To qualify a veteran must meet the following administrative requirements:

- Has a single or combined service-connected rating of 30 percent or more, or
- Veteran is in receipt of VA pension, or
- Previous calendar year income does not exceed maximum VA pension rate, or
- Projected income in travel year does not exceed maximum VA pension rate, or
- Projected income in travel year does not exceed maximum VA pension rate, or
- Travel is in connection with care for a service-connected disability, or
- Travel is for a Compensation and Pension exam, or
- Travel is to obtain a service dog, and
- A VA clinician must determine and document that special mode transportation is medically required

Unauthorized Ambulance Transport

Transport must be preauthorized by VA unless it is in relationship to a medical emergency. Veterans do not have to contact VA in advance of a medical emergency and are encouraged to call 911 or go to the nearest medical emergency room.

VA may pay for ambulance transport that's not preauthorized in the following situations:

- Transport from point of community emergency to a VA facility if the veteran meets administrative and eligibility criteria noted under "Preauthorized ambulance transport"
- Transport from point of community emergency to a community care facility if VA pays for the emergency care in the community care facility under the nonservice-connected or service-connected authorities detailed below.
- VA is contacted within 72 hours of care at a community care facility and retroactively authorizes the community care, and the veteran meets administrative and medical travel eligibility noted under "preauthorized

ambulance transport."

In order for VA to pay for unauthorized ambulance transport, the care associated with the transport must meet one of the following authorities for VA payment:

Emergent care for nonservice-connected conditions (38 United States Code (U.S.C.) 1725 ["Mill Bill"])

- Based on average knowledge of health and medicine, it is reasonably expected that a delay in seeking immediate medical attention would have been hazardous to life or health and
- The episode of care can't be paid under another VA authority and
- A VA or other federal facility/provider was not feasibly available and
- VA medical care was received within 24 months prior to the episode of emergency care and
- The services were furnished by an Emergency Department or similar facility that provides emergency care to the general public and
- Veteran is financial liable for the emergency care and
- Veteran has no other coverage under a health care plan including Medicare, Medicaid or Worker's Compensation, and
- There is no contractual or legal recourse against a third party that could, in whole, extinguish liability.

Emergent Care for Service-Connect Conditions (38 U.S.C. 1728)

- Care is for a service-connected disability or
- Care is for a nonservice-connected condition associated with and aggravating a service- connected condition or
- Care is for any condition of an active participant in the VA Chapter 31 Vocational Rehabilitation program and is needed to make a possible entrance into a course of training or to prevent interruption of a course of training, or
- Care is for any condition of a veteran rated as having a total disability permanent in nature resulting from a service-connected disability and
- Based on an average knowledge of health and medicine, it is reasonably expected that delay in seeking immediate medical attention would have been hazardous to life or health and
- A VA or other federal facility/provider was not feasibly available.

Retroactive Preauthorization (38 CFR 17.54)

In case of an emergency which existed at the time of treatment, VA may retroactively preauthorize the care if:

- An application for VA payment of care provided is made within 72 hours after the emergency care initiated and
- Veteran meets the eligibility criteria for community care at VA expense of 38 U.S.C. 1703

Reimbursement Considerations

- If the emergency room visit and/or admission meets eligibility for VA reimbursement, and the veteran meets beneficiary travel requirements, the

ambulance will be paid from the scene of the incident to the first community care facility providing necessary care
- If a veteran arrives via ambulance but leaves the hospital before being treated by a physician, the ambulance is not guaranteed to be covered by VA regardless of eligibility.
- Accepted VA payments are payments in full. Balance due billing of VA or veterans is prohibited. VA pays the authorized amount or not at all.

Documents Needed to Process Claims

To consider a claim for VA payment of emergency care provided and associated ambulance transport, VA needs the following documents:
- Documented request or application for VA payment of emergency transportation (usually a Health Care Financing Administration form or a bill). Unless transport is preauthorized, the application must be made within 30 days of transport.
- Ambulance trip report documenting circumstances of medical events and care provided by the ambulance service.
- Invoice from ambulance service and community care provider.
- Community care facility records of care provided to the veteran—VA will request these from the facility.

All required documents must be received prior to payment consideration. Payment for associated ambulance transport can't occur unless VA is providing or paying for emergency care.

Appeals

If a claim does not meet VA payment criteria (is not payable,) then it's denied and both the community care provider and veteran are provided an explanation of denial and notified of the right to appeal the decision (VA Form 4107, Notification of Rights to Appeal Decision).

Veterans Transportation Program

The Veterans Transportation Service (VTS) offers reliable transportation for veterans to and from VA and authorized non-VA health care appointments. It partners with Veterans Service Organizations (VSOs), local non-profits, and government agencies to meet veterans' transportation needs, especially those who are visually impaired, elderly, disabled, or live in rural areas.

VTS, in collaboration with the Office of Rural Health, is working to establish Mobility Managers at VA facilities to help veterans with transportation. Veterans eligible for VA health care can access VTS transportation based on the availability and guidelines at their local facility.

Highly Rural Transportation Grants

Highly Rural Transportation Grants (HRTG) is a grant-based program that helps veterans in highly rural areas travel to VA or VA-authorized health care facilities.

This program provides grant funding to Veteran Service Organizations and State Veterans Service Agencies to provide transportation services in eligible counties. HRTGs provide transportation programs in counties with fewer than seven people per square mile. There is no cost to participate in the program for veterans who live in an area where HRTG is available.

Overview of Health Services for Women Veterans

Women veterans come from diverse backgrounds, including professionals, mothers, retirees, and service members of varying ages, ethnicities, gender identities, and sexual orientations. The Department of Veterans Affairs (VA) provides a wide range of healthcare services to meet the unique needs of women veterans throughout different stages of life.

General and Specialized Health Services Primary Care and Preventive Services

Women veterans are eligible for comprehensive health care services, including routine screenings and wellness checks. Primary care providers at the VA offer preventive care and help manage short- and long-term health conditions. These services include:

- **Cancer Screenings**: Regular screenings for breast, cervical, colon, lung, and skin cancers based on age, risk factors, and family history.
    - *Breast Cancer*: Mammograms begin at age 45, with an option for biennial screenings after age 55.
    - *Cervical Cancer*: Pap tests begin at age 21, continuing every 3 years. After age 30, HPV testing may also be used in screening.
    - *Colon Cancer*: Screening starts at age 45.
    - *Lung Cancer*: Annual low-dose CT scans are recommended for women with significant smoking history, starting at age 50.
    - *Skin Cancer*: Screening is encouraged as skin cancer is treatable if detected early.
- **General Health Screenings**: Additional screenings include checks for anemia, blood pressure, cholesterol, diabetes, HIV, hepatitis C, and sexually transmitted infections (STIs). Women veterans are also screened for osteoporosis after age 65 and may be evaluated for abdominal aortic aneurysm if they have a smoking history.

Immunizations

The VA recommends various vaccines, including COVID-19, flu, pneumonia, shingles, HPV, tetanus, and respiratory syncytial virus (RSV) vaccinations, based on individual health needs.

Specialized Care for Women Veterans

In addition to general healthcare, the VA provides specialized care to address the unique health needs of women veterans:

- **Reproductive Health**: The VA offers a range of services, including family planning, maternity care, and infertility treatment.
- **Mental Health Services**: Services for conditions like PTSD, depression, and anxiety, including counseling and medications.
- **Military Sexual Trauma (MST)**: The VA provides confidential treatment for physical and mental health conditions related to MST. This care is available even if the veteran did not report the trauma at the time it occurred.
- **Gender-Specific Prosthetics**: The VA offers prosthetics and sensory aids designed for women, including post-mastectomy care.

Whole Health Approach

The VA's Whole Health model focuses on what matters most to the individual, rather than just treating illnesses. This holistic approach includes:

- Complementary therapies like meditation, yoga, massage, and acupuncture.
- Art, music, and equine therapy, which are offered to promote emotional and psychological well-being.

Accessing Services

Women Veterans Call Center (WVCC)

The Women Veterans Call Center is available to help women veterans navigate VA healthcare services. Veterans can contact the WVCC at **855-829-6636** to get assistance with:

- Enrollment in VA health care
- Scheduling medical appointments
- Understanding eligibility and benefits
- Referrals to local VA Medical Centers for coordinated care

The WVCC operates Monday through Friday from 8:00 a.m. to 10:00 p.m. ET and Saturday from 8:00 a.m. to 6:30 p.m. ET.

Reengagement and Training Resources

Women Veterans Health Reengagement Training (heaRT)

This training program is designed to help women veterans reconnect with the VA health care system and understand the benefits available to them. It provides information on how to enroll in VA services and access health care, particularly for those who have not utilized their benefits.

In Vitro Fertilization (IVF)

In 2025, the Department of Veterans Affairs (VA) announced an expansion of its fertility services to provide in vitro fertilization (IVF) to more veterans, including unmarried veterans and those in same-sex marriages. Additionally, the VA will now offer IVF services using donated sperm, eggs, or embryos for veterans whose ability to produce their own gametes has been affected by service-related injuries or health conditions. This marks a significant update from the previous policy, which restricted IVF access to legally married veterans who could produce their own eggs or sperm.

Under this update, eligible veterans with service-connected infertility can now receive IVF and other assisted reproductive technology (ART) services. These benefits extend to the spouses of qualifying veterans, who can also receive fertility counseling and ART services, including IVF. While IVF is typically excluded from the VA medical benefits package, it is authorized under 38 CFR 17.380 for certain veterans with disabilities resulting in infertility. These services are further defined in VHA Directive 1334.

In vitro fertilization (IVF) is a process where an egg and sperm are combined outside the body, creating embryos that are then implanted into the uterus. IVF is commonly used when other fertility treatments have not been successful or when a medical condition, such as blocked fallopian tubes or male infertility, is preventing conception. The procedure involves ovarian stimulation, egg retrieval, fertilization, and embryo transfer, and it is typically considered after less invasive treatments fail.

Spouses of eligible veterans may also access IVF and fertility treatments, as well as counseling, under the VA's expanded services.

However, non-veteran partners are not eligible for VA-funded infertility services unless they qualify for the Civilian Health and Medical Program of the Department of Veterans Affairs (CHAMPVA). In such cases, the veteran and non-veteran partner are responsible for the cost of treatment through outside providers.

This new policy ensures that more veterans can access the fertility care they need, helping them start families despite the challenges posed by service-connected disabilities.

Coverage for Indian Health Service and Tribal Health Programs

The VA provides coverage for eligible veterans receiving care at Indian Health Service (IHS), Tribal Health Programs, and Urban Indian Organization (I/T/U) facilities. This includes American Indian and Alaska Native veterans who are enrolled in VA health care and meet specific eligibility criteria. Here's what you need to know:

Eligible American Indian or Alaska Native Veterans

- If enrolled in VA health care, veterans can receive care through I/T/U

facilities with a reimbursement agreement with the VA.
- No prior approval or "preauthorization" is required for treatment.
- Veterans will not need to pay a VA copay for care received at these facilities.

Non-Eligible Veterans in Alaska

- Veterans who are not American Indian or Alaska Native may still be able to receive care at I/T/U facilities, but they must get preauthorization from the VA before treatment.
- A copay may be required for these veterans, depending on the situation.

For questions, veterans can contact the VA at tribal.agreements@va.gov.

Copay Exemptions for American Indian and Alaska Native Veterans

As of April 4, 2023, American Indian and Alaska Native veterans are no longer required to pay a copay for most VA health care services, including urgent care. Additionally, the VA will review any copays paid for covered services from January 5, 2022, onward and reimburse eligible amounts.

Services Covered by Copay Exemptions

Eligible veterans will no longer be billed for copays for the following services:
- Hospital care
- Outpatient prescription medications
- Urgent care visits

However, copays still apply for certain services like domiciliary care, nursing home care, and institutional geriatric evaluation.

Eligibility for Copay Exemption

Veterans may qualify for a copay exemption if they meet the following criteria:
1. They are an American Indian or Alaska Native veteran.
2. They provide documentation proving eligibility under the Indian Health Care Improvement Act.
3. They submit a completed Tribal Documentation Form (VA Form 10-334).

How to Apply for a Copay Exemption

To receive a copay exemption, veterans need to provide the following:
- A copy of an official tribal document (e.g., tribal enrollment card or certificate of Indian blood).
- A completed VA Form 10-334 (Tribal Documentation Form).

These documents can be sent to the following address:

VHA Tribal Documentation
PO Box 5100
Janesville, WI 53547-5100

It is important that only copies are sent, not originals.

What Happens After You Apply

Once the VA receives the completed form and tribal documents, they will review the information and notify veterans about their eligibility. If eligible, the VA will also reimburse veterans for any copays paid for covered services from January 5, 2022, onward.

Foreign Medical Program (FMP) Overview

The Foreign Medical Program (FMP) covers healthcare for eligible veterans with service-connected disabilities who are living or traveling outside the United States. The program reimburses veterans for care received in foreign countries related to their service-connected conditions. Here's what you need to know about FMP benefits and how to file a claim.

Eligibility for FMP

To be eligible for FMP, veterans must:

- Have a service-connected disability.
- Receive care in a foreign country for a service-connected condition, or for a condition that aggravates their service-connected disability.

Veterans do not need to be enrolled in VA health care to apply for FMP; however, they must be registered for the program to receive reimbursement.

What Care Is Covered?

FMP covers a variety of healthcare services that are medically necessary for treating service-connected conditions, including:

- Outpatient care (office visits)
- Inpatient care (hospital stays)
- Emergency and urgent care
- Medical equipment, devices, and supplies (e.g., prosthetics)
- Skilled nursing care
- Physical therapy
- FDA-approved prescription medications

However, FMP does not cover:

- Care for non-service-connected conditions (unless related to a service-connected condition).
- Long-term care in nursing homes or assisted living facilities.

- Non-medical home care, experimental treatments, or luxury medical equipment.

Filing FMP Claims

Veterans can file FMP claims directly if their provider does not submit the claim on their behalf.

Here's how to file:
1. Complete VA Form 10-7959f-2, the FMP Claim Cover Sheet.
2. Provide an itemized billing statement from the provider, including details of the care received, the health conditions treated, and proof of payment.
3. Fax or mail the form and supporting documents to the appropriate address based on where care was provided:
   - For care outside the U.S. (except Canada), mail to:
     VHA Office of Integrated Veteran Care
     Foreign Medical Program (FMP)
     PO Box 200
     Spring City, PA 19475
   - For care in Canada, mail to:
     Foreign Countries Operations (FCO)
     2323 Riverside Drive, 2nd Floor
     Ottawa, Ontario, Canada K1A OP5
   - Fax to 303-331-7803 (or 613-991-0305 for care in Canada).

Additional Documentation

Depending on the type of care, additional documentation may be required, such as:
- Inpatient hospital care: Send your discharge summary or operation report.
- Medical devices/equipment: Provide the prescription and details about the device.
- Prescription medications: Include the prescription and a receipt or billing statement.

When to File Your Claim

Claims must be filed within two years from the date the care was provided, or from the date of discharge if hospitalized. If the claim is related to inpatient care, it must be filed within two years of discharge from the hospital.

What Happens After You File a Claim?

After filing, the VA will review the claim and notify you of the decision:
- If approved, a U.S. Treasury check will be issued for the claim amount.
- If denied, you may appeal the decision within one year of the notification.

Contacting FMP

Veterans can contact FMP for questions or assistance via:

- Online through Ask VA
- Email: HAC.FMP@va.gov (please do not send sensitive information via email)
- Phone: +1-833-930-0816 (TTY: 711)
  Toll-free numbers are also available for veterans in specific countries.

Special Considerations

- COVID-19 Vaccines: Veterans can file claims for COVID-19 vaccines received abroad.
- Mail-order medications: FMP does not cover mail-order prescriptions from the U.S., but veterans can seek local pharmacies for prescriptions.

CHAPTER 2

NURSING HOME AND LONG-TERM CARE BENEFITS

Veterans may be able to get assisted living, residential or home health care through VA. The care is available in different settings, some of which are run by VA and others are run by state or community organizations the VA inspects and approves.

Standard Benefits

The following long-term care services are available to all enrolled veterans:

- **Geriatric Evaluation**
  - A geriatric evaluation is the comprehensive assessment of a veteran's ability to care for him/herself, his/her physical health, and the social environment, which leads to a plan of care. The plan could include treatment, rehabilitation, health promotion, and social services. These evaluations are performed by inpatient Geriatric Evaluation and Management (GEM) Units, GEM clinics, geriatric primary care clinics, and other outpatient settings.
- **Adult Day Health Care**
  - The adult day health care (ADHC) program is a therapeutic daycare program, providing medical and rehabilitation services to disabled veterans in a combined setting.
- **Respite Care**
  - Respite care provides supportive care to veterans on a short-term basis to give the caregiver a planned period of relief from the physical and emotional demands associated with providing care. Respite care can be provided in the home or other noninstitutionalized settings.
- **Home Care**
  - Skilled home care is provided by VA and contract agencies to veterans that are homebound with chronic diseases and include nursing, physical/occupational therapy, and social services.

- **Hospice/Palliative Care**
  - Hospice/palliative care programs offer pain management, symptom control, and other medical services to terminally ill veterans or veterans in the late stages of the chronic disease process. Services also include respite care as well as bereavement counseling to family members.

Financial Assessment for Long-Term Care Services

For veterans who are not automatically exempt from making copayments for long-term care services, a separate financial assessment must be completed to determine whether they qualify for cost-free services or to what extent they are required to make long term care copayments. For those veterans who do not qualify for cost-free services, the financial assessment for long term care services is used to determine the copayment requirement. Unlike copayments for other VA health care services, which are based on fixed charges for all, long-term care copayment charges are individually adjusted based on each veteran's financial status.

Limited Benefits

Nursing Home Care

While some veterans qualify for indefinite nursing home care services, other veterans may qualify for a limited period of time. Among those that automatically qualify for indefinite nursing home care are veterans whose service-connected condition is clinically determined to require nursing home care and veterans with a service-connected rating of 70% or more. Other veterans—with priority given to those with service-connected conditions—may be provided short-term nursing home care if space and resources are available.

The Department of Veterans Affairs (VA) provides both short-term and long-term care in nursing homes to veterans who aren't sick enough to be in the hospital but are too disabled or elderly to take care of themselves. Priority is given to veterans with service- connected disabilities.

Priority Groups

The VA is required to provide nursing home care to any veteran who

- Needs nursing home care because of a service-connected disability
- Has a combined disability rating of 70% or more, or
- Has a disability rating of at least 60% and is:
  - Deemed unemployable, or
  - Has been rated permanently and totally disabled.

Other veterans in need of nursing care will be provided services if resources are available after the above groups are taken care of.

Types of Nursing Care Available

Community Living Centers

Some VA Medical Centers have Community Living Centers (these used to be called Nursing Home Care Units or VA Nursing Homes). These centers are typically located within the VA Medical Center itself or in a separate building.

Contract Nursing Home Care

Nursing home care in public or private nursing homes is also available to some veterans. Stays in these nursing homes can be limited; however, for veterans with ratings less than 70% and for veterans who do not need care due to a service-connected disability.

State Veterans Homes

State Veterans Homes are nursing homes run by the state and approved by the VA. Sometimes the VA will pay for part of the care a veteran gets at a state veterans' home.

Eligibility for Community Living Centers (CLCS)

To receive care in a Community Living Center/VA nursing home, a veteran must:

- Be enrolled in the VA Health Care System
- Be psychiatrically and medically stable.
- Provide documentation specifying whether short or long-term care is needed, an estimation of how long the stay will be, and when discharge occurs, and
- Show priority for a stay in a CLC.

However, meeting the above criteria does not automatically ensure admission. CLCs make decisions about whether to admit a veteran based on the following factors:

- Availability of services in the CLC
- What sort of care the veteran needs, and
- Whether the CLC can competently provide the type of care the veteran needs.

Co-Pays

Veterans required to make co-pays are typically those:
- Without a service-connected disability rated at least 10%, and
- Whose income is higher than the VA's maximum annual pension rate.

How to Apply for CLC Care

Typically, a veteran's physician will submit the application requesting care in a CLC. Veterans who are not exempt from co-pays must complete VA Form 10-10EC, Application for Extended Care Services.

Eligibility for Contract Nursing Home Care

Any veteran who needs Contract Nursing Home Care for a service-connected disability or is receiving VA home health care after discharge from a VA hospital is eligible for direct admission. To be admitted, all that is required is for a VA physician or authorized private physician to determine that nursing home care is needed. Veterans rated 70%, or more service-connected should also be eligible.

Other veterans are eligible to be transferred into Contract Nursing Home Care (also called a Community Nursing Home) if the VA determines the care is needed and:

- The veteran is in a VA hospital, nursing home, domiciliary, or has been receiving VA outpatient care, or
- An active member of the Armed Forces who was in a DOD hospital needs nursing care and will be an eligible veteran upon discharge.

Time Limits for Contract Nursing Home Care

Veterans who are not in the priority groups are technically limited to six months of care, but this may be reduced to 30 to 60 days if resources are limited. Veterans in the priority groups are technically entitled to unlimited free care but again may receive shorter stays due to a lack of funding and resources to accommodate them.

Many veterans can extend their stay by relying on payments from Medicare and Medicaid.

How to Apply for Contract Nursing Home Care

Typically, an application will be made by a veterans' doctor, social worker or nurse, using VA Form 10-0415, Geriatrics and Extended Care (GEC) Referral.

Eligibility for State Veterans Homes

In some cases, the VA will help pay for a veteran's care at a State Veterans Home. The payments the VA will make are called per diem aid. A home must meet the VA standards for nursing home care to receive per diem aid. In addition, the VA will not pay more than half the cost of the veteran's care.

State homes provide hospital care, nursing home care, domiciliary care, and sometimes adult daycare. To receive per diem aid, veterans must meet VA eligibility requirements for the type of care they will receive.

States usually have their own eligibility requirements, in addition to the VA's requirements, such as residency requirements. The veterans' home will apply for VA aid for a veteran's care by submitting VA Form 10-10EZ, Application for Medical Benefits. The VA will pay per diem aid for a veteran's care indefinitely.

Reduction in Pension

Congress establishes the maximum annual Veterans Pension rates. Payments are reduced by the amount of countable income of the veteran, spouse, and dependent children. When a veteran without a spouse or a child is furnished nursing home or domiciliary care by VA, the pension is reduced to an amount not to exceed $90 per month after three calendar months of care. The reduction may be delayed if nursing-home care is being continued to provide the veteran with rehabilitation services.

Domiciliary Care

Domiciliary care provides rehabilitative and long-term, health maintenance care for veterans who require some medical care, but who do not require all the services provided in nursing homes. Domiciliary care emphasizes rehabilitation and return to the community. VA may provide domiciliary care to veterans whose annual income does not exceed the maximum annual rate of VA pension or to veterans who have no adequate means of support.

Services for Blind Veterans

Veterans with corrected central vision of 20/200 or less in both eyes, or field loss to 20 degrees or less in both eyes are considered to be blind.

Blind veterans may be eligible for many of the benefits detailed throughout this book, including, but not limited to: Disability Compensation, Health Insurance, Adaptive Equipment, and Training & Rehabilitation. In addition to these benefits, there are a number of miscellaneous benefits due veterans of all wars who were blinded as the result of their war service. Many individual states offer special programs and benefits for the blind.

Services are available at all VA medical facilities through Visual Impairment Services Team (VIST) coordinators.

The VIST Coordinator is a case manager who has major responsibility for the coordination of all services for legally blind veterans and their families. Duties include providing and/or arranging for appropriate treatment, identifying new cases of blindness, providing professional counseling, resolving problems, arranging annual healthcare reviews, and conducting education programs relating to blindness.

Blind veterans may be eligible for services at a VA medical center or for admission to a VA blind rehabilitation center or clinic. In addition, blind veterans entitled to receive disability compensation may receive VA aids for the blind, which may include:

- A total health and benefits review by a VA Visual Impairment Services team.
- Adjustment to blindness training;
- Home Improvements and Structural Alterations to homes (HISA Program);
- Specially adapted housing and adaptations;
- Low-vision aids and training in their use;
- Electronic and mechanical aids for the blind, including adaptive computers and computer-assisted devices;
- Guide dogs, including the expense of training the veteran to use the dog, and the cost of the dog's medical care;
- Talking books, tapes, and Braille literature, provided from the Library of Congress.

Guide Dogs/Service Dogs

As previously mentioned, VA may provide guide dogs to blind veterans. Additionally, Public Law 107-135 (signed by then-President Bush January 23, 2002) states that VA may provide:

- Service dogs trained for the aid of the hearing impaired to veterans who are hearing impaired, and are enrolled under Section 1705 of Title 38; and
- Service dogs trained for the aid of persons with spinal cord injury or dysfunction or other chronic impairment that substantially limits mobility to veterans with such injury, dysfunction, or impairment who are enrolled under section 1705 of Title 38.
- VA may also pay travel and incidental expenses for the veteran to travel to and from the veteran's home while becoming adjusted to the dog.

The VA operates nine blind rehabilitation centers in the United States and Puerto Rico. Rehabilitation centers offer comprehensive programs to guide individuals through a process that eventually leads to maximum adjustment to the disability, reorganization of the person's life, and return to a contributing place in the family and community.

To achieve these goals, the rehabilitation centers offer a variety of skill courses to veterans, which are designed to help achieve a realistic level of independence. Services offered at rehabilitation centers include:

- Orientation and mobility;
- Living skills;
- Communication skills;
- Activities of daily living;
- Independent daily living program;
- Manual skills;
- Visual skills;
- Computer Access Training Section;
- Physical conditioning;
- Recreation;
- Adjustment to blindness;

- Group meetings.

The VA also employs Blind Rehabilitation Outpatient Specialists (BROS) in several areas, including:

- Albuquerque, NM
- Ann Arbor, MI
- Bay Pines / St. Petersburg, FL
- Baltimore, MD
- Boston, MA
- Cleveland, OH
- Dallas, TX
- Gainesville, FL
- Los Angeles, CA
- Phoenix, AZ
- Portland, OR
- San Antonio, TX
- San Juan, PR
- Seattle, WA
- West Haven, CT

Home Improvements and Structural Alterations (HISA)

The HISA program offers medically necessary home modifications for veterans to improve accessibility and support medical equipment. These improvements may include:

- Accessible entrances, roll-in showers, or lowered counters/sinks
- Improvements to entrance paths or driveways (e.g., ramps)
- Plumbing or electrical upgrades for medical equipment

What HISA Covers:

- **Up to $6,800** for addressing service-connected disabilities, compensable disabilities treated as service-connected, or disabilities in veterans with at least a 50% service-connected rating.
- **Up to $2,000** for other eligible conditions.

What HISA Excludes:

- Exterior decking, spa/hot tubs, home security systems, and non-essential items like portable ramps or stair lifts.

Application Process:

- Submit a prescription from a VA physician, a completed VA Form 10-0103, cost estimates, and a photo of the unimproved area.
- If renting, include a notarized statement from the property owner.
- For detailed eligibility or to apply, contact your local Prosthetic and Sensory Aids Service.

CHAPTER 3

DENTAL BENEFITS

If you qualify for VA dental care benefits, you may be able to get some or all of your dental care through VA. Whether or not you can get VA dental care benefits for some, or all of your dental care depends on factors like your military service history, your current health, and your living situation. Based on this information, you are placed in a benefits class. You get specific benefits assigned to that class.

VA Outpatient Dental Benefits

Veteran dental care eligibility is categorized into classes. Recently discharged veterans may qualify for a one-time dental course if they apply within 180 days and were discharged under conditions other than dishonorable after 90+ days of active duty. Veterans not eligible for VA dental care can purchase insurance through the national VA Dental Insurance Program at a reduced cost.

Eligibility for outpatient care varies by class. Veterans in Class I, IIA, IIC, or IV are eligible for comprehensive dental care, including repeat treatments. Other classes have service and time limitations.

If You:	You Are Eligible For:	Through:
Have a service-connected compensable dental disability or condition	Any needed dental care	Class I
Are a former prisoner of war	Any needed dental care	Class IIC
Have service-connected disabilities rated 100% (total) disabling or are unemployable and paid at the 100% rate due to service-connected conditions	Any needed dental care (Note: veterans paid at the 100% rate based on a temporary rating are not eligible for comprehensive outpatient dental services based on this temporary rating)	Class IV

Request dental care within 180 days of discharge or release under conditions other than dishonorable from a period of active duty of 90 days or more	One-time dental care if your DD214 certificate of discharge does not indicate a complete dental exam and all appropriate treatment had been rendered prior to discharge	Class II
Have a service-connected noncompensable (0%) dental condition/disability resulting from combat wounds or service trauma	Any dental care necessary to provide and maintain a functioning dentition. A VA Regional Office Rating Decision Letter (VA Form 10-7131) or the historical Dental Trauma Rating (VA Form 10- 564-D) identifies the tooth/teeth/conditions that are trauma related	Class IIA
Have a dental condition clinically determined by VA to be associated with and aggravating a service-connected medical condition	Dental care to treat the oral conditions that are determined by a VA dental professional to have a direct and material detrimental effect to your service-connected medical condition	Class III
Are actively engaged in a Title 38, USC Chapter 31 Vocational Rehabilitation and Employment Program	Dental care to the extent determined by a VA dental professional to meet certain requirements.	Class V
Are receiving VA care or are scheduled for inpatient care and require dental care for a condition complicating a medical condition currently under treatment	Dental care to the treat the oral conditions that are determined by a VA dental professional to complicate your medical condition currently under treatment	Class VI
Are enrolled in a qualifying VA sponsored homeless residential rehabilitation program for at least 60 days	A one-time course of dental care that is determined medically necessary for certain reasons	Class IIB

VA Dental Insurance Program (VADIP)

If you can't get VA dental care benefits, you may be able to buy dental insurance at a reduced cost through the VA Dental Insurance Program (VADIP). You have to meet at least one of two requirements. The first is that you're signed up for VA health care, or you are signed up for CHAMPVA.

Insurance carriers may offer separate coverage options for dependents who aren't CHAMPVA beneficiaries.

VADIP provides coverage throughout the U.S. and its territories including Puerto Rico, Guam, the U.S. Virgin Islands, American Samoa, and the Commonwealth of the Northern Mariana Islands.

If you're not eligible for free VA dental care, VADIP can help you buy private dental insurance at a reduced cost. If you're eligible for free VA care for some of your dental needs, you can buy a VADIP plan if you want added dental insurance. If you sign up for VADIP, it doesn't affect your ability to get free dental care.

VADIP plans cover common dental procedures, which may include:

- Diagnostic services
- Preventive dental care
- Root canals and other services to manage oral health problems and restore function (called endodontic or restorative services)
- Dental surgery
- Emergency dental care

The costs of coverage depend on the insurance company and plan selected. Based on your plan, you'll pay the full insurance premium for each individual on your plan, and any required copays when you get care.

You can choose between a Delta Dental Plan or a MetLife Plan, and you enroll online with the company. Once you enroll you can use your insurance provider's website to manage your plan and benefits.

If you participated in the VADIP pilot program, that ended in 2017, so you need to enroll again to get new coverage.

TRICARE Retiree Dental Program

RDP ended in 2018 and was replaced by the Office of Personnel Management's Federal Employees Dental and Vision Insurance Program (FEDVIP). If you were eligible for TRDP, you might be able to enroll in a FEDVIP dental plan.

You must enroll in FEDVIP dental during the 2020 Open Season or after a FEDVIP Qualifying Life Event.

FEDVIP is a voluntary, enrollee-pay-all dental and vision program available to Federal employees and annuitants and certain uniformed service members. It is sponsored by the U.S. Office of Personnel Management (OPM) and offers eligible participants a choice between ten dental and four vision carriers.

BENEFEDS is the government-authorized and OPM-sponsored enrollment portal that eligible participants use to enroll in and manage their FEDVIP coverage. BENEFEDS also manages the billing systems and customer service functions necessary for the collection of FEDVIP premiums.

FEDVIP dental plans provide comprehensive dental coverage, including in-network preventive services covered 100%; no deductibles when using in-network dentists; no waiting period for major services such as crowns, bridges, dentures, and implants; and no 12-month waiting period or age limit for orthodontic coverage under some plans.

TRICARE Selected Reserve Dental Program Benefits

Individuals with at least one year of service commitment remaining who are serving in the Army Reserve, Naval Reserve, Air Force Reserve, Marine Corps Reserve, Coast Guard Reserve, Army National Guard or Air National Guard, may be eligible to enroll in the Tricare Selected Reserve Dental Program (TSRDP).

The Department of Defense works in conjunction with Humana Military Healthcare Services to offer and administer the TRICARE Selected Reserve Dental Program.

Coverage remains available as long as an individual maintains his or her Reserve status and is shown as eligible on the DEERS record.

The information provided in this section is intended only as a brief overview. Humana Military Healthcare Services has a staff of trained Beneficiary Services Representatives who are available to answer your questions.

TRICARE Dental Program Survivor Benefit Plan

If your sponsor died while serving on active duty, you may qualify for the TRICARE Dental Program Survivor Benefit Plan.

This includes 100% payment of monthly premiums, and TRICARE pays for cost shares for covered service.

If you were using the TRICARE Dental Program when your sponsor died, you're automatically transferred to the Survivor Benefit Plan. If not, you can enroll at any time. After three years, surviving spouses lose eligibility for the TRICARE Dental Program. They can purchase the TRICARE Retiree Dental Program only if their sponsor died while on active duty for more than 30 days.

Surviving children can remain enrolled in the TRICARE Dental Plan until they lose TRICARE eligibility for other reasons.

CHAPTER 4

TOXIC EXPOSURE

During military service, some servicemembers may have come in contact with hazardous materials and chemical hazards.

Exposures Include:

- **Agent Orange**: If you served in the Republic of Vietnam or in or near the Korean Demilitarized Zone (DMZ) during the Vietnam Era or in certain related jobs, you may have had contact with Agent Orange. Agent Orange is an herbicide, used for clearing trees and plants during war.
- **Asbestos**: If you worked in certain military jobs, you may have had contact with asbestos, which are toxic fibers that were once used in buildings and products.
- **Birth defects like spina bifida**: If you served in the Republic of Vietnam, in Thailand, or in or near the DMZ during the Vietnam Era and your child has spina bifida or certain other birth defects, your child could be eligible for disability benefits.
- **Burn pits and other specific environmental hazards**: If you served in Iraq, Afghanistan or other certain areas, you may have had contact with toxic chemicals in the air, water or soil.
- **Contact with mustard gas or lewisite**: If you served at the German bombing of Bari, Italy in World War II or worked in certain other jobs, you may have had contact with mustard gas.
- **Contaminated drinking water at Camp Lejeune**: If you served at Camp Lejeune or MCAS New River between August 1953 and December 1987, you may be at risk of certain illnesses believed to be caused by contaminants found in the drinking water during that time.
- **Gulf War Illnesses in Southwest Asia:** If you served in the Southwest Asia theater of operations, you may be at risk of certain illnesses or other conditions linked to the region.
- **Gulf War Illnesses in Afghanistan**: If you served in Afghanistan, you may be at risk of certain illnesses linked to this region.
- **Project 112/SHAD**: If you were part of warfare testing for Project 112 or Project Shipboard Hazard and Defense (SHAD) from 1962 to 1974, you may be at risk for illnesses believed to be caused by chemical testing.
- **Radiation exposure**: If you served in the post-WWII occupation of Hiroshima or Nagasaki, were imprisoned in Japan, worked with or near nuclear weapons testing, or served at a gaseous diffusion plant or in certain other jobs, you might be at risk of illnesses believed to be caused by radiation.

The PACT Act

The PACT Act is considered the largest expansion of health care and benefits in the history of VA. The full name of the legislation is The Sergeant First Class (SFC) Heath Robinson Honor Our Promise to Address Comprehensive Toxics (PACT) Act. You can find more about the details of The Pact Act in Chapter 9, The PACT Act and what it impacts.

Agent Orange Exposure and VA Disability Compensation

Agent Orange was a tactical herbicide the U.S. military used to clear leaves and vegetation for military operations, primarily during the Vietnam War. Veterans who were exposed to Agent Orange may have certain related cancers or other illnesses. If you have a health condition caused by exposure to Agent Orange during military service, you may be eligible for disability compensation and below is detailed how you can apply.

You may be eligible for VA disability benefits if you meet both requirements:

- You have a health condition caused by exposure to Agent Orange, and;
- You served in a location that exposed you to Agent Orange.

Eligibility is determined based on the facts of each veteran's claim, but the VA assumes that certain conditions and other illnesses are caused by Agent Orange. These are presumptive conditions. The VA assumes veterans who served in certain locations were exposed to Agent Orange, which is presumptive exposure.

Under the PACT Act, two new Agent Orange-related conditions have been added. These are:

- Hypertension (high blood pressure)
- Monoclonal gammopathy of undetermined significance (MGUS)

Under the PACT Act, five new Agent Orange presumptive locations were also added, which are detailed below.

Cancers caused by Agent Orange Exposure include:

- Bladder cancer
- Chronic B-cell leukemia
- Hodgkin's disease
- Multiple myeloma
- Non-Hodgkin's lymphoma
- Prostate cancer
- Respiratory cancers (including lung cancer)
- Some soft tissue sarcomas

Not included are osteosarcoma, chondrosarcoma, Kaposi's sarcoma or mesothelioma. Other illnesses caused by Agent Orange Exposure include:

- AL amyloidosis
- Chloracne or other types of acneiform disease like it (under the VA's rating regulations, the condition must be at least 10% disabling within a year of

herbicide exposure)
- Diabetes mellitus type 2
- Hypertension (high blood pressure)
- Hypothyroidism
- Ischemic heart disease
- Monoclonal gammopathy of undetermined significance (MGUS)
- Parkinsonism
- Parkinson's disease
- Peripheral neuropathy, early onset (under the VA rating regulations, the condition must be at least 10% disabling with a year of herbicide exposure)
- Porphyria cutanea tarda (under the VA rating regulation, the condition must be at least 10% disabling within a year of herbicide exposure)

If you have a cancer or illness not listed on the presumptive conditions, but you believe it was caused by exposure to Agent Orange, you can still file a claim for disability benefits, but you'll have to submit more evidence.

Service Requirements

The VA bases eligibility for disability compensation in part on whether you served in a location exposing you to Agent Orange—this is a presumption of exposure. You have a presumption of exposure if you meet the service requirements below.

Between January 9, 1962, and May 7, 1975, you must have served for any length of time in at least one of these locations:

- In the republic of Vietnam, or
- Aboard a U.S. military vessel that operated in the inland waterways of Vietnam, or
- On a vessel operating not more than 12 nautical miles seaward from the demarcation line of the waters of Vietnam and Cambodia

Or you must have served in at least one of these locations that have been added through the passage of the PACT Act:

- Any U.S. or Royal Thai military base in Thailand from January 9, 1962, through June 30, 1976, or
- Laos from December 1, 1965, through September 30, 1969, or
- Cambodia at Mimot or Krek, Kampong Cham Province, from April 16, 1969, through April 30, 1969, or
- Guam or American Samoa or in the territorial waters off Guam or American Samoa from January 9, 1962, through July 31, 1980, or
- Johnston Atoll or on a ship that called at Johnston Atoll from January 1, 1972, through September 30, 1977.

At least one of the following must be true:

- You served in or near the Korean DMZ for any length of time between September 1, 1967, and August 31, 1971, or
- You served on active duty in a regular Air Force unit location where a C-123 aircraft with traces of Agent Orange was assigned and had repeated contact with this aircraft due to your flight, ground or medical duties, or

- Were involved in transporting, testing, storing or other uses of Agent Orange during your military service, or
- You were assigned as a Reservist to certain flight, ground or medical crew duties at one of the locations listed.

Eligible Reserve locations, time periods and units include:

- Lockbourne/Rickenbacker Air Force Base in Ohio, 1969 to 1986 (906th and 907th Tactical Air Groups or 355th and 356th Tactical Airlift Squadrons)
- Westover Air Force Base in Massachusetts, 1972 to 1982 (731st Tactical Air Squadron and 74th Aeromedical Evacuation Squadron or 901st Organization Maintenance Squadron)
- Pittsburgh International Airport in Pennsylvania, 1972, to 1982 (758th Airlift Squadron)

The Bluewater (BWN) Vietnam Veterans Act 2019 (Public Law 116-23)

Public Law 116-23, The Blue Water Vietnam Veterans Act of 2019, went into effect on January 1, 2020. According to this new law, veterans who served as far as 12 nautical miles from the shore of Vietnam or who had served in the Korean Demilitarized zone, are presumed to have been exposed to herbicides such as Agent Orange and may be entitled to service compensation for any of the 14 conditions related to herbicide exposure. These conditions are:

- Chronic B-cell leukemia
- Hodgkin's disease
- Multiple myelomas
- Non-Hodgkin's lymphoma
- Prostate cancer
- Respiratory cancers including lung cancer
- Soft tissue sarcomas other than osteosarcoma, chondrosarcoma, Kaposi's sarcoma or mesothelioma
- AL amyloidosis
- Chloracne
- Diabetes mellitus type 2
- Ischemic heart disease
- Parkinson's disease
- Peripheral neuropathy
- Porphyria cutanea tarda

VA is now able to extend benefits to children with spina bifida whose BWN veteran parent may have been exposed while serving. Additionally, PL 116-23 made changes to the VA Home Loan Program. See Chapter 19 for more information about these changes. To be entitled to VA benefits, veterans must have served between January 9, 1962, and May 7, 1975, and have one or more of these conditions listed in section 3.309€ of title 38, Code of Federal Regulations.

You can apply for initial compensation claims with VA Form 21-526EZ. For initial DIC claims, submit a VA Form 21P-534EZ. For previously denied claims, submit a VA

Form 20-0995.

When filing a claim, you should state on your application that you're filing for one of the conditions related to presumed herbicide exposure such as Agent Orange. You should include any evidence you have of service in the offshore waters of the Republic of Vietnam during the required timeframe. Include the name of the vessels and the dates you served within 12 nautical miles of the Republic of Vietnam if you have that information. Provide medical evidence showing a diagnosis of a current condition related to exposure to herbicide such as Agent Orange or tell the VA where you're being treated.

Agent Orange Exposure from C-123 Aircraft

If you flew on—or worked with—C-123 aircraft in Vietnam or other locations, you may have had contact with Agent Orange. The U.S. military used this herbicide to clear trees and plants during the Vietnam War. C-123 aircraft sprayed Agent Orange during the war, and the planes still had traces of the chemical in them afterward while they were being used, up until 1986.

For active-duty service members, you may be able to get disability benefits if the following are true for you. First, you must have an illness the VA believes is caused by contact with Agent Orange (a presumptive disease). You also must have served in a regular Air Force unit location where a C-123 aircraft with traces of Agent Orange was assigned, and your flight, ground or medical duties must have put you in regular and repeated contact with C-123 aircraft that had traces of Agent Orange.

If you have an illness the VA determines to be caused by Agent Orange, you don't have to show your problem started during or got worse because of your military service, because it's a presumptive disease.

For reservists, you may be able to get disability benefits if you have a presumptive disease and you were assigned to certain flight, ground, or medical crew duties at one of the following locations:

You must have been assigned to one of these locations:

Lockbourne/Rickenbacker Air Force Base in Ohio, 1969-1986 (906th and 907th Tactical Air Groups or 355th and 356th Tactical Airlift Squadrons), or Westover Air Force Base in Massachusetts, 1972- 1982 (731st Tactical Air Squadron and 74th Aeromedical Evacuation Squadron, or 901st

Organizational Maintenance Squadron), or Pittsburgh International Airport in Pennsylvania, 1972- 1982 (758th Airlift Squadron)

You'll need to file a claim for disability compensation for these benefits. Supporting documents you can include with your online application are:
- Discharge or separation papers (DD214 or other separation documents)

- USAF Form 2096 (unit where you were assigned at the time of the training action)
- USAF Form 5 (aircraft flight duties)
- USAF Form 781 (aircraft maintenance duties)
- Dependency records (marriage certificate and children's birth certificates
- Medical evidence (like a doctor's report or medical test results)

You can get help filing your claim by calling the C-123 hotline at 800-749-8387 or emailing the St. Paul regional benefit office at VSCC123.VAVBASPL@va.gov.

How to Get Disability Benefits for Agent Orange-Related Claims

If you haven't filed a claim yet for a presumptive condition, you can file a new claim online. You can also file a claim by mail, in person or with the help of a trained professional.

If your claim for disability was denied in the past and now the VA considers your condition presumptive, you can file a supplemental claim, and the VA will review your case again.

You'll need to submit these records:
- A medical record that shows you have an Agent Orange-related health condition and
- Military records to show how you were exposed to Agent Orange during your service

If your condition isn't on the list of presumptive conditions, you'll also need to provide at least one of the below types of evidence:
- Evidence showing the problem started during or got worse because of your military service, or
- Scientific or medical evidence stating your condition is caused by Agent Orange. This scientific evidence could include a published research study or article from a medical journal.

You'll need to submit your discharge or separation papers that show your time and location of service, which may include your DD214 or other separation documents. You may also need more supporting documents for certain claims.

For claims related to C-123 aircraft you'll submit one or more of these forms:
- USAF Form 2096 (unit where you were assigned at the time of the training action)
- USAF Form 5 (flight aircraft duties)
- USAF Form 781 (aircraft maintenance duties)

Specific Environmental Hazards

VA disability compensation provides tax-free monthly payments. If you have a health condition caused by exposure to burn pits or other specific hazards in the air, soil or water during your service, you may be eligible.

You'll need to meet the following three requirements:
- You have a diagnosed illness or other health condition caused by exposure to a specific toxic hazard in the air, soil or water, and
- You served on active duty in a location that exposed you to the hazard, and
- You didn't receive a dishonorable discharge

Some of the ways a veteran could have had exposure to specific environmental hazards include:

- Burn pits and other toxic exposures in Afghanistan, Iraq and certain other areas
- A large sulfur fire at Mishraq State Sulfur Mine near Mosul, Iraq
- Hexavalent chromium at the Qarmat Ali water treatment plant in Basra, Iraq
- Pollutants from a waste incinerator near the Naval Air Facility at Atsugi, Japan

More than 20 burn pit and other toxic exposure presumptive conditions were added under the PACT Act passed in 2022. The changes from the PACT Act affects Gulf War era and post-9/11 veterans.

The following cancers are now presumptive:
- Brain cancer
- Gastrointestinal cancer of any type
- Glioblastoma
- Head cancer of any type
- Kidney cancer
- Lymphatic cancer of any type
- Lymphoma of any type
- Melanoma
- Neck cancer of any type
- Pancreatic cancer
- Reproductive cancer of any type
- Respiratory cancer of any type

The following illnesses are presumptive:
- Asthma diagnosed after service
- Chronic bronchitis
- Chronic obstructive pulmonary disease (COPD)
- Chronic rhinitis
- Chronic sinusitis

- Constrictive bronchiolitis or obliterative bronchiolitis
- Emphysema
- Granulomatous disease
- Interstitial lung disease (ILD)
- Pleuritis
- Pulmonary fibrosis
- Sarcoidosis

If you served in any of the locations and time periods below, the VA has determined you had exposure to burn pits or other toxins, which is a presumption of exposure.

On or after September 11, 2001, in any of the locations below:
- Afghanistan
- Djibouti
- Egypt
- Jordan
- Lebanon
- Syria
- Uzbekistan
- Yemen
- The airspace above any of these locations

On or after August 2, 1990, in any of these locations:

- Bahrain
- Iraq
- Kuwait
- Oman
- Qatar
- Saudi Arabia
- Somalia
- The United Arab Emirates (UAE)
- The airspace above any of these locations

Veterans Asbestos Exposure

Asbestos is a material once used in many buildings and products. If a veteran served in Iraq or other countries in the Middle East and Southeast Asia, they may have had contact with asbestos when old buildings were damaged.

This damage could have led to the release of toxic chemicals into the air.

A veteran could have also been exposed to asbestos if they worked in certain jobs or settings, such as construction, vehicle repair or shipyards.

You may be eligible for healthcare and disability compensation if you had contact with asbestos while serving in the military, and you didn't receive a dishonorable discharge.

You'll need to submit evidence that includes:
- Medical records stating your illness or disability, and
- Service records that list your job or specialty, and
- A doctor's statement that says there's a connection between your asbestos contact during your military service and your illness or disability

If you worked in certain jobs or with certain products, you should speak to your health care provider about testing for illnesses affecting your lungs.

Get tested if you worked in:
- Mining
- Milling
- Shipyards
- Construction
- Carpentry
- Demolition

Get tested if you worked with products like:
- Flooring
- Roofing
- Cement sheet
- Pipes
- Insulation
- Friction products like clutch facings and brake linings

Mustard Gas or Lewisite Exposure

If you had contact with mustard gas or lewisite, you may have certain related long-term illnesses. Mustard gas is also known as sulfur mustard, yperite, or nitrogen mustard. Lewisite is a natural compound that contains arsenic, a poison.

You may be eligible for disability benefits if you have a disability believed to be caused by contact with mustard gas or lewisite and your military record shows you had contact.

If you were in the Army and served in these places:
- Bari, Italy
- Bushnell, FL
- Camp Lejeune, NC
- Camp Sibert, AL
- Dugway Proving Ground, UT
- Edgewood Arsenal, MD
- Naval Research Lab, Washington, DC
- Ondal, India
- Rocky Mountain Arsenal, CO
- San Jose Island, Panama Canal Zone

If you were in the Navy and served in these places:
- Bari, Italy
- Camp Lejeune, NC
- Charleston, SC
- Great Lakes Naval Training Center, IL
- Hart's Island, NY
- Naval Training Center, Bainbridge, MD
- Naval Research Laboratory, VA
- Naval Research Laboratory, Washington D.C.
- USS Eagle Boat 58

Some service members who took place in testing in Finschhafen, New Guinean or Porton Down, England may be eligible, as can some select merchant seamen exposed at Bari, Italy.

You'll need to file a claim for disability compensation. You have to claim an actual disease or disability—it isn't sufficient to say you were exposed to mustard gas or lewisite during service. You have to apply based on the illnesses believed to be caused by your contact with one of these chemicals. When you send in a claim you should share any military records that show your contact with blistering agents.

Volunteering for Research Involving Chemical and Biological Testing

It's estimated that as many as 60,000 veterans volunteered for medical research for the U.S. Biological and Chemical Program. If you were involved in the research, you can get medical care through the U.S. Army if you meet both of the following requirements:
- You volunteered for research involving chemical and biological testing between 1942 and 1975, and
- You have an injury or disease caused directly by your participation in the testing.

Camp Lejeune Water Contamination

If a veteran served at Marine Corps Base Camp Lejeune or Marine Corps Air Station (MCAS) New River in North Carolina, they may have had contact with contaminants in the drinking water there. Both scientific and medical research show an association between exposure to these contaminants during military exposure, and the development of certain diseases later on.

If you have qualifying service at Camp Lejeune and a current diagnosis of a condition detailed below, you may be eligible for disability benefits.

You may be eligible for disability benefits if you meet all of the requirements below.

Both must be true:
- You served at Camp Lejeune or MCAS New River for at least 30 cumulative days from August 1953 through December 1987, and

- You didn't receive a dishonorable discharge when you separated from the military.

You must have a diagnosis of one or more of the following presumptive conditions:
- Adult leukemia
- Aplastic anemia and other myelodysplastic syndromes
- Bladder cancer
- Kidney cancer
- Liver cancer
- Multiple myeloma
- Non-Hodgkin's lymphoma
- Parkinson's disease

Veterans, reservists and guardsmen are covered. Health care and compensation benefits are available.

A veteran has to file a disability compensation claim, and provide the following evidence:
- Your military records showing you served at Camp Lejeune or MCAS New River for at least 30 days from August 1953 through December 1987 while on active duty or in the National Guard or Reserves, and
- Medical records stating that you have one or more of the eight illnesses on the presumptive conditions list, which is above.

Family Member Coverage

Veterans who served at Camp Lejeune or MCAS New River for at least 30 cumulative days from August 1953 through December 1987 as well as their family members can get health care benefits. The VA may reimburse you for your out-of-pocket health care costs related to any of the following conditions:
- Bladder cancer
- Breast cancer
- Esophageal cancer
- Female infertility
- Hepatic steatosis
- Kidney cancer
- Leukemia
- Lung cancer
- Miscarriage
- Multiple myeloma
- Myelodysplastic syndromes
- Neurobehavioral effects
- Non-Hodgkin's lymphoma
- Renal toxicity
- Scleroderma

For a family member to get benefits, they need to file a claim for disability compensation, and provide all of the following evidence:

- A document to prove the relationship with the veteran who served on active duty for at least 30 days at Camp Lejeune, like a birth certificate or marriage license, and
- A document to prove you lived at Camp Lejeune or MCAS New River for at least 30 days from August 1953 through December 1987. This evidence could include utility bills, military orders, base housing records or tax forms, as examples, and
- Medical records that show you have one of the 15 conditions listed above, and the date you were diagnosed and that you're being treated or have been treated in the past for the illness.

You'll also need to provide evidence that you paid health care expenses for your claimed condition during one of the time periods listed below:

- Between January 1, 1957, and December 31, 1987 (if you lived on Camp Lejeune during this time, the VA will reimburse you for care received on or after August 6, 2012, and up to two years before the date of your application), or
- Between August 1, 1953, and December 31, 1956 (if you lived on Camp Lejeune during this time period, the VA will reimburse you for care received on or after December 16, 2014, and up to two years before the date you apply for benefits).

Family members might also want to provide a Camp Lejeune Family Member Program Treating Physician Report (VA-Form 10-100068b). A family member has to get a doctor to fill out and sign the form before submission. It's not required by the VA but can provide information that's important to determine eligibility.

The Camp Lejeune Family Member program staff can be reached at (866) 372-1144.

Ionizing Radiation Exposure

There are some illnesses and cancers believed to be caused by contact with radiation during military service.

You may be eligible for benefits if you did not receive a dishonorable discharge, and meet both of the following requirements:

- You have an illness that's on the list of illnesses believed to be caused by radiation or that doctors say may be caused by radiation, and
- Your illness started within a certain period of time

Radiogenic disease is a term used to mean any disease that could be induced by ionizing radiation. This list includes:

- All forms of leukemia except chronic lymphocytic (lymphatic) leukemia
- Thyroid cancer

- Breast cancer
- Lung cancer
- Bone cancer
- Liver cancer
- Skin cancer
- Esophageal cancer
- Stomach cancer
- Colon cancer
- Pancreatic cancer
- Kidney cancer
- Urinary bladder cancer
- Salivary gland cancer
- Multiple myeloma
- Posterior subcapsular cataracts
- Non-malignant thyroid nodular disease
- Ovarian cancer
- Parathyroid adenoma
- Tumors of the brain and central nervous system
- Cancer of the rectum
- Lymphomas other than Hodgkin's disease
- Prostate cancer
- Any other cancer

You must have had contact with ionizing radiation in one of the following ways while serving in the military:

- You were part of atmospheric nuclear weapons testing, or
- You served in the postwar occupation of Hiroshima or Nagasaki, or
- You were a prisoner of war in Japan or,
- You worked as an X-ray technician, in a reactor plant, or in nuclear medicine or radiography (while on active duty or during active or inactive duty for training in the Reserves), or
- You did tasks like those of a Department of Energy employee that make them a member of the Special Exposure Cohort

You may also qualify for disability benefits if you served in at least one of these locations and capacities:

- You were part of underground nuclear weapons testing at Amchitka Island, Alaska, or
- You were assigned to a gaseous diffusion plant at Paducah, Kentucky, or
- You were assigned to a gaseous diffusion plant at Portsmouth, Ohio, or
- You were assigned to a gaseous diffusion plant at Area K-25 at Oak Ridge, Tennessee

Under the PACT Act, three new response efforts were added to the list of presumptive locations. These include:

- Cleanup of Enewetak Atoll, from January 1, 1977, through December 31, 1980.
- Cleanup of the Air Force B-52 bomber carrying nuclear weapons off the coast of Palomares, Spain, from January 17, 1966, through March 31,

1967.

- Response to the fire onboard an Air Force B-52 bomber carrying nuclear weapons near Thule Air Force Based in Greenland from January 21, 1968, to September 25, 1968.

If someone took part in any of the above efforts, the VA presumes they had exposure to radiation. You'll need to file a claim for disability compensation and provide the following evidence:

- Medical records that show you've been diagnosed with one of the illnesses on the list believed to be caused by radiation, or a condition your doctor states may have been caused by radiation exposure, and
- Service records show you were part of one of the radiation risk activities described above.

When a veteran files a claim, the VA will ask the military branch they served with, or the Defense Threat Reduction Agency to give a range of how much radiation they think the veteran may have come in contact with. The VA will then use the highest level of the range reported to decide on benefits.

Gulf War Illnesses Linked to Southwest Asia Service

If a veteran served in the Southwest Asia theater of military operations, they may suffer from illnesses or conditions the VA assumes are related to service in the region.

A veteran may be eligible for disability benefits if they served in the Southwest Asia theater of military operations during the Gulf War period and didn't receive a dishonorable discharge.

The illness or condition also has to meet certain requirements in terms of time period.

If your illness or condition was diagnosed while you were on active duty or before December 31, 2021, you can get benefits if both the descriptions are true for you and you have one of the presumptive conditions.

Both must be true:
- Your condition caused you to be ill for at least six months, and
- It resulted in a disability rating of 10% or more

You must have one of these presumptive diseases:
- Functional gastrointestinal disorders
- Chronic fatigue syndrome
- Fibromyalgia
- Other undiagnosed illnesses, including but not limited to muscle and joint pain, headaches and cardiovascular disease

If your illness or condition was diagnosed within one year of your date of separation you can get disability benefits if you have a disability rating of 10% or more, and you have one of the following presumptive diseases:

- Brucelliosis
- Camplobacter jejuni
- Coxiella burnetii (Q fever)
- Nontyphoid salmonella
- Shigella
- West Nile Virus
- Malaria

If your illness or condition was diagnosed at any time after your date of separation, you can get disability benefits if you have a disability rating of 10% or more, and you have one these presumptive conditions:

- Mycobacterium tuberculosis
- Visceral leishmaniasis

Included in the Southwest Asia theater of military operations are:

- Iraq, Kuwait, Saudi Arabia
- The neutral zone between Iraq and Saudi Arabia
- Bahrain, Qatar and the United Arab Emirates
- Oman
- The Gulf of Aden and the Gulf of Oman
- The waters of the Persian Gulf, the Arabian Sea, and the Red Sea
- The airspace above these locations

Birth Defects Linked to Agent Orange

Spina bifida is a spinal cord birth defect. A baby develops spina bifida while still in the womb. In some cases, a parent's past contact with specific chemicals causes this birth defect. If you served in Vietnam or Thailand, or in or near the Korean Demilitarized Zone (DMZ)—and your child has spina bifida or certain other birth defects—your child may be able to get disability benefits. VA recognizes that certain birth defects among veterans' children are associated with veterans' qualifying service in Vietnam or Korean.

Spina bifida except spina bifida occulta is a defect in the developing fetus, resulting in incomplete closing of the spine. It's associated with exposure to Agent Orange. Birth defects in children of women veterans associated with their military service in Vietnam, but not related to herbicide exposure may also be included. The affected child must have been conceived after the veteran entered Vietnam or the Korean demilitarized zone during the qualifying service period.

2025 Birth Defect Compensation Rates

Vietnam and Korea Veterans' Children with Spina Bifida

Disability Level	Monthly Payment
Level I (least disabling)	$418
Level II	$1,417
Level III (most disabling)	$2,411

Women Vietnam Veterans Children with Certain Other Birth Defects

Disability Level	Monthly Payment
Level I (least disabling)	$195
Level II	$418
Level III	$1,417
Level IV (most disabling)	$2,411

CHAPTER 5

MENTAL HEALTH

A veteran may experience difficult life experiences or challenges after leaving the military.

VA offers mental health treatment and care in different settings including in-person, through telehealth and online.

Starting January 17, 2023, VA announced it would pay for, provide or reimburse emergency care for certain veterans and individuals. This includes ambulance transportation costs and follow-up inpatient, or residential care related to the event for up to 30 days, and outpatient care for up to 90 days, including social work.

Notification as soon as possible is important, because VA must verify a veteran's eligibility for emergency suicide care if they aren't already enrolled or registered with VA. You should also contact your local VA medical center to coordinate follow-on care and transfer activities if needed.

If a veteran is already using VA medical services, they can ask their primary care provider to help them make an appointment with a VA mental health provider. If they aren't using VA medical services, they can contact their nearest Vet Center or VA medical center to find out how to enroll. VA also offers mental health support such as mental health apps, and Veteran Training.

Veteran Training is a self-help online portal that provides tools for overcoming everyday challenges. The portal has tools to help veterans with problem-solving skills, anger management, parenting skills and more, all in an anonymous environment. Mental health resources for veterans include:

National Call Center for Homeless Veterans

If you are or know a veteran who's homeless or at risk of becoming homeless, you can contact the National VA Call Center for Homeless Veterans. The resources are also available to veteran family and friends. You can dial 1-877-424-3838 and Press 1. The hotline is available 24/7.

QuitVet

QuitVet is a tobacco quitline. Any veteran receiving healthcare through VA is eligible to use the QuitVet quitline. You can call 1-855-QUIT-VET to talk to a tobacco cessation counselor.

Veterans Crisis Line

The Veterans Crisis Line connects veterans and service members in crisis and their families with qualified, caring VA responders through a confidential toll-free hotline or online chat. You can dial 911 and Press 1. This is available 24/7. You can also text 838255.

War Vet Call Center

You can call 1-877-927-8387 to reach the Vet Call Center. You can talk about concerns you have or your military experience. The team is made up of veterans from several eras and family members of veterans.

Women Veterans Call Center

The Women Veterans Call Center provides VA services and resources to women veterans, their families and caregivers. You can call 1-855-829-6636.

Real Warriors

Real Warriors is a program operated through the Defense Centers of Excellent for Psychological Health and Traumatic Brain injury. It provides resources about psychological health, traumatic brain injury and PTSD. You can call 1-866-966-1020.

Coaching Into Care

The Coaching Into Care program from the VA offers guidance to veterans' family members and friends to encourage a veteran they care about to reach out for support with mental health challenges. The program is available by calling 1-888-823-7458.

Vet Centers

If you're a combat veteran, you can visit a VA Vet Center for free, individual and group counseling for you and your family. You have access to these services even if you aren't enrolled in VA health care and aren't receiving disability compensation. Vet Centers offer services like:

- Military sexual trauma (MST) counseling
- Readjustment counseling
- Bereavement (grief) counseling
- Employment counseling
- Substance abuse assessment and referral

Mental Illnesses and VA Disability Benefits

The VA considers several categories of mental illness eligible for disability. The VA rates all service- connected mental illnesses by the severity of limitations and symptoms. These are rated according to the VA's Schedule of Rating Disabilities. After the VA establishes a mental health condition is related to military service, it rates the condition based on severity. The VA looks at medical records to determine the severity of clinical symptoms.

All mental health conditions are rated under the same criteria from the Diagnostic and Statistical Manual of Mental Disorders published by the American Psychiatric association.

In addition, the VA considers scores from a diagnostic tool—the Global Assessment of Functioning Scale (GAF). This is to determine the severity of a disability. GAF scores are designed to measure the ability of someone to function at work, socially and emotionally, and they range from 0-100. The higher someone's score, the better their ability to function. A lower score would mean a higher rating from the VA. A GAF score is assigned as part of a Compensation and Pension Exam.

Ratings for Mental Illness

VA Ratings for Mental Illness

The VA assigns disability ratings for mental health conditions based on the level of occupational and social impairment. Ratings are given in increments of 0%, 10%, 30%, 50%, 70%, and 100%, as outlined below:

0% Rating

- Diagnosis of a mental health condition with no significant symptoms that interfere with work or social life.
- Requires periodic evaluation but does not warrant compensation.

10% Rating

- Mild or transient symptoms that decrease work efficiency or ability to perform tasks only during periods of significant stress.
- Controlled by continuous medication.

30% Rating

- Symptoms cause occasional decrease in work efficiency and intermittent periods of inability to perform occupational tasks.
- Examples include:
  - Depressed mood
  - Anxiety
  - Panic attacks (weekly or less)
  - Chronic sleep impairment
  - Mild memory loss

77

50% Rating

- Reduced reliability and productivity due to symptoms such as:
  - Frequent panic attacks
  - Difficulty understanding complex commands
  - Impaired short- and long-term memory
  - Impaired judgment and abstract thinking
  - Difficulty maintaining social relationships

70% Rating

- Deficiencies in most areas, including work, school, family relations, judgment, and mood.
- Symptoms may include:
  - Suicidal ideation
  - Obsessive rituals interfering with routine activities
  - Speech intermittently illogical or irrelevant
  - Near-continuous panic or depression affecting functionality
  - Difficulty adapting to stressful circumstances
  - Inability to establish and maintain effective relationships

100% Rating

- Total occupational and social impairment.
- Symptoms may include:
  - Gross impairment in thought processes or communication
  - Persistent delusions or hallucinations
  - Grossly inappropriate behavior
  - Persistent danger of hurting self or others
  - Inability to perform activities of daily living
  - Disorientation to time or place
  - Severe memory loss, such as forgetting one's name or close relatives

The VA uses the General Rating Formula for Mental Disorders for all service-connected mental health conditions, including PTSD, anxiety, depression, and other related disorders.

The VA doesn't have set guidelines for mental health ratings. The VA instead uses discretion and examines all medical evidence on someone's symptoms and functional limitations to decide on a rating.

If you aren't entitled to a 100% rating under VA criteria because your symptoms aren't severe enough, you might be able to get payment at the 100% rate if you can't work a job that pays you enough to live above the poverty level. This is called Total Disability based on Employability or TDUI. You have to show you can't work as a result of your service-connected mental illness.

Eligibility for Emergency Mental Health Care

In most cases the VA will provide or cover the cost of emergency mental health care and up to 90 days of related service, even for individuals not enrolled in VA health care.

If a health care provider or trained crisis responder determines you're at risk of immediate self- harm, VA can provide or cover the cost of care if you meet at least one of the following requirements:

- You were sexually assaulted, battered or harassed while serving in the Armed Forces, or
- You served on active duty for more than 24 months and didn't get an honorable discharge, or
- You served more than 100 days under a combat exclusion or in support of a contingency operation, including as a member of the Reserve, and didn't get a dishonorable discharge. You meet this requirement if you served directly or if you operated an unmanned aerial vehicle from another location.

CHAPTER 6

CAREGIVERS

The Program of Comprehensive Assistance for Family Caregivers

The VA recognizes the role of family caregivers in supporting the health and wellness of veterans. As of October 1, 2022, the program is now open to family caregivers of all eligible veterans of all eras. This includes eligible veterans who served after May 7, 1975, and before September 11, 2001. Family caregivers of eligible veterans of all eras can now apply.

Eligibility

You may be eligible if both you and the veteran you're caring for meet all of the following requirements.

You must be at least 18 years old to be a caregiver, and at least one of the following must be true:
- You're a spouse, son, daughter, parent, stepfamily member or extended family member of the veteran, or
- You live full time with the veteran or you're willing to live full time with the veteran if the VA designates you as a family caregiver.

All of the following must be true for the veteran you're caring for:
- The veteran has a VA disability rating—individual or combined—of 70% or higher, and
- The veteran was discharged from the U.S. military or has a date of medical discharge, and
- The veteran needs at least six months of continuous in-person personal care services

Personal care services can include care or assistance to support health and well-being, everyday personal needs like feeding, bathing and dressing, and safety, protection or instruction in their living environment.

The veteran can appoint:
- 1 Primary Family Caregiver—this is the main caregiver

- Up to 2 Secondary Family Caregivers—these are people who serve as backup support to the primary caregiver when needed.

Eligible Primary and Secondary Family Caregivers can receive:
- Caregiver education and training
- Mental health counseling
- Travel, lodging, and financial assistance when traveling with the veteran to receive care

Eligible Primary Family Caregivers may also receive:

- A monthly stipend payment
- Access to health care benefits through the Civilian and Medical Program of the Department of Veterans Affairs (CHAMPVA)—if they don't already qualify for care or services under another health care plan
- At least 30 days of respite care per for the veteran.

Applying

A caregiver and veteran have to apply together for this program. Both have to be part of the application process to determine if they're eligible for the Program of Comprehensive Assistance for Family Caregivers. Both have to sign and date the application and completely answer all questions for their role. You can do this process online.

Every time a veteran wants to add a new family caregiver, the veteran and new caregiver have to submit a new application.

Along with applying online, you can also apply by mail. You fill out a joint Application for the Program of Comprehensive Assistance for Family Caregivers (VA Form 10-10CG).

You mail the form and supporting documents to:

Program of Comprehensive Assistance for Family Caregivers Health Eligibility Center 2957 Clairmont Road NE, Suite 200 Atlanta, GA 30329-1647

You can also bring your completed VA Form 10-10CG to your local VA medical center's Caregiver Support Coordinator. Contact the Caregiver Support Line at 855-260-3274 for more information.

You shouldn't send any medical records with the application. The VA will follow up after receiving the application.

If you're caring for a veteran who isn't eligible for the program, you may still be able to access support and resources. The VA Caregiver Support Program actually includes two programs. One is the Program of Comprehensive Assistance for

Family Caregivers, and the other is called the Program of General Caregiver Support Services.

Program of General Caregiver Support Services

The Program of General Caregiver Support Services is a program providing peer support mentoring, skills training, online programs, coaching, telephone services and referrals to available resources for caregivers of veterans. The veteran has to be enrolled in VA health care and be receiving care from a caregiver. Each VA facility is staffed with a CSP Team/Caregiver Support Coordinator who can help you figure out what services and resources are available to you. There's no formal application to enroll in the program.

Caregiver Support Line

The VA Caregiver Support Line is available at 1-855-260-3274. There are licensed professionals who staff the support line, and they can connect you with VA services, a Caregiver Support Coordinator.

Peer Support Mentoring

Caregivers of veterans are eligible to participate in the VA Caregiver Peer Support Mentoring Program, both as mentors and mentees. Mentors and mentees communicate using email, telephone, and letter writing.

Mentors receive training before being paired with another caregiver and are volunteers with their local VA medical center Voluntary Services department. Caregivers participating in the Caregiver Peer Support Mentoring Program agree to participate for six months, but many participate for much longer.

REACH VA

Mentoring in the areas of caregiving, stress management, mood management, and problem- solving is available through REACH VA. The program is available for caregivers of veterans diagnosed with ALS, dementia, MS, PTSD or spinal cord injury/disorder.

The REACH VA program is an opportunity for caregivers of veterans to take better care of themselves and their loved ones by providing them with important information in the areas of caregiving and building their skills in stress management and problem-solving.

The trained and certified REACH VA program coach usually provides four individual sessions with the caregiver over a period of two to three months, extending the session if both the coach and caregiver feel they need to do more work.

To be eligible for the REACH VA program, the caregiver must be caring for a veteran or a veteran caring for a loved one where the veteran is receiving services at the VA. Caregivers receive a Caregiver Notebook, which is the first resource for caregiver issues and challenges.

Approval and Designation of Primary and Secondary Family Caregivers

Eligibility for the Program of Comprehensive Assistance for Family Caregivers is determined by the VA Caregiver Support Coordinator, who may refer the application to the veteran's primary care team or a Clinical Eligibility Team for further evaluation. The eligibility process includes identifying qualifying injuries related to active military service after September 11, 2001, and assessing whether the injury necessitates caregiver services.

The Caregiver Support Coordinator considers input from the veteran and caregiver. If the veteran doesn't meet eligibility criteria, the coordinator will issue a determination of ineligibility. If eligibility remains unclear, the coordinator will refer the application for clinical evaluation to assess dependency and determine the applicable stipend.

Requirements of Primary Family Caregivers

Primary caregivers are expected to:

- Work closely with the veteran/servicemember's team to support, promote, and encourage the veteran/servicemember in attaining the highest level of independence possible.
- Promptly inform the veteran/servicemember's primary care team of any changes in their physical or mental health condition.
- Provide a written statement to the Caregiver Support Coordinator when the veteran/servicemember's address changes, to avoid disruption of stipend payment. This notification should be made anytime the veteran/servicemember moves.
- Demonstrate flexibility in scheduling home visits --- be physically present and participate during home visits and monitoring required by the Program of Comprehensive Assistance for Family Caregivers.
- Promptly inform the Caregiver Support Coordinator if you're no longer able to serve as the Primary Family Caregiver, or if the veteran/servicemember is admitted to the hospital or a long-term treatment facility.
- The stipend is not an entitlement—instead, it recognizes the care and support provided by the caregiver to the veteran/servicemember.

Caregiver Access to Military Commissaries, Exchanges and Recreation Facilities

According to the Department of Defense, starting January 1, 2020 the following: all service-connected veterans, Purple Heart recipients, former prisoners of war and individuals approved and designated as the primary family caregivers of eligible veterans under the Department of Veterans Affairs Program of Comprehensive

Assistance for Family Caregivers, can use commissaries, exchanges, and morale, welfare and recreational (MWR) retail facilities in-person and online.

Eligible caregivers will receive an eligibility letter from the VA Office of Community Care. Primary family caregivers who lose their eligibility letter can call 1-877-733-7927 to request a replacement.

Stipend Benefit for the Primary Family Caregiver

A Primary Family Caregiver stipend is monetary compensation paid for providing personal care services to an eligible veteran. The stipend benefit is not meant to replace career earnings, and the stipend payment doesn't create an employment relationship between the VA and the Primary Family Caregiver. Only the designated Primary Family Caregiver of an eligible veteran is entitled to receive a stipend. There can be only one Primary Family Caregiver designated at a time. The stipend is a VA enhanced service and is not considered taxable income.

The veteran's Patient Aligned Care Team at your assigned VA Medical Center makes a determination as far as the number of hours of personal care services a veteran requires. The PACT provides a clinical evaluation of the veteran's level of dependency, based on the degree to which the veteran is in need of supervision or protection based on symptoms or residuals of neurological or other impairment or injury.

As a result of the clinical evaluation and score, eligible veterans are rated as follows:

- **High Tier**: Equates to a maximum of 40 hours of care per week
- **Medium Tier**: Equates to a maximum of 25 hours of care per week
- **Low Tier**: Equates to a maximum of 10 hours of care per week

The stipend amount is based on the weekly number of hours of personal care services that an eligible veteran requires. It is calculated by multiplying the Bureau of Labor Statistics hourly wage for home health aides, Skill code 311011, for the geographic region in which the eligible veteran resides by the Consumer Price Index Cost of Living Adjustment (COLA), and then multiplying that total by the number of weekly hours of caregiver assistance required.

This is then multiplied by the average number of weeks in each month.

An Example: If an eligible veteran requires 10 hours of personal care services weekly (Tier 1) and the caregiver's hourly wage (including COLA) is $10 per hour, then the monthly stipend would be: (10 hours x $10) X 4.35=435.

The stipend is paid monthly for personal care services that a Primary Family Caregiver provided in the prior month. Once an application is approved, the stipend will be retroactive to the date the application was received at the VAMC.

The Caregiver Support Line can provide more information at 1-855-260-3274 Monday through Friday, 8 a.m. to 8 p.m. Eastern Standard Time. You can learn more by mail by contacting:

VHA Office of Community Care Caregiver Support Program
PO Box 460637
Denver CO 80246-0637

CHAMPVA Benefits for Primary Family Caregivers

CHAMPVA for the Primary Family Caregiver is a health care benefits program in which the Department of Veterans Affairs shares the cost of certain health care services and supplies with the Primary Family Caregiver, who is not entitled to care or services under a health-plan contract, including a health insurance plan, TRICARE, Medicare or Medicaid. CHAMPVA is managed by the VHA Office of Community Care.

Not all caregivers are eligible for CHAMPVA medical benefits. Only the designated Primary Family Caregiver who is without health insurance coverage is eligible for CHAMPVA benefits.

The Primary Family Caregiver is also eligible to receive health care at a VA facility through the CHAMPVA In-House Treatment Initiative Program if the VA facility has the excess capacity to provide care. Medical care and supplies received through a participating VA facility are not subject to cost shares or deductibles.

CHAPTER 7

TRICARE AND TRICARE FOR LIFE

TRICARE is the health care program from the Department of Defense. TRICARE serves 9.6 million active-duty service members, retired service members, National Guard and Reserve members, family members, and survivors. When you're a TRICARE beneficiary, you have access to health care wherever you are.

TRICARE brings together military hospitals and clinics with a network of civilian providers to offer medical, pharmacy and dental options.

TRICARE partners with civilian regional contractors to administer the benefit in two U.S. regions—East and West, as well as one overseas region. Your regional contractor is your go-to resource for information and help.

TRICARE meets the minimum essential coverage requirement under the Affordable Care Act.

Eligibility for TRICARE is determined by the services shown in the Defense Enrollment Eligibility Reporting System (DEERS). DEERS is a database of service members and dependents worldwide who are eligible for military benefits. To use TRICARE, first make sure your DEERS record is up to date.

TRICARE Regions Changing in 2025: Key Information for Beneficiaries

Starting on January 1, 2025, TRICARE implemented new regional contracts that will affect the way healthcare is delivered to beneficiaries.

While there will still be two main TRICARE regions, there will be significant changes regarding which states are part of each region. Notably, six states from the current East Region—Arkansas, Illinois, Louisiana, Oklahoma, Texas, and Wisconsin—will move to the West Region.

This transition is designed to balance the TRICARE population between the two regions and improve service quality for beneficiaries.

For those living in one of these states moving to the West Region, your TRICARE contractor will shift from Humana Military to TriWest Healthcare Alliance.

This change affects approximately 1.1 million eligible beneficiaries.

Continuing Care:
- Referrals and authorizations from Humana Military will remain valid until their expiration date (up to **June 30, 2025**). TriWest will work with Humana Military to ensure there is no disruption in care, especially for critical services such as cancer treatment, mental health, and disease management.

Provider Network:
- Most providers in these states will likely remain in the TRICARE network. However, each provider must confirm whether they will continue to work with TRICARE under the new contractor, TriWest.

TRICARE Covered Services

Generally, you have the same covered services, which includes preventative, maternity, pharmacy and mental health services with any TRICARE program option. Copayments or cost-sharing may apply for certain services depending on your program option and beneficiary status.

Your health care options can change if you move, have a life event like getting married or have a status change like a sponsor retiring from service.

Automatic Enrollment

If you're an Active-Duty Service Member, a family member of a new ADSM, a new family member of a current ADSM or your military sponsor has been called to active duty, you're automatically enrolled in TRICARE Prime if you live in a Prime Service Area (PSA). More details on Prime are below. Otherwise, active-duty family members are automatically enrolled in TRICARE Select. More details are available on page 95.

Active-duty service members must remain enrolled in TRICARE Prime. All others automatically enrolled have up to 90 days to change enrollment if eligible for other TRICARE plans.

TRICARE Prime

TRICARE Prime is a managed care plan available to eligible beneficiaries in designated Prime Service Areas. These areas are strategic locations across the U.S. that support the medical readiness of active-duty service members by supplementing the capacity of military hospitals and clinics. Prime Service Areas are also organized around Base Realignment and Closure sites.

To determine if you live in a Prime Service Area, check the Plan Finder.

Key Features

- Enrollment in TRICARE Prime is mandatory for eligible beneficiaries.
- Some participants are required to pay an annual enrollment fee.
- Additional TRICARE Prime options for active-duty service members and their families:
  - TRICARE Prime Remote
  - TRICARE Prime Overseas
  - TRICARE Prime Remote Overseas

Eligibility

- Active-duty service members and their families
- Retired service members and their families*
- Activated National Guard and Reserve members and their families (activated for more than 30 consecutive days)
- Non-activated National Guard and Reserve members and their families who qualify under the Transitional Assistance Management Program (TAMP)
- Retired National Guard and Reserve members at age 60 and their families*
- Surviving family members of service members
- Medal of Honor recipients and their families
- Qualified former spouses

*Retired service members and their families are no longer eligible for TRICARE Prime once they qualify for Medicare due to age.

How It Works

- Primary Care Manager (PCM): You will be assigned a PCM who is responsible for most of your healthcare needs.
  - Your PCM could be a military provider or a civilian network provider.
  - Your PCM will refer you to specialists when needed and coordinate any required authorizations and referrals.
  - Your PCM handles the submission of claims and will accept co-payments for services.

Costs

- Active-duty service members pay nothing out of pocket.
- Active-duty family members pay nothing unless they choose the point-of-service option.
- Other beneficiaries pay annual enrollment fees and network copayments.

Is TRICARE Prime Right for You?

- Active-duty service members must enroll in TRICARE Prime.
- Other beneficiaries can choose between TRICARE Prime and TRICARE Select.
- TRICARE Prime typically offers lower out-of-pocket costs compared to TRICARE Select but provides less provider flexibility.

- If you have other health insurance, TRICARE Prime might not be suitable.

Travel Reimbursement for Specialty Care

What is the Prime Travel Benefit?

The Prime Travel Benefit helps reimburse qualified travel expenses for TRICARE Prime enrollees traveling for specialty care. Covered expenses may include:
- Mileage
- Meals
- Tolls and parking
- Lodging
- Local transportation
- Public transportation tickets

Who Qualifies for the Prime Travel Benefit?

To qualify for reimbursement under the Prime Travel Benefit, you must meet the following conditions:
- Be enrolled in TRICARE Prime or TRICARE Prime Remote
- You are not an active-duty service member
- You are not an active-duty family member living with your active-duty sponsor on orders in Alaska or Hawaii (contact your nearest military hospital for separate overseas benefits)
- You are assigned a primary care manager (PCM) in the U.S.
- Your PCM refers you for medically necessary, non-emergency care covered by TRICARE
- Your referral is to a specialty care provider located more than 100 miles (one-way) from your PCM's office, or there is no suitable specialty care provider within 100 miles, including military, network, and non-network providers

Trips for services not covered by TRICARE will not qualify for reimbursement.

Does the Prime Travel Benefit Cover Non-Medical Attendants (NMAs)?

In certain cases, the travel expenses for a non-medical attendant (NMA) may also qualify for reimbursement. Requirements include:
- The NMA must be a parent, spouse, adult family member (21 or older), or legal guardian
- If the patient is over 18, a written statement from the referring or treating provider must verify that the NMA's presence is medically necessary
- The NMA must travel with the patient on a qualified trip
- You must submit itemized travel receipts for all expenses, including those under $75
- Shared expenses, such as lodging or car rental, cannot be reimbursed

Note: Active-duty service members are **not** eligible for the Prime Travel Benefit.
How Does the Prime Travel Benefit Work?

Once you receive a referral for specialty care that qualifies for the Prime Travel Benefit, follow these steps:

1. **Contact Your Prime Travel Office**
   a. If you have a military PCM, reach out to the travel representative at your military hospital or clinic.
   b. If you have a civilian PCM and your sponsor is active-duty or retired Coast Guard, contact the DHA Prime Travel Benefit office at:
      i. Email: dha.tricareptb@health.mil

2. **Make Your Travel Arrangements**
   a. Choose the least expensive travel option available, including:
      i. Economy class for air or train
      ii. Compact class for car rentals (unless pre-approved for a different class)
   b. Book only reasonable transportation, but your reimbursement will be capped at the most cost-effective amount as determined by the government.
   c. For trips over 400 miles one-way, contact your servicing Prime Travel Benefit office for confirmation before booking airfare or travel.

3. **Lodging and Meals**
   a. Reimbursement covers actual costs for lodging and meals, up to the government per diem rate for the location of your specialty care provider.
   b. Taxes and fees on lodging are reimbursable if itemized. If not, only the room cost is reimbursable.
   c. Meal allowance covers taxes and tips (excluding alcohol).

4. **Mileage**
   a. You will be reimbursed for mileage when driving your own vehicle.
   b. The standard Other Mileage Rate applies, unless the NMA is an active-duty service member or a Department of Defense employee, in which case the TDY Travel mileage rate applies.

5. **Submit Your Travel Documents**
   a. Obtain the required forms from the Prime Travel Reimbursement Instructions page.
   b. Complete the forms, sign where necessary, and attach all itemized receipts (tape receipts on plain paper, 8½ x 11 inches).
   c. Follow the submission instructions carefully.

TRICARE Prime Remote

TRICARE Prime Remote (TPR) is a managed care plan designed for service members and their families living in remote areas. To qualify for TPR, both your sponsor's home and work locations must be more than 50 miles or about one hour's drive from the nearest military hospital or clinic.

Key Details

- Enrollment is mandatory for TPR.
- No enrollment fees are required.
- You may be eligible for travel reimbursements, including costs for mileage, meals, tolls, parking, lodging, local transportation, and public transportation tickets, under the Prime Travel Benefit, provided you meet the requirements.
- If you are stationed in a remote overseas location, you may be eligible for TRICARE Prime Remote Overseas.

Who Can Enroll in TPR?

TRICARE Prime Remote is available for:

- Active-duty service members and their families
- Activated National Guard and Reserve members and their families (for service lasting more than 30 consecutive days)
- Active-duty family members who live with a sponsor enrolled in TPR
- Activated National Guard and Reserve families who reside in a designated remote location during their sponsor's activation

How TPR Works

- **Primary Care Manager (PCM):** Your PCM is responsible for most of your healthcare needs.
  - If available, you'll have a network PCM. If not, you can choose any TRICARE-authorized provider as your PCM.
  - Your PCM will refer you to specialists if needed and work with your regional contractor for approvals.
  - Your PCM will handle claims and provide guidance for accessing network specialists.

Costs

- There are no enrollment fees for TPR.
- No out-of-pocket costs for care as long as it's provided by your PCM or through a referral.
- If you seek care without a referral, point-of-service fees will apply.

Is TPR Right for You?

- TPR is specifically for active-duty service members and their families who live and work in designated remote areas.
- Active-duty service members must enroll in TPR if they live and work in a

remote location.

- Family members can choose between TRICARE Prime Remote or TRICARE Select.
  - o TPR generally has lower out-of-pocket costs compared to TRICARE Select but offers less provider choice.
  - o If you have other health insurance, TPR might not be suitable.

TRICARE Prime Option- US Family Health Plan

The US Family Health Plan (USFHP) is an alternative TRICARE Prime option, offered through networks of community-based, non-profit healthcare systems across six U.S. regions.

Who Can Enroll

USFHP is available to the following beneficiaries residing in designated service areas:

- Active-duty family members
- Retired service members and their families*
- Family members of activated National Guard and Reserve members (service of more than 30 days)
- Non-activated National Guard and Reserve members and their families qualifying for care under the Transitional Assistance Management Program (TAMP)
- Retired National Guard and Reserve members at age 60 and their families*
- Survivors
- Medal of Honor recipients and their families
- Qualified former spouses

*Note: Retired service members and their families lose eligibility for USFHP when they qualify for Medicare.

Where It's Available

You must live within a designated USFHP service area to enroll. USFHP is available in the following regions, each with its own provider network:

- **Maryland, Washington D.C., Pennsylvania, Virginia, Delaware, West Virginia:**
  - o Johns Hopkins Health Plans
  - o **Contact:** 800-808-7347

- **Maine, New Hampshire, Vermont, Upstate and Western New York, Northern and Western Pennsylvania, Northeastern and Central Ohio:**
  - o Martin's Point Health Care
  - o **Contact:** 888-241-4556

- **Massachusetts (including Cape Cod), Rhode Island, Northern Connecticut:**
    - Brighton Marine Health Center
    - **Contact:** 800-818-8589

- **New York City, Long Island, Lower Hudson Valley, New Jersey, Western Connecticut, Eastern Pennsylvania:**
    - St. Vincent Catholic Medical Centers
    - **Contact:** 800-241-4848

- **Central Texas, Coastal Bend Texas, Northeast and Southeast Texas,**
    - **Central Louisiana:** CHRISTUS Health
    - **Contact:** 800-678-7347

- **Western Washington State, Central and Eastern Washington State, Northern Idaho, Western Oregon, most of California:**
    - Pacific Medical Centers (PacMed Clinics)
    - **Contact:** 866-418-7346

How It Works

Under USFHP, you'll receive all your care, including prescription drug coverage, from a primary care provider (PCP) selected from the network of private physicians affiliated with the participating healthcare systems. Your PCP will also assist you in obtaining referrals to specialists and coordinate your care.

Important: When enrolled in USFHP, you will not receive care at military hospitals and clinics or from TRICARE network providers.

Costs
- **Active-duty family members**: No enrollment fees or out-of-pocket costs when receiving care from a USFHP provider.
- **Other beneficiaries**: Must pay annual enrollment fees and network copayments.

TRICARE Prime Overseas

TRICARE Prime Overseas is a managed care plan available in regions with military hospitals and clinics outside of the United States.

Key Details
- Enrollment is required.
- No enrollment fees.

Eligibility

TRICARE Prime Overseas is available to:

93

- Active-duty service members
- Command-sponsored active-duty family members
- Activated National Guard/Reserve members (who are called to active duty for more than 30 consecutive days)
- Command-sponsored family members of activated National Guard/Reserve members

Note: Retirees and their families are not eligible for TRICARE Prime Overseas.

How It Works

- Most of your care will be provided by your assigned primary care manager (PCM) at a military hospital or clinic.
- If needed, your PCM will refer you to a specialist and coordinate with International SOS for any necessary authorizations.

Costs

- No enrollment fees.
- No copayments for care received from your PCM or with a referral.
- Point-of-service fees apply for care received without a referral.

Is TRICARE Prime Overseas Right for You?

- TRICARE Prime Overseas is available only to active-duty service members and command-sponsored family members.
- Active-duty members must enroll if they are stationed in an area where TRICARE Prime Overseas is available.
- Family members must be command-sponsored to enroll.
- Family members who are not command-sponsored or who choose not to enroll may want to consider purchasing additional health insurance.

TRICARE Prime Remote Overseas

TRICARE Prime Remote Overseas is a managed care plan for beneficiaries living in designated remote overseas regions, including:

- Eurasia-Africa
- Latin America and Canada
- Pacific

TRICARE Prime Remote Overseas meets or exceeds the Affordable Care Act's minimum essential coverage requirements.

Eligibility

The following beneficiaries can enroll in TRICARE Prime Remote Overseas:

- Active-duty service members
- Command-sponsored active-duty family members

- Activated National Guard/Reserve members (serving more than 30 consecutive days)
- Command-sponsored family members of activated National Guard/Reserve members

Note: Retirees and their families are not eligible for TRICARE Prime Remote Overseas.

How It Works
- Most of your care will be provided by an assigned primary care manager (PCM).
- Your PCM will refer you to specialists when needed and work with International SOS for any required authorizations.

Costs
- No enrollment fees.
- No copayments for care received from your PCM or with a referral.
- Care received without a referral will incur point-of-service fees.

Overseas Point of Contact Program

When you enroll in TRICARE Prime Remote Overseas, you can reach out to an overseas point of contact (POC) for support. They can assist you with:
- Enrollment in a TRICARE plan overseas
- Scheduling appointments at overseas network facilities
- Filing medical and dental claims
- Answering questions about coverage and benefits
- Navigating TRICARE's electronic self-service options

To find your POC, contact your TRICARE Area Office.

Is TRICARE Prime Remote Overseas Right for You?

TRICARE Prime Remote Overseas is available to active-duty service members and their command-sponsored family members living in remote overseas locations.
- If you're on active duty, you must enroll in TRICARE Prime Remote Overseas where it is available.
- Family members must be command-sponsored to enroll.
- Family members who aren't command-sponsored or choose not to enroll may need to consider purchasing additional health insurance.

TRICARE Select

TRICARE Select is a self-managed health plan that operates as a preferred provider organization (PPO) within the U.S. It allows you to choose your healthcare providers and access a broad network of TRICARE-authorized providers.

To be eligible, you must be registered in the Defense Enrollment Eligibility Reporting System (DEERS), which tracks information about military members, their families, and other eligible personnel.

Enrollment

- Enrollment is required. Visit the TRICARE Select Enrollment page for more information.
- TRICARE Select Overseas is available to eligible beneficiaries living abroad.

Who Can Enroll?

TRICARE Select is available to:

- Active-duty family members
- Retired service members and their families
- Family members of activated National Guard and Reserve members (on active duty for more than 30 consecutive days)
- Non-activated National Guard and Reserve members and their families eligible under the Transitional Assistance Management Program (TAMP)
- Retired National Guard and Reserve members (age 60 or older) and their families
- Survivors
- Medal of Honor recipients and their families
- Qualified former spouses

How It Works

- You can schedule appointments with any TRICARE-authorized provider, either within the network or outside of it.
- Referrals are not needed for most primary care and specialist appointments. However, some services may require pre-authorization from your regional contractor.
- No TRICARE wallet card is issued under TRICARE Select. You simply need your Uniformed Services ID card as proof of coverage.

Costs

The costs for TRICARE Select vary based on your sponsor's military status. You will need to pay:

- An annual outpatient deductible
- Copayments or cost-shares for covered services
- Enrollment fees (applicable for Group A retirees as of January 1, 2021)

Is TRICARE Select Right for You?

TRICARE Select may be a suitable option if:

- You live in an area where TRICARE Prime is not available.
- You have other health insurance, such as Medicare or an employer-

sponsored health plan.
- You want to continue seeing a provider who is not in the TRICARE network and don't want to switch providers.

Note: Active-duty service members (including activated National Guard and Reserve members) are not eligible for TRICARE Select.

TRICARE Select Overseas

TRICARE Select Overseas offers comprehensive healthcare coverage for eligible beneficiaries living in overseas locations.

To be eligible, you must be registered in the Defense Enrollment Eligibility Reporting System (DEERS), which includes details of military personnel and their families. Registration in DEERS is necessary to access TRICARE benefits.

Enrollment
- Enrollment is required. For more details, visit the TRICARE Select Overseas Enrollment page.

Who Can Participate?

TRICARE Select Overseas is available to:
- Active-duty family members
- Retired service members and their families
- Family members of activated National Guard and Reserve members (on active duty for over 30 consecutive days)
- Non-activated National Guard and Reserve members and their families eligible under the Transitional Assistance Management Program (TAMP)
- Retired National Guard and Reserve members (age 60 or older) and their families
- Survivors
- Medal of Honor recipients and their families
- Qualified former spouses

How It Works
- You can make appointments with any TRICARE-authorized overseas provider.
- Referrals are generally not required for most care, though some services may need pre-authorization.
- You will not receive a TRICARE wallet card. Instead, use your Uniformed Services ID card as proof of coverage.

Costs

The costs associated with TRICARE Select Overseas depend on your sponsor's military status. You will be responsible for:

- Annual outpatient deductible
- Cost-shares (a percentage of the cost for covered services)
- Enrollment fees (Group A retirees pay fees starting January 1, 2021)
- You will need to pay for care upfront and submit claims to be reimbursed.

Is TRICARE Select Overseas Right for You?

TRICARE Select Overseas may be the best option if you live abroad. You also have the option to purchase additional health insurance.

If your sponsor is on active duty, you may be eligible for TRICARE Prime Overseas or TRICARE Prime Remote Overseas instead.

TRICARE For Life

TRICARE For Life (TFL) is a Medicare-wraparound coverage plan for TRICARE-eligible individuals who have Medicare Part A and B, regardless of age or location.

This plan is available only to those who are enrolled in Medicare and meet TRICARE eligibility criteria. TFL does not extend coverage to family members.

Key Details

- Enrollment is not required. TFL coverage is automatically activated once you have Medicare Part A and B.
- TFL coverage begins on the first day your Medicare Part A and B are in effect.
- Medicare Part B premiums are required.
- Worldwide coverage is available.

How Does TRICARE For Life Work?

- You don't need a special TRICARE For Life card. Your Medicare card and military ID serve as proof of coverage.
- You can visit any TRICARE-authorized provider. To find a provider, visit the Find a Doctor page.
- Typically, your provider will file your claims with Medicare first, and Medicare will pay its share. Then, the claim is forwarded to TRICARE For Life for payment.
- TRICARE For Life will pay the remaining balance for covered services.
- For services covered by both Medicare and TRICARE, you typically will have no out-of-pocket costs.
- If the service is not covered by either Medicare or TRICARE, you will need to pay out-of-pocket costs.

Does TRICARE For Life Work Overseas?

- Medicare provides coverage only in the U.S. and U.S. Territories. It does not cover overseas care.

- When using TRICARE For Life overseas, TRICARE becomes the primary payer, and you are responsible for paying TRICARE's annual deductible and cost shares.
- If you live overseas, Part B is still required for TRICARE eligibility, even though Medicare does not cover services abroad.

Enrollment Fees and Payments

- No enrollment fees for TRICARE For Life, but you must pay Medicare Part A and Part B premiums.
  - Medicare Part A premiums are covered by payroll taxes during your working years.
  - Part B premiums are based on income.
- For information on Part B premiums, you can visit the Medicare website or contact Social Security at 1-800-772-1213

Out-of-Pocket Costs

Type of Service	Medicare Pays	TRICARE Pays	You Pay
Covered by both Medicare and TRICARE	Medicare-authorized amount	Remaining balance	Nothing
Covered by Medicare only	Medicare-authorized amount	None	Medicare deductible and cost-share
Covered by TRICARE only	None	Tricare-allowable amount	TRICARE deductible and cost-share
Not covered by either Medicare or TRICARE	None	None	Billed charges (may exceed allowable)

Using TRICARE For Life with Other Health Insurance

If you have other health insurance, such as a Medicare supplement or employer-sponsored health insurance, TRICARE For Life will work as secondary coverage:

- Employer-sponsored insurance (current employment): The other insurance pays first, Medicare second, and TRICARE last. Your employer handles claim filing.
- Other health insurance (not tied to employment): Medicare pays first, followed by the other insurance, and TRICARE pays last. You must file a claim with the TRICARE For Life contractor, submitting a paper claim to WPS along with a copy of your Medicare Summary Notice and Explanation of Benefits from the other insurance.

You must file claims within one year from the care date. For more details, visit WPS website.

Can I Suspend My FEHB Coverage to Use TRICARE For Life?

Yes, you can suspend your Federal Employee Health Benefits (FEHB) coverage if you are eligible for TRICARE For Life. Contact the Office of Personnel Management at 1-888-767-6738 for the suspension form.

Who to Contact for Assistance

For any claims-related questions or customer service, TRICARE For Life contractors are available to assist:
- In the U.S. and U.S. Territories: Wisconsin Physicians Service (WPS)
- In all overseas locations: International SOS

TRICARE Reserve Select

TRICARE Reserve Select (TRS) is a premium-based health plan available worldwide, designed for qualified Selected Reserve members and their families.

Who Can Enroll?

TRICARE Reserve Select is available to:
- Selected Reserve members and their families who meet the following criteria:
    - Not on active-duty orders for more than 30 days
    - Not covered under the Transitional Assistance Management Program
    - Not eligible for or enrolled in Federal Employees Health Benefits (FEHB). If your spouse is a Selected Reserve member eligible for TRS, you may be covered under their plan if they qualify.
    - Survivor coverage is not impacted by FEHB eligibility.

Note: Members of the Individual Ready Reserve (including Navy Reserve Voluntary Training Units) are not eligible for TRICARE Reserve Select.

How It Works
- You can book an appointment with any TRICARE-authorized provider.
- If you visit a network provider, your cost-share is lower, and the provider will handle your claims.
- If you visit a non-network provider, you will pay higher cost shares and may need to file your own claims.
- Referrals are not required for most care, but some services may need pre-authorization from your regional contractor.
- Military hospital or clinic visits are possible if space is available, but you will need to make an appointment.
- You cannot have a Primary Care Manager (PCM) at a military treatment facility (MTF) if enrolled in TRS, but you can choose any TRICARE-authorized provider as your Primary Care Provider (PCP).

Costs

- Monthly premiums
- Annual deductible
- Cost-share (a percentage) for covered services
- For detailed cost information, visit the TRICARE Reserve Select Costs page.

Is TRICARE Reserve Select Right for You?

TRICARE Reserve Select may be the right choice if you:

- Are a member of the Selected Reserve but do not qualify for coverage under the following:
  - Active-duty orders for more than 30 days
  - The Transitional Assistance Management Program (TAMP)
  - Federal Employees Health Benefits (FEHB)

Note: If you don't qualify for TRS individually but have a family member who qualifies, you may be eligible for coverage through them.

How to Enroll

To enroll in TRICARE Reserve Select, visit the TRICARE Reserve Select Enrollment page.

For information on disenrollment or ending your coverage, visit the Ending TRICARE Reserve Select Coverage page.

Note: Family members must enroll under the same plan as the sponsor, and those overseas may request enrollment at a TRICARE Service Center.

Adding a Child to TRICARE Reserve Select

You have 90 days (or 120 days if overseas) from the date of your child's birth or adoption to add them to your coverage. Your child will not be covered until they are officially enrolled.

TRICARE Retired Reserve

TRICARE Retired Reserve is a premium-based health plan that provides comprehensive coverage for qualified retired members of the Reserve and their families, available worldwide.

Who Can Enroll?

TRICARE Retired Reserve is available to:

- Retired Reserve members who:
  - Are qualified for non-regular retirement under 10 U.S.C., Chapter

1223
- ○ Are under age 60
- ○ Are not eligible for or enrolled in Federal Employees Health Benefits (FEHB)
- Family members of qualified Retired Reserve members.
- Survivors of Retired Reserve members, if:
    - ○ The sponsor was enrolled in TRICARE Retired Reserve at the time of death.
    - ○ They are immediate family members (spouses who have remarried do not qualify).
    - ○ Coverage begins before the sponsor would have turned 60.

Note: Survivor coverage is unaffected by FEHB eligibility.

How It Works

- You can book an appointment with any TRICARE-authorized provider.
    - ○ If you visit a network provider, you'll pay lower cost shares, and the provider will handle your claims.
    - ○ If you visit a non-network provider, you'll pay higher cost shares and may need to file your own claims.
- Military hospital or clinic appointments are available if space permits.
- Referrals are not required, but some services may need pre-authorization from your regional contractor.

Costs

- Monthly premiums
- Annual deductible
- Cost-share (a percentage) for covered services

For full details on the costs, visit the TRICARE Retired Reserve Costs page.

Is TRICARE Retired Reserve Right for You?

TRICARE Retired Reserve is an excellent option for those who qualify. It offers full coverage upon retirement, without needing to wait until you turn 60 to access the plan. You also have the flexibility to keep your current providers without needing to switch.

TRICARE Young Adult

TRICARE Young Adult (TYA) is a health plan that provides coverage for qualified adult children after they age out of regular TRICARE eligibility, typically at age 21 (or 23 if enrolled in college). This plan is designed for unmarried children who no longer qualify for regular TRICARE coverage.

TYA offers comprehensive medical and pharmacy benefits, and you can choose between two options: TYA-Prime or TYA-Select, depending on how you want to access your care.

Before deciding on TYA, it's important to review all your healthcare options, both military and civilian.

Note: You are not eligible for TYA if you can get coverage through an employer-sponsored health plan.

Who Can Enroll?

To qualify for TRICARE Young Adult, you must meet the following criteria:
- You are an unmarried, adult child of an eligible sponsor.
- You are between the ages of 21 and 26.
- You are not eligible for any other form of TRICARE coverage.
- If you are enrolled in a full-time course of study at an approved institution and your sponsor provides more than 50% of your financial support, you may remain eligible until age 23 or until graduation (whichever comes first).
- You are not eligible for employer-sponsored health insurance based on your employment.

Eligible sponsors include:
- Active-duty service members
- Retired service members
- Activated National Guard and Reserve members
- Non-activated National Guard and Reserve members using TRICARE Reserve Select
- Retired National Guard and Reserve members using TRICARE Retired Reserve
- Unremarried former spouses registered in DEERS

Note: You can enroll in TYA without a valid Uniformed Services ID card. Once your coverage begins, visit an ID card office to get your new card, which you should present when seeing a provider.

How TRICARE Young Adult Works
- **TYA-Prime:** Functions similarly to TRICARE Prime, where you have a Primary Care Manager (PCM) who coordinates most of your care and refers you to specialists as needed. If you visit a network provider, they will handle the claims for you. If you see a non-network provider, you will pay higher out-of-pocket costs.
- **TYA-Select:** Works like TRICARE Select, giving you the flexibility to see any TRICARE-authorized provider. You don't need a referral for most types of care, though some services may require pre-authorization. If you visit a network provider, your out-of-pocket costs will be lower, and they will file your claims. If you visit a non-network provider, you may have higher costs and need to submit your claims.

What You Pay

- Monthly premiums
- Annual deductible
- Cost shares (percentage of covered services)

The costs vary depending on your sponsor's military status. For more details, check the TYA Costs page.

TRICARE Young Adult Options

1. **TYA-Prime:**
   o Care is coordinated by your assigned Primary Care Manager (PCM), who will refer you to specialists.
   o You will pay monthly premiums, TRICARE Prime copayments, and point-of-service fees for care without a referral.
2. **TYA-Select:**
   o You can visit any TRICARE-authorized provider, and you don't need a referral for most care.
   o You will pay monthly premiums, annual deductibles, and cost-shares for services.
3. **US Family Health Plan (USFHP) (for TYA-Prime option):**
   o Available in select regions through community-based, non-profit health care systems.
   o You'll receive all care from a primary care provider in the network.
   o There are no out-of-pocket costs for active-duty family members, but other beneficiaries pay annual fees and network copayments.

How to Enroll

- To enroll in TRICARE Young Adult, visit the TRICARE Young Adult Enrollment page.
- If you want to enroll in the US Family Health Plan (USFHP) under TYA-Prime, visit the USFHP enrollment page.

Dental Coverage Options

There are three primary dental plans available for eligible beneficiaries: the Active-Duty Dental Program, TRICARE Dental Program, and FEDVIP Dental. Each plan offers different coverage and eligibility requirements.

Active-Duty Dental Program

- **Description:** Provides coverage for civilian dental care for active-duty service members.
- **Eligibility:**
  o Active-duty service members
  o National Guard and Reserve members who are:
    ▪ On continuous active duty for over 30 days
    ▪ On federally funded orders for more than 30 days
    ▪ Transitioning from federal orders to state orders (e.g., during state disaster response duty)

- Early activation members (Reserve Component members with delayed-effective-date active-duty orders)
- Personnel in the Transitional Assistance Management Program (TAMP)
- Wounded warriors (active-duty members receiving inpatient care at a VA hospital)
- Family members of active-duty service members
- **Contact: United Concordia**

TRICARE Dental Program

- **Description:** A voluntary dental insurance plan for eligible beneficiaries, covering a range of dental services.
- **Eligibility:**
  - Family members of active-duty service members
  - National Guard and Reserve members not on active duty or covered by TAMP
  - Certain survivors
  - Retired service members and their families
  - Retired National Guard and Reserve members and their families
  - Medal of Honor recipients and their families
- **Contact:** United Concordia

FEDVIP Dental

- **Description:** A voluntary dental insurance plan available through the Federal Employees Dental and Vision Insurance Program (FEDVIP).
- **Eligibility:**
  - Retired service members and their families
  - Retired National Guard and Reserve members and their families
  - Medal of Honor recipients and their families
  - Certain survivors
- **Contact:** BENEFEDS

These dental plans offer flexibility based on service status and provide essential coverage for a variety of dental needs. Make sure to contact the respective program for more information and to determine which plan best suits your needs.

TRICARE Regions and Assistance

TRICARE is available worldwide, with services managed across three main regions. The U.S. is divided into two regions, and all areas outside of the U.S. are categorized as overseas.

Each region is managed by a specific regional contractor, and understanding your region will help you access the appropriate care and services.

U.S. Regions (Effective January 1, 2025)

- **East Region**
  Managed by Humana Military
  Contact: 800-444-5445
  Website: www.tricare.mil/east
- **West Region**
  Managed by TriWest Healthcare Alliance
  Contact: 888-TRIWEST (874-9378)
  Website: www.tricare.mil/west

Overseas Regions

- **Eurasia-Africa Area**
  Includes Europe, Africa, the Middle East, Pakistan, Russia, and former Soviet republics, including the Baltic States, Ukraine, Georgia, Kazakhstan, Kyrgyzstan, and Uzbekistan.
  Managed by International SOS
  Contact: +44-20-8762-8384 / 877-678-1207 (Stateside)
  Website: www.tricare-overseas.com
- **Latin America and Canada Area**
  Includes Central and South America, the Caribbean, Canada, Puerto Rico, and the Virgin Islands.
  Managed by International SOS
  Contact: +1-215-942-8393 / 877-451-8659 (Stateside)
  Website: www.tricare-overseas.com
- **Pacific Area**
  Includes Guam, Japan, Korea, Asia, Australia, New Zealand, India, and other Western Pacific regions.
  Managed by International SOS
  Contact: +65-6339-2676 / 877-678-1208/1209 (Stateside)
  Website: www.tricare-overseas.com

Other Contacts:

- For TRICARE For Life in the U.S. or U.S. Territories, visit www.tricare4u.com
- For US Family Health Plan coverage, visit www.tricare.mil/usfhp

If you are unsure which region you fall under, refer to the regional contractor or check the websites listed above to find the right plan and healthcare provider for your area.

Comparison of TRICARE Plans

TRICARE Plan	Eligibility	Key Features	Costs
TRICARE Prime	Active-duty service members, families, retirees under 65 (in Prime areas).	Managed care with assigned Primary Care Manager (PCM). Requires referrals for specialty care.	Low/no enrollment fees for active duty. Retirees may have annual enrollment fees and copayments.
TRICARE Select	Active-duty family members, retirees under 65, and certain others.	Fee-for-service plan. No assigned PCM; beneficiaries manage their own care and referrals.	Annual deductible and copayments/coinsurance. No enrollment fees for active-duty families.
TRICARE for Life	Medicare-eligible retirees (65+ with Medicare Part A and Part B).	Secondary coverage to Medicare. Covers services not fully paid by Medicare.	No enrollment fees. Pay Medicare Part B premiums and coinsurance after Medicare pays.
TRICARE Reserve Select	Selected Reserve members and families.	Premium-based plan similar to TRICARE Select. Manage own care and referrals.	Monthly premiums, annual deductible, and copayments.
TRICARE Retired Reserve	Retired Reserve members and families under age 60.	Premium-based plan similar to TRICARE Select. Available until the retiree reaches age 60.	Higher monthly premiums than Reserve Select, plus deductible and copayments.
TRICARE Young Adult	Adult children (21-26) who are not otherwise eligible.	Premium-based plan. Can choose Prime or Select options based on location and eligibility.	Monthly premiums, with varying costs for Prime vs. Select options.
TRICARE Overseas	Active duty, retirees, and eligible family members	Prime option for command-sponsored beneficiaries	Similar costs to Prime or Select based on plan type.

	stationed abroad.	and Select option for others. Covers overseas medical services.	
Tricare Pharmacy	All TRICARE beneficiaries.	Covers prescription medications via retail, mail order, and military pharmacies.	Copayments vary by pharmacy type and medication tier.

CHAPTER 8

CHAMPVA

If you are the spouse, surviving spouse or child of a veteran with disability or a veteran who died and you don't qualify for TRICARE, you may be eligible for health insurance through the Civilian Health and Medical Program of the Department of Veterans Affairs (CHAMPVA).

CHAMPVA Benefits Overview

The Civilian Health and Medical Program of the Department of Veterans Affairs (CHAMPVA) provides health care coverage for eligible family members and survivors of veterans with service-connected disabilities.

Eligibility for CHAMPVA

You may qualify for CHAMPVA if:

- You are the spouse or dependent child of a veteran with a permanent and total service-connected disability.
- You are the surviving spouse or dependent child of a veteran who died from a service-connected disability or who was rated as permanently and totally disabled at the time of their death.
- In some cases, you may qualify as the surviving spouse or dependent child of a service member who died in the line of duty (not due to misconduct).

Note: CHAMPVA is not available to those eligible for TRICARE.

Specific Eligibility Groups

- **Newborn Dependent Children:** You must enroll your newborn in CHAMPVA after birth by obtaining a Social Security number and adding the child as a dependent through your nearest VA office.
- **Surviving Spouses Who Remarry:** If you remarry after the age of 55, you can retain CHAMPVA benefits. However, if you remarry before 55, you lose benefits unless your remarriage ends, in which case benefits are reinstated the following month.
- **Veteran Spouses:** If both spouses are veterans, each can qualify for both VA health care and CHAMPVA. You can choose between these options when seeking care.

- **Dependent Children Aged 18-23:** Full-time students can keep CHAMPVA benefits until age 23. Benefits end if they marry or are no longer enrolled in school.
  - If the child is permanently disabled due to a condition before age 18, they can keep benefits after turning 18.
  - Stepchildren lose eligibility if they leave the veteran's household due to divorce or remarriage.
- **Eligibility with Medicare:** If you are eligible for Medicare, you must have Part A and Part B to receive CHAMPVA benefits.
- **Primary Family Caregivers:** Caregivers of veterans with disabilities may qualify for CHAMPVA if they are the primary caregiver and lack other health insurance.

How to Apply for CHAMPVA

You can apply for CHAMPVA in the following ways:
- **Online:** Apply directly through the CHAMPVA website.
- **By Mail**: Complete the VA Form 10-10d and send it along with supporting documents to VHA Office of Integrated Veteran Care, PO Box 137, Spring City, PA 19475.
- **By Fax**: Send your completed form and documents to 303-331-7809.

Supporting Documents

You may need to provide additional documents, such as:
- Proof of marriage (if applying as a spouse)
- Birth certificate (if applying as a child)
- Disability ratings for children with permanent disabilities
- School enrollment letters for children aged 18-23

After You Apply

Once approved, you'll receive a CHAMPVA ID card and program guide. If you need help or have questions about your application, you can contact the CHAMPVA support line at 800-733-8387 (TTY: 711).

CHAMPVA Benefits

The Civilian Health and Medical Program of the Department of Veterans Affairs (CHAMPVA) shares healthcare costs for eligible family members, survivors, and caregivers of veterans with service-connected disabilities. If you have additional health insurance, you may not be responsible for certain out-of-pocket costs.

Covered Services

CHAMPVA covers a broad range of health care services and supplies, including:
- Family Planning and Maternity Care

- Hospice Care
- Inpatient Care (hospital stays)
- Mental Health Care
- Outpatient Care (including office visits and procedures)
- Skilled Nursing Care (medically necessary recovery care)
- Ambulance Services
- Medical Equipment prescribed by a provider
- Organ Transplants
- Prescription Medications

For a complete list of covered services, refer to the CHAMPVA Program Guide.

Additional Coverage Details

- **Dental and Vision**: CHAMPVA does not provide routine dental or vision care. However, you can access dental insurance through the VA Dental Insurance Program (VADIP) at a discounted rate. Vision coverage is limited, and CHAMPVA only covers certain cases for eyeglasses and contact lenses.
- **Prescription Medications:**
  - Meds by Mail: CHAMPVA provides prescription medications through the Meds by Mail program, delivering regular prescriptions directly to your home with no out-of-pocket cost.
  - OptumRx: For urgent prescriptions, you can use a local pharmacy within the OptumRx network. You will pay 25% of the cost.
  - If you use non-OptumRx pharmacies, you must pay upfront and submit a claim for reimbursement (CHAMPVA will cover 75% of the cost).

Prior Authorization Requirements

While most services do not require prior approval, certain types of care require authorization:

- Inpatient Mental Health Care
- Care for Alcohol or Substance Use Disorders
- Dental Care (in limited cases)
- Organ Transplants

For approval of these services, contact CHAMPVA at 800-733-8387 or mail the necessary documentation to

CHAMPVA Authorization,
PO Box 500
Spring City, PA 19475.

Cost Sharing and Deductibles

- **Annual Deductible**: You will need to pay a $50 deductible per calendar year (or $100 max for families) for urgent prescriptions and outpatient care.

There is no deductible for inpatient care.

- **Cost Share:** You pay 25% of the allowable amount for most covered services, which is the amount CHAMPVA has agreed to pay for a specific service.
- **Out-of-Pocket Maximum:** You won't pay more than $3,000 per year. Once you reach this limit, CHAMPVA will pay 100% of covered services.

Finding CHAMPVA Providers

- There is no specific CHAMPVA network. However, you can see any healthcare provider who accepts CHAMPVA assignments. If a provider does not accept CHAMPVA, you will need to pay out of pocket and file a claim for reimbursement. CHAMPVA will cover the allowable amount, but you will need to pay any costs above that amount.
- Hospitals and Medicare Providers: Any hospital that accepts Medicare will also accept CHAMPVA. You can search for providers through the Medicare website.

CHAMPVA and Medicare

To continue receiving CHAMPVA benefits, you must have Medicare Part A and Part B (or a Medicare Advantage Plan). CHAMPVA acts as a secondary payer to Medicare, covering costs that are not paid by Medicare.

CHAMPVA and Other Insurance

If you have other health insurance, CHAMPVA will be your secondary payer. The primary insurer should pay for your care first, and then CHAMPVA will cover the remaining costs. If you have Medicare Part D for prescription coverage, you cannot use Meds by Mail, but you can still use OptumRx pharmacies.

CHAMPVA Coverage for Dependents Aged 18-23

If you are a dependent child under CHAMPVA:

- You can continue receiving benefits between ages 18-23 if enrolled full-time in high school, college, or another educational institution.
- Benefits end if you are no longer enrolled in school or if you marry before turning 23.
- Permanently disabled children may continue coverage after turning 18 if they are unable to support themselves.

How to Apply for CHAMPVA Benefits

You can apply for CHAMPVA benefits in three ways:

- **Online:** Apply directly on the CHAMPVA website.
- **By Mail:** Fill out the VA Form 10-10d and mail it to VHA Office of Integrated Veteran Care, CHAMPVA Eligibility, PO Box 137, Spring City, PA 19475.
- **By Fax:** Fax your completed VA Form 10-10d and documents to 303-331-

7809.

For Medicare beneficiaries, you will need to provide proof of your Medicare Part A and B coverage.

CHAMPVA ID Card and Services

Once approved, you will receive a CHAMPVA ID card and a program guide. If you lose your ID card or need a replacement, call 800-733-8387 (TTY: 711).

For additional questions or more details about CHAMPVA coverage, visit the CHAMPVA website or call 800-733-8387.

CHAPTER 9

THE PACT ACT

The PACT Act—An Overview

The PACT Act is a law expanding VA health care and benefits for veterans exposed to burn pits, Agent Orange and other toxic substances.

The PACT Act adds to the list of health conditions that the VA assumes or presumes are caused by exposure to these substances.

The PACT Act is considered the largest health care and benefit expansion in VA history. The full name of the legislation is The Sergeant First Class (SFC) Heath Robinson Honoring Our Promise to Address comprehensive Toxics (PACT) Act.

The PACT Act brought many major changes including expanding and extending eligibility for VA health care for veterans with toxic exposures and veterans of the Vietnam, Gulf War and post- 9/11 eras.

It adds more than 20 presumptive conditions for burn pits, Agent Orange and other toxic exposures. It adds more presumptive-exposure locations for Agent Orange and radiation and requires VA to provide a toxic exposure screening to every veteran enrolled in VA health care.

To get a VA disability rating, the disability must connect to a veteran's military service. For many health conditions, VA requires that the veteran prove their service caused their condition, but for some conditions, VA automatically assumes or presumes the veteran's service caused their condition.

These are presumptive conditions. If you have a presumptive condition, you don't have to prove your service caused the condition. You only have to meet the service requirements for the presumption.

Overview of the PACT Act (Honoring Our Promise to Address Comprehensive Toxics Act)

Category	Details
Purpose	Expands access to VA health care and benefits for veterans exposed to toxic substances during service.
Signed Into Law	August 10, 2022
Key Provisions	- Expands presumptions for toxic exposure-related conditions. - Enhances research and data collection on toxic exposures. - Provides additional funding for VA facilities and staffing.
Who It Affects	- Veterans who served in specific locations with known toxic exposures. - Survivors of affected veterans.
Conditions Covered	- Respiratory diseases (e.g., asthma, chronic bronchitis). - Cancers (e.g., lung cancer, head and neck cancer). - Other illnesses related to burn pits, Agent Orange, and radiation exposure.
Eligibility Expansion	- Includes veterans who served in previously excluded locations like Thailand, Laos, and Cambodia. - Adds new locations related to burn pits and other toxic exposures.
Presumptive Benefits	Veterans no longer need to prove a direct service connection for certain illnesses if they served in eligible locations.
Filing a Claim	Claims can be filed through the VA website, in person, or with the assistance of an accredited VA representative.
VA Health Care Access	Expands eligibility for VA health care services for veterans exposed to toxins.
Support Resources	Veterans can get help through: - VA's PACT Act webpage - Call 1-800-MYVA411 - Accredited Veterans Service Organizations (VSOs).

Gulf War Era and Post-9/11 Veteran Eligibility

If a veteran served in any of these locations and time periods, VA has determined you had exposure to burn pits or other toxins, which is called having a presumption of exposure.

On or after September 11, 2001, in any of these locations:

- Afghanistan
- Djibouti
- Egypt
- Jordan
- Lebanon
- Syria
- Uzbekistan
- Yemen
- The airspace above any of these locations

On or after August 2, 1990, in any of these locations:

- Bahrain
- Iraq
- Kuwait
- Oman
- Qatar
- Saudi Arabia
- Somalia
- The United Arab Emirates (UAE)
- The airspace above any of these locations

More than 20 burn pit and other toxic exposure presumptive conditions have been added based on The PACT Act. The cancers that are now presumptive include:

- Brain cancer
- Gastrointestinal cancer of any type
- Glioblastoma
- Head cancer of any type
- Kidney cancer
- Lymphoma of any type
- Melanoma
- Neck cancer of any type
- Pancreatic cancer
- Reproductive cancer of any type
- Respiratory cancer of any type

These illnesses are now presumptive:

- Asthma that was diagnosed after service
- Chronic bronchitis
- Chronic obstructive pulmonary disease (COPD)
- Chronic rhinitis
- Chronic sinusitis
- Constrictive bronchiolitis or obliterative bronchiolitis
- Emphysema
- Granulomatous disease

- Interstitial lung disease (ILD)
- Pleuritis
- Pulmonary fibrosis
- Sarcoidosis

VA health care eligibility was extended and expanded based on the PACT Act as well.

Eligibility depends on a veteran's service history and other factors, and veterans are encouraged to apply no matter their separation date.

If a veteran meets the listed requirements, they can get free VA health care for any condition related to their service for up to 10 years from the date of their most recent discharge or separation.

Veterans can also enroll at any time during this period and can get the care they needed, but they may owe a copay for some care.

At least one of these must be true for a veteran's active-duty service:

- The veteran served in a theater of combat operations during a period of war after the Persian Gulf War, or
- The veteran served in combat against a hostile force during a period of hostilities after November 11, 1998.

This must also be true:

- The veteran was discharged or released within 10 years.

If a veteran was discharged or released before October 1, 2013, VA currently says they'll share more information about opportunities to enroll in VA health care under The PACT Act soon.

Other factors like financial circumstances or having a service-connected disability can also make a veteran eligible for care. There are many paths to eligibility for VA health care, and VA says the best way to find out is applying.

Vietnam Era Veteran Eligibility

If a veteran served on active duty in any of the following locations during these time periods, they're now eligible to apply for VA health care:

- The Republic of Vietnam between January 9, 1962, and May 7, 1975
- Thailand at any U.S. or Royal Thai base between January 9, 1962, and June 30, 1976
- Laos between December 1, 1965, and September 30, 1969
- Certain provinces in Cambodia between April 16, 1969, and April 30, 1969
- Guam or American Samoa or their territorial waters between January 9, 1962, and July 31, 1980
- Johnston Atoll or on a ship that called at Johnston Atoll between January 1, 1972, and September 30, 1977

Based on The PACT Act, the VA has added two new Agent Orange Presumptive conditions.

The first is hypertension or high blood pressure. The second is monoclonal gammopathy of underdetermined significance or MGUS.

117

A veteran may also be eligible for disability compensation based on other Agent Orange presumptive conditions, which are detailed in Chapter 4 (Toxic Exposures).

Three new response efforts have been added to the list of radiation presumptive locations. These include:

- The cleanup of Enewetak Atoll from January 1, 1977, through December 31, 1980.
- Cleanup of the Air Force B-52 bomber carrying nuclear weapons off the coast of Palomares, Spain from January 17, 1966, through March 31, 1976.
- Response to the fire onboard an Air Force B-52 bomber carrying nuclear weapons near Thule Air Force Base in Greenland from January 21, 1968, to September 25, 1968.

If a veteran took part in any of the above efforts, the VA automatically presumes they had exposure to radiation under The PACT Act.

Getting Benefits

Veterans who haven't yet filed a claim for a presumptive condition can file one online now, or by mail, in person, or with the help of a trained professional. More information is available in Chapter 10 (Disability Compensation).

If VA previously denied your disability claim and the condition is now considered presumptive, you can submit a Supplemental Claim, and your case will be reviewed again. If you have a pending claim for a condition that's now presumptive, you don't have to do anything. The VA says it will consider it presumptive even if your condition was added after you filed a claim.

VA says it's working to process claims with the utmost urgency. The time it takes to review your claim depends on the type of claim filed, how many injuries or disabilities you claimed and how complex they are, and how long it takes the VA to collect the evidence needed to decide your claim.

Toxic Exposure Screenings

Toxic exposure screenings are available at VA health facilities across the country. Every veteran enrolled in VA health care will receive an initial screening and a follow-up screening at least once every five years.

Veterans who are not enrolled and who meet eligibility requirements will have an opportunity to enroll and receive the screening.

The screening asks veterans if they were exposed to any of these hazards while serving:

- Open burn pits and other airborne hazards
- Gulf War-related exposures
- Agent Orange
- Radiation
- Camp Lejeune contaminated water exposure
- Other exposures

Information for Survivors

Surviving family members of a veteran may be eligible for the following benefits:

- A monthly VA Dependency and Indemnity Compensation (VA DIC) payment. You could also qualify if you're the surviving spouse, dependent child or parent of a veteran who died from a service-connected disability.
- A one-time accrued benefits payment. You may qualify if you're the surviving spouse, dependent child or dependent parent of a veteran who the VA owed unpaid benefits at the time of their death.
- A Survivors Pension. You may qualify if you're the surviving spouse or child of a veteran with wartime service.

If you previously had the VA deny a DIC claim and you now think you're eligible, you can submit a new application for VA DIC.

Survivors may also be eligible for other VA benefits including:

- Burial benefits and memorial items like a gravesite in a VA national cemetery or a free headstone, marker or medallion.
- A burial allowance to help with the veteran's burial and funeral costs. You may qualify if you're the veteran's surviving spouse, partner, child or parent.
- Education and training. You may qualify if you're the survivor of a veteran who died in the line of duty or as a result of service-connected disabilities.
- Health care through the Civilian Health and Medical Program of the Department of Veterans Affairs (CHAMPVA). You may qualify if you're the survivor or dependent of a veteran with a service-connected disability.
- A VA-backed home loan. You may qualify if you're the surviving spouse of a veteran.

CHAPTER 10

DISABILITY COMPENSATION FOR SERVICE-CONNECTED DISABILITIES

VA disability compensation offers a monthly tax-free payment to veterans who got sick or injured while serving in the military, and to veterans whose service made an existing condition worse.

You may qualify for VA disability benefits for physical conditions, and mental health conditions that developed before, during or after service.

You may be eligible for VA disability benefits if you meet both of the following requirements:
- You have a current illness or injury that affects your mind or body, and
- You served on active duty, active duty for training, or inactive duty training.

At least one of these must be true:
- You got sick or injured while serving in the military and can link this condition to your illness or injury, called an in-service disability claim, or
- You had an illness or injury before you joined the military and serving made it worse, called a preservice disability claim, or
- You have a disability related to your active-duty service that didn't appear until after you end your service, known as a post service disability claim.

Presumed disabilities include chronic (long-lasting illnesses appearing within a year after discharge), an illness caused by contact with toxic chemicals or contaminants, or an illness caused by time spent as prisoner of war.

You may be able to get VA disability benefits for conditions including:
- Chronic back pain resulting in a current diagnosed back disability.
- Breathing problems stemming from a current lung disease or condition
- Severe hearing loss
- Scar tissue
- Loss of range of motion

- Ulcers
- Cancers caused by contact with toxic chemicals or other dangers
- Traumatic brain injury (TBI)
- Post-traumatic stress disorder (PTSD)
- Depression
- Anxiety

VA Disability Compensation Application Process Flowchart

Step	Description
1. Determine Eligibility	Confirm that your condition is related to your military service. Ensure you meet the criteria for VA disability compensation.
2. Gather Evidence	Collect necessary documentation, including: - Service records to verify your military service. - Medical records showing a current diagnosis. - Nexus evidence linking the condition to your service.
3. Submit an Application	Apply for VA disability compensation using one of the following methods: - Online via VA.gov. - Mail VA Form 21-526EZ to the VA Claims Intake Center. - Seek assistance from a VA-accredited representative or Veterans Service Organization (VSO).
4. VA Acknowledgment	The VA will confirm receipt of your claim and provide a claim number for tracking.
5. Claim Development	The VA will: - Request additional evidence if needed. - Schedule a Compensation & Pension (C&P) exam to assess your condition. - Review all evidence submitted to support your claim.
6. Claim Decision	The VA evaluates your claim and assigns a disability rating. A decision letter with details of the rating and benefits will be sent to you.
7. Appeal (if needed)	If you disagree with the decision, you can: - File a Supplemental Claim with new evidence. - Request a Higher-Level Review by a senior reviewer. - Appeal to the Board of Veterans' Appeals for further review.

How to File a Claim

You should find out if you're eligible for VA disability compensation and gather any evidence you're going to submit when you file your claim. Your claim should be filled out completely and you should have all your supporting documents ready.

The VA Fully Developed Claims Program can help you get a faster decision on your disability benefits.

You can submit a fully developed disability claim if you're applying for compensation for:

- An illness or injury caused by or one that got worse because of your active-duty service, or
- A condition caused by or made worse by a disability the VA has already determined is service connected.

For a claim to be considered fully developed, a veteran need to:

- Submit their completed Application for Disability Compensation and Related Compensation Benefits (VA Form 21-526EZ), and
- Submit all evidence (supporting documents), and
- Certify there's no more evidence the VA might need to decide the claim, and
- Go to any VA medical exams required for a claim decision. The VA lets the veteran know if they need any exams.

Evidence you'll need to submit along with your disability claim includes:

- All private medical records related to the claimed condition like reports from your own doctor, and
- Any records of medical treatment you received for the claimed condition while serving in the military, and
- Any military personnel records they have related to the claimed condition, and
- Information about any related health records that you don't have but that the VA can request on your behalf from a federal facility

If a veteran doesn't think their service records will include a description of their disability, they can also submit letters from family, friends, clergy members, law enforcement or the people they served with who can tell the VA more about their claimed condition, and how and when it happened.

Using the Fully Developed Claims program won't affect your benefits or how your claim is handled.

If the VA determines they need non-federal records to decide, they'll remove the claim from the Fully Developed Claims program and process it as a standard claim.

Once you start a Fully Developed Claim, you have up to a year to complete it. If the VA approves your claim, you'll be paid back to the day you started it.

Standard Disability Claims

To submit a standard disability claim, you'll need to:

- Submit your completed Application for Disability Compensation and Related Compensation Benefits (VA Form 21-526EZ), and
- Let the VA know about related records not held by a federal agency, and give the VA any information needed to get them, and
- Go to any medical exams the VA schedules, if they decide they're needed to make a decision on your claim.

You can start your online application, or you can file a claim by mail, in person, or with the help of a trained professional.

The process is slower for getting a decision on a standard disability claim because the VA gathers the evidence for your claim. If you want a faster decision, submit a fully developed claim, where you gather all the evidence and submit it with your claim.

If you aren't filing your disability compensation claim online, you can do it by mail.

You can print VA Form 21-526EZ, fill it out and send it to:

Department of Veterans Affairs Claims Intake Center
PO Box 4444
Janesville, WI, 53547-4444

You can also bring your application in person to the VA regional office nearest you.

Finally, you can work with a trained professional, called an accredited representative, to get help filing a disability compensation claim.

If you're going to file for disability compensation using a paper form, you might want to submit an intent to file form first.

This gives you time to gather evidence while avoiding a later potential start date, which is known as an effective date. If you notify the VA of an intent to file, you may be able to get retroactive benefits.

You don't need to notify the VA of an intent to file if you file for disability compensation online, because the effective date is automatically set when you start filling out your form online, before you submit it.

Evidence Needed for a Disability Claim

When you file a disability claim, the VA will review all available evidence to determine if you qualify. The VA is looking for evidence showing:

- A current physical or mental disability, and
- An event, injury or illness that happened while you were in the military to cause the disability.

You'll need to submit or give the VA permission to gather your DD214 or other separation documents, your service treatment records, and any medical evidence related to your illness or injury such as medical test results or X-rays.

The evidence you need to support a claim can vary depending on the type of claim you're filing.

- **Original claim**: This is your first claim you file for disability benefits. You'll need evidence of a current physical or mental disability from a medical professional or layperson, and an event, injury or disease that happened during active-duty service. You'll also need to show evidence of a link between your current disability and the event, injury or disease that happened during your service. If there's no evidence, but you have a chronic illness occurring within a year after discharge, an illness caused by time spent as a POW, or an illness caused by contact with hazardous materials, VA may conclude a link.
- **Increased claim**: These claims are for more compensation for a disability that has already been determined service-connected and has gotten worse. For this you'll need to submit current evidence from a medical professional or layperson that shows the disability has gotten worse.
- **New claim for added benefits or other benefit requests related to an existing service-connected disability**: For this type of claim you have to submit evidence of a current mental or physical disability from a medical professional or layperson, and an event injury or disease that happened during your active-duty service, and a link between your current disability and the event, injury or disease.
- **Supplemental claim**: These claims provide new evidence to support a disability claim that was denied.

Differences Between Pension Benefits and Disability Compensation

Pension benefits and disability compensation are both provided by the VA, but they have different eligibility requirements and methods for determining payment amounts.

- **Pension Benefits:** Pension benefits are available to veterans who served during wartime. Eligibility is determined based on financial need, which includes:
    - Your and your dependents' net worth and annual income.
    - Your age or the severity of any disabilities, which do not necessarily have to be service connected.

The amount of your pension is based on your income level.

- **Disability Compensation:** Disability compensation is for veterans who have a service-connected disability. Eligibility is based on the severity and type of disability, and it is not determined by income or net worth.

The amount of compensation you receive depends on your disability rating.

Note: Veterans cannot receive both pension benefits and disability compensation simultaneously. If you qualify for both, you will receive the benefit with the higher payment amount.

Selected Reserve and National Guard

Since September 11, 2001, numerous members of the Armed Forces Reserves have been called to active duty. Some of these individuals had already filed claims for VA compensation, based on earlier periods of active service. In September 2004, the VA General Counsel issued a precedent opinion that discussed the effect of a return to active service on a pending disability compensation claim.

In general, a veteran's return to active duty does not affect his or her claim for VA benefits and does not alter either the veteran's right or the VA's duty to develop and adjudicate the claim.

If the veteran is temporarily unable to report for a medical examination or take some other required action because of his or her return to active duty, the VA must defer processing the claim until the veteran can take the required action.

The VA cannot deny the claim because a veteran is temporarily unavailable due to a return to active duty.

A veteran is not entitled to receive both active duty pay and VA disability compensation for the same period of time. However, the higher monetary benefit is usually paid. If a veteran with a pending claim dies on active duty before the claim is decided, an eligible survivor may be entitled to any accrued benefits payable.

Concurrent Military Retired Pay and VA Disability Compensation

Military retirees generally cannot receive both VA Disability Compensation and military retired pay concurrently.

Typically, retirees must waive their military retirement pay to receive VA disability benefits. This rule is outlined in Title 38, U.S.C., sections 5304 and 5305.

However, a limited exception allows certain retirees to receive both military retired pay and VA Disability Compensation at the same time.

This exception is referred to as Concurrent Retirement and Disability Pay (CRDP), though the term is not legally defined. CRDP applies to specific retirees under certain conditions.

Eligibility Criteria

- **For Retirees Not Under Chapter 61 for Disability**:
  To receive concurrent benefits, you must:
    o Be eligible for both military retired pay and VA Disability Compensation in the same month.
    o Have a service-connected disability rated at 50% or higher by the VA.
- **For Retirees Under Chapter 61 for Disability**:
  If you retired under Chapter 61, you must:
    o Have at least 20 years of service (creditable under 10 U.S.C. § 1405 or 10 U.S.C. § 12732) at the time of retirement.
    o Be eligible for both military disability retired pay and VA Disability Compensation.
    o Have a service-connected disability rated at 50% or higher by the VA.

If you do not have 20 years of service under Chapter 61, you are not eligible for concurrent pay and must waive military retired pay to receive VA Disability Compensation.

CRDP Implementation

- **For Retirees Not Under Chapter 61**:
  Since January 1, 2014, eligible retirees can receive full concurrent payments, including both military retired pay and VA Disability Compensation. The phase-in period, which began in 2004, ended on December 31, 2013.
- **For Chapter 61 Retirees**:
  If you retired under Chapter 61 for disability, you must waive the amount of your military disability pay that exceeds the military retirement pay you would have received if you had retired for length of service. Retirees under Chapter 61 who did not reach eligibility age for retirement may have to wait until reaching the required age to receive concurrent pay.

Applying for Concurrent Retired Pay

DFAS typically processes concurrent pay automatically if the VA shares relevant data. Retirees who believe they qualify but do not receive concurrent pay should submit a **DD Form 827** (Application for Arrears in Pay) to DFAS.

Retroactive Concurrent Retired Pay

If your VA disability rating increases, you may be eligible for retroactive pay. DFAS will audit your account to determine the retroactive amount, potentially backdated to **January 1, 2004**, depending on the specifics of your case.

For any retroactive payments owed by the VA, DFAS will forward your information to the VA for processing.

Contact Information

For questions on military retired pay, contact DFAS at **800-321-1080**. For inquiries about disability ratings or compensation, contact the VA at **800-827-1000**.

Concurrent Receipt Overview Table

Category	Details
What is Concurrent Receipt?	A policy allowing eligible veterans to receive both military retirement pay and VA disability compensation without offset.
Eligibility Criteria	Veterans must be rated at least 50% disabled by the VA.
	Must be receiving military retirement pay based on length of service or Chapter 61 medical retirement.
Key Programs	**Concurrent Retirement and Disability Pay (CRDP):**
	For retirees with 20 or more years of service.
	No application required; payments are automatic if eligible.
	Combat-Related Special Compensation (CRSC):
	For retirees with combat-related disabilities (verified through service records).
	Requires an application to the respective service branch.
Benefits	Veterans receive full VA disability compensation without a reduction in their retirement pay.
	Provides financial improvement for eligible veterans.
Limitations	CRSC requires proof of combat-related injury or condition.
	CRDP and CRSC cannot be received simultaneously; veterans must choose which benefits them most.
How to Apply	CRDP is automatic; no action is needed if eligible.
	CRSC applications are submitted to the retiree's branch of service with supporting documentation.

Disability Compensation Effective Dates

When the VA decides to pay a disability, benefit based on a claim, there is an effective date assigned to the claim. The effective date is the day the veteran can start to get their disability benefits, and it varies with the type of benefit they're applying for, and the nature of their claim.

How Does the VA Decide Effective Dates?

The VA bases effective dates on the situation.

Direct Service Connection

The effective date for a disability that was caused or made worse by military service is whichever of the following comes later:

- The date the VA gets your claim, or
- The date you first got your illness or injury, also known as the date your entitlement arose.

If the VA gets your claim within a year of the day you left active service, the effective date can be as early as the day following separation.

Presumptive Service Connection

In most cases, if VA believes your disability is related to your military service, known as a presumptive service connection, and they get your claim within a year of your separation from active service, then the effective date is the date you first got your illness or injury.

If the VA gets your claim more than a year after your separation from active service, the effective date is the date the VA got your claim or when you first got your illness or injury—whichever is later.

Reopened Claims

The effective date for a reopened claim is the date the VA gets the claim to reopen, or the date you first got your illness or injury, whichever is later.

Liberalizing Law Change

If there's a change in law or VA regulation that allows the VA to pay disability compensation, the effective date could be assigned in one of these ways:

- If the VA gets your claim within a year of a law or regulation changing, the effective date may be the date the law or regulation changed.
- If the VA reviews your claim or you request a review, more than one year after the law or regulation changed, the effective date may be up to one year before the date the VA got your request or the date the VA decides to pay benefits on your claim.

Dependency and Indemnity Compensation (DIC)

For claims based on a veteran's death in service, the effective date is the first day of the month in which the veteran died or was presumed to have died. This is true only if the VA gets the claim within a year of the date of the report of the veteran's actual or presumed death.

Otherwise, the effective date is the date the VA gets the claim. If the veteran's death happened after service and the VA gets the claim within a year of their death, the effective date is the first day of the month in which the veteran died.

If the death happened after service and the VA gets the claim more than one year after the veteran's death, the effective date is the date the VA gets the claim.

Error In a Previous Decision

If the VA finds a clear and unmistakable error in a prior decision, the effective date of the new decision will be the date from which benefits would have been paid if there hadn't been an error in the prior decision.

Difference of Opinion

A decision that's based on a difference of opinion will have an effective date of the original decision, had it been favorable.

Increases in the Disability

The VA dates back increases in the disability rating to the earliest date when a veteran can show there was an increase in disability. This is only if the VA gets the new claim request within a year from that date. Otherwise, the effective date is the date the VA gets the claim.

Disability or Death Due to a Hospital Stay

If the VA gets a claim within a year after the date the veteran suffered an injury, or their existing injury got worse, the effective date is the date the injury happened or when it began to get worse.

If the VA gets a claim within a year of the date of a veteran's death, the effective date is the first day of the month in which the veteran died. If the VA gets a claim more than a year after a veteran suffered an injury, their injury got worse, or they died, the effective date is the date the VA gets the claim.

Disabilities That Appear Within One-Year After Discharge

A veteran may be able to get disability benefits if they have signs of an illness like hypertension, arthritis, diabetes, or peptic ulcers that started within a year after they were discharged from military service. If the symptoms appear within a year after discharge, even if they weren't there while the veteran was serving, they VA concludes they're related to service.

You may be eligible for benefits if you have an illness that's at least 10% disabling and appears within one year after discharge, and you meet two requirements. First, the illness has to be listed in Title 38, Code of Federal Regulations, 3.309(a), and you didn't receive a dishonorable discharge.

If you have an illness listed in Title 38, Code of Federal Regulations, 3.309(a), you don't have to show the problem started during or got worse because of your military service.

These are presumptive diseases.

The following diseases are covered even if they appeared more than a year after you separated from service:

- Hansen's disease can appear within three years after discharge
- Tuberculosis can appear within three years after discharge
- Multiple sclerosis can appear within seven years after discharge
- Amyotrophic lateral sclerosis (ALS), also known as Lou Gehrig's can appear any time after discharge.

Detailed Rates of Disability Compensation Rates
Effective December 1, 2024

Dependent Status	Disability Rating									
	10%	20%	30%	40%	50%	60%	70%	80%	90%	100%
Veteran Alone	$175.51	$346.95	$537.42	$774.16	$1102.04	$1395.93	$1759.19	$2044.89	$2297.96	$3831.30
Veteran & Spouse	$175.51	$346.95	$601.42	$859.16	$1208.04	$1523.93	$1908.19	$2214.89	$2489.96	$4044.91
Veteran, Spouse &1 Child	$175.51	$346.95	$648.42	$922.16	$1287.04	$1617.93	$2018.19	$2340.89	$2630.96	$4201.35
Veteran, No Spouse & 1 Child	$175.51	$346.95	$579.42	$831.16	$1173.04	$1480.93	$1858.19	$2158.89	$2425.96	$3974.15
	10%	20%	30%	40%	50%	60%	70%	80%	90%	100%
Veteran & Spouse & No Children and 1 parent	$175.51	$346.95	$652.42	$927.16	$1293.04	$1625.93	$2028.19	$2351.89	$2643.96	$4216.35
Veteran & Spouse & 1 Child & 1 parent	$175.51	$346.95	$699.42	$990.16	$1372.04	$1719.93	$2138.19	$2477.89	$2784.96	$4372.79
Veteran & Spouse & No Child & 2 Parents	$175.51	$346.95	$703.42	$995.16	$1378.04	$1727.93	$2148.19	$2488.89	$2797.96	$4387.79
Veteran & Spouse & 1 Child & 2 Parents	$175.51	$346.95	$750.42	$1058.16	$1457.04	$1821.04	$2258.19	$2614.89	$2938.96	$4544.23
Veteran & No Spouse & No Children & 1 Parent	$175.51	$346.95	$588.42	$842.16	$1187.04	$1497.93	$1879.19	$2181.89	$2451.96	$4002.74
Veteran & No Spouse & 1 Child & 1 Parent	$175.51	$346.95	$630.42	$899.16	$1258.04	$1582.93	$1978.19	$2295.89	$2579.96	$4145.59
Veteran & No Spouse &No Children & 2 Parents	$175.51	$346.95	$639.42	$910.16	$1272.04	$1599.93	$1999.19	$2318.89	$2605.96	$4174.18
Veteran & No Spouse & 1 Child & 2 Parents	$175.51	$346.95	$681.42	$967.16	$1343.04	$1684.93	$2098.19	$2432.89	$2733.96	$4317.03

Benefits Rates for Service-Connected Disability Compensation

VA compensation and pension benefits cost of living allowance (COLA) is paid based on the Social Security Administration (SSA) COLA. By statute, compensation COLA may not be more than the SSA COLA; and pension COLA is equal to the SSA COLA.

This year SSA increased COLA by 2.5%		
Basic Rates of Disability Compensation **Effective December 1, 2024**		
	Disability Rating	**Monthly Benefit**
(a)	10%	$175.51
(b)	20%	$346.95
(c)	30%	$537.42
(d)	40%	$774.16
(e)	50%	$1102.04
(f)	60%	$1395.93
(g)	70%	$1759.19
(h)	80%	$2044.89
(i)	90%	$2297.96
(j)	100%	$3831.30

Additional Amounts Payable for Spouse Requiring Aid & Attendance Rates Effective December 1, 2024								
Disability Rating	30%	40%	50%	60%	70%	80%	90%	100%
Monthly Benefit	$58	$78	$98	$117	$137	$157	$176	$195.92

Additional Amount Payable for Each Additional Child Under 18 Rates Effective December 1, 2024								
Disability Rating	30%	40%	50%	60%	70%	80%	90%	100%
Monthly Benefit	$31	$42	$53	$63	$74	$84	$95	$106.14

Additional Amount Payable for Each Additional Child Over Age 18 Attending School Rates Effective December 1, 2024								
Disability Rating	30%	40%	50%	60%	70%	80%	90%	100%
Monthly Benefit	$102	$137	$171	$205	$239	$274	$308	$342.85

Notes: Rates for Children over age 18 attending school are shown separately in the above chart. All other entries in the above charts reflect rates for children under age 18, or helpless.

Higher Statutory Awards for Certain Multiple Disabilities

VA special monthly compensation or SMC is a higher rate of compensation paid to veterans, spouses and surviving spouses, and parents with certain needs or disabilities.

Special monthly compensation rate payment variations—effective December 1, 2024

Levels K and Q are special rates called SMC rate variations. VA may add level K to your basic SMC rate.

SMC Letter Designation	Monthly payment	How this payment variation works
SMC-K	$136.06	If you qualify for SMC-K, VA adds this rate to the basic disability compensation rate for any disability rating from 0-100%. VA may also add this rate to all SMC basic rates except SMC-O, SMC-Q and SMC-R. You may receive 1 to 3 SMC-K awards in addition to basic and SMC rates.
SMC-Q	$67.00	This is a protected rate the VA hasn't awarded since August 19, 1968. If a veteran is awarded an SMC-Q designation, it pays this rate in place of the basic disability compensation rate.

Special monthly compensation rates for veterans without children—effective December 1, 2024

Levels L through O cover specific disabilities and situations. Level R may apply if you need help daily from another person for basic needs like dressing, bathing and eating. Level S may apply if you aren't able to leave the house because of service-connected disabilities.

SMC-L through SMC-N Rates

Start with the Basic SMC rates table and find the dependent status in the left column best describing you. Then find your SMC letter designation in the top row.

Your monthly basic rate is where your dependent status and SMC letter meet.

If you have more than one child or your spouse receives Aid and Attendance benefits, also check the Added Amounts table, and then add them to your amount from the basic SMC rates table.

Basic SMC Rates

Dependent Status	SMC-L in U.S. $	SMC-L ½ in U.S.$	SMC-M in U.S.$	SMC-M ½ in U.S.$	SMC-N in U.S.$
Veteran alone	4767.34	5014.00	5261.21	5623.00	5985.06
With Spouse	4980.95	5227.61	5474.85	5836.61	6198.67
With spouse and 1 parent	5152.39	5399.05	5646.29	6008.05	6370.11
With spouse and 2 parents	5323.83	5570.49	5817.73	6179.49	6541.55
With 1 parent	4938.78	5185.44	5432.68	5794.44	6156.50
With 2 parents	5110.22	5356.88	5604.12	5965.88	6327.94

Added Amounts

Dependent Status	SMC-L in U.S.$	SMC-L ½ in U.S.$	SMC-M in U.S.$	SMC-M ½ in U.S.$	SMC-N in U.S.$
Spouse receiving Aid and Attendance	195.92	195.92	195.92	195.92	195.92

SMC-N ½ through SMC-S Basic SMC Rates

Dependent Status	SMC-N ½ in U.S.$	SMC-O/P in U.S. $	SMC-R.1 in U.S.$	SMC-R.2/T in U.S.$	SMC-S in U.S.$
Veteran Alone	6337.00	6689.81	9559.22	10,964.66	4288.45
With Spouse	6550.61	6903.42	9772.83	11,178.27	4502.06
With Spouse and 1 Parent	6722.05	7074.86	9944.27	11,349.71	4673.50
With Spouse and 2 Parents	6893.49	7246.30	10,115.71	11,521.15	4844.94
With 1 Parent	6508.44	6861.25	9730.66	11,136.10	4459.89
With 2 Parents	6679.88	7032.69	9902.10	11,307.54	4631.33

Added Amounts

Dependent Status	SMC-N ½ in U.S.$	SMC-O/P in U.S.$	SMC-R.1 in U.S.$	SMC-R.2/T in U.S.$	SMC-S in U.S.$
Spouse Receiving Aid and Attendance	195.92	195.92	195.92	195.92	195.92

Special monthly compensation rates for veterans with dependents including children— effective December 1, 2024

L through O cover specific disabilities and situations.

Level R may apply if you need help from another person for basic needs.

Level S may apply if you can't leave the house because of your service-connected disabilities

SMC-L through SMC-N Basic SMC Rates

Start with the Basic SMC rates table and find the dependent status in the left column that best describes you. Then find your SMC letter designation in the top row.

Your monthly basic rate is where your dependent status and SMC letter meet.

If you have more than one child or your spouse receives Aid and Attendance benefits, be sure to check the Added Amounts table and add those to your amount from the Basic SMC rates table.

Dependent Status	SMC-L in U.S.$	SMC-L ½ in U.S.$	SMC-M in U.S.$	SMC-M ½ in U.S.$	SMC-N in U.S.$
Veteran with 1 Child	4910.19	5156.85	5404.09	5765.85	6127.91
With 1 Child and Spouse	5137.39	5384.05	5631.29	5993.05	6355.11
With 1 Child, Spouse and 1 Parent	5308.83	5555.49	5802.73	6164.49	6526.55
With 1 Child, Spouse and 2 Parents	5480.27	5726.93	5974.17	6335.93	6697.99
With 1 Child and 1 Parent	5081.63	5328.29	5575.53	5937.29	6299.35
With 1 Child and 2 Parents	5253.07	5499.73	5746.97	6108.73	6470.79

Added Amounts

Dependent Status	SMC-L in U.S.$	SMC-L ½ in U.S.$	SMC-M in U.S.$	SMC-M ½ in U.S.$	SMC-N in U.S.$
Each additional child under age 18	106.14	106.14	106.14	106.14	106.14

Each additional child over age 18 in a qualifying school program	342.85	342.85	342.85	342.85	342.85
Spouse receiving Aid and Attendance	195.92	195.92	195.92	195.92	195.92

SMC-N ½ through SMC-S

Dependent Status	SMC-N ½ in U.S.$	SMC-O/P in U.S.$	SMC-R.1 in U.S.$	SMC-R.2/T in U.S.$	SMC-S in U.S.$
Veteran with 1 Child	6479.85	6832.66	9702.07	11,107.51	4431.30
With 1 Child and Spouse	6707.05	7059.86	9929.27	11,334.71	4658.50
With 1 Child, Spouse and 1 Parent	6878.49	7231.30	10,100.71	11,506.15	4829.94
With 1 Child, Spouse and 2 Parents	7049.93	7402.74	10,272.15	11,677.59	5001.38
With 1 Child and 1 Parent	6651.29	7004.10	9873.51	11,278.95	4602.74
With 1 Child and 2 Parents	6822.73	7175.54	10,044.95	11,450.39	4774.18

Added Amounts

Dependent Status	SMC-N ½ in U.S.$	SMC-O/P in U.S.$	SMC-R.1 in U.S.$	SMC-R.2/T in U.S.$	SMC-S in U.S.$
Each additional child under age 18	106.14	106.14	106.14	106.14	106.14
Each additional child over age 18 in a qualifying school program	342.85	342.85	342.85	342.85	342.85
Spouse receiving Aid and Attendance	195.92	195.92	195.92	195.92	195.92

How VA Assigns SMC Levels L Through O

The SMC levels are assigned based on very specific situations and combinations of situations, including:

- The amputation of one or more limbs or extremities
- The loss of use of one or more limbs or extremities
- The physical loss of one or both eyes
- The loss of sight or total blindness in one or both eyes
- Being permanently bedridden
- Needing daily help with basic needs also called Aid and Attendance

You may receive an SMC-L designation if any of these situations are true:

- You've had both feet amputated, or
- You've had one foot amputated and have lost the use of the other foot, or
- You've had one hand and one foot amputated, or
- You've had one foot amputated and have lost the use of one hand, or
- You've had one hand amputated and have lost the use of one foot, or
- You've lost the use of both feet, or
- You've lost the use of one hand and one foot, or
- You've lost sign in both eyes, or
- You're permanently bedridden, or
- You need help with daily basic needs

You may receive an SMC-L ½ designation if any of these situations are true for you:

- You've had one foot and the other knee amputated, or
- You've had one foot amputated, and have lost the use of the other knee, or
- You've had one foot and one elbow amputated, or
- You've had one foot amputated and have lost the use of one elbow, or
- You've had one knee and one hand amputated, or
- You've had one knee amputated and have lost the use of one hand, or
- You've lost the use of one foot and have had the other knee amputated, or
- You've lost the use of one foot and had one elbow amputated, or
- You've lost the use of one foot and one elbow, or
- You've lost the use of one knee and have had one hand amputated, or
- You've lost the use of one knee and one hand, or
- You have blindness in one eye and total blindness in the other eye with only the ability to perceive light, or
- You have blindness in both eyes and have lost the use of one foot—rated as less than 50% disabling

You may receive an SMC-M designation if any of these are true for you:

- You've had both hands amputated, or
- You've had one hand amputated and have lost the use of the other hand, or
- You've had both knees amputated, or
- You've had one elbow and one knee amputated, or
- You've had one foot amputated and have lost the use of one arm at the shoulder, or
- You've had one foot amputated and have had one leg amputated so close to the hip that you can't wear a prosthesis, or
- You've had one foot amputated and have had one arm amputated so close to the shoulder that you can't wear a prosthesis, or
- You've had one hand amputated and have had one leg amputated so close to the hip that you can't wear a prosthesis, or
- You've lost the use of both hands, or
- You've lost the use of both knees, or
- You've lost the use of one elbow and one knee, or
- You've lost the use of one foot and the use of one arm at the shoulder, or
- You've lost the use of one foot, and you have had one leg amputated so close to the hip that you can't wear a prosthesis, or
- You've lost the use of one foot, and have had one arm amputated so close to the shoulder that you can't wear a prosthesis, or
- You've lost the use of one hand and have had one leg amputated so close to the hip that you can't wear a prosthesis

Or you have blindness in one eye, and:

- You've physically lost the other eye, or
- You have total blindness without the ability to perceive light in the other eye,

or

- You have total blindness in the other eye with only the ability to perceive light and have total deafness in one ear, or
- You have total blindness in the other eye with only the ability to perceive light and have lost the use of one foot rated as less than 50% disabling, or
- You have blindness in both eyes considered total blindness, with only the ability to perceive light, or
- You have blindness in both eyes that requires you to have daily help with basic needs

Or you have blindness in both eyes, and:
- You have deafness in both rated as 30% or more disabling, or
- You've had one hand amputated, or
- You've lost the use of one hand, or
- You've had one foot amputated, or
- You've lost the use of one foot—rated as 50% or more disabling

You may receive an SMC-M ½ designation if any of these situations are true for you:
- You've had one knee amputated, and have had one leg amputated so close to the hip that you can't wear a prosthesis, or
- You've had one knee amputated, and have had one arm amputated so close to the shoulder that you can't wear a prosthesis, or
- You've had one elbow amputated, and have had one leg amputated so close to the hip that you can't wear a prosthesis, or
- You've had one hand and one elbow amputated, or
- You've had one hand amputated, and have lost the use of one elbow, or
- You've lost the use of one knee, and have had one leg amputated so close to the hip that you can't wear a prosthesis, or
- You've lost the use of one knee, and have had one arm amputated so close to the shoulder that you can't wear a prosthesis, or
- You've lost the use of one elbow, and have had one leg amputated so close to the hip that you can't wear a prosthesis, or
- You've lost of use of one hand, and have had one elbow amputated, or
- You've lost the use of one hand and of one elbow

Or you have total blindness with only the ability to perceive light:
- In one eye, and have physically lost the other eye, or
- In one eye, and have total blindness without the ability to perceive light in the other eye, or
- In both eyes, and have lost the use of one foot (rated as less than 50% disabling)
- Or you have blindness in one eye, and:
- You've physically lost the other eye, and have total deafness in one ear, or
- You have total blindness without the ability to perceive light in the other eye, and have total deafness in one ear, or

- You have total blindness with only the ability to perceive light in the other eye, and have deafness in both ears (rated as 30% or more disabling), or
- You have total blindness with only the ability to perceive light in the other eye, and have had one foot amputated, or
- You have total blindness with only the ability to perceive light in the other eye, and have lost the use of one foot (rated as 50% or more disabling), or
- You have total blindness with only the ability to perceive light in the other eye, and have had one hand amputated, or
- You have total blindness with the only ability to perceive light in the other eye, and have lost the use of one hand, or
- You have blindness in both eyes and total deafness in one ear, or
- You have blindness in both eyes that requires you to have daily help with basic needs (like eating, bathing, and dressing), and have lost the use of one foot (rated as less than 50% disabling)

You may receive an SMC-N designation if any of these situations are true for you:
- You've had both elbows amputated, or
- You've had both legs amputated so close to the hip that you can't wear a prosthesis, or
- You've had one arm and one leg amputated so close to the shoulder and hip that you can't wear a prosthesis on either, or
- You've had one hand amputated, and one arm amputated so close to the shoulder that you can't wear a prosthesis, or
- You've lost the use of both elbows, or
- You've lost the use of one hand, and have had one arm amputated so close to the shoulder that you can't wear a prosthesis, or
- You've physically lost both eyes, or
- You have total blindness without the ability to perceive light

Or you have total blindness with only the ability to perceive light in one eye, and:
- You've physically lost the other eye, and have deafness in both ears (rated as 10% or 20% disabling), or
- You have total blindness without the ability to perceive light in the other eye, and have deafness in both ears (rated as 10% or 20% disabling), or
- You've physically lost the other eye, and have lost the use of one foot (rated as less than 50% disabling), or
- You have total blindness without the ability to perceive light in the other eye, and have lost the use of one foot (rated as less than 50% disabling)

Or you have total blindness with only the ability to perceive light in both eyes, and:
- You have deafness in both ears (rated as 30% or more disabling), or
- You've had one hand amputated, or
- You've lost the use of one foot, or

- You've lost the use of one hand, or
- You've had one foot amputated, or
- You've lost the use of one foot (rated as 50% or more disabling)

Or you have blindness in one eye, and:

- You've physically lost the other eye, and have deafness in both ears (rated as 30% or more disabling), or
- You have total blindness without the ability to perceive light in the other eye, and
    - have deafness in both ears (rated as 30% or more disabling)

Or you have blindness in both eyes that requires you to have daily help with basic needs and:

- You have deafness in both ears (rated as 30% or more disabling), or
- You've had one hand amputated, or
- You've lost the use of one hand, or
- You've had one foot amputated, or
- You've lost the use of one foot (rated as 50% disabling)

You may receive an SMC-N ½ designation if any of these situations are true for you:

- You've had one elbow amputated, and have had one arm amputated so close to the shoulder that you can't wear a prosthesis, or
- You've lost the use of one elbow, and have had one arm amputated so close to the shoulder that you can't wear a prosthesis, or
- You've physically lost both eyes, and have lost the use of one foot (rated as less than 50% disabling), or
- You have total blindness without the ability to see light, and have lost the use of one foot (rated as less than 50%)

Or you have total blindness with only the ability to perceive light in one eye, have physically lost the other eye, and:

- You have deafness in both ears (rated as 30% or more disabling), or
- You've had one foot amputated, or
- You've lost the use of one foot (rated as 50% or more disabling), or
- You've had one hand amputated, or
- You've lost the use of one hand

Or you have total blindness with only the ability to perceive light in one eye and total blindness without the ability to perceive light in the other eye, and:

- You have deafness in both ears (rated as 30% or more disabling), or
- You've had one foot amputated, or
- You've lost the use of one foot (rated as 50% or more disabling), or
- You've had one hand amputated, or
- You've lost the use of one hand

You may receive SMC-O designation if any of these situations are true for you:

- You've had both arms amputated so close to the shoulder that you can't wear a prosthesis, or
- You have complete paralysis of both legs that's resulted in being unable to control your bladder or bowels, or
- You have hearing loss in both ears (with at least one ear's deafness caused by military service) that's rated as 60% or more disabling, and you have blindness in both eyes, or
- You have hearing loss in both ears (with at least one ear's deafness caused by military service) that's rated as 40% or more disabling, and you have blindness in both eyes with only the ability to perceive light, or
- You have total deafness in one ear as well as blindness in both eyes with only the ability to perceive light

Or you have total blindness without the ability to see light, and:

- You have deafness in both ears (rated as 30% or more disabling), or
- You've had one foot amputated, or
- You've lost the use of one foot (rated as 50% or more disabling), or
- You've had one hand amputated, or
- You've lost the use of one hand

Or you have physically lost both eyes, and:

- You have deafness in both ears (rated as 30% or more disabling), or
- You've had one foot amputated, or
- You've lost the use of one foot (rated as 50% or more disabling), or
- You've had one hand amputated, or
- You've lost the use of one hand

Presumptive Service Connection

The U.S. Department of Veterans Affairs (VA) provides presumptive service connection for certain disabilities that veterans may develop due to their military service. This means that specific health conditions are automatically assumed to be related to service under certain circumstances, simplifying the process for Veterans to receive disability compensation.

What Are Presumptive Conditions?

Veterans diagnosed with certain conditions are presumed to have developed those conditions during their service. Here are the main categories:

- **Chronic Diseases:** Conditions like arthritis, diabetes, and hypertension that appear within one year of discharge may qualify for disability benefits.
- **Amyotrophic Lateral Sclerosis (ALS):** Veterans who served at least 90 days of continuous active duty and develop ALS are eligible for benefits.

Specific Groups with Presumptive Disability Benefits

1. **Former Prisoners of War (POWs):**
   - Veterans who were POWs and have conditions like psychosis, post-traumatic osteoarthritis, heart disease, and stroke may qualify for presumptive conditions.
   - If imprisoned for more than 30 days, additional conditions like beriberi, chronic dysentery, and osteoporosis are included.

2. **Vietnam Veterans:**
   - Veterans exposed to Agent Orange or who served in specific areas during the Vietnam War may have conditions presumed to be service connected.
   - Common conditions include Type 2 diabetes, Hodgkin's disease, ischemic heart disease, non-Hodgkin's lymphoma, prostate cancer, and respiratory cancers.

3. **Atomic Veterans:**
   - Veterans who participated in nuclear tests or were near sites of nuclear activity are presumed to have conditions like leukemia, thyroid cancer, and multiple myeloma.

4. **Gulf War Veterans:**
   - Veterans who served in the Southwest Asia theater, including Iraq, Kuwait, and surrounding areas, are eligible for presumptive benefits for conditions such as chronic fatigue syndrome, fibromyalgia, and respiratory disorders.
   - Specific infectious diseases and cancers linked to their service are also covered.

5. **Post-9/11 Veterans:**
   - Veterans serving in regions like Afghanistan, Djibouti, and Syria may qualify for benefits due to conditions like respiratory diseases, cancers, and neurological disorders.

How to Apply for Presumptive Benefits

To apply for presumptive disability benefits, veterans should submit their claim with supporting medical documentation. If diagnosed with one of the presumptive conditions, veterans do not need to prove that the condition was caused by service; they only need to meet the service and diagnosis requirements.

Key Points:

- If a veteran meets the criteria for a presumptive condition, they do not need to prove service connection.
- The VA recognizes specific conditions tied to service during wartime, exposure to Agent Orange, radiation, and more.

145

- Conditions like cancer, respiratory diseases, and neurological issues may be linked to specific service periods or locations.
- For more information and to apply for benefits, veterans can visit the VA website or contact the VA claims office.

Additional Compensation for Dependents

Any veteran entitled to peacetime disability compensation, and whose disability is rated as 30% or greater, will be entitled to additional monthly compensation for dependents in the same amounts payable for Wartime Disability Compensation.

Please refer to the charts presented earlier in this chapter.

Adjudication

Adjudication means a judicial decision made by the Veterans Administration in claims filed within their jurisdiction. There is an Adjudication Division in each regional office, under the direction of an adjudication officer, who is responsible for the preparation of claims.

Upon the receipt of an original application in the Adjudication Division, it will be referred to the Authorization Unit for review and development in accordance with established procedures.

All reasonable assistance will be extended to a claimant in the prosecution of his or her claim, and all sources from which information may be elicited will be thoroughly developed before the submission of the case to the rating board.

Every legitimate assistance will be rendered to a claimant in obtaining any benefit to which he or she is entitled, and the veteran will be given every opportunity to substantiate his or her claim. Information and advice to claimants will be complete and will be given in words that the average person can understand.

VA personnel must always give claimants and other properly interested and recognized individuals courteous and satisfactory service, which is essential to good public relations. It is incumbent upon the claimant to establish his or her case following the law. This rule, however, should not be highly technical and rigid in its application.

The general policy is to give the claimant every opportunity to substantiate the claim, to extend all reasonable assistance in its prosecution, and to develop all sources from which information may be obtained. Information and advice to claimants will be complete and expressed, so far as possible, in plain language, which can be easily read and understood by people not familiar with the subject matter.

Benefits for Persons Disabled by Treatment or Vocational Rehabilitation

Compensation shall be awarded for an additional qualifying disability or a qualifying death of a veteran in the same manner as if such additional disability or death were service connected, provided:

The disability or death was caused by hospital care, medical or surgical treatment, or examination was furnished under any law administered by the VA, either by a VA employee, on a VA facility, and the proximate cause of the disability or death was:

- Carelessness, negligence, lack of proper skill, error in judgment, or similar instance of fault on the part of the VA in furnishing the hospital care, medical treatment, surgical treatment, or examination; or
- An event not reasonably foreseeable.
- The disability or death was proximately caused by the provision of training and rehabilitation services by the VA (including a service-provider used by the VA) as part of an approved rehabilitation program.

Effective December 1, 1962, if an individual is awarded a judgment against the United States in a civil action brought pursuant to Section 1346(b) of Title 28, or enters into a settlement or compromise under Section 2672 or 2677 of Title 28 by reason of a disability or death treated pursuant to this section as if it were service-connected, then no benefits shall be paid to such individual for any month beginning after the date such judgment, settlement, or compromise on account of such disability or death becomes final until the aggregate amount of benefits which would be paid out for this subsection equals the total amount included in such judgment, settlement, or compromise.

Aggravation

A preexisting injury or disease will be considered to have been aggravated by active military, naval, or air service, if there is an increase in disability during such service unless there is a specific finding that the increase in disability is due to the natural progress of the disease.

Consideration to be Accorded Time, Place and Circumstances of Service

Consideration shall be given to the places, types, and circumstances of each veteran's service. The VA will consider the veteran's service record, the official history of each organization in which such veteran served, such veteran's medical records, and all pertinent medical and lay evidence. The provisions of Public Law 98-542 – Section 5 of the Veterans' Dioxin and Radiation Exposure Compensation Standards Act shall also be applied.

In the case of any veteran who engaged in combat with the enemy in active service with a military, naval, or air organization of the United States during a period of war, campaign, or expedition, the Secretary shall accept as sufficient proof of service- connection of any disease or injury alleged to have been incurred in or aggravated by such service, if consistent with the circumstances, conditions, or hardships of such service. This provision will apply even if there is no official record of such incurrence or aggravation in such service. Every reasonable doubt in such instances will be resolved in favor of the veteran.

The service-connection of such injury or disease may be rebutted only by clear and convincing evidence to the contrary. The reasons for granting or denying service-connection in each case shall be recorded in full.

Disappearance

If a veteran who is receiving disability compensation disappears, the VA may pay the compensation otherwise payable to the veteran to such veteran's spouse, children, and parents. Payments made to such spouse, child, or parent should not exceed the amounts payable to each if the veteran died from a service-connected disability.

Combination of Certain Ratings

If the VA finds that a veteran has multiple disabilities, they use a Combined Ratings Table to calculate combined disability rating. Disability ratings are not additive, meaning that if a veteran has one disability rated 60% and a second disability 20%, the combined rating is not 80%.

This is because subsequent disability ratings are applied to an already disabled veteran, so the 20% disability is applied to a veteran who is already 60% disabled.

The following outlines how the VA combines ratings for more than one disability:

The disabilities are first arranged in the exact order of their severity, beginning with the greatest disability combined with use of the Combined Ratings Table. The degree of one disability will be read in the left column of the table, and the degree of the other in the top row, whoever is appropriate. The figures appearing in the space where the column and row intersect will represent the combined value of the two.

This combined value is rounded to the nearest 10%. If there are more than two disabilities, the combined value for the first two will be found as previously described for two disabilities.

The exact combined value—without yet rounding—is combined with the degree of the third disability. The process continues for subsequent disabilities, and the final number is rounded to the nearest 10%.

Example of Combining Two Disabilities: If a veteran has a 50 percent disability and a 30 percent disability, the combined value will be found to be 65 percent, but the 65 percent must be converted to 70 percent to represent the final degree of disability. Similarly, with a disability of 40 percent, and another disability of 20 percent, the combined value is found to be 52 percent, but the 52 percent must be converted to the nearest degree divisible by 10, which is 50 percent.

Example of Combining Three Disabilities: If there are three disabilities ratable at 60 percent, 40 percent, and 20 percent, respectively, the combined value for the first two will be found opposite 60 and under 40 and is 76 percent. This 76 will be found in the left column, then the 20 rating in the top row. The intersection of these two ratings is 81. Thus, the final rating will be rounded to 80%.

Tax Exemption

Compensation and pension may not be assigned to anyone and are exempt from taxation (including income tax). No one can attach, levy, or seize a compensation or pension check either before or after receipt. Property purchased with money received from the government is not protected.

Disabled veterans may be eligible to claim a federal tax refund based on an increase in the veteran's percentage of disability from the Department of Veterans Affairs (which may include a retroactive determination) **or** the combat-disabled veteran applying for, and being granted, Combat-Related Special Compensation, after an award for Concurrent Retirement and Disability.

To do so, the disabled veteran will need to file the amended return, Form 1040X, Amended U.S. Individual Income Tax Return, to correct a previously filed Form 1040, 1040A, or 1040EZ. An amended return cannot be e-filed. It must be filed as a paper return. Disabled veterans should include all documents from the Department of Veterans Affairs and any information received from Defense Finance and Accounting Services explaining proper tax treatment for the current year.

Please note: It is only in the year of the Department of Veterans Affairs reassessment of disability percentage (including any impacted retroactive year) or the year that the CRSC is initially granted or adjusted that the veteran may need to file amended returns.

Under normal circumstances, the Form 1099-R issued to the veteran by Defense Finance and Accounting Services correctly reflects the taxable portion of compensation received. No amended returns would be required since it has already been adjusted for any non-taxable awards.

If needed, veterans should seek assistance from a competent tax professional before filing amended returns based on a disability determination. Refund claims based on an incorrect interpretation of the tax law could subject the veteran to interest and/or penalty charges.

Protection of Service Connection

Service connection for any disability or death granted under this title which has been in force for ten or more years shall not be severed on or after January 1, 1962, unless it is shown that the original grant of service connection was based on fraud, or it is clearly shown from military records that the person concerned did not have the requisite service or character of discharge. The mentioned period shall be computed from the date determined by the VA as the date on which the status commenced for rating purposes.

Preservation of Ratings

Public Law 88-445, approved August 19, 1964, effective the same date, amends Section 110, Title 38, U.S. Code as follows:

The law provides that a disability that has been continuously rated at or above a given percentage for 20 years or longer for service connection compensation under laws administered by the VA shall not after that be rated at any lesser percentage except upon showing that the rating was based on fraud.

Special Consideration for Certain Cases of Loss of Paired Organs or Extremities

If a veteran has suffered any of the following, the VA shall assign and pay to the veteran the applicable rate of compensation, as if the combination of disabilities were the result of a service- connected disability:

- Blindness in one eye as a result of a service-connected disability, and blindness in the other eye as a result of a non-service-connected disability not the result of the veteran's own willful misconduct; or
- The loss or loss of use of one kidney as a result of a service-connected disability, and involvement of the other kidney as a result of a non-service-connected disability not the result of the veteran's own willful misconduct; or
- Total deafness in one ear as a result of a service-connected disability, and total deafness in the other ear as the result of non-service-connected disability not the result of the veteran's own willful misconduct; or
- The loss or loss of use of one hand or one foot as a result of a service-connected disability and the loss or loss of use of the other hand or foot as a result of non- service-connected disability not the result of the veteran's own willful misconduct; or
- Permanent service-connected disability of one lung rated 50% or more disabling, in combination with a non-service-connected disability of the other lung that is not the result of the veteran's own willful misconduct.

If a veteran described above receives any money or property of value according to an award in a judicial proceeding based upon, or a settlement or compromise of, any cause of action for damages for the non-service-connected disability, the increase in the rate of compensation otherwise payable shall not be paid for any month following a month in which any such money or property is received until the total of the amount of such increase that would otherwise have been payable equals the total of the amount of any such money received, and the fair market value of any such property received.

Payment of Disability Compensation in Disability Severance Cases

The deduction of disability severance pay from disability compensation, as required by Section 1212(c) of Title 10, shall be made at a monthly rate, not more than the rate of compensation to which the former member would be entitled based on the degree of such former member's disability, as determined on the initial VA rating.

Trial Work Periods and Vocational Rehabilitation for Certain Veterans with Total Disability Ratings

The disability rating of a qualified veteran who begins to engage in a substantially gainful occupation after January 31, 1985, may not be reduced based on the veteran having secured and followed a substantially gainful occupation unless the veteran maintains such an occupation for 12 consecutive months.

("Qualified Veteran" means a veteran who has a service-connected disability or disabilities, not rated as total, but who has been awarded a rating of total of disability because of inability to secure or follow a substantially gainful occupation as a result of such disability or disabilities.)

Counseling services, placement, and post-placement services shall be available to each qualified veteran, whether or not the veteran is participating in a vocational rehabilitation program.

Naturalization

Veterans who served before September 11, 2001, are eligible to file for naturalization based on their U.S. military service.

An applicant who served three years in the U.S. military and is a lawful permanent resident is excused from any specific period of required residence, period of residence in any specific place, or physical presence within the United States if the application for naturalization is filed while the applicant is still serving in the military or within six months of honorable discharge.

Applicants who file for naturalization more than six months after termination of three years of U.S. military service may count any periods of honorable service as residence and physical presence in the United States.

Aliens and non-citizen nationals with honorable service in the U.S. armed forces during specified periods of hostilities may be naturalized without having to comply with the general requirements for naturalization. This is the only section of the Immigration and Nationality Act, as amended, which allows persons who have not been lawfully admitted for permanent residence to apply for naturalization.

Any person who has served honorably during qualifying time may apply at any time in his or her life if, at the time of enlistment, reenlistment, extension of enlistment or induction, such person shall have been in the United States, the Canal Zone, American Samoa or Swain's Island, or, on or after November 18, 1997, aboard a public vessel owned or operated by the United States for non- commercial service, whether or not lawful admittance to the United States for permanent residence has been granted.

Certain applicants who have served in the U.S. Armed Forces are eligible to file for naturalization based on current or prior U.S. military service. Such applicants should file the N-400 Military Naturalization Packet.

Benefits for Former Prisoners of War (POWs)

Former prisoners of war (POWs) may be eligible for VA disability compensation if they have a health condition related to their captivity. These benefits provide tax-free monthly payments. Read on to learn more about eligibility and the types of conditions covered.

Am I Eligible for VA Disability Compensation?

To qualify for disability compensation, you must meet the following requirements:

- You have a health condition linked to your time as a POW.
- The condition became at least 10% disabling after your active-duty service.

If you receive a disability rating, you may also qualify for VA health care and other benefits.

Presumptive Conditions for Former POWs

The VA assumes certain conditions are connected to your time as a POW. If you have one of these presumptive conditions, you don't need to prove that your service caused the condition; you only need to meet the service requirements.

Conditions for All Former POWs

For veterans held as POWs for any length of time, the following conditions are considered presumptive:
- Osteoporosis (if diagnosed with PTSD after October 10, 2008)
- Frostbite damage
- Posttraumatic osteoarthritis (joint pain and swelling from previous injuries)
- Stroke or complications (memory loss, speech problems, weakness)

- Hypertensive vascular disease (including heart disease and related issues like blood clots)

For mental health, the following conditions are also covered:
- Neuropsychiatric disorders
- Psychosis
- Persistent depressive disorder (dysthymic disorder)
- Anxiety disorders (including PTSD)

Conditions for POWs Held for 30 Days or More

If you were held captive for 30 days or more, additional presumptive conditions include:
- Osteoporosis (if your claim was filed after September 28, 2009, and you don't need to have PTSD)
- Helminthiasis (intestinal parasitic infections)
- Peripheral neuropathy (nerve damage, excluding infection-related cases)
- Peptic ulcer disease
- Chronic dysentery
- Irritable bowel syndrome
- Cirrhosis of the liver

For nutritional deficiencies, the following are covered:
- Avitaminosis (vitamin deficiencies)
- Beriberi (including beriberi heart disease)
- Malnutrition (including optic atrophy due to malnutrition)
- Pellagra

How to File a Claim for Compensation

To file for VA disability compensation, you can apply online, by mail, in person, or with the help of a trained representative.

Steps to File:
1. **Online**: Submit your claim through the VA's online portal.
2. **By Mail**: Complete the necessary forms and mail them to the appropriate address.
3. **In Person**: Visit your local VA office to file your claim.

Be sure to include documentation proving your time as a POW and a medical report confirming your condition and its disabling impact. You will need a doctor's statement showing the condition is at least 10% disabling to complete your claim.

For further assistance, consult a Veterans Service Officer or a trained professional to help with your claim.

How To Avoid Overpayments

A VA overpayment is when a veteran receives more VA benefits than he or she is entitled to and therefore must pay the money back to the VA. This may happen if a veteran is delayed in submitting paperwork or forgets to update records.

When discovered those funds are owed to the VA and may lead to a deduction in future monthly benefit amounts until the debt is repaid. You can make changes if anything happens that could impact your benefits by calling 1-800-827-1000.

Common overpayment situations include:
- A veteran in the Reserves may be called up for active duty and still receiving benefits from VA
- A veteran receiving education benefits doesn't complete the course requirement
- A veteran has a change in marital status and doesn't notify VA
- The veteran doesn't report a school-age child remarries
- A dependent passes away and VA isn't notified
- A veteran receives care at a VA medical facility and doesn't pay a required co-pay
- A veteran or beneficiary is incarcerated by still receives benefits during that time
- Veterans or beneficiaries receiving an income-based pension don't report a change in income
- The Vocational Rehabilitation program purchased a service or tools for a veteran who leaves the program without a valid reason

CHAPTER 11

SPECIAL CLAIMS & MISCELLEANOUS BENEFITS

If a veteran has a disability not listed as being linked to military service, they may still be able to get disability compensation or other benefits. If a veteran has a disability that the VA has concluded is because of an illness or injury caused or made worse by active-duty service, they may be able to get special compensation to help with disabilities.

Commissary Access

As of January 1, 2020, service-connected veterans, Purple Heart recipients, former prisoners of war (POWs), and primary family caregivers of eligible veterans under the Program of Comprehensive Assistance for Family Caregivers (PCAFC) can access commissaries, exchanges, and MWR facilities both in-person and online.

Eligibility:
Eligible individuals include Purple Heart recipients, POWs, veterans with 0-90% service-connected disability ratings, and PCAFC-approved primary caregivers.

Required Credentials:
Veterans must have a Veteran Health Identification Card for in-person access, which shows their eligibility status. Those not enrolled in VA healthcare or without the card will not have in-person access but can shop online. Medal of Honor recipients and veterans with 100% service-connected disabilities are also eligible.

Caregivers:
Eligible caregivers receive an eligibility letter from VA's Office of Community Care. If lost, caregivers can request a replacement by calling 1-877-733-7927.

2025 VA Special Benefit Allowance Rates

Benefit	Monthly Payment	Effective Date
Automobile Allowance Money to help you buy a specially equipped vehicle if your service-connected disability prevents you from driving.	Up to $26,417.20 paid once.	October 1, 2024
Clothing Allowance Money to help you replace clothes damaged by a medicine or prosthetic or orthopedic device related to your service-connected disability	$1024.50 paid once or once each year	December 1, 2024
Medal of Honor Pension Added compensation if you received the Medal of Honor	$1712.94 paid once each month	December 1, 2024

Automobile Assistance Program

The VA offers a one-time payment of up to $26,417.20 to eligible veterans or active-duty members with service-connected disabilities, to help purchase an automobile or conveyance.

This amount is adjusted annually based on the Consumer Price Index. The program requires VA approval before purchasing a vehicle or adaptive equipment.

Eligibility:

Veterans eligible for Disability Compensation under Chapter 11 of Title 38 due to the permanent loss of use of one or both feet, hands, or severe vision impairment (e.g., central visual acuity of 20/200 or worse in the better eye) may qualify.

Adaptive Equipment:

In addition to the one-time payment, the VA covers the cost of adaptive equipment installation, repairs, and replacements necessary for vehicle operation and state licensure.

Eligibility Requirements for Receipt of Adaptive Equipment
- The loss or permanent loss of use of one or both feet; or
- The loss or permanent loss of use of one or both hands; or
- The permanent impairment of vision of both eyes of the following status:
    - Central visual acuity of 20/200 or less in the better eye, with

corrective glasses, or central visual acuity of more than 20/200 if there is a field defect in which the peripheral field has contracted to such an extent that the widest diameter of visual field subtends an angular distance no greater than twenty degrees in the better eye; or
- Ankylosis (immobility) of one or both knees; or
- Ankylosis (immobility) of one or both hips.

Adaptive Equipment Available for Installation

The term adaptive equipment generally means any equipment which must be part of or added to a vehicle manufactured for sale to the general public to make it safe for use by the claimant and to assist him or her in meeting the applicable standards of licensure of the proper licensing authority.

Following is a partial list of adaptive equipment available under this program:
- Power steering;
- Power brakes;
- Power window lifts;
- Power seats;
- Special equipment necessary to assist the eligible person into and out of the automobile or other conveyance;
- Air-conditioning equipment, if such equipment is necessary to the health and safety of the veteran and the safety of others, regardless of whether the automobile or other conveyance is to be operated by the eligible person or is to be operated for such person by another person;
- Any modification of the size of the interior space of the automobile or other conveyance if necessary, for the disabled person to enter or operate the vehicle;
- Other equipment, not described above, if determined necessary by the Chief Medical Director or designee in an individual case.

Eligible veterans are not entitled to adaptive equipment for more than two vehicles at any one time during any four years. (In the event an adapted vehicle is no longer available for use by the eligible veteran due to circumstances beyond his or her control, loss due to fire, theft, accident, etc., an exception to this four-year provision may be approved.

Clothing Allowance

In 2011, a final regulation was published in the Federal Register, expanding the eligibility criteria for veterans with multiple prosthetic and orthopedic devices or those who use prescription medications for service-related skin conditions.

The new regulation provides the criteria for more than one annual clothing allowance in situations where distinct garments are affected. Payment for more than one clothing allowance for eligible veterans began in 2012.

The VA shall pay a clothing allowance of $1024.50 per year (rate effective

December 1, 2024, and payable beginning August 1, 2025) to each veteran who:

- Because of a service-connected disability, wears or uses a prosthetic or orthopedic appliance (including a wheelchair) which the VA determines tends to wear out or tear the clothing of the veteran; or

- Uses medication prescribed by a physician for a skin condition that is due to a service- connected disability, and which the VA determines causes irreparable damage to the veteran's outer garments.

Medal of Honor Pension

The VA pays a lump sum to Medal of Honor recipients equal to the special pension they would have received from the first month after the award until the month their special pension begins. The pension amount is based on the rate in effect for each month.

Eligibility for the Medal of Honor is determined by the Department of the Army, Navy, Air Force, or Transportation, who will send certification to the VA. The special pension is in addition to other U.S. government payments, but recipients may only receive one special pension, even if awarded multiple Medals of Honor.

The Medal of Honor Pension rate was updated to $1,712.94 on December 1, 2024.

Hearing Aids

To receive hearing aids through the VA, you must first register at the health administration/enrollment section of the VA Medical Center of your choice. You will need to bring a copy of your DD214, a driver's license and health insurance information if available.

You can do this in person at any VA medical center or clinic, or online by filling out the form 10- 10EZ. You can also mail the completed Form 10-10EZ to the medical center of your choice.

Once registered you can schedule an appointment at the Audiology and Speech Pathology Clinic for a hearing evaluation. The audiologist then makes a clinical determination on the need for hearing aids. If hearing aids are recommended and fit, hearing aids, repairs and future batteries will be available at no charge to you if you remain VA healthcare eligible.

Ordering Batteries

If you are authorized to receive batteries from the VA, you can request them in a few different ways.

You can request them by mail using VA Form 2346, Request for Batteries and Accessories. You should have received the card/envelope with your most recent battery order. You can then complete the form and mail it to:

VA Denver Acquisition and Logistics Center
PO Box 25166
Denver, CO 80225-0166

You can also order batteries over the phone by calling the Denver Acquisition and

Logistics center at 303-273-6200.

A third way to order new batteries is to use the eBenefits website. You have to apply for a Premium Account on eBenefits. Once you're logged in as a Premium User, you can go to the category "Manage Health." From there, navigate to the subcategory which is "Hearing Aid Batteries and Prosthetic Socks."

Once you order your batteries, they should arrive within 7 to 10 days.

Recovery From Surgery or an Immobilizing Disability (Convalescence)

If a veteran is recovering from a surgery or disability related to their military service that left them unable to move, they may be able to get a temporary 100% disability rating, and disability compensation or benefits.

You could be eligible for disability benefits if you had surgery or another treatment at a VA hospital, approved hospital, or an outpatient center for a disability related to your military service (service-connected disability).

If you had surgery, both of the following most be true:

- The surgery required a recovery time of at least one month or reports show that the surgery or treatment was for a service-connected disability, and
- The surgery resulted in severe injuries, like:
  - Surgical wounds that haven't totally healed
  - Stumps of recent amputations
  - Being unable to move due to being put in splints or casts to help with healing, known as therapeutic immobilizations
  - Being unable to leave your house, known as house confinement
  - Being required to use crutches or a wheelchair

If you didn't have surgery, you must have had one or more major joints immobilized by a cast.

You may be eligible for health care, added compensation while you recover, and a temporary 100% disability rating.

You'll need to file a claim for disability compensation.

Recovery time from either surgery or joint immobilization by a cast without surgery requires a temporary 100% disability rating for a service-connected disability.

The temporary 100% rating may continue for 1 to 3 months, depending on your specific case. You may be able to get an extension for up to 3 more months if your case is severe.

Increased Disability Rating for Time in a Hospital

If a veteran spent time in a VA hospital or a VA-approved hospital for a disability that's service-connected, they may be able to get added disability compensation or benefits with a temporary 100% disability rating for the time spent in the hospital.

A veteran may be eligible for disability benefits if they meet one of the following requirements:

- The veteran spent more than 21 days in a VA hospital or other approved hospital for a service-connected disability, or
- The veteran was under hospital observation for more than 21 days at the VA's expense for a service-connected disability

If you qualify, you'll need to file a claim for disability compensation. If you weren't in a VA hospital when you file your claim, you have to provide the VA with a hospital discharge summary showing the length and cause of the hospital stay.

VA Temporary Disability (Prestabilization Rating)

If a veteran recently ended their military service and they have a service-connected disability, they might be able to get temporary disability compensation or benefits right away. If a veteran qualifies for these benefits, they get a prestabilization rating. The rating may be 50% or 100%, depending on the severity of the disability. The prestabilization rating continues for one year after discharge from active service.

Both of the following must be true:

- The veteran must have a severe service-connected disability that's unstable, meaning an illness or injury that will change or hasn't yet been fully treated, and
- Your disability is expected to continue for an unknown amount of time.

You'll need to file a claim for disability compensation. When you file, you have to so show the VA you have a severe, service-connected disability that's unstable and is expected to continue for an unknown amount of time. The information will be part of your Service Treatment Record.

VA Title 38 U.S.C. 1151 Claims

If a veteran suffered an added disability or an existing injury or disease got worse while they were getting VA medical care or taking part in a VA program designed to help the veteran find, get or keep a job, they may be able to get compensation.

At least one of the three must have led directly to an added disability or to the injury or disease getting worse:

- VA carelessness or negligence, or
- VA medical or surgical treatment, or
- A VA health exam, or
- A VA vocational rehabilitation course under 38 U.S.C. Chapter 31, or
- VA compensated work therapy under 38 U.S.C. 1718

It's necessary to file a claim for disability compensation. When a veteran files, they have to show the added disability happened because of VA medical care or a VA medical program designed to help them find, get or keep a job.

The VA will award compensation payments in the same way it would if the disability was related to military service (a service-connected disability).

Individual Unemployability

If you can't work because of a disability related to your service in the military, you may qualify for Individual Unemployability, meaning you may be able to get disability compensation or benefits at the same level as a veteran with a 100% disability rating.

You have to meet both of the following:

- You have at least one service-connected disability rated at 60% or more disabling, or two or more service-connected disabilities with at least one rated at 40% or more disabling and a combined rating of 70% or more, and
- You can't hold down a steady job that supports you financially, known as substantially gainful employment because of your service-connected disability. Odd jobs, known as marginal employment, don't count.

In some cases, for example, if you often have to be in the hospital, you could qualify at a lower disability rating.

You'll need to file a claim for disability compensation. When you file, you'll have to provide evidence showing your disability prevents you from holding down a steady job. The VA will also review your work and education history.

When you file a disability claim you also need to file A Veteran's Application for Increased Compensation Based on Unemployability (VA Form 21-8940) and A Request for Employment Information in Connection with Claim for Disability Benefits (VA Form 21-4192).

CHAPTER 12

EDUCATION BENEFITS OVERVIEW

The Department of Veterans Affairs provides education benefits to eligible servicemembers, veterans and certain dependents and survivors. You may receive financial support for undergraduate and graduate degrees, technical training, licensing and certification tests, apprenticeships, on-the-job training and more.

As of March 2023, VA simplified the Post-9/11 GI Bill application experience. There is now a streamlined application to use transferred Post-9/11 GI Bill benefits available on VA.gov. There are options, once logged in, to pre-fill sponsor details, add transferee direct deposit information, and the application is shorter with fewer questions.

You may be eligible for one or more of the following VA education benefit programs:
- Post-9/11 GI Bill
- Montgomery GI Bill-Active Duty (MGIB-AD)
- Montgomery GI Bill-Selected Reserve (MGIB-SR)
- Reserve Educational Assistance Program (REAP
- Post-Vietnam Era Educational Assistance Program (VEAP)
- National Call to Service (NCS)
- Survivors' and Dependents' Educational Assistance (DEA)

You may be eligible to receive funds for:
- School tuition and fees for public, private or foreign schools, flight programs, correspondence training and distance learning
- Books and supplies
- License or certification tests
- National exams including SATs, ACTs, GMATs and LSATs
- On-the-job and apprenticeship training
- Distance learning/correspondence school
- Vocational/technical training
- Relocating from highly rural areas
- A monthly housing allowance

Each program offers different amounts of financial assistance and has varying eligibility requirements. If you are eligible for more than one educational benefit, choose the one that's right for you. You can't choose more than benefit program at a time to receive payment under.

Overview of VA Education Benefits

Benefit Program	Purpose	Eligibility	Key Features
Post-9/11 GI Bill	Provides education and training benefits to veterans, service members, and their families.	Served at least 90 days active duty after 9/10/2001.	Covers tuition and fees, housing allowance, and supplies.
		Honorable discharge required.	Transferable to dependents.
Montgomery GI Bill (MGIB-AD/SELRES)	Offers education benefits for those on active duty or in the Selected Reserve.	Active-duty service for MGIB-AD; Selected Reserve service for MGIB-SR.	Monthly benefit payments for approved programs.
		Contributions to the MGIB program required.	
Veteran Readiness and Employment (VR&E)	Assists veterans with service-connected disabilities to prepare for and find employment.	Veterans with service-connected disabilities rated at 10% or more.	Tuition, fees, and training supplies covered.
			Includes employment services and counseling.
Survivors' and Dependents' Educational Assistance (DEA)	Offers education benefits to dependents	Dependents of veterans who are permanently	Covers degree, certification, and training

	of disabled or deceased veterans.	disabled due to service-connected conditions or deceased.	programs.
Yellow Ribbon Program	Helps cover tuition costs that exceed the Post-9/11 GI Bill cap for private schools.	Eligible under the Post-9/11 GI Bill at 100% benefit level.	Participating schools and VA share tuition costs.
Fry Scholarship	Provides education benefits to children and spouses of service members who died in the line of duty.	Surviving dependents of service members who died in the line of duty after 9/10/2001.	Covers tuition, housing allowance, and supplies similar to the Post-9/11 GI Bill.
Veteran Rapid Retraining Assistance Program (VRRAP)	Helps veterans pursue high-demand occupations.	Unemployed veterans who are not eligible for other VA education benefits.	Covers tuition and housing during training for approved programs.
State-Specific Programs	Additional benefits offered by individual states for veterans.	Varies by state; usually requires residency.	May include tuition waivers, scholarships, or grants.

2025 Update: Rudisill Decision

If you are a veteran with two or more qualifying periods of active duty, you may now qualify for up to 48 months of combined entitlement under the Post-9/11 GI Bill (PGIB) and the Montgomery GI Bill Active Duty (MGIB-AD). This additional benefit is available even if you previously relinquished your MGIB-AD benefits.

What's Changed?

The Supreme Court's ruling on April 16, 2024, now allows veterans who served during two different qualifying periods, one that qualifies for MGIB and another that qualifies for PGIB—to receive additional GI Bill benefits.

Previously, veterans had to waive MGIB eligibility to access PGIB benefits, and PGIB entitlement was limited to the amount remaining in their MGIB entitlement. This ruling revokes that requirement and extends the benefits accordingly.

Eligibility for Additional Benefits

To be eligible for the expanded benefits under the Rudisill decision, you must meet two criteria:

1. You have served at least two eligible periods of active duty—one qualifying for MGIB and another qualifying for PGIB.

2. You previously waived MGIB benefits to use PGIB benefits.

Veterans who are affected by the decision can follow the chart or decision tree provided by the VA to determine the next steps.

How to Apply for Additional Benefits

If your last decision for education benefits was made after August 15, 2018, you will automatically be reviewed for additional benefits, and the VA will notify you of your eligibility. If your decision was made before August 15, 2018, you will need to submit a claim using VA Form 22-1995 and indicate that you are requesting a Rudisill review.

New Delimiting Date

If your claim is approved, the VA will calculate a new delimiting date based on your application date. This means that the date your benefits expire will be adjusted. If you are not ready to use your benefits, it is recommended that you wait to apply to prevent your benefits from expiring before use.

The deadline for recalculating your delimiting date is October 1, 2030. After this date, veterans can still submit a claim, but normal delimiting date rules will apply.

Key Questions

Q: How is VA notifying veterans impacted by these changes?

A: VA is contacting affected veterans. If you believe you may be impacted but haven't received notification, you should check the eligibility section on the VA website or contact them for further guidance.

Q: Will I be able to transfer additional benefits to my spouse or dependents?

A: Your eligibility for transferring benefits to family members remains unchanged by the Rudisill decision. Transfer of Entitlement eligibility still applies based on existing rules.

Q: Will my new delimiting date be adjusted?

A: Yes, if you are eligible, the VA will recalculate your benefits expiration date. For example, if you had seven years remaining on your MGIB when you forfeited it, the VA will add that seven years to your new delimiting date, along with an additional 90 days.

Q: Can I waive MGIB benefits to get a refund?

A: Yes, veterans can still voluntarily waive their MGIB benefits to receive a refund of their $1,200 contribution and PGIB kicker payments.

Q: Will the Rudisill decision change my Veteran Readiness & Employment (VR&E) benefits?

A: If you were participating in the VR&E program and were granted retroactive PGIB benefits, you may now be eligible for the higher BAH subsistence rate, which is typically greater than the standard Chapter 31 rate.

Deadlines and Appeals

Veterans have until October 1, 2030, to submit a claim to receive the recalculated delimiting date. After that date, the VA will apply standard delimiting date rules. If your claim is denied, you can file an appeal within one year from the original decision.

For any questions or assistance with your claim, the VA is available through various contact methods, including online support and direct assistance via phone or email.

Post-9/11 GI Bill

The Post-9/11 GI Bill provides up to 36 months of education benefits to eligible servicemembers and veterans. The benefits may include financial support for school tuition and fees, books and supplies, and housing. You might also receive reimbursement for license or certification tests such as CPA, national tests like SAT or GMAT, or assistance for apprenticeships/on-the-job training. A one-time payment to help you relocate from certain rural areas to attend school is also available.

Each type of benefit, such as tuition or books, has a maximum rate. Based on the length of your active service, you are entitled to a percentage of the maximum total benefit.

You may be eligible for the Post-9/11 GI Bill benefits if you:
- Have at least 90 aggregate days of qualifying active service after September 10, 2001, or
- Were honorably discharged from active duty for a service-connected disability after serving at least 30 continuous days after September 10, 2001

If you are in the Armed forces, you may be able to transfer your Post-9/11 GI Bill benefits to your spouse and children. Generally, you must use these benefits within 15 years from your last period of active service of at least 90 days.

Montgomery GI Bill-Active Duty

Montgomery GI Bill-Active Duty (MGIB-AD) or Chapter 30, provides up to 36 months of financial assistance for educational pursuits including college, vocational, or technical training, correspondence courses, apprenticeships and on-the-job training, flight training, high-tech training, licensing and certification tests, entrepreneurship training, and national exams. Generally, your MGIB-AD benefits are paid directly to you each month.

You may be eligible for MGIB-AD benefits while you are on or after you separate from active duty. At a minimum you must have a high school diploma or GED. To receive benefits after separating, you must have received an honorable discharge. You generally have 10 years from your last date of separation from active duty to use your MGIB-AD benefits.

Montgomery GI Bill-Selected Reserve

Montgomery GI Bill-Selected Reserve (MGIB-SR) or Chapter 1606 provides up to 36 months of financial assistance for educational pursuits. MGIB-SR benefits are available to members of the Selected Reserve of the Army, Navy, Air Force, Marine Corps or Coast Guard or the Army or Air National Guard. Generally, MGIB-SR benefits are paid directly to you on a monthly basis.

You may be eligible for MGIB-SR benefits if you have a six-year obligation to serve in the Selected Reserve, complete your Initial Active Duty for Training, serve in a drilling unit and remain in good standing, and obtain a high school diploma or equivalency.

The Guard and Reserves decide if you are eligible, while the VA makes the payments for the program. Generally, your eligibility for MGIB-SR benefits end on the day you leave the Selected Reserve.

Veterans' Educational Assistance Program

The Veterans' Educational Assistance Program (VEAP) helps Veterans continue their education by using contributions made from their military pay. This government program offers a $2-to-$1 match to assist with educational costs.

Am I Eligible for VEAP?

You may qualify for VEAP benefits if you meet all of the following criteria:
- You entered military service for the first time between January 1, 1977, and June 30, 1985 (for all branches except the Air Force), and
- You contributed between $25 and $2,700 to your VEAP account before April 1, 1987, and
- You completed your first period of service and did not receive a dishonorable discharge.

Additional Criteria for Air Force Veterans:

- You entered service for the first time between December 1, 1980, and September 30, 1981, and
- You enlisted in one of the designated Air Force specialties and locations listed by the Department of Defense.

Note: If you're currently active duty, you must have at least three months of VEAP contributions available to use this benefit.

What Benefits Are Available Under VEAP?

VEAP provides tuition assistance to help cover the cost of qualifying education or training programs.

How to Apply for VEAP Benefits

- **If You Haven't Started Training:**
  Submit an Application for VA Education Benefits (VA Form 22-1990) online, or by mail, in person, or with the help of a representative. Active-duty members must have their Education Services Officer and Commanding Officer approve the enrollment.
- **If You've Already Started Training:**
  Bring your VA Form 22-1990 and a copy of your DD214 (Certificate of Release or Discharge) to your school or employer, who will complete VA Form 22-1999 (Enrollment Certification) and send it to VA.

What Programs Does VEAP Cover?

VEAP can be used for:
- Undergraduate and graduate degree programs
- Non-degree programs (technical or vocational)
- Flight training
- Co-op training
- On-the-job training or apprenticeships
- Licensing and certification exams
- National tests and prep courses
- Entrepreneurship training
- Correspondence courses

VEAP may also cover:
- Remedial courses to build basic skills
- Deficiency courses needed for college admission
- Refresher courses to review knowledge

How Many Months of Benefits Are Available?

You may receive up to 36 months of benefits, depending on the amount you contribute. You have 10 years from your release from active duty to use your VEAP benefits. If unused after 10 years, your contributions will be refunded.

Can I Withdraw My Contributions?

Yes, if you don't meet the eligibility requirements or if you want to request a refund, you can withdraw your VEAP contributions by completing an Application for Refund of Educational Contributions (VA Form 22-5281).

For more information, contact the VA Education Call Center at 888-442-4551 (TTY: 711).

National Call to Service

The National Call to Service Program offers an alternative to the Montgomery GI Bill (MGIB) for eligible service members. It provides benefits for veterans who have completed national service as part of their military or other government service commitments.

Eligibility Criteria

To qualify for this program, veterans must meet the following conditions:
* Complete initial entry training and serve on active duty for at least 15 months in a designated military occupational specialty.
* Continue service without a break, either with additional active duty or 24 months in the Selected Reserve or another qualifying national service program.

Additionally, veterans must meet one of the following:
* Complete their service in the Armed Forces, Selected Reserve, Individual Ready Reserve, or a designated domestic national service program.

Available Benefits

Eligible participants can choose from the following benefits upon enlistment:
* $5,000 cash bonus.
* Up to $18,000 student loan repayment.
* Educational assistance for 12 months equal to the 3-year MGIB Active-Duty rate.
* Educational assistance for 36 months equal to 50% of the less-than-3-year MGIB Active-Duty rate.

How to Apply

To apply for these benefits, veterans should complete VA Form 22-1990n and mail it to the appropriate VA regional processing office based on their school address or home address.

Additional Information

For more details, veterans can check the current MGIB-AD payment rates or contact the VA Education Call Center for guidance.

Survivors' and Dependents' Educational Assistance

Survivors' and Dependents' Educational Assistance (DEA) or Chapter 35, provides assistance for degree and certificate programs, apprenticeships/on-the-job training, correspondence courses, and other programs. You must be the son, daughter or spouse of:

- A veteran who died or is permanently and totally disabled as the result of a service-connected disability. The disability must arise from active service in the Armed Forces.
- A veteran who died from any cause while such permanent and total service-connected disability existed.
- A servicemember who died during active military service.
- A servicemember missing in action or captured in the line of duty by a hostile force.
- A service member forcibly detained or interned in the line of duty by a foreign government or power.
- A servicemember who is hospitalized or receiving outpatient treatment for a service- connected permanent and total disability and is likely to be discharged for that disability.

The program offers up to 45 months of education benefits. If you are the child, you generally must use your benefits between the ages of 18 and 26. If you are the spouse, your benefits end 10 years from the date VA finds you eligible or from the date of death of your spouse.

A surviving spouse who meets the criteria below may be eligible for benefits for 20 years from the date of death:

- VA rated your spouse permanently and totally disabled with an effective date within three years from discharge or
- Your spouse died on active duty

Edith Nourse Rogers STEM Scholarship

The Edith Nourse Rogers STEM Scholarship provides additional educational benefits for veterans using the Post-9/11 GI Bill or dependents using the Fry Scholarship. This scholarship helps fund education in high-demand fields like Science, Technology, Engineering, and Mathematics (STEM) and offers up to 9 months of benefits, with a maximum of $30,000.

Eligibility Criteria

To be eligible for this scholarship, you must meet one of the following criteria:

- Undergraduate STEM Degree Program: You must be enrolled in an undergraduate STEM degree program requiring at least 120 semester credit hours (or 180 quarter credit hours) and have completed at least 60 standard credit hours. Additionally, you should have no more than 6 months of benefits left under the Post-9/11 GI Bill or the Fry Scholarship.

- Graduate Clinical Training for Healthcare: If you have a qualifying STEM degree and are enrolled in a covered, post-graduate clinical training program for healthcare professionals (not part of a graduate degree program), you may also qualify, provided you have no more than 6 months of GI Bill or Fry Scholarship benefits remaining.
- Teaching Certification: If you have earned a STEM degree and are working toward a teaching certification, you can also apply, provided you have 6 months or less of GI Bill or Fry Scholarship benefits left.

Approved Fields of Study

The scholarship is applicable to the following fields of study:

- Agriculture science and natural resources
- Biological or biomedical science
- Computer and information science
- Engineering and related fields
- Healthcare-related fields
- Mathematics and statistics
- Physical science
- Science technologies and technicians

Benefits

If approved, the scholarship provides:

- Up to 9 months of additional educational benefits or $30,000, whichever comes first.
- Monthly housing allowance (MHA) sent directly to you, contingent on monthly verification of enrollment.

Application Process

To apply, complete the VA Form 22-1990n online. It typically takes about 15 minutes to fill out the application. After submission, the VA will review your eligibility and notify you of their decision. If approved, you will receive a Certificate of Eligibility (COE), which should be submitted to your school's VA certifying official.

Additional Information
- Deadline: You must start using your scholarship within 6 months of approval.
- Work-Study Program: Veterans receiving the Rogers STEM Scholarship are eligible to apply for the Veterans Work-Study Program.
- Transferability: The benefits are not transferable to dependents.

CHAPTER 13

EDUCATION BENEFITS - MONTGOMERY G.I. BILL (MGIB-AD), CHAPTER 30

2025 Update: You might be eligible for additional benefits under the Rudisill ruling. If you've completed two or more periods of qualifying active-duty service, you could be entitled to up to 48 months of educational benefits. To qualify, you must be eligible for both the Post-9/11 GI Bill and the Montgomery GI Bill Active Duty (MGIB-AD).

Note: If you previously waived your MGIB-AD benefits (known as "relinquishing" them), you may now be able to access some of that entitlement.

The Montgomery GI Bill Active Duty (MGIB-AD) can help pay for education and training programs for veterans who served at least two years on active duty. You may be eligible for education benefits through this program if you were honorably discharged and you meet the requirements of one of the following categories.

Category I

All of these are true:
- You have a high school diploma, GED or 12 hours of college credit, and
- You entered active duty for the first time after June 30, 1985, and
- You had your military pay reduced by $100 a month for the first 12 months of service.

And you served continuously for at least one of these time periods:
- 3 years, or
- 2 years if that was your agreement when you enlisted, or
- 4 years if you entered the Selected Reserve within a year of leaving active duty—this is called the 2 by 4 program.

Category II

All of these are true:

- You have a high school diploma, GED, or 12 hours of college credit, and
- You entered active duty before January 1, 1977 (or before January 2, 1978, under a delayed enlistment program contracted before January 1, 1977), and
- You served at least 1 day between October 19, 1984, and June 30, 1985, and stayed on active duty through June 30, 1988 (or through June 30, 1987, if you entered the Selected Reserve within 1 year of leaving active duty and served 4 years, and
- You had at least 1 day of entitlement left under the Vietnam Era GI Bill (Chapter 34) as of December 31, 1989.

Category III

All of these are true:
- You have a high school diploma, GED, or 12 hours of college credit, and
- You don't qualify for MGIB under categories I or II, and
- You had your military pay reduced by $1,200 before separation.

And one of these is true:
- You were on active duty on September 30, 1990, and involuntary separated not by your choice after February 2, 1991, or
- You were involuntarily separated on or after November 30, 1993, or
- You chose to voluntarily separate under either the Voluntary Separation Initiative (VSI) program or the Special Separation Benefit (SSB) program.

Category IV

Both of these are true:
- You have a high school diploma, GED or 12 hours of college credit, and
- You had military pay reduced by $100 a month for 12 months or made a $1,200 lump sum contribution.

And one of these is true:
- You were on active duty on October 9, 1996, had money left in a VEAP account on that date, and you chose MGIB before October 9, 1997, or
- You entered full-time National Guard duty under title 32, USC, between July 1, 1985, and November 28, 1989, and chose MGIB between October 9, 1996, and July 9, 1997

The amount a veteran will receive through this education program depends on:
- Their length of service
- The type of education or training program they choose
- Their category (I, II, III or IV)
- Whether they qualify for a college fund or kicker
- How much the veteran paid into the $600 Buy-Up program

You usually have 10 years to use your MGIB-AD benefits, but this can change depending on your situation.

The transferability option under the Post-9/11 GI Bill allows Servicemembers to transfer all or some unused benefits to their spouse or dependent children. The request to transfer unused GI Bill benefits to eligible dependents must be completed while serving as an active member of the Armed Forces.

The Department of Defense (DoD) determines whether or not you can transfer benefits to your family. Once the DoD approves benefits for transfer, the new beneficiaries apply for them at VA. To find out more, visit DoD's website or apply now.

Overview of the Montgomery GI Bill (MGIB)

Feature	Active Duty (MGIB-AD)	Selected Reserve (MGIB-SR)
Purpose	Provides education benefits to active-duty service members and veterans.	Offers education benefits to members of the Selected Reserve.
Eligibility	Active duty for at least two years.	Six-year service obligation in the Selected Reserve.
	High school diploma or equivalent.	Completion of initial active-duty training (IADT).
	Honorable discharge.	Actively drilling in the Selected Reserve.
Time Limit to Use Benefits	10 years from separation date.	Generally, benefits expire 10 years after eligibility begins.
Benefit Amount	Monthly payments based on enrollment status (e.g., full-time, part-time).	Monthly payments while in an approved education program.
Programs Covered	College degree programs.	College degree programs.
	Technical and vocational courses.	Technical and vocational training.
	Flight training, apprenticeships, and on-the-job training (OJT).	-Flight training, apprenticeships, and OJT.
	Correspondence courses.	Correspondence

		courses.
Contribution Requirement	$1,200 deduction from active-duty pay.	No monetary contribution required.
Key Features	Can be combined with other VA education benefits under specific circumstances.	Limited to Selected Reserve members actively drilling.
How to Apply	File VA Form 22-1990 through VA.gov or eBenefits.	File VA Form 22-1990 through VA.gov or eBenefits.

Eligible Servicemembers may transfer all 36 months or the portion of unused Post-9/11 GI Bill benefits (unless DoD or the Department of Homeland Security has limited the number of transferable months). If you're eligible, you may transfer benefits to the following individuals:

- Your spouse
- One or more of your children
- Any combination of spouse and child

Available Benefits and Eligibility

Family members must be enrolled in the Defense Eligibility Enrollment Reporting System (DEERS) and be eligible for benefits at the time of transfer to receive transferred benefits.

The option to transfer is open to any member of the armed forces active duty or Selected Reserve, officer or enlisted who is eligible for the Post-9/11 GI Bill, and meets the following criteria:

- Has at least six years of service in the armed forces (active duty and/or Selected
  Reserve) on the date of approval and agrees to serve four additional years in the armed forces from the date of election.
- Has at least 10 years of service in the armed forces (active duty and/or Selected Reserve) on the date of approval, is precluded by either standard policy (by Service Branch or DoD) or statute from committing to four additional years and agrees to serve for the maximum amount of time allowed by such policy or statute.
- Transfer requests are submitted and approved while the member is in the armed forces.
- Effective 7/20/19, eligibility to transfer benefits will be limited to sevicemembers with less than 16 years of active duty or selected reserve service.

Transfer Process

While in the armed forces, transferors use the Transfer of Education Benefits (TEB) website to designate, modify, and revoke a Transfer of Entitlement (TOE) request. After leaving the armed forces, transferors may provide a future effective date for use of TOE, modify the number of months transferred, or revoke entitlement transferred by submitting a written request to VA.

Upon approval, family members may apply to use transferred benefits with VA by applying online or by printing, completing, and mailing the VA Form 22-1990e to your VA Regional processing office of jurisdiction. VA Form 22-1990e should only be completed and submitted to VA by the family member after DoD has approved the request for TEB. Do not use VA Form 22-1990e to apply for transfer of education benefits.

Other Factors to Consider

Marriage and Divorce
- A child's subsequent marriage will not affect his or her eligibility to receive the educational benefit; however, after an individual has designated a child as a transferee under this section, the individual retains the right to revoke or modify the transfer at any time.
- A subsequent divorce will not affect the transferees eligibility to receive educational benefits; however, after an individual has designated a spouse as a transferee under this section, the eligible individual retains the right to revoke or modify the transfer at any time.

Reallocation of Benefits

If a veteran or servicemember wants to reallocate transferred benefits they can do so using the TEB Portlet in MilConnect.

Reallocation of Benefits if a Family Member Dies

The Harry W. Colmery Veterans Assistance Act of 2017 allows for designation and transfer of Post-9/11 GI Bill benefits to eligible dependents of the Veteran/servicemember upon the death of the veteran/servicemember or of a dependent who had unused transferred benefits.

Nature of Transfer

Family member use of transferred educational benefits is subject to the following rules:

Spouses:
- May start to use the benefit immediately.
- May use the benefit while the member remains in the Armed Forces or after

separation from active duty.
- Are not eligible for the monthly housing allowance while the member is serving on active duty.
- If servicemember's last discharge was before January 1, 2013, can use the benefit for up to 15 years after the last separation from active duty. If the servicemember's last discharge is after January 1, 2013, there is no time limit to use benefits.

Children

- May start to use the benefit only after the individual making the transfer has completed at least 10 years of service in the armed forces.
- May use the benefit while the eligible individual remains in the armed forces or after separation from active duty.
- May not use the benefit until he or she has attained a secondary school diploma (or equivalency certificate), or he or she has reached age 18.
- Is entitled to the monthly housing allowance stipend even though the eligible individual is on active duty.
- Is not subject to the 15-year delimiting date but may not use the benefit after reaching 26 years of age.

Discharges and Separations

As previously mentioned, if the veteran is separated from active duty, the character of discharge must specifically be listed as "Honorable." "Under Honorable Conditions," or a "General" discharge do not establish eligibility. A discharge for one of the following reasons may result in a reduction of the required length of active duty to qualify for benefits under the MGIB:
- Convenience of the Government; or
- Disability; or
- Hardship; or
- Medical conditions existing before entry into Service; or
- Force reductions; or
- Medical condition, which is not a disability due to misconduct, but which prevents satisfactory performance of duty.

The following types of active duty do not establish eligibility for MGIB benefits:
- Time assigned by the military to a civilian institution to take the same course provided to civilians.
- Time served as a cadet or a midshipman at a service academy.
- Time spent on active duty for training in the National Guard or Reserve.

Please note: Time assigned by the military to a civilian institution, and time served at a service academy does not break the continuity of active duty required to establish eligibility for MGIB benefits. Active duty for training does count toward the four years in the Selected Reserve under the 2 by 4 program.

Approved Courses

This program provides veterans up to 36 months of education benefits. The benefits may be used for:

- Undergraduate or graduate degrees from a college or university;
- Cooperative training programs;
- Accredited independent study programs leading to standard college degrees;
- Courses leading to certificates or diplomas from business, technical or vocational schools;
- Vocational flight training (from September 30, 1990 only – Individuals must have a private pilot's license and meet the medical requirements for a desired license before beginning training, and throughout the flight training program);
- Apprenticeship / job training programs offered by a company or union;
- Correspondence courses.

VA may approve programs offered by institutions outside of the United States, when they are pursued at educational institutions of higher learning, and lead to an associate or higher degree, or the equivalent. Individuals must receive VA approval prior to attending or enrolling in any foreign programs.

Restrictions on Training

- Bartending and personality development courses
- Non-accredited independent study courses;
- Any course given by radio;
- Self-improvement courses such as reading, speaking, woodworking, basic seamanship, and English as a second language;
- Any course which is avocational or recreational in character;
- Farm cooperative courses;
- Audited courses;
- Courses not leading to an educational, professional, or vocational objective;
- Courses an individual has previously completed;
- Courses taken by a Federal government employee under the Government Employees' Training Act;
- Courses paid for in whole or in part by the Armed Forces while on active duty;
- Courses taken while in receipt of benefits for the same program from the Office of Workers' Compensation Programs.

The VA must reduce benefits for individuals in Federal, State or local prisons after being convicted of a felony.

An individual may not receive benefits for a program at a proprietary school if he or she is an owner or official of the school. Benefits are generally payable for 10 years following a veteran's release from active duty.

Part-Time Training

Individuals unable to attend school full-time should consider going part-time. Benefit rates and entitlement charges are pro-rated as follows:
- Individuals who are on active duty or training at less than one-half time, will receive the lesser of:
- The monthly rate based on tuition and fees for the course(s); or
- The maximum monthly rate based on training time.
- Individuals training at less than one-half time will receive payment in one sum for the whole enrollment period.

Remedial, Deficiency and Refresher Training

Remedial and deficiency courses are intended to assist a student in overcoming a deficiency in a particular area of study. In order for such courses to be approved, the courses must be deemed necessary for pursuit of a program of education.

Refresher training is for technological advances that occurred in a field of employment. The advance must have occurred while the student was on active duty, or after release. There is an entitlement charge for these courses.

Tutorial Assistance

Students may receive a special allowance for individual tutoring, if attending school at one-half time or more. To qualify, the student must have a deficiency in a subject. The school must certify the tutor's qualifications, and the hours of tutoring. Eligible students may receive a maximum monthly payment of $100.00. The maximum total benefit payable is $1,200.00.

There is no entitlement charge for the first $600.00 of tutorial assistance. To apply for tutorial assistance, students must submit VA Form 22-1990t, "Application and Enrollment Certification for Individualized Tutorial Assistance." The form should be given to the certifying official in the office handling VA paperwork at the school for completion.

Months of Benefits/Entitlement Charged

Individuals who complete their full period of enlistment may receive up to 36 months of MGIB benefits.

Individuals are considered to have completed their full enlistment period if they are discharged for the convenience of the government after completing 20 months of an enlistment of less than three years; or 30 months of an enlistment of three years or more Individuals will earn only one month of entitlement for each month of active duty after June 39, 1985, if they are discharged for other specific reasons (i.e. service- connected disability, reduction in force, hardship, etc.) before completing the enlistment period.

Individuals will earn one month of entitlement for each four months in the Selected Reserve after June 30, 1985. Individuals qualifying for more than one VA education program may receive a maximum of 48 months of benefits. For example, if a student used 30 months of Dependents' Educational Assistance, and is eligible for chapter 1606 benefits, he or she could have a maximum of 18 months of entitlement remaining.

Individuals are charged one full day of entitlement for each day of full-time benefits paid. For correspondence and flight training, individuals use one month of entitlement each time the VA pays the equivalent of one month of full-time benefits. Individuals pursuing a cooperative program use one month for each month of benefits paid.

For apprenticeship and job-training programs, the entitlement charge during the first 6 months is 75% full-time. For the second six months, the charge is 55% of full-time. For the rest of the program, the charge is 35% of full-time. VA can extend entitlement to the end of a term, quarter, or semester if the ending date of an individual's entitlement falls within such period. If a school does not operate on a term basis, entitlement can be extended for 12 weeks.

Rates of Educational Assistance After Separation from Active Duty

The basic monthly rates increase October 1 every year with the Consumer Price Index (CPI) increase. While in training, students receive a letter with the current rates when the increase goes into effect each year. The rates may increase at other times by an act of Congress.

Basic Monthly Rates for College and Vocational Training

For approved programs in college and vocational or technical schools, basic payments are monthly, and the rates are based on training time.

When students train at less than half time, they will be paid tuition and fees. But if tuition and fees amount to more than would be paid at the half- time rate (or the quarter-time rate if training at quarter-time or less), payments will be limited to the half time (or the quarter-time rate).

For on-the-job training (OJT) and apprenticeship programs, rates are monthly and based on the length of time in the program. MGIB rates decrease as the student's wages increase according to an approved wage schedule.

Rates for Other Types of Training

For correspondence courses, students receive 55% of the approved charges for the course. For flight training, students receive 60% of the approved charges for the course. For reimbursement of tests for licenses or certifications, students receive 100% of the charges up to a maximum of

$2,000 per test.

Rates of Educational Assistance While on Active Duty

If a service member goes to school while on active duty, he or she may have two options for using MGIB benefits. They may be eligible to receive:
- "Regular" MGIB; or
- Tuition Assistance plus MGIB, or
- Tuition Assistance "Top-Up"

Using "Regular" MGIB While on Active Duty

If a service member uses "regular" MGIB while on active duty, VA can pay whichever is less:
- The monthly rate based on tuition and fees for your course(s); or
- The maximum monthly MGIB rate (basic rate plus any increases he or she may qualify for).

The basic monthly rates increase October 1 every year with the Consumer Price Index (CPI) increase. While in training, students receive a letter with the current rates when the increase goes into effect each year. The rates may increase at other times by an act of Congress.

Using Tuition Assistance Top-Up

If a student is on active duty, he or she may be eligible to receive Tuition Assistance (TA) from his or her branch of service. If the student has been on active duty for two years, he or she may also be eligible to use MGIB to supplement, or "top up," the TA. Top-up covers the remaining percentage of costs approved for TA that TA alone doesn't cover—**up to specified limits**. For example, if a student's service authorizes 75% of costs, top-up can pay the remaining 25% of costs approved for TA.

DETAILED Rates of Educational Assistance—
The rates effective October 1, 2024, are detailed in the following charts:

Basic Monthly Rates Effect October 1, 2024, Montgomery G.I. Bill – Active Duty (MGIB), Chapter 30					
Type of Training	Full-Time	¾ Time	½ Time	Less Then ½ Time but More than 1/4	¼ Time
Institutional	$2438.00	$1828.50	$1219.00	$1219.00	$609.50
Cooperative Training	$2438.00				
Correspondence Training	VA pays 55% of the established cost for the number of lessons completed. You have to submit completed lessons to receive				

	payments.
Apprenticeship On-The-Job Training-	First six months: $1828.50 for each full month Second six months: $1340.90 for each full month Remainder of program: $853.30 for each full month
Flight Training	VA will pay 60% of approved charges.

Basic Monthly Rates Effective October 1, 2024
For persons who's initial active-duty obligation was less than three years and who served less than three years
(excluding 2x4 participants)

Type of Training	Full- Time	¾ Time	½ Time	Less Then ½ Time but More Than ¼	¼ Time
Institutional	$1978.00	$1483.50	$989.00	Tuition & Fees, not to exceed $989.00	$494.50
Correspondence Training	VA will pay 55% of the established cost of lessons completed.				
Apprenticeship On-The-Job Training-	First six months: $1483.50 for each full month Second six months: $1087.90 for each full month Remainder of program: $692.30 for each full month				
Flight Training	VA will pay for 60% of the approved charges.				
Cooperative Training	$1913.00 (Full-Time Only)				

Special Notes:

Cooperative Training is full time only.

Individuals taking correspondence courses will receive 55% of the approved charges for the course. Individuals taking flight training will receive 60% of the approved charges for the course, including solo hours.

Increased Above Basic Rates

Individuals may qualify for the following increases above their basic monthly rates. These increases don't apply to correspondence courses, the test for a license or certification, or flight training.

College Fund

Certain branches of service may offer the College Fund. The College Fund money, or "kicker," is an additional amount of money that increases the basic MGIB monthly benefit and is included in the VA payment.

Important: Students can't receive College Fund money without receiving MGIB. A common misunderstanding is that the College Fund is a separate benefit from MGIB. The College Fund is an add-on to the MGIB benefit.

Accelerated Payments for Education Leading to Employment in High Technology

If you're enrolled in a high-tech program, you may be eligible for a larger, one-time payment—often called a "lump sum" or "accelerated" payment—to help cover the higher costs of these programs.

Am I eligible for this benefit?

Eligibility depends on your service status, the type of program you're enrolled in, and the cost of tuition.

- **Active-Duty Eligibility:**
  To qualify, you must meet all of these conditions:
  - Be eligible for the Montgomery GI Bill Active Duty (MGIB-AD).
  - Be enrolled in a qualifying high-tech degree or non-degree program.
  - Your tuition and fees must exceed 200% of the monthly educational assistance you would otherwise receive during the enrollment period.

- **Reserves Eligibility:**
  To qualify, you must meet all of these conditions:
  - Be a current Reserve Educational Assistance Program (REAP) recipient or using the Montgomery GI Bill Selected Reserve (MGIB-SR).
  - Be enrolled in a qualifying high-tech, non-degree program that lasts 2 years or less.
  - Your tuition and fees must exceed 200% of the monthly educational assistance you would otherwise receive during the enrollment period.

Note: This benefit is not available under the Post-9/11 GI Bill, Dependents' Educational Assistance (DEA) program, or Veterans' Educational Assistance Program (VEAP).

What does this benefit cover?

The benefit provides a lump-sum payment covering 60% of your tuition and fees for high-cost, high-tech programs. These accelerated payments replace the monthly GI Bill benefits you would typically receive.

How do I apply for this benefit?

Request the accelerated payment through your school when they submit your enrollment details. Ensure that your program falls into one of these categories:

- Life sciences or physical sciences
- Engineering (all fields)
- Mathematics
- Engineering and science technology
- Computer specialties

Additionally, you must certify that you plan to seek employment in one of these industries:

- Biotechnology
- Life science technologies
- Optoelectronics
- Computers and telecommunications
- Electronics
- Computer-integrated manufacturing
- Material design
- Aerospace
- Weapons
- Nuclear technology

Miscellaneous Information

For Montgomery GI Bill benefits verify your enrollment if both of these are true for you:

- You're enrolled in an institution of higher learning or a non-college degree program, like training for HVAC repair or truck driving, and
- You're enrolled half-time or more
- You don't need to verify your enrollment if you're completing an apprenticeship, or on-the-job, flight, or correspondence training.

If you don't verify your enrollment, VA won't send your monthly benefits payment.

You'll need to verify your enrollment at the end of every month after your school starts. For example, if your school starts on August 5, you'll need to verify your enrollment on or after August 31.

If you were enrolled in school for any part of the month, you'll need to verify your enrollment for that month. For example, if your school ends on May 5, you'll need to verify your enrollment for the month of May on or after May 5.

Application for Benefits

Follow these steps to apply for VA education benefits:
- **Ensure Program Approval**
  Before enrolling, confirm that your program is approved for VA benefits.
  You can do this by contacting your school or using the GI Bill Comparison
  Tool. If you need assistance, you can call the VA Education Call Center at
  888-442-4551 (TTY: 711) or submit a question via Ask VA online.
  1. GI Bill Comparison Tool
  2. Contact Ask VA

Important: If your program isn't approved, your school must request the approval
on your behalf. The VA cannot take action until the request comes from an official
at your school. Without approval, you will be responsible for all costs, including
tuition and fees.

- **Submit Your Application**
  Complete the VA Form 22-1990 (Application for VA Benefits) online, or
  apply by mail, in person, or with the help of a professional.
- **Get Enrollment Certification from Your School**
  Your school's certifying official (usually in the financial aid, Veterans
  Affairs, registrar, admissions, or counseling office) will certify your
  enrollment. If you're in an on-the-job training program or apprenticeship,
  the certifying official could be in the training, finance, or human resources
  department.
- **Verify Your Enrollment**
  To continue receiving payments, you will need to verify your enrollment at
  the end of each month. Learn how to verify your enrollment.

For more information or assistance, contact the VA or your school's certifying
official.

How Education Payments Work

When Will I Receive My First GI Bill Payment?

If you set up direct deposit during your application for education benefits, your
payment will be deposited into your bank account within 7 to 10 business days
after you confirm your enrollment. This is the fastest way to receive your payment.
If you opted to receive payments by check, expect your first check in the mail
approximately 14 days after you verify your school enrollment.

What Should I Do If My GI Bill Payment is Late?

If your payment is delayed, reach out to the VA. You can call 888-442-4551 (TTY:
711) for assistance, Monday through Friday, from 8:00 a.m. to 7:00 p.m. ET.
If you receive your payment by check and it's been at least 3 weeks since the check
was issued, you can request a replacement. Please note that it may take up to 6

weeks to process a replacement.

Why Is My Monthly GI Bill Payment Lower Than Expected?

Your payment may be less than the expected amount for several reasons:
- **Partial Month Attendance:** If you attended classes for only part of the month, your payment will be prorated for that period. For instance, if your monthly rate is $800, and your classes start on August 19, you'll receive $320 for August 19 to 31.
    - Note: The monthly payment is calculated based on a 30-day period, so the rate is the same for months with 30 or 31 days.
- **Overpayment Adjustments**: If an overpayment occurred in a previous month, the VA may reduce the current payment to adjust for that.
- **Reduction in Enrollment Hours:** If you dropped classes or reduced your enrollment after your award was granted, your payment amount will be adjusted accordingly.

Will I Get Monthly Housing Allowance (MHA) During School Breaks?

No, the VA does not provide MHA during school breaks, including between semesters, quarters, or terms. Be sure to plan accordingly to cover your housing costs during these breaks.

If your enrollment begins after the first day of the month or ends before the last day, your housing allowance will be prorated for the portion of the month you're enrolled.

Can I Request an Advance GI Bill Payment?

The possibility of receiving an advance payment depends on the GI Bill program you're using:
- Post-9/11 GI Bill: Advance payments are not available.
- Other GI Bill Programs: You may be eligible for an advance payment if you meet these conditions:
    - You have an advance payment request on file at your school.
    - You're enrolled at least half-time.
    - There is a gap of at least 30 days before the term starts.

How to Request an Advance GI Bill Payment:

First, check with your school's Veterans benefits office (usually the registrar's or financial aid office) to confirm they will accept an advance payment. If so, they will provide a request form for you to complete.

Once your eligibility is confirmed, the VA will send the advance payment to your school. You can then pick up the check from the office. The payment will cover the first partial month and the first full month of your enrollment.

For example, if your enrollment starts on August 25, the advance payment will cover August 25 through September 30. Your next payment for October will be processed in early November.

Note: If you stop taking some or all of your classes after receiving an advance, you may be required to repay the amount.

CHAPTER 14

EDUCATION BENEFITS: POST-9/11 G.I. BILL, CHAPTER 33

The Post-9/11 GI Bill (PGIB), also known as Chapter 33, assists with funding your education or training costs for a new career. If you served on active duty after September 10, 2001, you could be eligible for this benefit.

2025 Update: You may be eligible for additional benefits under the Rudisill decision.

If you have two or more qualifying periods of active duty, you could now be eligible for up to 48 months of entitlement. To qualify, you must be eligible for both the Post-9/11 GI Bill and the Montgomery GI Bill Active Duty (MGIB-AD).

Note: Even if you previously waived your rights to use MGIB-AD benefits (referred to as "relinquishing" your benefits), you may now be eligible to access some of those benefits.

Eligibility

You may be eligible if you meet at least one of these requirements:
- You served at least 90 days on active duty, either all at once or with breaks in service on or after September 11, 2001, or
- You received a Purple Heart on or after September 11, 2001, and were honorably discharged after any amount of service, or
- You served for at least 30 continuous days, all at once without a break in service on or after September 11, 2001, and were honorably discharged with a service-connected disability, or
- You're a dependent child using benefits transferred by a qualifying veteran or service member.

Note: If you're a member of the Reserves who lost education benefits when the Reserve Educational Assistance Program (REAP) ended in November 2015, you might qualify to receive restored benefits under the Post-911 GI Bill.

You can only use 1 education benefit for a period of service, so you have to choose which one you want to use. After you make the choice, you can't change your mind.

Non-Qualifying Periods of Service

The VA does consider certain periods of service to be "non-qualifying," meaning those periods do not count toward eligibility for the Post-9/11 GI Bill.

Non-qualifying periods of service include situations where:
- The service member was assigned by their branch of service to a civilian school for courses that are similar to those available to civilians.
- The service member served as a cadet or midshipman at a service academy.
- The service member enlisted in the Army National Guard, Air National Guard, or Reserve and received training under section 12103(d) of Title 10 (initial skills and training).
- The service member was called to active duty from the Reserve under any section of Title 10 other than sections 688, 12301(a), 12301(d), 12301(g), 12301(h), 12302, 12304, 12304a, or 12304b, or section 3713 of Title 14.
- The President called the service member to full-time service in response to a national emergency supported by federal funds, but not under section 502(f) of Title 32.
- The service member served full-time in the National Guard for purposes other than organizing, administering, recruiting, instructing, or training under section 502(f) of Title 32.

Additionally, the VA considers any service period related to the following Department of Defense (DoD) programs as non-qualifying:
- Loan Repayment Program (LRP)
- Reserve Officers' Training Corps (ROTC) Scholarship
- Service Academy Graduation

What if I'm eligible for multiple VA education benefits?

If you qualify for more than one VA education benefit, you may be able to use more than one, depending on how many qualifying periods of active duty you've completed.

For one qualifying period of active duty:

Active Duty Starting on or After August 1, 2011:

If your active duty started on or after August 1, 2011, you can only use one education benefit. You will need to choose which benefit you wish to use, and once you make that choice, you will forfeit the ability to use the other benefit. You can use up to 36 months of education benefits.

- **Choosing the Post-9/11 GI Bill** means you cannot later switch to:
    - Montgomery GI Bill Active Duty (MGIB-AD or Chapter 30)
    - Montgomery GI Bill Selected Reserve (MGIB-SR or Chapter 1606)

Similarly, if you choose to use MGIB-AD or MGIB-SR, you cannot later switch to the Post-9/11 GI Bill.

If you use Post-9/11 GI Bill benefits and deplete your entitlement, the VA may refund some or all of the payments you made into MGIB-AD, with a maximum refund of $1,200.

Active Duty Starting Before August 1, 2011:

If your active duty started before August 1, 2011, you may use MGIB-AD or MGIB-SR benefits and later switch to the Post-9/11 GI Bill. Here's what happens when you switch:
- You forfeit the right to use your MGIB-AD or MGIB-SR benefits.
- If switching from MGIB-AD to Post-9/11 GI Bill benefits, you can only use the remaining MGIB-AD entitlement when starting the Post-9/11 benefits. For example, if you have 6 months left of MGIB-AD benefits, you'll have 6 months of Post-9/11 GI Bill benefits available.
- You cannot switch from Post-9/11 GI Bill benefits back to MGIB-AD or MGIB-SR because choosing the Post-9/11 GI Bill means you forfeit those options.

For two or more qualifying periods of active duty:

If you have completed two or more qualifying periods of active duty, you may be eligible for a total of up to 48 months of education benefits, provided you qualify for both the Post-9/11 GI Bill and MGIB-AD.

Recent Changes Under the Rudisill Decision:

If you previously gave up your MGIB-AD benefits when switching to the Post-9/11 GI Bill, you might now qualify for up to 12 months of additional MGIB-AD benefits.
- If you're currently using MGIB-AD benefits and switch to Post-9/11 GI Bill benefits, you're no longer limited to the remaining MGIB-AD entitlement.

Note: A reenlistment is considered a new period of active duty, but an extension does not count as a separate period.

How to Get Additional Entitlement (If Eligible)
- If you received an education claim decision on or after **August 15, 2018**, no action is needed. The VA will automatically review your entitlement and notify you if there are any changes.

- If you received an education claim decision before August 15, 2018, you'll need to submit a Request for Change of Program or Place of Training (VA Form 22-1995) to request additional entitlement.

When the VA receives your request, they will review your entitlement and notify you of any changes. Be sure to specify if your request is related to the Rudisill decision.

Benefits

Benefits available through the Post-9/11 GI Bill include:
- **Tuition and fees:** If you qualify for the maximum benefit, the VA will cover the full cost of public, in-state tuition and fees. The VA caps the rates for private and foreign schools, and those rates are updated each year.
- **Money for housing:** If you're in school for more than half-time, VA will base your monthly housing allowance on the cost of living where your school is located.
- **Money for books and supplies**: You can receive up to the maximum stipend per school year.
- **Money to help you move from a rural area to go to school**: You might qualify for a one-time payment if you live in a county with six or fewer people per square mile, and you're either moving at least 500 miles to go to school or have no other option but to fly by plane to get to your school.

Your award of benefits is based on how long you served on active duty or certain other forces. You can start using your Post-911 GI Bill benefits while you're on active duty if you served at least 90 days.

You're eligible for 100% of the full benefit if you meet at least one of these requirements:
- You served on active duty for a total of at least 1,095 days (at least 36 months)
- You served on active duty and received a Purple Heart on or after September 11, 2001, or
- You served on active duty for at least 30 continuous days without a break and the VA discharged you because of a service-connected disability

Expiration

If your service ended before January 1, 2013, your Post-9/11 GI Bill benefits will expire 15 years after your last separation date from active service. You must use all of your benefits by that time, or you'll lose what's left.

If your service ended on or after January 1, 2013, your benefits won't expire because of a law called the Forever GI Bill—Harry W. Colmery Veterans Educational Assistance Act.

How VA Determines Post-9/11 GI Bill Coverage

Post-9/11 GI Bill benefits cover in-state tuition and rates and public schools at the percentage a veteran is eligible for. Even if someone is an out-of-state student, they may be able to get the in-state tuition rate. Post-9/11 GI Bill benefits cover tuition at private schools at the current national maximum amount.

To determine how much of a veteran's tuition and fees will be covered at a public school, the veteran will need the following information:
- How much the school they want to attend charges for in-state tuition and fees.
- Whether the school they want to attend offers the in-state tuition rate to veterans who live out-of-state.
- What percentage of Post-9/11 GI Bill benefits you're eligible for.

If you want to attend a public school in the state where you live, the state will offer you in-state tuition. Your Post-9/11 GI Bill benefits will cover you at the percentage you're eligible for.

Member Serves	Percentage of Maximum Benefit Payable
At least 36 months	100%
At least 30 continuous days on active duty and discharged due to service-connected disability	100%
At least 30 months, but less than 36 months	90%
At least 24 months, but less than 30 months	80%
At least 18 months, but less than 24 months	70%
At least 12 months, but less than 18 months	60%
At least 6 months, but less than 12 months	50%
At least 90 days, but less than 6 months	40%

As an example, if the in-state tuition at a public school is $22,000, the amount that the VA will cover depends on the percentage you're entitled to. If you're entitled to 100% of your Post-9/11 GI Bill benefits, the VA will cover the full cost of tuition and fees. If you're entitled to 70%, the VA would cover $15,400 of your tuition and fees, and you'd be responsible for the rest.

If you want to go to an out-of-state public school that offers VA-approved programs, under the Veterans Choice Act, the school must offer you the in-state rate, and your benefits will cover you at your eligible percentage.

If you want to attend an out-of-state public school that doesn't offer in-state rates to veterans, the school will charge the out-of-state tuition rate. Your Post-9/11 Gi Bill benefits will cover you at the percentage you're eligible for only up to the amount of the in-state tuition rate.

If you qualify for the Yellow Ribbon Program, you may be able to get additional payments to help you cover the remaining amount.

Enrollment Verification

If you're receiving education benefits through the Post-9/11 GI Bill, you can easily verify your enrollment using the VA's online tool.

Sign In to Confirm Your Enrollment

To get started, sign in using your existing ID.me or Login.gov account. If you don't have either account, you can quickly create a free account with either service.

What Information Will Be Verified?

When verifying your enrollment, VA will ask you to confirm two key details:
- Your credit hours or clock hours
- The start and end dates of your enrollment for the current month

Other Ways to Verify Your Enrollment
- **By Text** Once your program begins, the VA may send a text asking if you would like to verify your enrollment. If you opt-in, they will send a monthly text reminder to confirm your enrollment.
- **By Email** If you prefer not to receive text messages or don't use texting, the VA can send you an email instead. They will send this email to the address they have on file for you.
- **Online through Ask VA** Enrollment verification can also be done through Ask VA. When using this method, make sure to include your enrollment dates in your message.
- **By Phone** You can also verify your enrollment by calling the VA at 888-442-4551 (TTY: 711). They are available Monday through Friday, from 8:00 a.m. to 7:00 p.m. ET.

Overview of the Post-9/11 GI Bill

Feature	Details
Purpose	Provides education benefits to veterans, service members, and their families who served after Sept. 10, 2001.
Eligibility	At least 90 days of active-duty service after Sept. 10, 2001.
	Honorable discharge or discharge due to a service-connected disability.
	Includes active-duty National Guard and Reserve members.
Time Limit to Use Benefits	Generally, 15 years from separation date for those discharged before Jan. 1, 2013.
	No time limit for those discharged on or after Jan. 1, 2013.
Benefit Amount	Covers up to 100% of in-state tuition and fees at public institutions.
	Monthly housing allowance (MHA) based on location of the school.

	Up to $1,000 annually for books and supplies.
	Yellow Ribbon Program for costs exceeding public tuition rates (participating schools only).
Programs Covered	College degree programs.
	Non-college degree programs, vocational training, and certifications.
	Flight training, correspondence courses, and licensing exams.
	On-the-job training (OJT), apprenticeships, and entrepreneurial training.
Transfer of Benefits	Eligible service members can transfer unused benefits to spouses or dependents.
	Requires six years of service with an agreement to serve four more years.
Housing Allowance	Based on location of school and enrollment status (full-time vs. part-time).
	Not available for those taking all online courses.
Key Features	No monetary contribution required from service members.
	Includes benefits for active-duty members, veterans, and their families.
How to Apply	File VA Form 22-1990 through VA.gov or eBenefits.

Transferring Post-9/11 GI Bill Benefits

You may be able to transfer your Post-9/11 GI Bill benefits if you're on active duty or in the Selected Reserve and you meet all of these requirements:
- You've completed at least 6 years of service on the date your request is approved, and
- You agree to add 4 more years of service, and
- The person getting benefits has enrolled in the Defense Enrollment Eligibility Reporting System (DEERS)

If DoD approves the Transfer of Entitlement, a spouse or dependent children can apply for up to 35 months of benefits, including money for tuition, housing, books and supplies.

Spouses:
- May use the benefit right away
- May use the benefit while the veteran is on active duty or after they've separated from service
- Don't qualify for the monthly housing allowance while you're on active duty
- May use the benefit for up to 15 years after the veteran's separation from active duty

Children:
- May start to use the benefit only after the veteran has finished at least 10 years of service

- May use the benefit while the veteran is on active duty or after they've separated from service
- May not use the benefit until they've gotten a high school diploma or equivalency certificate or have reached the age of 18
- Qualify for the monthly housing allowance even when you're on active duty
- Don't have to use the benefit within 15 years after your separation from active duty, but can't use the benefit after they've turned 26 years old

Your dependents may still qualify even if a child marries or you and your spouse divorce. Servicemembers and veterans can cancel or change a TOE at any time. If a veteran wants to revoke benefits for a dependent and they're still in the service, they should turn in another transfer request for the dependent through milConnect. If a dependent's transfer eligibility has been totally revoked, the veteran can't transfer benefits again to that dependent.

While you're still on active duty, you request a transfer, change or revocation of TOE through milConnect and not the VA. If the DoD approves the TOE, family members may apply for benefits.

If your family member is able to apply for benefits, they can apply online or by mail. They should fill out an Application for Family Member to Use Transferred Benefits (VA Form 22-1990E) and mail it to the nearest VA regional office.

Full Rates for School and Training Programs— Effective August 1, 2024, to July 31, 2025

VA sends tuition and fees directly to the school or training program. The amounts listed are full monthly rates. If you're eligible for a percentage of the full benefit, you should multiple the rate by your percentage to find the amount of your monthly payment.

Public Institution of Higher Learning (Like a State University or Community College)

VA will pay the net tuition and mandatory fees. You may be eligible for in-state tuition rates at a public school even if you haven't lived in the state where the school is located.

Private Institution of Higher Learning

VA will pay the net tuition and mandatory fees up to $28,937.09.

Foreign Institution of Higher Learning (Outside of the U.S. Whether Public or Private)

VA will pay the net tuition and mandatory fees up to $28,937.09 in U.S. dollars.

Non-College Degree Programs

VA will pay the net tuition and mandatory fees up to $28,937.09.

Flight Training

VA will pay the net tuition and mandatory fees up to $16,535.46.

Money For Books and Supplies

You may be eligible for up to $1,000 each academic year for books and supplies. This is based on how many courses you're enrolled in for the year and the percentage of benefits you're eligible for. VA pays the benefit at the start of each term.

Monthly Housing Allowance

You may be eligible for money to help pay your housing while you study. If you're eligible for a monthly housing allowance (MHA) you're paid at the end of each month. The VA pays a percentage of the full monthly housing allowance based on two factors—the percentage of Post- 9/11 GI Bill benefits you're eligible for and how many credits you're taking.

If you're taking online classes only, VA will pay a housing allowance that's half the national average.

If you're taking flight or correspondence training, you aren't eligible for MHA.

If you need money to help you relocate from a highly rural area so you can attend school, the VA may give you a one-time payment of $500 to help with your moving expenses. You must live in a county with no more than six people per square mile, as determined by the most recent U.S. Census.

You need to physically relocate at least 500 miles away from your home to attend school or you need to travel by air to physically attend school because you don't have the option to travel by car, train, bus or other ground transportation.

Covered Expenses

Benefit Payments for Test Fees and Prep Courses

Effective from August 1, 2024, to July 31, 2025

Licensing and Certification Test Fees and Prep Courses
- **Test Fees:**
  VA will cover up to **$2,000** for qualifying licensing and certification test fees. Your entitlement will be charged at a rate of **1 month** for every **$2,414.18** in fees paid for licensing and certification tests.

- **Prep Courses:**
  For prep courses that help you prepare for licensing or certification tests, your entitlement will be charged at a rate of **1 month** for every **$2,348.36** in fees paid for these courses.

College Funds

If the member is eligible for a "kicker," such as the Army or Navy College Fund, or a Reserve "Kicker," he or she will still receive the extra monthly benefit under the new GI bill. This monthly amount will be paid to the member, not to the university.

VEAP & the Post-9/11 Benefit

If someone is eligible for both VEAP and the Post-9/11 GI Bill he or she may un-enroll from VEAP and receive a refund of contributions or leave the remaining contributions in the VEAP account and remain eligible for both benefit programs.

NOTE: Students may not receive benefits under more than one program at the same time.

Yellow Ribbon Program

The Yellow Ribbon Program can help pay for higher out-of-state, private school, foreign school or graduate school tuition and fees not covered by the Post-9/11 GI Bill.

To be eligible you must qualify for the Post-9/11 Bill at a 100% benefit level, and at least one of the following has to be true:
- You served at least 36 months on active duty—this can be all at once, or with breaks in the service, and you were honorably discharged, or
- You received a Purple Heart on or after September 11, 2001, and were honorably discharged after any amount of service, or
- You served at least 30 continuous days, all at once without a break on or after September 11, 2001, and were discharged or released from active duty for a service- connected disability, or
- You're an active-duty service member who has served at least 36 months on active duty either all at once or with breaks in service, or
- You're a spouse using the transferred benefits of an active-duty service member who has served at least 36 months on active duty, or
- You're a dependent child using benefits transferred by a veteran, or
- You're a Fry Scholar

Your school has to meet certain requirements. All of the following has to be true of your school:
- Your school is an institution of higher learning, and
- Your school offers the Yellow Ribbon Program, and
- Your school hasn't offered the Yellow Ribbon benefit to more than the maximum number of students in their agreement with VA, and

- Your school has certified your enrollment with VA and provided Yellow Ribbon Program information

If you qualify for the Yellow Ribbon program, your school contributes a certain amount toward your additional tuition and fees through a grant, scholarship or similar program. The VA will match the contribution.

If you qualify for Post-9/11 GI Bill benefits, you'll get a Certificate of Eligibility or COE. You turn your COE into your school's certifying official, or the financial aid, military liaison or appropriate office. You then ask to apply for the Yellow Ribbon program at the school.

The school will make a decision based on whether it's already enrolled the maximum number of students for the program period, and how much funding you would receive.

Work-Study Program

The veterans work-study program allows you to earn money while enrolled in a college, vocational school, or professional training program.

Eligibility

To participate, you must meet these criteria:

- Be enrolled at least 3/4-time in an approved education or training program.
- Complete the work-study contract while still eligible for education benefits.
- Use an approved VA education program, such as the Post-9/11 GI Bill, Montgomery GI Bill, VEAP, or other qualifying programs.

Benefits

You can earn money working part-time while you study, with jobs related to VA or veterans' services.

How to Apply
Complete the **VA Form 22-8691** (Application for Work-Study Allowance). For questions, contact your VA regional processing office or your school's financial aid office.

Job Locations

Eligible job sites include:
- VA facilities, regional offices, and health care centers
- Educational institutions and state Veterans agencies
- Veterans Service Organizations (VSOs)
- Hospitals and state Veterans homes

If using Montgomery GI Bill Selected Reserve benefits, you may also work at Department of Homeland Security or Defense Department locations.

Pay

You'll earn at least the federal or state minimum wage, whichever is higher. If your school pays more, they may cover the difference.

Payment

You can choose to receive advance payment for up to 40% of your work-study hours or 50 hours, whichever is less. Afterward, you'll receive payments for every 50 hours worked or every other week.

Work Hours

You can work during or between enrollment periods, with a maximum of 25 times the number of weeks in your enrollment period (e.g., 375 hours for a 15-week semester).

CHAPTER 15

EDUCATION BENEFITS - MONTGOMERY G.I. BILL – SELECTED RESERVE (MGIB- SR), CHAPTER 1606

The Montgomery GI Bill-Selected Reserve Program is for members of the Selected Reserve, including the Army Reserve, Navy Reserve, Air Force Reserve, Marine Corps Reserve, Coast Guard Reserve, Army National Guard and Air National Guard. While the reserve components decide who is eligible for the program, VA makes the payments for the program. Chapter 1606 is the first educational program that does not require service in the active Armed Forces in order to qualify.

Eligibility Requirements

You could be eligible for benefits under the MGIB-SR program if one of the following is true:
- You have a 6-year service obligation in the Selected Service, meaning you agreed to serve 6 years, or
- You're an officer in the Selected Reserve and you agreed to serve 6 years in addition to your initial service obligation.

Your obligation must have started after June 30, 1985, or for some types of training after September 3, 1990. All of these have to be true too:
- You complete your initial active duty for training (IADT), and
- You get a high school diploma or certificate of equal value like a GED before finishing IADT—you can't use 12 hours toward a college degree to meet this requirement, and
- You remain in good standing while you're serving in an active Selected Reserve unit—you'll still be eligible if you're discharged from Selected Reserve service due to a disability not caused by misconduct.

You can receive benefits until your eligibility period ends or you use all of your entitlement—whichever comes first. Entitlement is the number of months of benefits you may receive. The VA might extend the eligibility period if you're called to active duty. If this were to happen, the VA would extend your eligibility for the amount of time you're mobilized plus four months.

Your eligibility for the program typically ends the day you leave the Selected Reserve, with a few exceptions. You can still qualify for MGIB-SR benefits for up to 14 years from the date of your first 6-year obligation if at least one of the following is true for you:
- You separated because of a disability not caused by misconduct, or
- Your unit was deactivated between October 1, 2007, and September 30, 2014, or
- You involuntarily separated for reasons other than misconduct between October 1, 2007, and September 30, 2014

ROTC (Reserve Officers' Training Corps) scholarship under section 2107 of title 10, Code:

An individual can't be eligible for MGIB–SR if he or she is receiving financial assistance through the Senior ROTC program under this section of the law.

Note: However, an individual may still be eligible for MGIB – SR if he or she receives financial assistance under **Section 2107a** of title 10, U.S. Code. This financial assistance program is for specially selected members of the Army Reserve and National Guard only. Individuals should check with their ROTC advisor for more information.

Note: There's no restriction on service academy graduates receiving MGIB – SR. Service academy graduates who received a commission aren't eligible under MGIB – AD.

If an individual enters Active Guard and Reserve (AGR) status, his or her eligibility for MGIB – SR will be suspended. He or she may be eligible for MGIB – AD. The individual may resume MGIB – SR eligibility after AGR status ends.

Approved Courses

Individuals may receive benefits for a wide variety of training, including:
- Undergraduate degrees from a college or university;
- Beginning November 30, 1993, graduate degrees from a college or university;
- Accredited independent study programs leading to standard college degrees;
- Technical courses for a certificate at a college or university.

Individuals with 6-year commitments beginning after September 30, 1990 may take the following types of training:
- Courses leading to a certificate or diploma from business, technical, or vocational schools;

- Cooperative training;
- Apprenticeship or job training programs offered by companies;
- Correspondence training;
- Independent study programs;
- Flight training (Individuals must have a private pilot's license, and must meet the medical requirements for the desired license program before beginning training, and throughout the flight training program.)

VA may approve programs offered by institutions outside of the United States, when they are pursued at educational institutions of higher learning, and lead to a college degree. Individuals must receive VA approval prior to attending or enrolling in any foreign programs.

Eligibility for this program is determined by the Selected Reserve components. Payments for the program are made by the VA. A state agency or VA must approve each program offered by a school or company. If an individual is seeking a college degree, the school must admit the individual to a degree program by the start of the individual's third term.

Restrictions on Training

Benefits are not payable for the following courses: Courses paid by the military Tuition Assistance program, if student is enrolled at less than ½ time;

- Courses taken while student is receiving a Reserve Officers' Training Corps scholarship;
- Non-accredited independent study courses;
- Bartending and personality development courses;
- Any course given by radio;
- Self-improvement courses such as reading, speaking, woodworking, basic seamanship, and English as a 2nd language;
- Any course which is avocational or recreational in character;
- Farm-cooperative courses;
- Audited courses;
- Courses not leading to an educational, professional, or vocational objective;
- Courses previously taken and successfully completed;
- Courses taken by a Federal government employee under the Government Employee's Training Act;
- Courses taken while in receipt of benefits for the same program from the Office of Workers' Compensation Programs.

VA must reduce benefits for individuals in Federal, State, or local prisons after being convicted of a felony.

An individual may not receive benefits for a program at a proprietary school if he or she is an owner or official of the school.

Part-Time Training

Individuals unable to attend school full-time should consider going part-time. Benefit rates and entitlement charges are less than the full-time rates. For example, if a student receives full-time benefits for 12 months, the entitlement charge is 12 months. However, if the student receives ½ time benefits for 12 months, the charge is 6 months. VA will pay for less than ½ time training if the student is not receiving Tuition Assistance for those courses.

Remedial, Deficiency and Refresher Training

Remedial and deficiency courses are intended to assist a student in overcoming a deficiency in a particular area of study. Individuals may qualify for benefits for remedial, deficiency, and refresher courses if they have a 6-year commitment that began after September 30,1990. In order for such courses to be approved, the courses must be deemed necessary for pursuit of a program of education.

Refresher training is for technological advances that occurred in a field of employment. The advance must have occurred while the student was on active duty, or after release. There is an entitlement charge for these courses.

Tutorial Assistance

Students may receive a special allowance for individual tutoring performed after September 30, 1992, if they entered school at one-half time or more. To qualify, the student must have a deficiency in a subject. The school must certify the tutor's qualifications, and the hours of tutoring. Eligible students may receive a maximum monthly payment of $100.00. The maximum total benefit payable is $1,200.00.

There is no entitlement charge for the first $600.00 of tutorial assistance.

To apply for tutorial assistance, students must submit VA Form 22-1990t, "Application and Enrollment Certification for Individualized Tutorial Assistance." The form should be given to the certifying official in the office handling VA paperwork at the school for completion.

Months of Benefits/Entitlements Charged

Eligible members may be entitled to receive up to 36 months of education benefits. Benefit entitlement ends 10 years from the date the member becomes eligible for the program, or on the day the member leaves the Selected Reserve. (If a member's Reserve or National Guard unit was deactivated during the period October 1, 1991, through September 30, 1999, or if the member was involuntarily separated from service during this same period, eligibility for MGIB-SR benefits is retained for the full 10-year eligibility period. Eligibility for MGIB-SR benefits is also retained if a member is discharged due to a disability that was not caused by misconduct. Eligibility periods may be extended if a member is ordered to active duty.)

Individuals qualifying for more than one VA education program may receive a maximum of 48 months of benefits. For example, if a student used 30 months of Dependents' Educational Assistance, and is eligible for chapter 1606 benefits, he or she could have a maximum of 18 months of entitlement remaining.

Individuals are charged one full day of entitlement for each day of full-time benefits paid. For correspondence and flight training, one month of entitlement is charged each time VA pays one month of benefits. For cooperative programs, one month of entitlement is used for each month of benefits paid.

For apprenticeship and job training programs, the entitlement charge changes every 6 months. During the first 6 months, the charge is 75% of full time. For the second 6 months, the charge is 55% of full time. For the remainder of the program, the charge is 35% of full time.

Rates of Educational Assistance Pay

The following basic monthly rates are effective October 1, 2024, to September 30, 2025

Basic Monthly Rates Montgomery GI Bill Selected Reserve (MGIB-SR), Chapter 1606				
Type of Training	**Full-Time**	**¾ Time**	**½ Time**	**Less Than ½ Time**
Institutional	$481.00	$360.00	$240.00	$120.25
Cooperative Training	$481.00 (Full-Time Only)			
Correspondence Training	Entitlement charged at the rate of one month for each $481.00 paid (Payment for correspondence courses is made at 55% of the approved charges for the course.)			
Apprenticeship On-The-Job Training	First six months: $360.75 for each full month Second six months: $264.55 for each full month Remainder of program: $168.35 for each full month			
Flight Training	Entitlement charged at the rate of one month for each $481.00 paid (Payment for flight training is made at 60% of the approved charges for the course, including solo hours.)			

Eligibility Periods

Under previous law, benefits typically ended upon separation from the Reserves. Section 530 of the National Defense Authorization Act of 2008 increased the time period that a reservist may use MGIB-SR benefits to ten years after separation from the Reserves, as long as the member's discharge characterization is honorable. This revision has been backdated to October 28, 2004.

For individuals who separated from the Selected Reserve prior to 10/28/2004, generally benefits end the day of separation. For individuals who stayed in the Selected Reserve, generally benefits ended 14 years from the date the individual became eligible for the program.

Exceptions: If an individual stayed in the Selected Reserve, VA could generally extend the 14-year period if:
- The individual couldn't train due to a disability caused by Selected Reserve service; or
- The individual was activated for service in the Persian Gulf Era (which hasn't ended for purposes of VA education benefits); or
- The individual's eligibility expired during a period of his or her enrollment in training.

Application for Benefits

To apply for these benefits, follow these steps:
1. **Obtain your Notice of Basic Eligibility (DD Form 2384-1)**
   Your unit will provide this form and will also input your eligibility into the Department of Defense (DoD) system to verify it.
2. **Ensure your program is approved**
   Before you enroll, check with your school or use the GI Bill Comparison Tool to confirm that your program is approved for VA education benefits. If you have any questions, contact the VA directly at 888-442-4551 (TTY: 711) or submit a query online.

Note: If your program is not yet approved, ask your school to request approval from the VA. The VA will not take action until the school submits this request. Until the program is approved, you will be responsible for covering all costs, including tuition and fees.

1. **Submit your application for MGIB-SR benefits**
   a. *If you haven't started training yet*: Complete and submit the Application for VA Education Benefits (VA Form 22-1990) online.
   b. *If you've already begun training*: Download and complete VA Form 22-1990.
2. **Submit your forms to your school or employer**
   Provide your application and your Notice of Basic Eligibility to your school or employer. Ask them to complete VA Form 22-1999 and submit all the forms to the VA.
3. **Certify your enrollment**
   Your school or training program must certify your enrollment. This can be done by an official from your school's financial aid, Veterans Affairs, registrar, admissions, or counseling office. If you are in an on-the-job training or apprenticeship program, the official may be from the training, finance, or human resources department.

Note: Remember to verify your enrollment at the end of each month to continue receiving payments.

Verifying Enrollment

To receive Montgomery GI Bill benefits, you must verify your enrollment if both of these apply to you:
1. You are enrolled in a higher education institution or a non-college degree program (such as HVAC repair or truck driving training).
2. You are enrolled at least half-time.

You do not need to verify your enrollment if you are participating in an apprenticeship, on-the-job training, flight training, or correspondence courses. Keep in mind that without verifying your enrollment, your monthly benefits payment will not be sent.

When do I need to verify my enrollment?

You must verify your enrollment at the end of each month after your classes begin. For example, if your classes start on August 5, you should verify your enrollment on or after August 31.

If you were enrolled for any part of a month, you must verify your enrollment for that month. For instance, if your school ends on May 5, you'll need to verify your enrollment for May on or after May 5.

How do I check my enrollment details?

You can view your enrollment information by signing in to the online tool. You can also find this information in your education decision letter.

What if my enrollment information is incorrect?

If there are any discrepancies in your enrollment details, contact your School Certifying Official (SCO) to update the information promptly. Once your enrollment is verified, your benefit payment will be processed, and it may take up to 5 days for the payment to reach you.

How do I update my contact information for enrollment verification?

You can update your contact information by:
• Contacting the VA through Ask VA
• Calling the VA at 888-442-4551 (TTY: 711), or +1-918-781-5678 if you're outside the U.S.

Additionally, you can update your contact and direct deposit details online.

Note: Changes made using this tool will only affect your contact and direct deposit information related to Montgomery GI Bill benefits. To update other benefit-related information, you'll need to access your VA.gov profile.

CHAPTER 16

CAREERS & EMPLOYMENT

If a veteran has a service-connected disability limiting their ability to work, or one that prevents them from working, the Veteran Readiness and Employment program can help. The program was formerly called Vocational Rehabilitation and Employment, and it's also known as Chapter 31 or VR& E.

The program helps veterans explore employment options, address training and education needs, and in some cases, family members can qualify for benefits.

There are several tracks available.

Reemployment Track

This track is available to veterans with a service-connected disability. It's meant to help a veteran return to their former job and support their employer in meeting their needs. Veterans are protected under the Uniformed Services Employment and Reemployment Rights Act or USERRA. You can't be disadvantaged in your civilian career because of your service.

A Vocational Rehabilitation Counselor or VRC can help provide a veteran with a full range of services and can direct the veteran to the Department of Labor to start the process.

You may be eligible if you're a veteran with a service-connected disability, and you meet all of the following requirements:
- You have an employment barrier or handicap, and
- Your enrolled in Veteran Readiness and Employment (VR&E), and
- You'd like to return to your former job.

Note: Having an employment handicap means your service-connected disability limits your ability to prepare for, obtain and maintain suitable employment (a job that doesn't make your disability worse, is stable and matches your abilities aptitudes and interests).

You may be eligible for benefits related to helping you return to the job you held before you deployed.

You'll need to first apply for VR&E benefits. Then, you'll work with your Vocational

Rehabilitation Counselor.

You can get training and hands-on work experience through programs including:
- The VR&E Special Employer Incentive Program or SEI, which is for eligible veterans who face challenges getting a job.
- The VR&E Non-Paid Work Experience program or NPWE for eligible veterans and service members who have an established career goal and learn easily in a hands-on environment or are having trouble getting a job due to a lack of work experience.

Rapid Access to Employment Track

If a veteran wants to follow an employment path using their existing skill set, the Rapid Access to Employment Track can help them. Counseling and rehabilitation services are available.

You may be eligible if you're a servicemember or veteran with a service-connected disability and you meet all of the following requirements:
- You have an employment handicap or barrier, and
- You're enrolled in VR&E, and
- You already have experience, education or training in your field of interest.

Available benefits include tools to help with the job search, professional or vocational counseling, help with writing a resume and preparing for interviews, and help determining if you're eligible for Veterans' Preference.

You'll first need to apply for VR&E benefits, and then work with your Vocational Rehabilitation Counselor.

Self-Employment Track

If a servicemember or veteran has a service-connected disability and employment barrier, but the strong desire, skills and drive to run a business, they could be interested in the Self-Employment track.

You maybe be eligible if you're a servicemember or veteran with a service-connected disability, and you meet all of the following requirements:
- You have an employment barrier or handicap, and
- You're enrolled in VR&E, and
- Your service-connected disability makes it hard for you to prepare for, obtain and maintain suitable employment. Suitable employment is a job that doesn't worsen your disability, is stable, and matches your abilities, aptitudes and interests.

Benefits available through the VR&E Self-Employment Tract include:
- Coordination of services and help in the creation of a proposed business plan
- Analysis of your business concept
- Training in small business operations, marketing and finances

- Guidance in getting the right resources to implement a business plan

After you develop a business plan, the VA will review it and evaluate whether self-employment and the proposed business are viable options.

To get these benefits, first you have to apply for VR&E benefits. Then you begin to work with your Vocational Rehabilitation Counselor.

Employment Through Long-Term Services Track

If you have a service-connected disability that makes it hard to succeed in your employment path, you might be interested in the Employment Through Long-Term Services track. The VA can help you get education and training needed to find work in a different filed, better suiting your current interests and abilities.

You may be eligible for both VR&E training and GI bill benefits, so you have to decide which benefit you want to use.

Available benefits through this VR&E tract include:
- A complete skills assessment
- Career guidance
- Job market evaluation
- Education and training for a professional or vocational field that's a good fit for you
- Apprenticeship, on-the-job training and volunteer opportunities
- Employment assistance

To be eligible, the following must be true:
- You have an employment barrier or handicap, and
- You're enrolled in VR&E, and
- Your service-connected disability makes it hard for you to prepare for, obtain and maintain suitable employment.

Independent Living Track

Under the VR&E Independent Living Track, if your service-connected disability limits your ability to perform activities of daily living such as bathing, dressing or interacting with others, and you can't return to work right away, you might qualify for independent living services through the Independent Living track. You might also receive the services as you work on finding a job, if that's your goal that you've created with your Vocational Rehabilitation Counselor (VRC). In both scenarios, your VRC can help restore your activities of daily living.

You may be eligible for independent living services if you are a servicemember or veteran with a service-connected disability who's eligible for VR&E benefits, and you meet all of the following requirements:
- You have a serious employment handicap (SEH), and
- Your disabilities prevent you from looking for or returning to work, and
- You're in need of services to live as independently as possible

Depending on your needs, services may include:
- Evaluation and counseling to identify needs and goal
- Referral to support resources
- Evaluation to see if you're eligible for the VR&E home adaptation grant. The grant is part of a rehabilitation plan to improve accessibility features in the home.
- Guidance to help you understand if you're eligible for the VA's adaptive housing programs. These programs help people make changes to their home, such as widening doorways or adding ramps, so they can live more independently.

The services generally last up to 24 months. In some cases, you could be able to use services for longer.

Support for a Veteran-Owned Small Business

If someone has a Veteran-Owned Small Business, they may qualify for advantages when bidding on government contracts and access to other resources and support through the Vets First Verification Program.

The Vets First Verification Program is run by the Office Small & Disadvantaged Business Utilization (OSDBU). Registering through OSDBU will let the veteran work with the VA.

You may be eligible if you're a veteran and you or another veteran at your company meet the following requirements. All of the following must be true of you or another veteran at your company:

- One of you owns 51% or more of the company you want to register, and
- One of you has full control over the day-to-day management, decision-making and strategic policy of the business, and
- One of you has the managerial experience needed to manage the business, and
- One of you is the highest-paid person in the company or can provide a written statement explaining why your taking lower pay helps the business, and
- One of you works full time for the business, and
- One of you holds the highest officer position in the company

To be considered a veteran, at least one of these must be true:
- You served on active duty with the Army, Air Force, Navy, Marine Corps or Coast Guard for any length of time and didn't receive a dishonorable discharge, or
- You served as a Reservist or member of the National Guard and were called to federal active duty or disabled from a disease or injury that started or got worse in the line of duty or while in training status

You may be eligible to register your business as a Service-Disabled Veteran-Owned Small Business (SDVOSB) if you meet all of the requirements of a VOSB listed above, and either you or another veteran owner of the company meet at least one requirement listed below:

- A disability rating letter from VA confirming you have a service-connected disability rating between 0 and 100%, or
- A disability determination from the Department of Defense

If you received an other than honorable, bad conduct or dishonorable discharge you may not be eligible for VA benefits. You can try to apply for a discharge upgrade or learn about the VA Character of Discharge Review Process.

The U.S. Small Business Administration (SBA) can also provide you with resources to help you grow or start a business, and many universities or nonprofits also offer free or low-cost entrepreneur and business-focused courses for veterans and military family members.

SBA Support for Veteran-Owned Businesses

The SBA offers support for veterans as they enter the world of owning a business.

The Office of Veterans Business Development is devoted exclusively to the promotion of veteran entrepreneurship. The OVBD facilitates the U.S. of all SBA programs by veterans, service-disabled veterans, reservists, active-duty service members, transitioning service members, and their dependents or survivors.

SBA programs provide access to capital and preparation for small business opportunities, and they can connect veteran small business owners with federal procurement and commercial supply chains.

The Veterans Business Outreach Center Program is an initiative that oversees Veteran Business Outreach Centers (VBOC) across the country.

You can use SBA tools including Lender Match to connect with lenders.

SBA also makes special consideration for veterans through programs including the Military Reservist Economic Injury Disaster Loan Program. This program provides loans of up to $2 million to cover operating costs that can't be met due to the loss of an essential employee called to active duty in the Reserves or National Guard

Veteran Contracting Assistance Programs

Every year the federal government awards a portion of contracting dollars specifically to businesses owned by veterans. Small businesses owned by veterans may also be eligible to buy surplus property from the federal government.

Veteran Small Business Certification (VetCert) Program

Certification with SBA allows service-disabled veteran-owned small businesses (SDVOSBs) to compete for federal sole-source and set-aside contracts across the federal government. Certified veteran-owned small businesses (VOSBs) have additional opportunities to pursue sole-source and set-aside contracts at the VA under the VA's Vet First Program.

SBA's Veteran Small Business Certification program implemented changes from the National Defense Authorization Act for Fiscal Year 2021 (NDAA 2021) which transferred the certification function from the VA to SBA on January 1, 2023.

The transfer provides veterans with central support for their small business certification needs, and the final rule was published in the Federal Register on November 29, 2022.

Benefits include the ability to compete for sole-source and set-aside contracts across the federal government. Self-certified firms seeking these restriction competition opportunities had to apply to SBA for certification by December 31, 2023.

To apply for certification with SBA as a VOSB or SDVOSB, a firm has to meet the following requirements:
- Be considered a small business as defined by the size standard corresponding to any NAICS code listed in the businesses' SAM profile
- Have no less than 51% of the business owned and controlled by one or more veterans.
- For certification as a SDVOSB, have no less than 51% of the business owned and controlled by one or more veterans rated as service-disabled by the VA.
- For veterans who are permanently and totally disabled and unable to manage the daily business operations of their business, their business may still qualify for their spouse or appointed, permanent caregiver is assisting in the management.

Certification Transfer from the VA and One-Year Extension
- Firms certified by the VA Center for Verification and Evaluation (CVE) as of January 1, 2023, were automatically granted certification by the SBA for the remainder of the firm's eligibility period.
- SBA granted a one-time, one-year extension of certification to current VOSBs and SDVOSBs verified by the VA as of the transfer date on January 1, 2023. The additional year was added to the existing eligibility period of a current participant.
- New applications certified by SBA after January 1, 2023, received the standard three- year certification period.

Grace Period for Self-Certified Firms
- The NDAA 2021 granted a one-year grace period for self-certified SDVOSBs until January 1, 2024. During the grace period, self-certified businesses had one year to file an application for SDVOSB certification and could continue to rely on their self-certification to compete for non-VA SDVOSB set-aside contracts.
- Self-certified SDVOSBs that applied before January 1, 2024, kept eligibility through the expiration of the grace period until SBA issues a final eligibility

decision.
- VOSBs and SDVOSBs seeking sole-source and set-aside opportunities with the VA must be certified. There is no grace period.

How to Apply for Certification

SBA started accepting applications for certification on January 9, 2023, through the application portal available from the SBA.

Surplus Personal Property for Veteran-Owned Small Business Programs

Veteran-owned small businesses can access federally owned personal property no longer in use through the General Service Administration's Federal Surplus Personal Property Donation Program. GSA oversees the reuse and donation of federal personal property.

State Agency for Surplus Property operations manage surplus property disbursement.

VOSBs may get federal surplus property in the state where the property will be primarily located and used. You have to agree in writing that your VOSB:
- Is located and operated within the state
- Is unconditionally owned and controlled by one or more eligible veterans, service- disabled veterans or surviving spouses
- Has registered and is in verified status in the VA's Vets First Verification Program database
- After January 1, 2023, to be eligible, a VOSB had to show certified status in SBA's VetCert database
- Will use the property in the normal conduct of its business activities—personal or not- business use isn't allowed
- Will not sell, transfer, loan, lease, encumber or otherwise dispose of the property during the period of restriction unless with express written authorization
- Will get permission from donating SASP before permanently removing the property from the state
- Will use the property as intended within one year of receipt
- Will maintain VOSB eligibility with VA and SASP for the duration of the applicable federal period of restriction for donated property
- Will give SBA, GSA and SASP access to inspect the property and all pertinent records

Subsistence Allowance

In some cases, veterans who participate in the VR&E program might receive a subsistence allowance while they pursue their educational or training program to prepare for a future career. The subsistence allowance is paid every month and is based on the rate of attendance in a training program—full time, three-quarter time or half-time. It's also based on the number of dependents and the type of training.

If a veteran qualifies for the Post-9/11 GI Bill, they might be eligible to receive the Basic Allowance for Housing (BAH) rate for subsistence.

The following Subsistence Allowance rates are paid for training in an Institution of Higher Learning for FY 2025, based on a 3.2% CPI Increase.

Number of Dependents	Full Time	¾ Time	½ Time	¼ Time
No Dependents	$793.01	$595.86	$398.69	$199.32
One Dependent	$983.65	$738.81	$493.97	$247.02
Two Dependents	$1159.17	$866.65	$580.64	$290.33
Each Additional Dependent	$84.47	$64.98	$43.34	$21.62

Subsistence Allowance is paid for full time training only, in the following training programs:

Non-pay or nominal pay on-job training in a federal, state, local, or federally recognized Indian tribe agency; training in the home; vocational course in a rehabilitation facility or sheltered workshop; institutional non-farm cooperative.

Number of Dependents	Full Time
No Dependents	$793.01
One Dependent	$983.65
Two Dependents	$1159.17
Each Additional Dependent	$84.47

Subsistence Allowance is paid for full time training only in the following training programs:
Farm cooperative, apprenticeship, or other on-job training

Number of Dependents	Full Time
No Dependents	$793.34
One Dependent	$983.65
Two Dependents	$1159.17
Each Additional Dependent	$84.47

Subsistence Allowance is paid at the following rates for combined training programs:
Combination of Institutional and On-Job Training
(Full Time Rate Only).

Number of Dependents	Institutional Greater than one half
No Dependents	$793.01
One Dependent	$983.65
Two Dependents	$1159.17
Additional Dependents	$84.47

Subsistence Allowance is paid at the following rates for Non-farm Cooperative Training:
Non-farm Cooperative Institutional Training and Non-farm Cooperative On-Job Training
(Full Time Rate Only).

Number of Dependents	FT Non-farm Coop/Institutional
No Dependents	$693.34
One Dependent	$838.47
Two Dependents	$966.3
Each Additional Dependent	$62.84

Subsistence Allowance is paid at the following rates for Independent Living programs:

A subsistence allowance is paid each month during the period of enrollment in a rehabilitation facility when a veteran is pursuing an approved Independent Living Program plan. Subsistence allowance paid during a period of Independent Living Services is based on rate of pursuit and number of dependents.

	Full-Time	¾ Time	½ Time	¼ Time
No dependents	$793.01	$595.86	$386.32	$193.14
One dependent	$983.65	$738.81	$493.97	$247.02
Two dependents	$1159.17	$866.65	$580.64	$290.33
Each additional dependent	$84.87	$64.98	$43.34	$21.62

Programs for Unemployable Veterans

Veterans awarded 100% disability compensation based upon unemployability may still request an evaluation, and, if found eligible, may participate in a vocational rehabilitation program and receive help in getting a job. A veteran who secures employment under the special program will continue to receive 100% disability compensation until the veteran has worked continuously for at least 12 months.

Election of Alternate Subsistence Allowance Under Public Law 111- 377

This option is included for your use in comparing subsistence allowance rates that may be available to certain veterans participating in the Chapter 31 program. The VA is authorized to allow a veteran, entitled to both a Chapter 31 subsistence allowance and Post 9/11 GI Bill Chapter 33 educational assistance, to elect to receive a replacement in an alternate amount instead of the regular Chapter 31 subsistence allowance.

The alternate payment will be based on the military basic allowance for housing (BAH) for an E-5 with dependents residing in the zip code of the training facility. Training in foreign institutions and training that is solely on-line or in-home will be based on the national average BAH.

Paralympic Veteran Benefit

Some veterans in training for the U.S. Paralympics may qualify for a monthly subsistence allowance from VA. The allowance is pegged to the subsistence allowance for participants in a fulltime institutional program under chapter 31 of title 38 of the U.S. Code. According to the rule, the VA will pay the allowance to a veteran with a service-connected or non-service-connected disability if the veteran is invited by the U.S. Paralympics to compete for a slot on the U.S. Paralympic team or is residing at the U.S. Paralympic training center for training or competition.

Applications for the allowance must be submitted through the U.S. Paralympics. Through the program, VA will pay a monthly allowance to a veteran with a service-connected or non-service-connected disability if the veteran meets the minimum military standard or higher (e.g., Emerging, Talent Pool, National Team) in his or her respective sport at a recognized competition. Besides making the military standard, an athlete must also be nationally or internationally classified by his or her respective sport federation as eligible for Paralympic competition within six or 12 months of a qualifying performance.

Athletes must also have established training and competition plans and are responsible for turning in monthly and quarterly reports in order to continue receiving a monthly assistance allowance. The monthly allowance rate for an athlete approved for monetary assistance is the same as the 38 U.S.C. Chapter 31 Vocational Rehabilitation & Employment Rate (VR&E), which in FY 2025 starts at $693.35 and increases depending on the number of dependents.

Vocational Training for Children with Spina Bifida

To qualify for entitlement to a vocational training program an applicant must be a child:

- To whom VA has awarded a monthly allowance for spina bifida; and
- For whom VA has determined that achievement of a vocational goal is reasonably feasible.

A vocational training program may not begin before a child's 18th birthday, or the date of completion of secondary schooling, whichever comes first. Depending on the need, a child may be provided up to 24 months of full-time training.

Vocational Training for Children of Female Vietnam Veterans Born with Certain Birth Defects

Section 401of P.L. 106-416, which became law on November1, 2000 directed the Secretary of VA to identify birth defects of children of female Vietnam veterans that: (1) are associated with service during the Vietnam era; and (2) result in the permanent physical or mental disability of such children.

The law excludes from such defects familial or birth-related defects or injuries. The law further directs the Secretary to provide such children a monthly monetary allowance, as well as necessary health care to address the defect and any associated disability.

Veterans' Preference

Veterans' Preference gives eligible veterans preference in appointment over many other applicants. Veterans' Preference applies to all new appointments in the competitive service and many in the excepted service. Veterans' preference doesn't guarantee veterans a job, and it doesn't apply to internal agency actions like promotions, transfers, reassignments or reinstatements.

Applying for Benefits

Interested veterans can apply by filling out "VA Form 28-1900", "Application for Veteran Readiness and Employment for Claimants with Service-Connected Disabilities," and mailing it to the VA regional office serving his or her area.

Resources for Military and Veteran Family Members

If you're a military spouse or surviving spouse, you may be eligible for the Department of Defense's Spouse Education Career Opportunities (SECO) program.

One of the following must be true:
- You're the spouse of an active-duty, National Guard or Reserve service

member in the Army, Marine Corps, Navy or Air Force.
- You are the spouse of a service member who has been separated from active duty, National Guard or Reservists for less than 180 days.
- You are the surviving spouse of a service member who died while on active duty.

Through the Department of Defense's Spouse Education Career Opportunities (SECO) program, spouses can use government-sponsored career and education resources, take advantage of networking opportunities and work with employment counselors. SECO also partners with the Military Spouse Employment Partnership (MSEP) and My Career Advancement Account (MyCAA) scholarship program. These organizations and others, such as Blue Star Families, offer assistance for spouses interested in connecting with employers committed to hiring military spouses and pursuing additional education and/or training.

CHAPTER 17

VETERANS PENSION

The Veterans Pension program provides monthly payments to wartime veterans who meet certain age or disability requirements, and who have income and net worth within certain limits.

You may be eligible if you meet both of these requirements:
- You didn't receive a dishonorable discharge, and
- Your yearly family income and net worth meet certain limits set by Congress. Your net worth includes all personal property you own except your house, car and most home furnishings, minus any debt you owe. Your net worth includes the net worth of your spouse.

At least one of the following must be true about your service:
- You started on active duty before September 8, 1980, and you served at least 90 days on activity duty with at least one day during wartime, or
- You started on active duty as an enlisted person after September 7, 1980, and served at least 24 months or the full period for which you were called to active with some exceptions with at least one day during wartime, or
- You were an officer and started on active duty after October 16, 1981, and you hadn't previously served on active duty for at least 24 months.

At least one of the following must be true:
- You're at least 65 years old, or
- You have a permanent and total disability, or
- You're a patient in a nursing home for long-term care because of a disability, or
- You're getting Social Security Disability Insurance or Supplemental Security income.

Under current law, the VA recognizes the following wartime periods to decide eligibility for VA pension benefits:
- Mexican Border period (May 9, 1916, to April 5, 1917, for Veterans who served in Mexico, on its borders, or in adjacent waters)
- World War I (April 6, 1917, to November 11, 1918)
- World War II (December 7, 1941, to December 31, 1946)
- Korean conflict (June 27, 1950, to January 31, 1955)
- Vietnam War era (November 1, 1955, to May 7, 1975, for Veterans who served in the Republic of Vietnam during that period. August 5, 1964, to

May 7, 1975, for veterans who served outside the Republic of Vietnam.)
- Gulf War (August 2, 1990, through a future date to be set by law or presidential proclamation)

To apply for tax-free VA pension benefits as a veteran, you'll need this information:
- Social Security number or VA file number
- Military history
- Your financial information
- The financial information of your dependents
- Work history
- Bank account direct deposit information
- Medical information

You can apply online, or by mail. If you're applying by mail, you fill out an Application for Pension (VA Form 21P-527EZ). You mail the completed form to the pension management center at:

Department of Veterans Affairs
Pension Intake Center
PO Box5365
Janesville, WI 53547-5365

You can also bring your application to a VA regional office, or you can work with an accredited representative to help when you're applying for VA pension benefits.

VA Aid and Attendance Benefits and Housebound Allowance

VA Aid and Attendance or Housebound benefits provide monthly payments added to the amount of a monthly VA pension for qualified veterans and survivors. You may be eligible if you get a VA pension, and you meet at least one of these requirements:
- You need another person to help you with daily activities like dressing, feeding or bathing, or
- You have to stay in bed or spend a large portion of the day in bed because of illness, or
- You are a patient in a nursing home due to the loss of mental or physical abilities related to a disability, or
- Your eyesight is limited (even with contact lenses or glasses you have only 5/200 or less in both eyes, or concentric contraction of the visual field to 5 degrees or less).

You may be eligible for housebound allowance if you get a VA pension and spend most of your time in your home because of a permanent disability.

You can't get Aid and Attendance and Housebound benefits at the same time.

You can send a complete VA Form 21-2680 (Examination for Housebound Status or Permanent Need for Regular Aid and Attendance) to the PMC for your state.

Your doctor should fill out the examination information section.

You can include other evidence like a doctor's report, details about what you normally do during the day, or details that show what kind of illness or disability affects your ability to do things on your own.

If a veteran is in a nursing home, they'll need to fill out a Request for Nursing Home Information in Connection with Claim for Aid and Attendance (VA Form 21-0779).

VA Pension Rates for Veterans

If you qualify for pension benefits, the VA bases the payment amount on the difference in your countable income and a limit set by Congress, called the Maximum Annual Pension Rate or MAPR. Your countable income is how much you earn. This includes your Social Security benefits, investment and retirement payments, and income your dependents receive. Some expenses, like non-reimbursable medical expenses, may reduce your countable income.

Your MAPR amount is the maximum amount of pension payable. MAPR is based on how many dependents you have, if you're married to another veteran who qualifies for a pension, and if your disabilities qualify you for Housebound or Aid and Attendance benefits. MAPRs are adjusted every year for cost-of-living increases.

Example: You're a qualified veteran with a dependent, non-veteran spouse and no children.

You also qualify for Aid and Attendance benefits based on your disabilities. You and your spouse have a combined yearly income of $10,000.

Your MAPR amount = $31,714 Your yearly income = $10,000
Your VA pension = $21,714 for the year (or $1,809 paid each month)

Net Worth Limit

From December 1, 2024, to November 30, 2025, the net worth limits to be eligible for Veterans Pension benefits is $159,240.

On October 18, 2018, the VA changed the way it assesses net worth to make pension entitlement rules clearer. Net worth includes the veteran and their spouse's assets and annual income.

If the veteran's child's net worth is more than the net worth limit, they aren't considered as a dependent when determining pension.

Assets

Assets include the fair market value of all real and personal property, minus the amount of any mortgages. Real property means land and buildings the veteran may own. Personal property assets can include investments like stocks and bonds, furniture and boats.

Assets don't include your primary residence where you live most of the time, your car, or basic home items like appliances that you wouldn't take with you if you moved to a new house.

Annual Income

For purposes of pensions, annual income is defined as the money earned in a year from a job or from retirement or annuity payments. It includes salary or hourly pay, bonuses, commissions, overtime and tips. The VA will subtract certain expenses from a veteran's annual income when assessing net worth. These are known as applicable deductible expenses, and they include educational expenses and medical expenses you aren't reimbursed for.

3-Year Look-Back Period

When VA receives a pension claim, they review the terms and conditions of any assets the veteran may have transferred in the three years before filing the claim. If a veteran transfers asset for less than fair market value during the look-back period, and those assets would have pushed the veteran's net worth above the limit for a VA pension, they may be subject to a penalty period of up to five years. The veteran isn't eligible for benefits during this time.

This policy took effect on October 18, 2018. If a veteran filed a claim before this date, the look- back period doesn't apply.

A penalty period is the length of time when a veteran isn't eligible for pension benefits because the transferred assets for less than fair market value during the look-back period. The penalty period rate is $2,795.

2025 VA Pension Rates for Veterans

Date of Cost-of-Living Increase: December 1, 2024, Increase Factor: 2.5%
Standard Medicare Deduction: The actual amount will be determined by SSA based on individual income.

For veterans with no dependents

If You Have No Dependents and...	Your Maximum Annual Pension Rate (MAPR) Amount is
You don't qualify for Housebound or Aid and Attendance benefits	$16,695
You qualify for Housebound benefits	$20,732
You qualify for Aid and Attendance Benefits	$28,300

Note: If You have medical expenses, you may deduct only the amount that's above 5% of your MAPR amount ($848 for a veteran with no spouse or child).

For veterans with at least 1 dependent child or spouse

If You Have 1 Dependent and...	Your MAPR Amount Is
You don't qualify for Housebound or Aid and Attendance benefits	$22,216
You qualify for Housebound benefits	$25,982
You qualify for Aid and Attendance benefits	$33,548

Notes:
- If you have more than one dependent, add $2,902 to your MAPR amount for each additional dependent.
- If you have a child who works, you may exclude their wages up to $15,000.
- If you have medical expenses, you may deduct only the amount that's above 5% of your MAPR amount ($1,110 for a veteran with one dependent).

For 2 veterans who are married to each other

If You're 2 Veterans Who Are Married to Each Other and...	Your MAPR Amount Is
Neither of you qualifies for Housebound or Aid and Attendance benefits	$22,216
One of you qualifies for Housebound benefits	$25,982
Both of you qualify for Housebound benefits	$29,747
One of you qualifies for Aid and Attendance benefits	$33,548
One of you qualifies for Housebound benefits and one of you qualifies for Aid and Attendance benefits	$37,305
Both of you qualify for Aid and Attendance benefits	$44,886

Notes:
- If you have more than one dependent, add $2,902 to your MAPR amount for each additional child.
- If you have a child who works, you may exclude their wages up to $15,000.
- If you have medical expenses, you may deduct only the amount that's above 5% of your MAPR amount ($1,110 for a veteran with 1 dependent).

2025 VA Protected Pension Rates

A veteran may be eligible for protected rates if they began receiving VA disability pension payments before December 31, 1978, and they haven't elected to change to the current, improved pension programs. That means a veteran will continue to receive payments at the rates under the old program as well as a cost-of-living increase.

To qualify for protected rates, your yearly income for 2024 must be at or below a certain amount. This is the income limit. Income is any money you earn in a year, including your salary, investment and retirement payments and income from dependents.

Some expenses, like non-reimbursable medical expenses may work to reduce your countable income. VA bases a veteran's income limit on the specific pension benefits they're eligible to receive, and whether they have eligible dependents, and their yearly income.

Eligible dependents may include a veteran's spouse, and the VA recognizes same-sex and common-law marriages.

Dependents may also include biological, step or adopted children who are unmarried and meet at least one of the following requirements:
- The child is unmarried and under 18 years old, or
- The child is unmarried and between 18 and 23 years old and enrolled in qualified school full time, or
- The child is unmarried and was seriously disabled before age 18 and can't care for themselves.

Section 306 Disability Pension Rates

The non-service-connected pension program was available from July 1, 1960, through December 31, 1978.

Section 306 Disability Pension Yearly Income Limits for Veterans without Dependents

Pension Benefit	2024 Yearly Income Limit (Effective December 1, 2024)
Basic monthly payment (veteran only, no dependent spouse or children)	Your yearly income must be $19,295 or less to continue receiving this benefit.
Special Aid and Attendance allowance, if your income is more than $19,295	Your yearly income must be $19,990 or less to continue receiving this benefit
Hospital reduction rate for Special Aid and Attendance, if you're hospitalized on or after January 1, 2024	Your yearly income must be $19,990 or less to continue receiving this benefit.

Note: the hospital reduction rate is a reduced rate of Special Aid and Attendance the VA will pay if you're hospitalized and meet certain requirements.

Section 306 Disability Pension Yearly Income Limits for Veterans with Dependents

Pension Benefit	2024 Yearly Income Limit
Basic monthly payment for a veteran with a spouse or one or more dependent children	Your yearly income must be $25,936 or less to continue receiving this benefit
Special Aid and Attendance allowance, if your income is more than $24,936	Your yearly income must be $26,628 or less to continue receiving this benefit.
Hospital reduction rates, if you're hospitalized on or after January 1, 2024	Your yearly income must be $26,628 or less

Note: If you're married, the VA will include some of your spouse's income when determining if your yearly income is at or below the income limit. The current Section 306 disability pension spouse income exclusion limit is $6,164. The VA won't include the first $6,164 of a veteran's spouse's income but will include any amount above that unless the veteran can prove they don't have access to the income or that including it would cause financial hardship.

Old Law Disability Pension Rates

Effective December 1, 2024.

This non-service-connected pension program was available before July 1, 1960.

The below income limits include a 3.2% cost-of-living increase for the year.

Veteran Status	2024 Yearly Income Limit
Veteran alone (no spouse or dependent children)	The veteran's yearly income must be $16,898 or less to continue receiving this benefit.
Veteran with a spouse or one or more dependent children	The veteran's yearly income must be $24,351 or less to continue receiving this benefit.

Old Law Disability Pension Monthly Payments

Pension Benefit	Monthly Payment
Basic veteran pension	$66.15
Pension for veteran with 10 years of service who is at least 65 years old	$78.75
Aid and Attendance (if entitled)	$135.45

Housebound allowance (if entitled)	$100.00

Combination of Ratings

The VA shall provide that, for the purpose of determining whether or not a veteran is permanently and totally disabled, ratings for service-connected disabilities may be combined with ratings for non-service-connected disabilities. Where a veteran is found to be entitled to a Non-Service- Connected Disability Pension and is also entitled to Service-Connected Disability Compensation, the VA shall pay the veteran the greater benefit.

Vocational Training for Certain Pension Recipients

In the case of a veteran who is awarded a Non-Service-Connected Disability Pension, the VA shall base on information on file with the VA, make a preliminary finding whether such veteran, with the assistance of a vocational training program, has a good potential for achieving employment. If such potential is found to exist, the VA shall solicit from the veteran an application for vocational training. If the veteran after that applies for such training, the VA shall provide the veteran with an evaluation, which may include a personal interview, to determine whether the achievement of a vocational goal is reasonably feasible.

If the VA, based on the evaluation, determines that the achievement of a vocational goal by a veteran is reasonably feasible, the veteran shall be offered and may elect to pursue a vocational training program.

If the veteran elects to pursue such a program, the program shall be designed in consultation with the veteran to meet the veteran's individual needs and shall be outlined in an individualized written plan of vocational rehabilitation.

A vocational training program under this section:
- May not exceed 24 months unless, based on a determination by the VA that an extension is necessary for the veteran to achieve a vocational goal identified in the written plan formulated for the veteran, the VA grants an extension for a period not to exceed 24 months.
- May not include the provision of any loan or subsistence allowance or any adaptive automobile equipment.
- May include a program of education at an institution of higher learning, only in a case in which the Secretary of the VA determines that the program involved is predominantly vocational in content.
- When a veteran completes a vocational training program, the VA may provide the veteran with counseling, placement, and post-placement services for a period not to exceed 18 months.

A veteran may not begin pursuit of a vocational training program under this chapter after the later of:
- December 31, 1995; or
- The end of a reasonable period of time, as determined by the VA, following either the evaluation of the veteran or the award of pension to the veteran.

In the case of a veteran who has been determined to have a permanent and total non- service- connected disability and who, not later than one year after the date the veteran's eligibility for counseling under this chapter expires, secures employment within the scope of a vocational goal identified in the veteran's individualized written plan of vocational rehabilitation (or in a related field which requires reasonably developed skills, and the use of some or all of the training or services furnished the veteran under such plan), the evaluation of the veteran as having a permanent and total disability may not be terminated because of the veteran's capacity to engage in such employment until the veteran first maintains such employment for a period of not less than 12 consecutive months.

Protection of Healthcare Eligibility

In the case of a veteran whose entitlement to pension is terminated after January 31, 1985, because of income from work or training, the veteran shall retain for a period of three years, beginning on the date of such termination, all eligibility for care and services that the veteran would have had if the veteran's entitlement to pension had not been terminated.

Disappearance

When a veteran receiving a non-service-connected disability pension from the VA disappears, the VA may pay the pension otherwise payable to such veteran's spouse and children. Payments made to a spouse or child shall not exceed the amount to which each would be entitled if the veteran died of a non-service-connected disability.

CHAPTER 18

SURVIVOR BENEFITS: PENSIONS

If you qualify for VA survivors' pensions as a surviving spouse or dependent child, the VA bases your payment amount on the difference between your countable income and a limit that congress sets. The limit Congress sets is called the Maximum Annual Pension Rate or MAPR.

Your **countable income** is how much you earn including your salary, investment and retirement payments. Countable income also includes any income you may have from your dependents. Some expenses, like non-reimbursable medical expenses may reduce your countable income. Non-reimbursable medical expenses are paid medical expenses not covered by your insurance provider.

Your **MAPR amount** is the maximum amount of pension payable to a veteran, surviving spouse or child. Your MAPR is based on how many dependents you have and whether you qualify for Housebound or Aid and Attendance benefits. MAPRs are adjusted each year for cost-of-living increases.

As an example, if you're a qualified surviving spouse with one dependent child, and you also qualify for Aid and Attendance and have a yearly income of $10,000, your MAPR amount is $18,867. Your yearly income is $10,000. Your VA pension is $8,867 for the year, or $739 paid each month.

Net Worth Limit to Be Eligible for Survivors Pension Benefits

From December 1, 2024, to November 30, 2025, the net worth limits to be eligible for Survivors Pension benefit is $159,240.

On October 18, 2018, the VA changed the way they assess net worth to make pension entitlement rules clearer. Net worth includes assets and annual income. When you apply for Survivors Pension benefits, you'll need to report all your assets and income.

If your child's net worth is more than the net worth limit, VA doesn't consider them to be dependent when determining pension.

Assets

Assets include the fair market value of all your real and personal property, minus the amount of any mortgages you may have. Real property means any land and buildings you may own.

Your personal property assets can include any of the following items:
- Investments like stocks and bonds
- Furniture
- Boats

Assets don't include your primary residence, your car or basic home items like appliances.

Annual Income

Annual income is the money earned in a year from a job or from retirement or annuity payments. Annual income includes salary or hourly pay, bonuses and commissions. It also includes overtime and tips.

VA subtracts certain expenses from your annual income when assessing net worth. These are called applicable deductible expenses. They include medical expenses you aren't reimbursed for and educational expenses.

Three-Year Look-Back Period for Asset Transfers

When VA receives a pension claim, it reviews the terms and conditions of any assets the survivor may have transferred in the three years before filing the claim. If you transfer assets for less than fair market value during the look-back period, and those assets would have pushed your net worth above the limit for VA Survivors Pension you may be subject to a penalty period of up to five years. You won't be eligible for pension benefits during this time.

The new policy took effect on October 18, 2018. If you filed your claim before this date, the look back period doesn't apply.

A penalty period is a length of time when a survivor isn't eligible for pension benefits because they transferred assets for less than fair market value during the look-back period. This may apply if those transferred assets would have caused the survivor's net worth to be over the limit mentioned above, but not every asset transfer is subject to the penalty.

Maximum Annual Pension Rate (MAPR) Amount

Date of cost-of-living increase: December 1, 2024
Increase Factor: 2.5%
Standard Medicare Deduction: Actual amount will be determined by SSA, based on individual income.

For qualified surviving spouses with at least 1 dependent

If you have one dependent child and...	Your MAPR amount is:
You don't qualify for Housebound or Aid and Attendance benefits	$14,893
You qualify for Housebound benefits	$17,414
You qualify for Aid and Attendance benefits	$21,696
You qualify for Aid and Attendance benefits and you're the surviving spouse who served in the Spanish American War	$22,353

Notes:

- The Survivor Benefit Plan (SBP)/Minimum Income Annuity (MIW) limitation is $11,380.
- **If you have more than 1 child**, add $2,902 to your MAPR amount for each additional child.
- **If you have a child who works**, you may exclude their wages up to $15,000.
- **If you have medical expenses**, you may deduct only the amount that's above 5% of your MAPR amount ($744 for a surviving spouse with 1 dependent).

For qualified surviving spouses with no dependents

If you have no dependents and...	Your MAPR amount is:
You don't qualify for Housebound or Aid and Attendance benefits	$11,380
You qualify for Housebound benefits	$13,908
You qualify for Aid and Attendance benefits	$18,187

You qualify for Aid and Attendance benefits and you're the surviving spouse of a veteran who served in the Spanish-American War	$18,923

Notes:
- The Survivor Benefit Plan (SBP)/Minimum Income Annuity (MIW) limitation is $11,380.
- **If you have medical expenses**, you may deduct only the amount that's above 5% of your MAPR amount ($569 for a surviving spouse with no dependent child).
- If you're a qualified surviving child, your MAPR amount is $2,902.

Protected Death Pension Rates

This non-service-connected pension program was available from July 1, 1960, through December 31,1978.

Section 306 Death Pension Yearly Income Limits

Survivor Status	2024 Yearly Income Limit
Surviving spouse alone— no dependent children	Your yearly income must be $19,295 or less to continue receiving this benefit
Surviving spouse with one or more dependent children	Your yearly income must be $25,936 or less to continue receiving this benefit
Each surviving dependent child— if the veteran has no surviving spouse	Your yearly income must be $15,778 or less to continue receiving this benefit

An annuity is a fixed sum of money paid to the plan's beneficiary every year. If you're part of a Section 306 survivor benefit plan, the VA will pay you up to $11,380 this year, effective December 1, 2024. This is the minimum income widow provision. The rate includes a 2.5% cost-of-living increase.

Old Law Death Pension Rates

This non-service-connected pension program was available before July 1, 1960. The following rates are effective December 1, 2024.

Old Law Death Pension Yearly Income Limits

Survivor Status	2024 Yearly Income Limit
Surviving spouse alone— no children	Your yearly income must be $16,898 or less

	to continue receiving this benefit
Each surviving dependent child when the veteran has no surviving spouse	Your yearly income must be $16,898 or less to continue receiving this benefit
Surviving spouse with one or more children	Your yearly income must be $24,351 or less to continue receiving this benefit

An annuity is a fixed sum of money paid to the plan's beneficiary each year. If you're the beneficiary of old law death pension survivor benefit plan—also called the minimum income window provision—the VA will pay you up to $11,380 for the year.

VA Survivors Pension Eligibility

You may be eligible for this benefit if you haven't remarried after the veteran's death and if the deceased veteran didn't receive a dishonorable discharge, and their service meets at least one requirement below.

At least one of the following must be true:
- The veteran entered active duty on or before September 7, 1980, and served at least 90 days on active military service with at least one day during a covered wartime period, or
- The veteran entered active duty after September 7, 1980, and served at least 24 months or the full period for which they were called or ordered to active duty with at least one day during a covered wartime period, or
- The veteran was an officer and started on active duty after October 16, 1981, and hadn't previously served on active duty for at least 18 months.

Your yearly family income and net worth must meet certain limits set by Congress. You may be eligible for a VA Survivors Pension as the child of a deceased wartime veteran if you're unmarried and meet at least one of three criteria. You are under the age of 18, or you're under the age of 23 attending a VA-approved school, or you're unable to care for yourself due to a disability that happened before age 18.

How To Apply for VA Survivors Pension

You can apply in one of a few ways.
- You can work with a trained professional called an accredited representative to get help filing a claim.
- You can use the direct upload tool through AccessVA to upload your form online.
- You can fill out an Application for DIC, Death Pension, and/or Accrued Benefits (VA Form 21P-534EZ).
- You may want to submit an intent to file form before you apply. This can give you time to gather the evidence you need but avoid a later potential start date. The start date is also called an effective date. When you notify VA of intent to file, you may be able to get retroactive payments.

CHAPTER 19

HOME LOAN GUARANTEES

The VA home loan program helps servicemembers, veterans and eligible surviving spouses become homeowners. The home loan guarantee benefit is available, and there are other housing-related programs to help you buy, build, repair, keep or adapt a home. VA home loans are provided by private lenders, like banks and mortgage companies. VA guarantees a portion of the loan, which enables the lender to provide you with more favorable terms.

Major features of the VA home loan benefit include:
- No required down payment—some lenders may require down payments for some borrowers using the VA home loan guarantee, but VA doesn't require a down payment.
- Competitively low interest rates
- Limited closing costs
- No need for Private Mortgage Insurance (PMI)
- The VA home loan is a lifetime benefit that can be used multiple times

Benefits

Purchase Loans help veterans purchase a home at a competitive interest rate, often without requiring a down payment or private mortgage insurance. Cash-Out Refinance loans let eligible veterans take cash out of their home equity to pay off things such as debt, to, make home improvements or to fund education. To be eligible veterans must have satisfactory credit, sufficient income to meet the expected monthly obligations, and a valid Certificate of Eligibility (COE).

Interest Rate Reduction Refinance Loans (IRRRL) are also called the Streamline Refinance Loan, and they can help veterans obtain a lower interest rate by refinancing an existing VA loan. This can be used only for veterans with an existing VA guaranteed loan on a property.

Native American Direct Loan (NADL) Program helps eligible Native American veterans finance the purchase, construction or improvement of homes on Federal Trust Land or reduce the interest rate on a VA loan. The veterans' tribal organization must participate in VA direct loan program, and the veteran must have a valid COE.

Cash-OUT Refinance Loan is a VA-backed cash-out refinance loan that lets you replace your current loan with a new one under different terms. If you want to take cash out of your home equity or refinance a non-VA loan into a VA-backed loan, a

VA-backed cash-out refinance loan might be right for you. You must qualify for a VA-backed home loan Certificate of Eligibility and meet VA's and your lender's standards for credit, income and other requirements and live in the home you're refinancing.

Adapted Housing Grants help veterans with a permanent and total service-connected disability purchase or build an adapted home or to modify an existing home to account for their disability.

Other resources may be available to veterans depending on their state of residency, including property tax reductions.

General Information

The purpose of the VA loan guaranty program is to help veterans and active-duty personnel finance the purchase of homes with competitive loan terms and interest rates.

The VA does not actually lend the money to veterans. VA guaranteed loans are made by private lenders, such as banks, savings & loans, or mortgage companies. The VA guaranty means the lender is protected against loss if the veteran fails to repay the loan.

The VA Loan Guaranty Service is the organization within the VA that has the responsibility of administering the home loan program.

In 2011 the VA announced that those veterans who qualify and submit to a short sale or deed-in-lieu of foreclosure may be eligible to receive $1,500 in relocation assistance. The VA has instructed mortgage lenders to provide the funds in order to help borrowers cover the cost of moving or other expenses incurred during the process.

In 2012 Under Public Law 112-154, veterans in specially adapted housing or those in receipt of VA home loans, which have property hindered or destroyed by a natural disaster, became eligible to receive VA assistance. The law also extended the VA's authority to extend the guarantee of timely payment of principal and interest of mortgage loans. The VA's authority was also extended with regard to the collection of loan fees and adjustment of maximum home loan guarantee amounts.

PL 116-23 and the VA Home Loan Program

The Blue Water Navy Vietnam Veterans Act of 2019 (PL 116-23) extended the presumption of herbicide exposure, such as Agent Orange, to veterans who served in the offshore waters of the Republic of Vietnam between January 9, 1962, and May 7, 2975.

Beginning January 1, 2020, veterans who served as far as 12 nautical miles from the shore of Vietnam or who had served in the Korean Demilitarized Zone are presumed to have been exposed to herbicides.

Additionally, PL 116-23 made changes to the VA Home Loan Program, including:

- VA-guaranteed home loans will no longer be limited to the Federal Housing Finance Agency Conforming Loan Limits. Veterans are now able to obtain a no-down-payment home loan in all areas, regardless of loan amount.
- The law exempts Purple Heart recipients currently serving on active duty from the VA Home Loan funding fee
- VA removed the loan limit for Native American Veterans seeking to build or purchase a home on Federal Trust Land
- At this time, there is a temporary change to the VA funding Fee, which is a congressionally mandated fee associated with the VA Home Loan. Veterans and service members will see a slight increase of 0.15 to 0,30% in their funding fee, while National Guard and Reserve members will see a slight decrease in their fee to align with the fee paid by 'Regular Military' borrowers. Veterans with service-connected disabilities, some surviving spouses and other potential borrowers are exempt from the VA loan funding fee and won't be impacted by the change.

Features of VA Guaranteed Home Loans

- Equal opportunity for all qualified veterans to obtain a VA guaranteed loan.
- No downpayment (unless required by the lender or the purchase price is more than the reasonable value of the property).
- The buyer's interest rate is negotiable.
- Buyer can finance the VA funding fee (plus reduced funding fees with a down payment of at least 5% and exemption for veterans receiving VA compensation).
- Closing costs are comparable with other financing types (and may be lower).
- No mortgage insurance premiums are necessary.
- An assumable mortgage may be available.
- The buyer has the right to prepay without penalty.

VA Guaranteed Loans Do Not Do the Following:

- Guarantee that a home is free of defects
- VA only guarantees the loan. It is the veteran's responsibility to assure that he or she is satisfied with the property being purchased. Veterans should seek expert advice as necessary, before legally committing to a purchase agreement.
- If a veteran has a home built, VA cannot compel the builder to correct construction defects, although VA does have the authority to suspend a builder from further participation in the VA home loan program.
- VA cannot guarantee the veteran is making a good investment.
- VA cannot provide a veteran with legal service.

Uses for VA Loan Guarantees

VA loan guarantees can be used for the following:
- To purchase, construct, or improve a home.
- To purchase and improve a home concurrently.
- To purchase a residential condominium or townhouse unit in a VA approved project. (If one veteran is purchasing the property, the total number of separate units cannot be more than 4.)
- To purchase a manufactured home or a manufactured home and manufactured home lot.
- To purchase and improve a manufactured home lot on which to place a manufactured home which the veteran already owns and occupies.
- To refinance an existing home loan.
- To refinance an existing VA loan to reduce the interest rate and make energy-efficient improvements.
- To refinance an existing manufactured home loan in order to acquire a lot.
- To improve a home by installing a solar heating and/or cooling system or other energy-efficient improvements.

Veterans must certify that they plan to live in the home they are buying or building in order to qualify for a VA loan guaranty.

VA loan guarantees are available only for property located in the United States, its territories, or possessions (Puerto Rico, Guam, Virgin Islands, American Samoa, and Northern Mariana Islands).

VA loan guarantees are not available for farm loans unless there is a home on the property, which will be personally occupied by the veteran. Non-realty loans for the purchase of equipment, livestock, machinery, etc. are not made. Other loan programs for farm financing may be available through the Farmers Home Administration, which gives preference to veteran applicants. (Interested veterans should refer to the local telephone directory for the phone number of the local office.)

Although business loans are not available through VA, the Small Business Administration (SBA) has a number of programs designed to help foster and encourage small business enterprises, including financial and management assistance. Each SBA office has a veteran affairs officer available to speak with. (Interested veterans should refer to the local telephone directory for the phone number of a local SBA office, or call (800) 827- 5722.

Eligibility Requirements

Individuals may qualify for VA home loan guarantees if their service falls within any of the following categories:

Vietnam Eligibility Requirements
- Active duty on or after August 5, 1964, and prior to May 8, 1975. (For

those serving in the Republic of Vietnam, the beginning date is February 28, 1961.); and
- Discharge or separation under other than dishonorable conditions; and
- At least 90 days of total service, unless discharged earlier for a service-connected disability.
- Unremarried widows of above-described eligible individuals who died as a result of service.
- Widows of above-described eligible individuals who died as a result of service who remarried after age 57.

Post-Vietnam Eligibility Requirements for Veterans with Enlisted Service Between May 8, 1975, AND September 7, 1980 (if enlisted) Or October 16, 1981 (if officer):
- At least 181 days of continuous service, all of which occurred on or after May 8, 1975, unless discharged earlier for a service-connected disability; and
- Discharge or separation under other than dishonorable conditions.
- Unremarried widows of above-described eligible individuals who died as a result of service.
- Widows of above-described eligible individuals who died as a result of service who remarried after age 57.

Post-Vietnam Eligibility Requirements for Veterans Separated from Enlisted Service between September 7, 1980 (October 17,1981, for officers) and August 1, 1990:
- At least 24 months of continuous active duty, or the full period (at least 181 days) for which individual was called or ordered to active duty, and discharged or separated under other than dishonorable conditions; or
- At least 181 days of continuous active duty, and discharged due to:
  - a hardship; or
  - a service-connected, compensable disability; or
  - a medical condition which preexisted service, and has not been determined to be service connected; or
  - the convenience of the government as a result of a reduction in force; or a physical or mental condition not characterized as a disability, and not the result of misconduct, but which did interfere with the performance of duty.
- Early discharge for a service-connected disability.
- Unremarried widows of above-described eligible persons who died as the result of service.
- Widows of above-described eligible individuals who died as a result of service who remarried after age 57.

Persian Gulf War Eligibility Requirements
- At least 24 months of continuous active duty on or after August 2, 1990, or the full period for which the individual was called or ordered to active duty, and discharged or separated under other than dishonorable conditions; or
- At least 90 days of continuous active duty, and discharged due to:
  - A hardship; or

- o A service-connected, compensable disability; or
- o A medical condition which preexisted service, and has not been determined to be service connected; or
- o The convenience of the government as a result of a reduction in force; or
- o A physical or mental condition not characterized as a disability, and not the result of misconduct, but which did interfere with the performance of duty.
- Early discharge for a service-connected disability.
- Unremarried widows of above-described eligible individuals who died as the result of service.
- Widows of above-described eligible individuals who died as a result of service who remarried after age 57.

When law or Presidential Proclamation ends the Persian Gulf War, a minimum of 181 days of continuous active duty will be required for those who did not serve during wartime.

Members of the Reserve and National Guard are eligible if activated after August 1, 1990, served at least 90 days, and discharged or separated under other than dishonorable conditions.

Active-Duty Personnel Requirements

Individuals who are now on regular duty (not active duty for training) are eligible after having served 181 days (90 days during the Gulf War), unless discharged or separated from a previous qualifying period of active-duty service.

Eligibility Requirements for Members of the Selected Reserve
- At least 6 years in the Reserves or National Guard, or discharged earlier due to a service-connected disability; and
- Discharged or separated under other than dishonorable conditions; or
- Placed on the retired list; or
- Transferred to an element of the Ready Reserve other than the Selected Reserve; or
- Continue to serve in the Selected Reserve.
- Unremarried widows of above-described eligible persons who died as the result of service.
- Widows of above-described eligible individuals who died as a result of service who remarried after age 57.

Eligibility Requirements for Other Types of Service
- Certain U.S. citizens who served in the armed forces of a U.S. ally in World War II. Members of organizations with recognized contributions to the U.S. during World War II (Questions about this type of service eligibility can be answered at any VA regional office.)
- Spouses of American servicemen who are listed as missing-in-action, or prisoners-of-war for a total of 90 days or more.

Certificate of Eligibility

The Certificate of Eligibility is the medium by which VA certifies eligibility for A VA loan guaranty.

Individuals may request a Certificate of Eligibility by completing "VA Form 26-1880 Request for a Certificate of Eligibility for VA Home Loan Benefits." The completed form should be submitted to a VA Eligibility Center along with acceptable proof of service.

Veterans separated after January 1, 1950, should submit DD Form 214, Certificate of Release or Discharge from active duty.

Veterans separated after October 1, 1979, should submit copy 4 of DD Form214.

Since there is no uniform document like the DD Form 214 for proof of service in the Selected Reserve a number of different forms may be accepted as documentation of service in the Selected Reserve:
- For those who served in the Army or Air National Guard and were discharged after at least 6 years of such service, NGB Form 22 may be sufficient.
- Those who served in the Army, Navy, Air Force, Marine Corps or Coast Guard Reserves may need to rely on a variety of forms that document at least 6 years of participation in paid training periods or have paid active duty for training.
- Often it will be necessary to submit a combination of documents, such as an Honorable Discharge certificate together with a Retirement Points Statement. It is the reservist's responsibility to obtain and submit documentation of 6 years of honorable service.

In addition, if an individual is now on active duty, and has not been previously discharged from active-duty service, he or she must submit a statement of service that includes the name of the issuing authority (base or command) and is signed by or at the direction of an appropriate official. The statement must identify the individual, include the social security number, provide the date of entry on active duty and the duration of any lost time.

The Certificate of Eligibility should be presented to the lender when completing the loan application. (However, if an individual does not have a Certificate, the lender may have the forms necessary to apply for the Certificate of Eligibility.)

Procedures for Obtaining Loans
- Find a real estate professional to work with.
- Locate a lending institution that participates in the VA program. You may want to get "pre-qualified" at this point - that is, find out how big a loan you can afford. Lenders set their own interest rates, discount points, and closing points.
- Obtain your Certificate of Eligibility. The lender can probably get you a

certificate online. Or you can apply online yourself. To get your Certificate of Eligibility (COE) online, please go to the eBenefits portal at this link. If you need any assistance, please call the eBenefits Help Desk at 1-800-983-0937. Their hours are Monday-Friday, 8am to 8pm EST.

- You find a home you want to buy.
- When you negotiate, make sure the purchase and sales agreement contain a "VA option clause."
- You may also want the agreement to allow you to "escape" from the contract without penalty if you can't get a VA loan.
- You formally apply to the lender for a VA-backed loan. The lender will complete a loan application and gather the needed documents such as pay stubs and bank statements.
- The lender orders a VA appraisal and begins to "process" all the credit and income information.
- The lending institution reviews the appraisal and all the documentation of credit, income, and assets. The lender then decides whether the loan should be granted.
- Finally, the closing takes place and the property is transferred. The lender chooses a title company, an attorney, or one of their own representatives to conduct the closing. This person will coordinate the date and time.
- If a lender cannot be located, the local VA regional office can provide a list of lenders active in the VA program.

A VA loan guaranty does not guarantee approval of a loan. The veteran must still meet the financial institution's income and credit requirements. If a loan is approved, the VA guarantees the loan when it's closed.

Guaranty or Entitlement Amount

A key aspect of these benefits is the VA's loan limit policy, which determines the maximum loan amount the VA will guarantee.

Full Entitlement:

As of 2020, veterans with full entitlement have no VA loan limit for loans over $144,000. This means you can borrow without a down payment, and the VA guarantees up to 25% of the loan amount to your lender if you default. To have full entitlement, you must meet at least one of the following criteria:

- You haven't used your home loan benefit.
- You've paid a previous VA loan in full and sold the property.
- You've used your home loan benefit but had a foreclosure or short sale and repaid the VA in full.

Remaining Entitlement:

If you have remaining entitlement, your VA home loan limit is based on the county loan limit where you live. This means that if you default on your loan, the VA will pay your lender up to 25% of the county loan limit minus the amount of your entitlement you've already used. You can use your remaining entitlement—either on its own or together with a down payment—to take out another VA home loan.

County Loan Limits:

County loan limits are determined by the Federal Housing Finance Agency (FHFA) and can vary based on the county where the property is located. These limits affect the maximum loan amount the VA will guarantee for a specific area. You can check your county's loan limit on the FHFA website.

Hybrid Adjustable-Rate Mortgages

An Adjustable-Rate Mortgage means the interest rate changes with changes in the market. The first-year rate, which is also referred to as a teaser rate, is generally a couple of percentage points below the market rate. The "cap" is the upper limit of the interest rate. If a teaser rate is 4%, and there is a five-point cap, then the highest that an interest rate could go would be 9%.

The amount that the interest rate can rise each year is usually limited to one or two percentage points per year, but the frequency at which the rate adjusts can vary. If interest rates go up, an ARM will adjust accordingly.

Down Payments

The VA does not require a down payment be made, provided that:
- The loan is not for a manufactured home or lot (a 5% down payment is required for manufactured home or lot loans); and
- The purchase price or cost does not exceed the reasonable value of the property, as determined by VA; and
- The loan does not have graduated payment features. (Because with a graduated-payment mortgage, the loan balance will be increasing during the first years of the loan, a down payment is required to keep the loan balance from going over the reasonable value or the purchase price.)

Even though the VA may not require a down payment, the lender may require one.

Closing Costs and Fees

When obtaining a VA-backed home loan, it's essential to understand the various closing costs involved and who is responsible for paying them.

Determining Loan Details

The specifics of your home loan, such as the interest rate, discount points, and other closing costs, are primarily set by your chosen lender. These terms can vary between lenders, so it's advisable to compare offers to find the best fit for your financial situation.

Seller Concessions

The seller can contribute to certain closing costs, known as seller concessions. The

VA allows sellers to pay up to 4% of the loan amount toward these costs. However, this 4% cap applies only to specific fees, such as the VA funding fee, and does not include standard closing costs like loan discount points.

Common Closing Costs

Both buyers and sellers may be responsible for various closing costs, including:
- **VA Funding Fee**: A one-time payment to help fund the VA loan program.
- **Loan Origination Fee**: Charged by the lender for processing the loan.
- **Loan Discount Points**: Fees paid to the lender at closing to reduce the interest rate.
- **Credit Report Fees**: Costs for obtaining your credit report.
- **VA Appraisal Fee**: Charged for the VA-required appraisal of the property.
- **Hazard Insurance and Real Estate Taxes**: Prepaid amounts for insurance and taxes.
- **State and Local Taxes**: Applicable taxes based on the property's location.
- **Title Insurance**: Protects against potential title issues.
- **Recording Fees**: Charges for recording the new deed and mortgage.

It's important to note that while the seller can contribute up to 4% of the loan amount toward these costs, this limit does not cover all fees. For instance, the seller cannot pay for loan discount points, which are considered a buyer's expense.

Negotiating Closing Costs

Buyers can negotiate with sellers to cover certain closing costs. However, the total seller concessions cannot exceed the 4% limit set by the VA. Understanding which costs are eligible for seller concessions and which are not can help in negotiations.

Funding Fees

A VA funding fee is payable at the time of loan closing. This fee may be included in the loan and paid from the loan proceeds. The funding fee does not have to be paid by veterans receiving VA compensation for service-connected disabilities, or who but for the receipt of retirement pay, would be entitled to receive compensation for service-connected disabilities, or surviving spouses of veterans who died in service or from a service-connected disability.

The VA funding fee is a one-time payment that helps lower the cost of the loan for U.S. taxpayers, since the VA home loan program doesn't require down payments or monthly mortgage insurance. If you're using a VA home loan to buy, build, improve or repair a home or to refinance a mortgage, you'll need to pay the VA funding fee unless you meet certain requirements.

You won't have to pay a VA funding fee if any of the following are true for you:
- You're receiving VA compensation for a service-connected disability, or
- You're eligible to receive VA compensation for a service-connected disability, but you're receiving retirement or active-duty pay instead, or

- You're receiving Dependency and Indemnity Compensation (DIC) as the surviving spouse of a veteran, or
- You're a servicemember who has received a proposed or memorandum rating before the loan closing date that says you're eligible to get compensation because of a pre- discharge claim, or
- You're a servicemember on active duty who, before or on the loan closing date, provides evidence of having received the Purple Heart.

You may be eligible for a refund of the VA funding fee if you're later awarded VA compensation for a service-connected disability. The effective date of your VA compensation must be retroactive to before the date of your loan closing. If you get a proposed or memorandum rating after your loan closing date, you'll still need to pay the funding fee. You won't be eligible for a refund based on this rating.

You pay the funding fee when you close your VA-backed or VA direct home loan. You can pay it in a couple of ways. The options include having it as part of your loan that you pay off over time or paying the full fee all at once at closing.

The amount of the funding fee depends on the amount of your loan and other factors including the type of loan you get and the total amount of your loan. Depending on the type of loan you get, the VA may also base the fee on other factors including your down payment amount, and whether it's your first time using a VA-backed or VA direct home loan.

A lender also charges interest on a loan in addition to closing fees.

The following VA funding fees are effective as of April 7, 2023. The funding fee applies only to the loan amount, not the purchase price of the home.

VA-Backed Purchase and Construction Loans

Rates for veterans, active-duty service members, and National Guard and Reserve members

	If your down payment is...	Your VA funding fee will be...
First Use	Less than 5%	2.15%
	5% or more	1.5%
	10% or more	1.25%
After first use	Less than 5%	3.3%
	5% or more	1.5%
	10% or more	1.25%

Note: If you used a VA-backed or VA direct home loan to purchase only a manufactured home in the past, you'll still pay the first-time funding fee.

VA-Backed Cash-Out Refinancing Loans

Rates for veterans, active-duty service members, and National Guard and Reserve Members

First Use	After First Use
2.15%	3.3%

Note: The VA funding fee rates for refinancing loans don't change based on your down payment amount. If you used a VA-backed or VA direct home loan to purchase only a manufactured home int eh past, you'll still pay the first-time funding fee.

Native American Direct Loan (NADL)

Type of Use	VA Funding Fee
Purchase	1.25%
Refinance	0.5%

Note: The VA funding fee for this loan doesn't change based on your down payment amount or whether you've used the VA home loan program in the past.

Other VA Home Loan Types

Loan Type	VA Funding Fee
Interest Rate Reduction Refinancing Loans (IRRRLs)	0.5%
Manufactured home loans (not permanently affixed)	1%
Loan assumptions	0.5%
Vendee loan, for purchasing VA-acquired property	2.25%

Note: The VA funding fees for these loans don't change based on down payment amount or whether the home loan program has been used in the past.

Flood Insurance

If the dwelling is in an area identified by the Department of Housing and Urban Development as having special flood hazards, and the sale of flood insurance under the national program is available, such insurance is required on loans made since March 1, 1974. The amount of insurance must be equal to the outstanding loan balance, or the maximum limit of coverage available, whichever is less.

Interest Rates

The interest rate on VA loans varies due to changes in the prevailing rates in the mortgage market. One a loan is made, the interest rate set in the note remains the same for the life of the loan. However, if interest rates decrease, a veteran may apply for a new VA loan to refinance the previous loan at a lower interest rate.

Repayment Period

The maximum repayment period for VA home loans is 30 years and 32 days. However, the exact amortization period depends upon the contract between the lender and the borrower.

The VA will guarantee loans with the following repayment terms:
- Traditional Fixed Payment Mortgage
- Equal monthly payments for the life of the loan
- Graduated Payment Mortgage – GPM
- Smaller than normal monthly payments for the first few years – usually 5 years, which gradually increase each year, and then level off after the end of the "graduation period" to larger than normal payments for the remaining term of the loan. The reduction in the monthly payment in the early years of the loan is accomplished by delaying a portion of the interest due on the loan each month, and by adding that interest to the principal balance.

Buydown
The builder of a new home or seller of an existing home may "buy down" the veteran's mortgage payments by making a large lump sum payment up front at closing that will be used to supplement the monthly payments for a certain period, usually 1 to 3 years.

Growing Equity Mortgage (GEM)
Provides for a gradual annual increase in monthly payments, with all of the increase applied to the principal balance, resulting in early payoff of the loan.

Prepayment of Loan
A veteran or serviceman may pay off his entire loan at any time without penalty or fee or make advance payments equal to one monthly installment or $100, whichever is the lesser amount. Individuals should check with the mortgage holder for the proper procedure.

Loan Defaults

If a veteran fails to make payments as agreed, the lender may foreclose on the property. If the lender takes a loss, the VA must pay the guaranty to the lender, and the individual must repay this amount to the VA. If the loan closed on or after January 1, 1990, the veteran will owe the VA in the event of default, only if there was fraud, misrepresentation, or bad faith on the veteran's part.

The US Department of Veterans Affairs urges all veterans who are encountering problems making their mortgage payments to speak with their loan servicers as soon as possible to explore options to avoid foreclosure. Depending on a veteran's specific situation, servicers may offer any of the following options to avoid foreclosure:

- **Repayment Plan**: The borrower makes regular installment each month plus part of the missed installments.
- **Special Forbearance**: The servicer agrees not to initiate foreclosure to allow time for borrowers to repay the missed installments. An example would be when a borrower is waiting for a tax refund.
- **Loan Modification**: Provides the borrower a fresh start by adding the delinquency to the loan balance and establishing a new payment schedule.
- **Additional time to arrange a private sale**: The servicer agrees to delay foreclosure to allow a sale to close if the loan will be paid off.
- **Short Sale**: When the servicer agrees to allow a borrower to sell his/her home for a lesser amount than what is currently required to pay off the loan.
- **Deed-in-Lieu of Foreclosure**: The borrower voluntarily agrees to deed the property to the servicer instead of going through a lengthy foreclosure process

Release of Liability

Any veteran who sells or has sold a home purchased with a VA loan guaranty may request release from liability to the VA. (If the VA loan closed prior to March 1, 1988, the application forms for a release of liability must be requested from the VA office that guaranteed the loan. If the VA loan closed on or after March 1, 1988, then the application forms must be requested from the lender to whom the payments are made.) The loan must be current, the purchaser must assume full liability for the loan, and the purchaser must sign an Assumption of Liability Agreement. The VA must approve the purchaser from a credit standpoint.

For loans closed on or after March 1, 1988, the release of liability is not automatic. To approve the assumer and grant the veteran release from liability, the lender or VA must be notified, and release of liability must be requested.

If the loan was closed prior to March 1, 1988, the purchaser may assume the loan without approval from VA or the lender. However, the veteran is encouraged to request a release of liability from VA, regardless of the loan's closing date. If a veteran does not obtain a release of liability, and VA suffers a loss on account of a default by the assumer, or some future assumer, a debt may be established against the veteran. Also, strenuous collection efforts will be made against the veteran if a debt is established.

The release of a veteran from liability to the VA does not change the fact that the VA continues to be liable on the guaranty.

Restoration of Entitlement

Veterans who have used all or part of their entitlement may restore their entitlement amount to purchase another home, provided:

- The property has been sold, and the loan has been paid in full; or
- A qualified veteran buyer has agreed to assume the outstanding balance on the loan and agreed to substitute his entitlement for the same amount of entitlement the original veteran owner used to get the loan. (The veteran buyer must also meet the occupancy, income, and credit requirements of the VA and the lender.)
- If the veteran has repaid the VA loan in full but has not disposed of the property securing that loan, the entitlement may be restored ONETIME ONLY.

Restoration of entitlement does not occur automatically. The veteran must apply for restoration by completing "Form 26, 1880." Completed forms may be returned to any VA regional office or center (A copy of the HUD-1, Closing Statement, or other appropriate evidence of payment in full should also be submitted with the completed Form 26, 1880.) Application forms for substitution of entitlement can be requested from the VA office that guaranteed the loan.

If the requirements for restoration of entitlement cannot be met, veterans who had a VA loan before may still have remaining entitlement to use for another VA loan. The current amount of entitlement available to eligible veterans has been increased over time by changes in the law.

For example, in 1974 the maximum guaranty entitlement was $12,500. Today the maximum guaranty entitlement is $36,000 (for most loans under $144,000). So, if a veteran used the $12,500 guaranty in 1974, even if that loan is not paid off, the veteran could use the $23,500 difference between the $12,500 entitlement originally used and the current maximum of $36,000 to buy another home with a VA loan guaranty.

Direct Home Loans

VA direct home loans are only available to:

- Native American veterans who plan to buy, build, or improve a home on Native American trust land; or
- Certain eligible veterans who have a permanent and total service-connected disability, for specially adapted homes.

Native American Veterans Living on Trust Lands

A VA direct loan can be used to purchase, construct, or improve a home on Native American trust land. These loans may also be used to simultaneously purchase and improve a home, or to refinance another VA direct loan made under this program in order to lower the interest rate. VA direct loans are generally limited to the cost of the home or $80,000, whichever is less.

To qualify for a VA direct loan, the tribal organization or other appropriate Native American group must be participating in the VA direct loan program. The tribal organization must have signed a Memorandum of Understanding with the Secretary of Veterans Affairs that includes the conditions governing its participation in the program.

Veterans should contact their regional VA office for specific information regarding direct home loans.

Resale of Repossessed Homes

The VA sells homes that it acquires after foreclosure of a VA guaranteed loan. These homes are available to veterans and non-veterans.

The properties are available for sale to the general public through the services of private sector real estate brokers. The VA cannot deal directly with purchasers. Real estate brokers receive the keys to the properties and assist prospective purchasers in finding, viewing, and offering to purchase them.

Participating brokers receive instructional material regarding the sales program and are familiar with VA sales procedures. VA pays the sales commission. Offers to purchase VA acquired properties must be submitted on VA forms. Offers cannot be submitted on offer forms generally used in the real estate industry.

VA financing is available for most, but not all, property sales. The down payment requirements are usually very reasonable, the interest rate is established by VA based on market conditions. Any prospective purchaser who requests VA financing to purchase a VA-owned property must have sufficient income to meet the loan payments, maintain the property, and pay all other obligations. The purchaser must have acceptable credit and must also have enough funds remaining for family support.

Anyone interested should consult a local real estate agent to find out about VA-acquired properties listed for sale in the area.

HUD / FHA Loans

Veterans are not eligible for VA financing based on service in World War I, Active Duty for Training in the Reserves, or Active Duty for Training in the National Guard (unless "activated" under the authority of Title 10, U.S. Code). However, these veterans may qualify for a HUD / FHA veteran's loan.

The VA's only role in the HUD / FHA program is to determine the eligibility of the veteran, and issue a Certificate of Veteran Status, if qualified. Under this program, financing is available for veterans at terms slightly more favorable than those available to non-veterans.

A veteran may request a "Certificate of Veteran Status" by completing "VA form

26-8261a." The completed form and required attachments should be submitted to the veteran's regional VA office for a determination of eligibility.

Disability Housing Grants

The U.S. Department of Veterans Affairs (VA) offers housing grants to assist veterans and service members with certain service-connected disabilities in purchasing, building, or modifying homes to enhance accessibility and independence.

Types of Housing Grants:

1. **Specially Adapted Housing (SAH) Grant:** Designed for veterans with specific permanent and total service-connected disabilities, this grant helps in building, purchasing, or modifying a home to meet individual needs. Qualifying disabilities include the loss or loss of use of more than one limb, blindness in both eyes with 20/200 visual acuity or less, and certain severe burns. For fiscal year 2024, the maximum grant amount is $117,014.
2. **Special Home Adaptation (SHA) Grant:** Aimed at veterans with specific service-connected disabilities, this grant assists in adapting an existing home. Qualifying disabilities include the loss or loss of use of both hands, certain severe burns, and certain respiratory or breathing injuries. The maximum grant amount for fiscal year 2024 is $23,444.
3. **Temporary Residence Adaptation (TRA) Grant:** For veterans who qualify for an SAH or SHA grant and are temporarily living in a family member's home, the TRA grant provides funding to adapt that residence. The maximum amounts for fiscal year 2024 are $47,130 for SAH and $8,415 for SHA.

Eligibility Criteria:

- **SAH Grant:** Eligibility requires ownership or intent to own a permanent home and a qualifying service-connected disability. Notably, only 120 veterans and service members each fiscal year can qualify for a grant based on the loss of one extremity after September 11, 2001, as set by Congress.
- **SHA Grant:** Eligibility requires ownership or intent to own a permanent home and a qualifying service-connected disability.
- **TRA Grant:** Eligibility requires living temporarily in a family member's home that needs changes to meet the veteran's needs and qualifying for an SAH or SHA grant.

Application Process:

- **Online Application:** Veterans can apply through the VA's eBenefits portal.
- **By Mail:** Complete VA Form 26-4555, "Application in Acquiring Specially Adapted Housing or Special Home Adaptation Grant," and mail it to:
- Department of Veterans Affairs
  Claims Intake Center
  PO Box 4444
  Janesville, WI 53547-4444
- **In Person:** Submit the completed application at a local VA regional office.

- **Required Documentation:**
    1. Social Security number
    2. VA file or claim number (if applicable)
    3. Medical records supporting the service-connected disability
    4. Proof of homeownership or intent to purchase
    5. For comprehensive information and assistance, veterans are encouraged to contact the VA's Specially Adapted Housing staff at 877-827-3702 (TTY: 711) or via email at sahinfo.vbaco@va.gov.

CHAPTER 20

SPECIAL VETERAN GROUPS

The United States military has long been a diverse institution, encompassing individuals from various backgrounds, identities, and experiences. Recognizing this diversity, the Department of Veterans Affairs (VA) has developed specialized programs and benefits to address the unique needs of specific veteran populations, including women, LGBTQ+ individuals, minorities, Native Americans, and other distinct groups.

Elderly Veterans

As veterans age, they encounter unique challenges that necessitate specialized support and resources. The Department of Veterans Affairs (VA) offers a range of benefits tailored to meet the evolving needs of elderly veterans, addressing both health-related concerns and financial assistance.

VA Benefits for Elderly Veterans

Elderly veterans may be eligible for various benefits, including:

- **Disability Compensation**: Monthly payments for veterans with service-connected disabilities.
- **Pension**: Financial assistance for low-income veterans who served during wartime.
- **Health Care**: Access to VA medical facilities and services.
- **Home Loans**: Assistance in purchasing homes with favorable terms.
- **Insurance**: Life insurance options for veterans and their families.
- **Burial and Memorial Services**: Support for funeral and burial expenses.

Additional Benefits for Elderly Veterans

Beyond the standard benefits, elderly veterans may qualify for:

- **Aid and Attendance (A&A)**: An increased monthly pension for veterans who require assistance with daily activities, are bedridden, reside in a nursing home, or have limited eyesight.

- **Housebound Allowance**: An increased monthly pension for veterans substantially confined to their immediate premises due to a permanent disability.

VA Health Care for Elderly Veterans

The VA provides specialized health care services for elderly veterans, including:

- **Geriatrics Program**: Focused on the health care needs of elderly veterans with complex conditions.
- **Long-Term Care**: Services such as nursing homes, assisted living, and home health care.

Eligibility for these services depends on factors like service-connected disability status and income.

How to Apply

To access these benefits, veterans can:

- **Apply Online**: Use the VA's online portal to submit applications.
- **Work with an Accredited Representative**: Seek assistance from organizations accredited by the VA.
- **Visit a VA Regional Office**: Receive in-person assistance at a local office.

For more details on the application process, refer to our guide on applying for benefits.

Gulf War Veterans

The Gulf War era, encompassing operations from August 2, 1990, to the present, has seen over 650,000 service members participate in missions such as Desert Shield and Desert Storm. This extended period qualifies all active-duty personnel during this time as Gulf War veterans, making them eligible for various benefits.

Available Benefits

Gulf War Veterans have access to a comprehensive range of benefits, including:
- **Disability Compensation**: Financial support for service-related injuries or illnesses.
- **Pension**: Assistance for low-income veterans with limited or no income.
- **Education and Training**: Opportunities for further education and vocational training.
- **Health Care**: Access to medical services for service-connected conditions.
- **Home Loans**: Assistance in purchasing homes with favorable terms.
- **Insurance**: Life insurance options tailored for veterans.
- **Vocational Rehabilitation and Employment**: Support for transitioning to civilian employment.

- **Burial**: Benefits related to funeral and burial services.

Health Conditions Associated with Gulf War Service

Gulf War veterans may experience a range of health issues, some of which are recognized as presumptive conditions linked to their service.

These include:

- **Medically Unexplained Illnesses**: Conditions such as chronic fatigue, headaches, joint pain, and memory problems that lack a clear diagnosis.
- **Infectious Diseases**: Certain diseases contracted during service in the Gulf region.
- **Amyotrophic Lateral Sclerosis (ALS)**: Also known as Lou Gehrig's disease, ALS is presumed service-connected for veterans with 90 days or more of continuous active service.

Application Process

To apply for these benefits, Gulf War veterans can:
1. **Online Application**: Submit applications through the official government website.
2. **Assistance from Accredited Representatives**: Seek help from accredited organizations or agents.
3. **In-Person Assistance**: Visit a regional office for direct support.

Homeless Veterans

Homelessness among veterans is a critical issue that demands immediate attention and action. Many veterans face unique challenges that can lead to housing instability, including mental health conditions, substance abuse, and difficulties transitioning to civilian life. Recognizing the diverse needs of homeless veterans, various programs and services have been established to provide comprehensive support.

Health Care Services

Access to quality health care is essential for homeless veterans. Numerous health care programs are available to address both physical and mental health needs, ensuring that veterans receive the necessary medical attention to improve their well-being.

Housing Assistance

Securing stable housing is a fundamental step toward ending homelessness. Several housing assistance programs offer support, including rental assistance and case management, to help veterans find and maintain permanent housing.

Employment Support

Employment is a key factor in achieving long-term stability. Employment assistance programs provide job training, resume development, and job placement services to help homeless veterans re-enter the workforce and regain financial independence.

Foreclosure Prevention

For veterans at risk of losing their homes, foreclosure prevention programs offer counseling and financial assistance to help manage mortgage payments and avoid foreclosure.

How to Access These Services

Veterans seeking assistance can contact the National Call Center for Homeless Veterans at 1-877-4AID-VET (1-877-424-3838) for immediate support. Additionally, local VA medical centers and community resource centers offer outreach and support services tailored to the needs of homeless veterans.

Incarcerated Veterans

Veterans who become involved with the criminal justice system and face incarceration encounter unique challenges that can impact their well-being and access to benefits. Understanding how incarceration affects eligibility for various benefits and the programs available to assist in reintegration is crucial for these individuals.

Impact of Incarceration on VA Benefits

Incarceration can influence the availability and amount of certain benefits for veterans. For instance, disability compensation payments may be reduced if a veteran is convicted of a felony and imprisoned for more than 60 days.

Veterans rated at 20% or more may see their payments limited to the 10% disability rate during incarceration.

Similarly, pension benefits are typically discontinued after 61 days of imprisonment for a felony conviction. It's important to note that these reductions do not apply to work release programs or halfway house placements.

Programs Supporting Justice-Involved Veterans

Several initiatives aim to support veterans involved in the criminal justice system:

- **Health Care for Re-entry Veterans (HCRV) Program**: This program assists incarcerated veterans in planning for their transition back into the community, focusing on preventing homelessness and ensuring continuity of care.

- **Veteran Justice Outreach (VJO) Initiative**: The VJO initiative connects eligible justice-involved veterans with VA health care services, including mental health and substance use treatment, to address issues that may contribute to legal challenges.

Reintegration and Support Services

Upon release, veterans can access various support services to aid in reintegration:

- **Employment Assistance**: Programs are available to help veterans secure employment, providing job training and placement services tailored to their needs.
- **Housing Assistance**: Support is offered to prevent homelessness, including assistance with finding stable housing and financial support.
- **Health Care Services**: Continued access to health care, including mental health services, is available to address ongoing health needs.

Maintaining Eligibility and Accessing Benefits

It's essential for incarcerated veterans to inform the appropriate authorities of their incarceration status to ensure accurate benefit distribution and to prevent overpayments. Upon release, veterans should promptly contact VA services to reinstate or adjust their benefits as needed.

Korean War Veterans

An estimated 5.7 million U.S. veterans served during the Korean War. These veterans, particularly those exposed to harsh winter conditions, are at a higher risk of developing health issues related to cold injuries. The severe cold during the winter of 1950-1951 led to significant casualties, with over 5,000 soldiers requiring evacuation due to cold-related injuries. Many of these veterans, due to battlefield circumstances, were unable to receive proper medical care for these injuries.

VA Benefits for Korean War Veterans

Korean War veterans are eligible for various benefits, similar to those available to all U.S. military veterans. These include disability compensation, pension, health care, education, home loans, life insurance, vocational rehabilitation, and burial benefits.

Cold-Related Injury Benefits for Korean War Veterans

Veterans who suffered cold-related injuries may experience long-term health effects, such as arthritis, skin cancer from frostbite scars, and complications like cold sensitization. As these conditions worsen over time, veterans with other health issues, such as diabetes or vascular disease, are at an increased risk of serious complications, including the potential need for amputations.

If you are dealing with cold-related injuries, you may be eligible for VA disability compensation. The VA can help you receive compensation for conditions resulting from these injuries, which could be linked to service-related health problems.

Ionizing Radiation Exposure

Korean War veterans who were exposed to ionizing radiation during their service may qualify for health care and compensation. The VA offers services such as health exams through the Ionizing Radiation Registry, as well as clinical treatment at the War Related Illness and Injury Study Centers. If you have developed cancers due to this exposure, you may be eligible for additional disability compensation.

Radiation-Risk Activities

Korean War veterans who participated in specific activities involving radiation risk, such as nuclear weapons testing, may be eligible for similar benefits. These veterans, often referred to as "Atomic Veterans," may be entitled to both health care and disability compensation, particularly if they have developed cancers linked to their service-related radiation exposure.

How to Apply

Veterans interested in applying for these benefits can do so through several methods. You can apply online, work with an accredited representative, or visit a VA regional office for assistance. The VA offers a range of services tailored to help Korean War veterans access the benefits they are entitled to.

Lesbian, Gay, Bisexual and Transgender (LGBT) Servicemembers and Veterans

The Department of Veterans Affairs (VA) is committed to serving all eligible service members, veterans, and their families, recognizing the diversity within this community, including those who identify as lesbian, gay, bisexual, transgender, queer, or questioning (LGBTQ+). VA strives to provide outreach to diverse service member and veteran populations and has provided guidance on how, under current federal law, VA may recognize marriage.

In June 2015, the Supreme Court's decision in Obergefell v. Hodges mandated that the Fourteenth Amendment of the U.S. Constitution requires states to license and recognize marriages between two people of the same sex, regardless of where the marriage was performed.

Consequently, VA now recognizes all same-sex marriages without regard to a veteran's state of residence. Veterans in same-sex marriages who believe they are entitled to benefits should promptly apply for them. Additionally, veterans whose claims were previously denied based on prior guidance should re-apply for benefits.

The Department of Defense, in its ongoing review of military benefits following the repeal of "Don't Ask, Don't Tell," identified several VA benefits for which service members may designate beneficiaries of their choosing, regardless of sexual orientation.

These benefits include:
- Servicemembers Group Life Insurance (SGLI)
- Veterans' Group Life Insurance (VGLI)
- Post Vietnam-era Veterans Assistance Program (VEAP)
- Montgomery GI Bill
- Presentation of the Flag of the United States

Additionally, there are other benefits for service members provided by the Department of Defense for which LGBTQ+ service members may designate a beneficiary regardless of sexual orientation.

Minority Veterans

The Department of Veterans Affairs (VA) is committed to serving all eligible service members, veterans, and their families, recognizing the rich diversity within this community.

Minority veterans—those identified as African American, Asian American/Pacific Islander, Hispanic, Native American/Alaska Native, and Native Hawaiian—may face unique challenges and have specific needs. To address these, the VA offers a range of benefits and programs tailored to support minority veterans.

VA Benefits for Minority Veterans

Minority veterans are eligible for a comprehensive array of benefits available to all U.S. military veterans, including:
- **Disability Compensation**: Financial support for veterans with service-connected disabilities.
- **Pension**: Income assistance for low-income veterans with wartime service.
- **Education and Training**: Opportunities for further education and vocational training.
- **Health Care**: Access to medical services through VA facilities.
- **Home Loans**: Assistance in purchasing homes with favorable terms.
- **Insurance**: Life insurance options tailored for veterans.
- **Vocational Rehabilitation and Employment**: Support for veterans seeking employment or job training.
- **Burial**: Benefits related to funeral and burial services.

Programs and Resources for Minority Veterans

To enhance outreach and support for minority veterans, the VA has established several initiatives:

- **Center for Minority Veterans (CMV)**: Established in 1994, the CMV serves as the principal advisor to the Secretary on policies and programs affecting minority veterans. It conducts outreach to promote awareness and utilization of VA benefits among minority veterans.
- **Minority Veterans Program Coordinators (MVPCs)**: Each VA Regional Office has designated MVPCs to assist minority veterans in understanding and accessing VA benefits. They provide information, help with applications, and connect veterans to additional resources.
- **Special Emphasis Programs**: The VA has implemented programs focusing on specific minority groups, such as the Black/African American Special Emphasis Program, Hispanic Employment Program, and LGBT Departmental Special Emphasis Program. These initiatives aim to address disparities and promote equal opportunities within the VA workforce and for veterans.

Applying for Benefits

Minority veterans can apply for VA benefits through various channels:
- **Online**: Utilize the VA's online portal to submit applications.
- **Assistance**: Work with accredited representatives or agents who can guide you through the application process.
- **In-Person**: Visit a VA regional office for direct assistance.

For personalized guidance, contact your local MVPC or reach out to the CMV for support.

Native American Veterans

Native American veterans have a distinguished history of service in the U.S. Armed Forces, with American Indians and Alaska Natives among the most highly represented groups. The Department of Veterans Affairs (VA) collaborates with tribal governments to enhance access to services and benefits for these veterans and their families. VA is dedicated to ensuring that Native American veterans can fully utilize all the benefits and services to which they are entitled.

VA Benefits

Native American veterans may be eligible for a comprehensive range of benefits available to all U.S. military veterans. These benefits include disability compensation, pension, education and training, health care, home loans, insurance, vocational rehabilitation and employment, and burial services.

VA Benefits and Programs for Native American Veterans
- **Native American Direct Loan (NADL) Program**: This program assists eligible Native American veterans in financing the purchase, construction, or improvement of homes on Federal Trust Land or in reducing the interest rate on such a VA loan. Veterans can use these direct loans to simultaneously purchase and improve a home or refinance another VA

direct loan made under NADL to lower the interest rate.

- **Office of Tribal Government Relations (OTGR)**: OTGR consults with American Indian and Alaska Native tribal governments to develop partnerships that enhance access to services and benefits for veterans and their families. OTGR also sponsors regional training sessions for tribal leaders, veteran service organizations, and tribal organizations to increase access to VA healthcare and benefits through informative presentations and interactive discussions.
- **VA Recognition as a Tribal Organization**: VA has regulations governing which organizations can assist veterans and survivors with their benefit claims. Formal recognition allows tribal organizations to expand their support to veterans within their communities.

Other Programs for Native American Veterans

- **Alaska Native Veterans Land Allotment Program of 2019**: The John D. Dingell, Jr., Conservation, Management, and Recreation Act of 2019 provides the opportunity for eligible Vietnam-era veterans or their heirs to select 2.5 to 160 acres of Federal land in Alaska. Veterans or their heirs have five years to select and apply for land. The program is open to all eligible Alaska Natives who served between August 5, 1964, and December 31, 1971, and it removes the requirement for personal use or occupancy mandated under previous laws.

How to Apply

To apply for VA benefits, Native American veterans can:

- **Apply online**: Visit the official VA website to submit applications for various benefits.
- **Work with an accredited representative or agent**: Seek assistance from accredited representatives who can guide you through the application process.
- **Visit a VA regional office**: Locate the nearest VA regional office to receive in-person assistance from VA employees.

Former Prisoners of War

Former prisoners of war (FPOWs) are veterans who endured captivity during their military service. The Department of Veterans Affairs (VA) offers a range of benefits to support their health and well-being.

Presumptive Conditions for FPOWs

FPOWs are presumed to have service-connected disabilities for certain conditions, including:

- **Psychiatric Disorders**: Psychosis, anxiety states, dysthymic disorder, and depressive neurosis.
- **Musculoskeletal Issues**: Post-traumatic osteoarthritis.
- **Cardiovascular Diseases**: Atherosclerotic heart disease, hypertensive

vascular disease, and related complications.

- **Neurological Conditions**: Organic residuals of frostbite, stroke, and osteoporosis.
- **Nutritional Deficiencies**: Avitaminosis, beriberi (including heart disease), chronic dysentery, cirrhosis of the liver, helminthiasis, malnutrition, pellagra, and other nutritional deficiencies.
- **Gastrointestinal Disorders**: Peptic ulcer disease, irritable bowel syndrome.
- **Peripheral Neuropathy**: Except where directly related to an illness caused by an infection.
- **Other Conditions**: Peripheral neuropathy, except where directly related to an illness caused by an infection, on or after September 28, 2009.

These presumptions apply if the conditions manifest to at least a minimally compensable degree of 10% or more after discharge or release from active military service.

Medical Benefits

FPOWs with service-connected disabilities are eligible for VA hospital, nursing home, and outpatient treatment. Those without service-connected disabilities can receive VA hospital and nursing home care without regard to their ability to pay and are eligible for outpatient care on a priority basis.

While receiving treatment in an approved outpatient program, FPOWs are eligible for necessary medications, glasses, hearing aids, prostheses, and all needed dental care. There is no co-payment requirement for FPOWs at VA pharmacies.

Benefits for Survivors

Surviving spouses, children, and parents of FPOWs may be eligible for Dependency and Indemnity Compensation (DIC) if the FPOW:
- Died on active duty.
- Died from service-related disabilities.
- Died after September 30, 1999, and was continuously rated totally disabled for a service-connected condition for at least 1 year immediately preceding death.

DIC is terminated for a surviving spouse who remarries but can be resumed if the remarriage ends in death, divorce, or annulment.

Additional Benefits

FPOWs and their dependents may also be entitled to:
- Pension (income-based).
- Medical care.
- Education and training.

- Home loan guaranty.
- Burial benefits.
- Survivors' pension.
- Burial in a national cemetery.

Special Assistance

Each VA Regional Office has a FPOW Veterans Outreach Coordinator to assist FPOWs with benefits and services. To find your local coordinator, contact your nearest VA regional benefit office.

How to Apply

To apply for benefits, you can:
- Contact your local FPOW Veterans Outreach Coordinator at your nearest VA regional benefit office.
- Apply online using the VA's official website.
- Work with an accredited representative or agent.
- Visit a VA Regional Office for assistance.

Veterans Living Overseas

Veterans living outside the U.S. are entitled to the benefits earned during their military service, regardless of where they reside. Most VA benefits remain accessible to veterans abroad, including disability compensation, pension, education, healthcare, home loans, insurance, and more.

What You Need to Know

- **Direct Deposit**: After payments are made from the U.S., the timing of your deposit depends on your foreign bank's processing system.
- **VA Claim Exam**: If you need a disability claim exam, it will be scheduled as close to your location as possible. It's crucial to provide your physical address, not just your mailing address, to ensure proper communication and avoid delays. Keep your contact details updated to prevent issues with your claim.
- **Currency Conversion**: While there's no fee for converting currency for VA payments, your bank might impose a fee.
- **Foreign Schools**: Veterans can use their education benefits to attend approved foreign schools. Find approved programs and learn more about eligibility.
- **Specially Adaptive Housing**: Disabled veterans may qualify for grants to modify or build homes to accommodate their disabilities. The property must be owned by the Veteran, and all modifications must be pre-approved by the VA.

Healthcare Abroad

Veterans living abroad can access care for service-connected disabilities through the VA's Foreign Medical Program. This program covers necessary treatments, and more details are available through the VA's website.

Setting Up an eBenefits Account

To manage your benefits online, set up an eBenefits account. If you're a dependent without a Social Security number, you can contact the Defense Manpower Data Center to receive a generated number for registration.

For additional help, contact VA's support team or visit a VA office nearest to you.

Vietnam Veterans

The Vietnam War, officially known as the Second Indochina War, spanned from November 1, 1955, to April 30, 1975. During this period, approximately 2.7 million U.S. military personnel served in Vietnam. The conflict resulted in over 58,000 American military deaths and approximately 153,000 wounded. Additionally, 766 U.S. service members were taken as prisoners of war, with 114 dying in captivity.

VA Benefits for Vietnam Veterans

Vietnam veterans may be eligible for a variety of benefits available to all U.S. military veterans. These benefits include disability compensation, pension, education and training, health care, home loans, insurance, vocational rehabilitation and employment, and burial services.

Disability Compensation for Veterans Exposed to Agent Orange

The Department of Veterans Affairs (VA) presumes that certain health conditions in veterans were caused by exposure to Agent Orange during military service. Veterans who served in Vietnam between January 9, 1962, and May 7, 1975, are presumed to have been exposed to herbicides, including Agent Orange. As a result, they may be eligible for disability compensation for diseases associated with this exposure.

Children of Veterans Exposed to Agent Orange

Children of veterans exposed to Agent Orange who have certain birth defects, such as spina bifida, may be entitled to VA benefits. These benefits can include monetary compensation, health care, and vocational rehabilitation services.

Women Veterans

Women have been integral to the United States military since the Revolutionary War, serving across all branches and achieving significant milestones. Today, women veterans are entitled to a comprehensive array of benefits and services through the Department of Veterans Affairs (VA).

VA Benefits for Women Veterans

Women veterans may qualify for various benefits available to all U.S. military veterans, including:

- **Disability Compensation**: Financial support for veterans with service-connected disabilities.
- **Pension**: Income assistance for low-income veterans.
- **Education and Training**: Opportunities for further education and skill development.
- **Health Care**: Access to comprehensive medical services.
- **Home Loans**: Assistance in purchasing homes with favorable terms.
- **Insurance**: Life insurance options tailored for veterans.
- **Vocational Rehabilitation and Employment**: Support for career development and job placement.
- **Burial**: Benefits related to funeral and burial services.

Specialized Programs for Women Veterans

The VA offers programs specifically designed to address the unique needs of women veterans:

- **Center for Women Veterans**: Established in 1994, this center monitors and coordinates VA's administration of benefit services and programs for women veterans. It advocates for cultural transformation within the VA and the general public, recognizing the service and contributions of women veterans and women in the military.
- **Women Veterans Call Center:** A dedicated resource providing information and assistance to women veterans. Representatives are available Monday through Friday, 8:00 a.m. to 10:00 p.m. ET, and Saturday, 8:00 a.m. to 6:30 p.m. ET.
- **Women Veterans Program Managers:** Located at each VA medical center, these managers coordinate care and advocate for women veterans, ensuring access to necessary health services.

Health Care Services for Women Veterans

The VA provides comprehensive health care services tailored to women veterans, including:

- **Primary and Specialty Care**: Routine check-ups, cancer screenings, and specialized treatments.
- **Reproductive Health Care:** Maternity care, family planning, and menopause management.
- **Mental Health Services:** Support for conditions such as PTSD, depression, and anxiety.
- **Preventive Care**: Immunizations, wellness exams, and health education.

Applying for VA Benefits

Women veterans can apply for VA benefits through several channels:

- **Online**: Use the VA's official website to apply for health care and other benefits.
- **In Person**: Visit a local VA regional office for assistance.
- **By Phone**: Contact the Women Veterans Call Center at 1-855-829-6636 for guidance.

World War II Veterans

World War II (WWII) was the most widespread conflict in history, with over 100 million people serving in military units worldwide. Veterans who were part of the Occupation Forces assigned to Hiroshima and Nagasaki, Japan, shortly after the atomic bombings, and those American prisoners of war (POWs) held near these cities, are sometimes referred to as "Atomic Veterans."

VA Benefits

WWII veterans may be eligible for a variety of benefits available to all U.S. military veterans. These benefits include disability compensation, pension, education and training, health care, home loans, insurance, vocational rehabilitation and employment, and burial.

Benefits for WWII Veterans Exposed to Ionizing Radiation

WWII-era veterans may qualify for health care and compensation benefits if they were exposed to ionizing radiation during military service. Health care services include an Ionizing Radiation Registry health exam and clinical treatment at VA's War Related Illness and Injury Study Centers. You may also be entitled to disability compensation benefits if you have certain cancers as a result of exposure to ionizing radiation during military service.

Benefits for WWII Veterans Who Participated in Radiation-Risk Activities

WWII-era veterans may qualify for health care and compensation benefits if they participated in certain radiation-risk activities, such as nuclear weapons testing, during military service. These veterans may be informally referred to as "Atomic Veterans." Health care services include an Ionizing Radiation Registry health exam and clinical treatment at VA's War Related Illness and Injury Study Centers. You may also be entitled to disability compensation benefits if you have certain cancers as a result of your participation in a radiation-risk activity during military service.

Benefits for Survivors of Veterans with Radiation Exposure

Surviving spouses, dependent children, and dependent parents of veterans who died as a result of diseases related to radiation exposure during military service may be eligible for survivors' benefits.

CHAPTER 21

SERVICEMEMBERS' CIVIL RELIEF ACT

Congress and state legislatures have long recognized that military service can often place an economic and legal burden on servicemembers. The Soldiers' and Sailors' Civil Relief Act of 1918 was passed in order to protect the rights of service members while serving on active duty.

Servicemembers were protected from such things as repossession of property, bankruptcy, foreclosure or other such actions while serving in the military. This Act remained in effect until shortly after World War I when it expired. The Soldiers' and Sailors' Civil Relief Act of 1940 (SSCRA) was passed in order to protect the rights of the millions of service members activated for World War II. The SSCRA has remained in effect until the present day and has been amended many times since 1940 to keep pace with the changing military.

In December 2003, Congress passed legislation renaming SSCRA as the Servicemembers' Civil Relief Act (SCRA). The SCRA updates and strengthens the civil protections enacted during World War II.

The SCRA is designed to protect active-duty military members, reservists who are in active federal service, and National Guardsmen who are in active federal service. Some of the benefits under the SCRA extend to dependents of active-duty military members as well.

Public Law 107-330 extended protections under the SCRA to members of the National Guard who are called to active service authorized by the President or the Secretary of Defense, or a state governor for a period of more than 30 consecutive days, for purposes of responding to a national emergency declared by the President and supported by Federal funds.

The SCRA can provide many forms of relief to military members. Below are some of the most common forms of relief.

Protection from Eviction

If a military member is leasing a house or apartment and his or her rent is below a certain amount, the SCRA can protect the individual from being evicted for a period of time, usually three months. The dwelling place must be occupied by either the active-duty member or his or her dependents and the rent on the premises **cannot exceed $9,106.46 a month.**

This rent ceiling will be adjusted annually for consumer price index (CPI) changes. Additionally, the military member must show that military service materially affects his or her ability to pay rent. If a landlord continues to try to evict the military member or does actually evict the member, he or she is subject to criminal sanctions such as fines or even imprisonment.

Termination of Pre-Service Residential Leases

The SCRA also allows military members who are just entering active-duty service to lawfully terminate a lease without repercussions. To do this, the service member needs to show that the lease was entered into prior to the commencement of active-duty service, that the lease was signed by or on behalf of the service member, and that the service member is currently in military service or was called to active-duty service for a period of 180 days or more. Proper written notice with a copy of orders must be provided to the landlord.

Termination of Residential Leases During Military Service

The SCRA allows military members who receive permanent change of station (PCS) orders or are deployed for a period of 90 days or more to terminate a lease by providing written notice to the landlord along with a copy of the military orders. The termination of a lease that provides for monthly payment of rent will occur 30 days after the first date on which the next rental payment is due and payable after the landlord receives proper written notice.

Mortgages

The SCRA can also provide military members temporary relief from paying their mortgage. To obtain relief, a military member must show that their mortgage was entered into prior to beginning active duty, that the property was owned prior to entry into military service, that the property is still owned by the military member, and that military service materially affects the member's ability to pay the mortgage.

Mortgage foreclosures or lien actions initiated during your military service or within nine months after the end of your military service must be stayed upon your request. This applies only to obligations that you have undertaken before entering active duty. A court may instead "adjust the obligations in a way that preserves the interests of all parties." Note that the nine-month period reverts to 90 days as of January 1, 2013, unless further extended.

No sale, foreclosure, or seizure of property for a breach of a pre-service mortgage-type obligation is valid if made during or within 9 months after the period of active duty, unless pursuant to a valid court order. This provides the service member tremendous protections from foreclosure in the many states that permit foreclosures to proceed without involvement of the courts. Service members who miss any mortgage payments should immediately see a legal assistance attorney.

Maximum Rate of Interest

Under the SCRA, a military member can **cap the interest rate at 6% for all obligations** entered into before beginning active duty if the military service materially affects his or her ability to meet the obligations. This can include interest rates on credit cards, mortgages, and even some student loans (except for Federally guaranteed student loans), to name a few. To qualify for the interest rate, cap the military member has to show that he or she is now on active duty, that the obligation or debt was incurred prior to entry on active duty, and that military service materially affects the members' ability to pay.

To begin the process, the military member needs to send a letter along with a copy of current military orders to the lender requesting relief under the SCRA. The interest rate cap lasts for the duration of active-duty service. The interest rate cap will apply from the first date of active-duty service. The military member must provide written notice to the creditor and a copy of military orders not later than 180 days after the service member's termination or release from military service.

Termination of Automobile Leases During Military Service

The SCRA allows military members to terminate pre-service automobile leases if they are called up for military service of 180 days or longer. Members who sign automobile leases while on active duty may be able to terminate an automobile lease if they are given orders for a permanent change of station outside the continental United States or to deploy with military unit for a period of 180 days or longer.

Stay of Proceedings

If a military member is served with a complaint indicating that they are being sued for some reason, they can obtain a "stay" or postponement of those proceedings if the military service materially affects their ability to proceed in the case. A stay can be used to stop the action altogether or to hold up some phase of it.

According to the SCRA, military members can request a "stay" during any stage of the proceedings. However, the burden is on the military member to show that their military service has materially affected their ability to appear in court. In general, individuals can request a stay of the proceedings for a reasonable period of time (30-60 days).

For example, if they are being sued for divorce, they can put off the hearing for some period of time, but it is unlikely that a court will allow the proceedings to be put off indefinitely. The stay can be granted in administrative proceedings.

Default Judgments

A default judgment is entered against a party who has failed to defend against a claim that has been brought by another party.

To obtain a default judgment, a plaintiff must file an affidavit (written declaration of fact) stating that the defendant is not in the military service and has not requested a stay. If someone is sued while on active duty and fails to respond, and as a result a default judgment is obtained against them, they can reopen the default judgment by taking several steps.

First, they must show that the judgment was entered during their military service or within 30 days after they've left the service.

Second, they must write to the court requesting that the default judgment be reopened while they are still on active duty or within 90 days of leaving the service.

Third, they must not have made any kind of appearance in court, through filing an answer or otherwise, prior to the default judgment being entered. Finally, they must indicate that their military service prejudiced their ability to defend their case and show that they had a valid defense to the action against them.

Insurance

Under SCRA, the U.S. Department of Veterans Affairs (VA) will protect, from default for nonpayment of premiums, up to $250,000 of life insurance for servicemembers called to active duty. (This amount was previously $10,000.) The protection provided by this legislation applies during the insured's period of military service and for a period of two years thereafter. The following are conditions for eligibility for protection:
- The policy must be whole life, endowment, universal life or term insurance.
- The policy must have been in force on a premium-paying basis for at least six months at the time the servicemember applies for benefits.
- Benefits from the policy cannot be limited, reduced or excluded because of military service.
- Policies for which an additional amount of premium is charged due to military service are not eligible for protection under SCRA.

The servicemember must apply for protection of their life insurance by filing "VA Form 29-380 "Application For Protection Of Commercial Life Insurance Policy" with his/her insurance company and forwarding a copy of the application to VA.

Benefits of SCRA Life Insurance Protection

Once the servicemember has applied for protection of their life insurance policy and VA determines that the policy is eligible for protection under SCRA:

- The servicemember is still responsible for making premium payments. However, the policy will not lapse, terminate, or be forfeited because of the servicemember's failure to make premium payments or to pay any indebtedness or interest due during their period of military service or for a period of two years thereafter.
- The rights of the servicemember to change their beneficiary designation or select an optional settlement for a beneficiary are not affected by the provisions of this Act.

Limitations of SCRA Life Insurance Protection

Once the servicemember has applied for protection of their life insurance policy and VA determines that the policy is eligible for protection under SCRA:

- Premium payments are deferred only, not waived. During this period, the government does not pay the premiums on the policy but simply guarantees that the premiums will be paid at the end of the servicemember's period of active duty.
- A servicemember cannot receive dividends, take out a loan, or surrender the policy for cash without the approval of VA. (Dividends or other monetary benefits shall be added to the value of the policy and will be used as a credit when final settlement is made with the insurer.)
- If the policy matures as a result of the insured's death, or any other means, during the protected period, the insurance company will deduct any unpaid premiums and interest due from the settlement amount.

Termination of Period Under SCRA

The servicemember has up to two years after their military service terminates to repay the unpaid premiums and interest to the insurer.

If the amount owed is not paid before the end of the two years, then:

- The insurer treats the unpaid premiums as a loan against the policy.
- The government will pay the insurer the difference between the amount due and the cash surrender value (if the cash surrender value of the policy is less than the amount owed.)
- The amount the United States government pays to the insurance company under the SCRA Act becomes a debt due the government by the insured.
- If the policy matures as a result of the insured's death, or any other means, during the protected period, the insurance company will deduct any unpaid premiums and interest due from the settlement amount.

Taxation

A servicemember's state of legal residence may tax military pay and personal property. A member does not lose residence solely because of a transfer to another state pursuant to military orders.

For example, if an Illinois resident who is a member of Illinois Army National Guard is activated to federal military service and sent to California for duty, that person remains an Illinois resident while in California. The service member is not subject to California's authority to tax his/her military income. However, if the service member has a part-time civilian job in California, California will tax his/her non-military income earned in the state.

The Servicemembers Civil Relief Act also contains a provision preventing servicemembers from a form of double taxation that can occur when they have a spouse who works and is taxed in a state other than the state in which they maintain their permanent legal residence. The law prevents states from using the income earned by a servicemember in determining the spouse's tax rate when they do not maintain their permanent legal residence in that state. Public Law 111-98, which became law on November 11, 2009, provides that when a service member leaves his or her home state in accord with military or naval orders, the service member's spouse may retain residency in his or her home state for voting and tax purposes, after relocating from that state to accompany the service member.

Right to Vote

In addition to the protections involving debt payments and civil litigation, the act guarantees service members the right to vote in the state of their home of record and protects them from paying taxes in two different states.

Caution

The SCRA does not wipe out any of an individual's obligations. Rather, it temporarily suspends the right of creditors to use a court to compel an individual to pay, only if the court finds that the inability to pay is due to military service. The obligation to honor existing debts remains, and someday the individual must "pay up."

It is important to remember that the SCRA affords no relief to persons in the Service against the collection of debts or other obligations contracted or assumed by them after entering such Service.

The Servicemembers' Civil Relief Act is highly technical. The above summary is intended only to give a general overview of the protection available. The specific nature of all the relief provided under the law is a matter about which an individual may need to contact an attorney. The Act is designed to deal fairly with military personnel and their creditors. While relief is very often available, individuals are expected and required to show good faith in repayment of all debts.

Veterans Benefits Act of 2010 Overview

This law amended the Servicemembers Civil Relief Act (SCRA) to prohibit lessors from charging early termination fees with respect to residential, business, agricultural, or motor vehicle leases entered into by servicemembers who subsequently enter military service or receive orders for a permanent change of station or deployment in support of a military operation.

It allows a servicemember to terminate a contract for cellular or home telephone service at any time after receiving military orders to deploy for at least 90 days to a location that does not support the contract. The law requires the return of any advance payments made by a deploying servicemember under such a contract.

It also allows the Attorney General to bring a civil suit against any violator of the SCRA and gives servicemembers a "private right of action" to file their own lawsuits against those who violate their legal rights.

CHAPTER 22

NATIONAL GUARD AND RESERVE

Members of the National Guard and Reserve, both current and former, may be eligible for a variety of benefits through the Department of Veterans Affairs (VA). These benefits encompass disability compensation, pensions, home loan guarantees, education, health care, insurance, vocational rehabilitation and employment, and burial services. Understanding your eligibility and the application process is essential to accessing these resources.

Qualifying Service in the National Guard and Reserve

Generally, all National Guard and Reserve members discharged or released under conditions other than dishonorable are eligible for some VA benefits.

Eligibility for specific benefits may depend on factors such as the length of service, type of service (e.g., active duty or full-time National Guard duty), and duty status.

Active Service

Eligibility for several VA benefits requires a certain length of active service. Active service in the National Guard or Reserve includes:

- **Active Duty (Title 10):** Full-time duty in the Armed Forces, such as unit deployment during war, including travel to and from such duty, except active duty for training.
- **Full-Time National Guard Duty (Title 32):** Duty performed for which you are entitled to receive pay from the federal government, such as responding to a national emergency or performing duties as an Active Guard Reserve (AGR) member.

It's important to note that service on State Active Duty, such as in response to a natural or man-made disaster, is based on state law and does not qualify as "active service" for VA benefits. Unlike full-time National Guard duty, National Guard members on State Active Duty are paid with state funds as opposed to federal funds.

Traditional and Technician Service

Traditional National Guard and Reserve members typically serve one weekend per month and two weeks per year. Traditional members may become eligible for some VA benefits by fulfilling a service commitment.

Eligibility for disability compensation requires that a disability was the result of an injury or disease incurred or aggravated in the line of duty during active duty or active duty for training. For inactive duty training, the disability must have resulted from injury, heart attack, or stroke. Other benefit programs require a specified number of days of active service.

Military technicians are civilian employees of the Department of the Army or Department of the Air Force who are required to maintain membership in the National Guard or Reserve in order to retain employment.

Similar to traditional National Guard and Reserve members, military technicians are normally in a military status one weekend a month and two weeks a year and are eligible for some VA benefits. They may establish eligibility for additional benefits based on the length of Guard, Reserve, or active service.

Serving on active duty under Title 10 or full-time National Guard duty under Title 32 may qualify you for additional VA benefits.

A state or territory's governor may activate certain National Guard members for State Active Duty, such as in response to a natural or man-made disaster. State Active Duty is based on state law and funding and does not qualify as active duty for VA benefits.

However, National Guard members may also qualify for additional benefits through their state. Contact your state's veteran's agency office for more information. Home Loans.

Home Loan Guaranty

The VA's Home Loan Guaranty Program assists eligible service members and veterans in purchasing, retaining, or adapting homes. National Guard and Reserve members may qualify if they meet one of the following conditions:

- **Six years of service in the Selected Reserve**, and either:
    o Discharged honorably,
    o Placed on the retired list,
    o Transferred to the Standby Reserve or another element of the Ready Reserve after honorable service,
    o Continue to serve in the Selected Reserve beyond six years.
- **Served for 90 days or more on active duty (Title 10) during a wartime period**, or
- **Served at least 90 days of active-duty service**, including at least 30 consecutive days, with activation under specific U.S. Code sections.
- **Discharged or released from active duty for a service-connected disability**.

Education Benefits

The VA offers several education programs for National Guard and Reserve members:

- **Post-9/11 GI Bill**: Eligible if you have at least 90 aggregate days of active service after September 10, 2001, or were discharged with a service-connected disability after serving at least 30 consecutive days.
- **Montgomery GI Bill-Selected Reserve (MGIB-SR)**: Available to those with a six-year obligation to serve in the Selected Reserve, who have completed Initial Active Duty for Training (IADT), serve in a drilling unit and remain in good standing, and have a high school diploma or equivalency.
- **Reserve Educational Assistance Program (REAP)**: For members who served on active duty for at least 90 consecutive days after September 10, 2001.

Life Insurance

The VA provides life insurance options tailored for service members and veterans:

- **Servicemembers' Group Life Insurance (SGLI)**: Automatic coverage for National Guard or Reserve members scheduled to perform at least 12 periods of inactive duty training per year, or Individual Ready Reserve members who volunteer for a mobilization category.
- **Veterans' Group Life Insurance (VGLI)**: Available to those separating, retiring, or being released from Reserve or National Guard assignments and already covered by SGLI. Applications must be submitted within one year and 120 days from discharge.
- **Family Servicemembers' Group Life Insurance (FSGLI)**: Coverage for spouses and dependent children of active-duty service members covered by full-time SGLI.
- **SGLI Traumatic Injury Protection (TSGLI)**: Provides financial assistance to service members who suffer traumatic injuries.

Disability Compensation

Disability compensation is a monthly tax-free benefit for veterans with disabilities resulting from injuries or diseases incurred or aggravated during active duty or active duty for training. Eligibility requires a disability rating of at least 10%. Additional benefits may include automobile allowance, clothing allowance, and Specially Adapted Housing (SAH) or Special Home Adaptation (SHA) grants.

Health Care

VA health care benefits encompass necessary inpatient and outpatient services to promote, preserve, or restore health. Eligibility requires that you served on active duty under a federal order and completed the full period for which you were called or ordered. If you served on active duty in a theater of combat operations after November 11, 1998, you are eligible for free VA health care benefits for up to 5 years from the date of discharge or release.

Burial Benefits

The VA offers burial and memorial services to honor deceased veterans, including:
- Burial in a national cemetery.
- An inscribed headstone, marker, or medallion.
- A burial and/or plot allowance to partially reimburse burial and funeral costs.
- A Presidential Memorial Certificate.
- An American flag to drape the casket.

Eligibility requires that the veteran was serving on active duty, or their death was due to an injury or disease that developed or was aggravated during active duty, active duty for training, or inactive duty training.

Frequently Asked Questions

Do I qualify for VA benefits as a National Guard or Reserve member?

Yes, generally, all National Guard and Reserve members qualify for some VA benefits. Different VA benefits may consider different factors to determine eligibility, such as length of service, type of service (e.g., active duty or full-time National Guard duty), wartime service, and/or service-related disability.

What is the difference between serving as a Traditional National Guard or Reserve member and as an Active Guard Reserve member?

Traditional National Guard and Reserve members typically serve one weekend a month and two weeks a year. Active Guard Reserve members are full-time members of a Reserve component for which they are entitled to receive pay from the federal government. As an AGR, you establish eligibility for certain VA benefits by your active service under either Title 10 or Title 32.

What qualifies as a wartime period?

Under current law, VA recognizes the following wartime periods:
- World War I (April 6, 1917 – November 11, 1918)
- World War II (December 7, 1941 – December 31, 1946)
- Korean conflict (June 27, 1950 – January 31, 1955)
- Vietnam era (February 28, 1961 – May 7, 1975, for veterans who served in the Republic of Vietnam during that period; otherwise August 5, 1964 – May 7, 1975)
- Gulf War (August 2, 1990 – through a future date to be set by law or Presidential Proclamation)

CHAPTER 23

LIFE INSURANCE

VA insurance programs were developed to provide insurance benefits for veterans and servicemembers who may not be able to get insurance from private companies because of a service-connected disability or because of the extra risks involved in military service. VA has responsibility for veterans' and servicemembers' life insurance programs.

In October 2023, VA reduced premiums for most veterans and servicemembers insured under the Veterans' Mortgage Life Insurance program. Through the VMLI program, eligible veterans and servicemembers with severe disabilities can purchase up to $200,000 in mortgage life insurance. Starting October 1, 2023, most VMLI policyholders saw a reduction between 6% and 36% on their premiums, depending on their age.

VALife Veterans Affairs Life Insurance

Veterans Affairs Life Insurance (VALife) provides guaranteed acceptance whole life coverage of up to $40,000 to veterans with service-connected disabilities. Lesser amounts are available, in increments of $10,000. Under the plan, the elected coverage will take effect two years after enrollment, as long as premiums are paid during the two-year period.

All veterans aged 80 and under who have a disability rating from the VA of 0-100% are eligible to apply for the program, with no time limit to apply.

Veterans who are 81 or older and have applied for VA Disability Compensation before age 81 but who didn't receive the rating for a new service-connected condition until after turning 81 are also eligible if they apply within two years of their rating.

The two-year waiting period that's part of this life insurance program replaces the need for medical underwriting. If the insured dies within the two-year period, the beneficiary receives all premiums they've paid plus interest.

The premium rate you pay each month or annually for coverage depends on your age and the amount of coverage you elect. The premiums for VALife are fixed, and they're based on your age when you enroll. There are no premium waivers for this program.

VALife took effect January 1, 2023, and the application became available on the VA's site after that date.

As a result of VALife, S-DVI programs are closed to new enrollment. No new applications are being accepted. If you have S-DVI you can apply for VALife.

If you apply before December 31, 2025, you can keep S-DVI during the initial two-year enrollment period for VALife. You don't have to switch to VALife—you can stay in the S-DVI program.

Servicemembers' Group Life Insurance

Servicemembers' Group Life Insurance (SGLI) provides affordable term life coverage to eligible service members. If you meet the required criteria, you will be automatically enrolled. Here's what you need to know about your eligibility and how to manage your coverage.

Am I Eligible For SGLI?

You may qualify for full-time SGLI coverage if you meet at least one of the following conditions:
- You are an active-duty member of the Army, Navy, Air Force, Space Force, Marine Corps, or Coast Guard.
- You are a commissioned officer with the National Oceanic and Atmospheric Administration (NOAA) or the U.S. Public Health Service (USPHS).
- You are a cadet or midshipman at one of the U.S. military academies.
- You are a member of the Reserve Officers Training Corps (ROTC) engaged in authorized training or practice cruises.
- You are a member of the Ready Reserve or National Guard, assigned to a unit, and scheduled for at least 12 periods of inactive training per year.
- You are a volunteer in an Individual Ready Reserve (IRR) mobilization category.

If you are in a nonpay status with the Ready Reserve or National Guard, you may still qualify for full-time SGLI if you meet both of the following:
- You are scheduled for 12 periods of inactive training for the year.
- You are drilling for points, not pay. (Note: Premiums must be paid directly in this case.)

What Benefits Are Available with SGLI?

SGLI provides benefits such as:
- Coverage up to $500,000 in increments of $50,000.
- 120 days of free coverage after leaving the military.
- Up to 2 years of free coverage if you're totally disabled when leaving the military.
- Part-time coverage for Reserve members who do not qualify for full-time

SGLI coverage.

How Do I Get SGLI Benefits?

If you meet the criteria, you will automatically be enrolled in SGLI through your service branch. For more information, check with your unit's personnel office.

Can I Make Changes to My SGLI Coverage?

Yes, you can adjust your coverage level or decline coverage completely. You can also select and update your beneficiaries (those who will receive the payout from your life insurance policy in the event of your death).

How to update your SGLI coverage:

You can update your coverage and beneficiaries through the SGLI Online Enrollment System (SOES):
1. Go to milConnect and sign in.
2. Select "Manage my SGLI."
3. Review your coverage and beneficiary information and make any necessary updates.

You can log in using your CAC or DS Logon as soon as you are notified that SOES is available for you.

How much does SGLI cost?

SGLI premiums are deducted automatically from your base pay each month. The current rate is 6 cents per $1,000 of coverage, plus an additional $1 per month for Traumatic Injury Protection (TSGLI).

Here's a breakdown of monthly premiums:

Coverage Amount	Premium	TSGLI Premium	Total Monthly Premium
$500,000	$30.00	$1.00	$31.00
$450,000	$27.00	$1.00	$28.00
$400,000	$24.00	$1.00	$25.00
$350,000	$21.00	$1.00	$22.00
$300,000	$18.00	$1.00	$19.00
$250,000	$15.00	$1.00	$16.00
$200,000	$12.00	$1.00	$13.00
$150,000	$9.00	$1.00	$10.00
$100,000	$6.00	$1.00	$7.00
$50,000	$3.00	$1.00	$4.00

Converting SGLI Coverage When Leaving the Military
Upon separation from the military, you have the option to convert your SGLI coverage:
- **Convert to VGLI:** You can apply for Veterans' Group Life Insurance (VGLI) within 1 year and 120 days of discharge, maintaining up to the amount of coverage you had under SGLI.
- **Convert to individual insurance**: You can also convert your SGLI coverage to a permanent, individual policy (like whole life insurance) within

120 days of discharge without providing proof of good health.

Free SGLI Extension For Disabled Servicemembers

If you are totally disabled when leaving the military, you may qualify for up to 2 years of free SGLI coverage. You must meet one of the following conditions:
- You are unable to work due to your disability at the time of discharge, or
- You have permanent (long-lasting) loss of hearing in both ears, loss of speech, or the use of both hands, feet, or eyes.

How to apply for the SGLI Disability Extension

To apply, complete the SGLI Disability Extension Application (SGLV 8715) and submit it to the Office of Servicemembers' Group Life Insurance (OSGLI).

Additional support

If you have any questions or need assistance with your SGLI benefits, you can contact the OSGLI at 800-419-1473 or email Prudential Insurance Company for help.

Beneficiary Forms:
- SGLV 8283: For death benefits claims.
- SGLV 8600: For traumatic injury benefits.
- SGLV 8284: For accelerated benefits claims.

Family Servicemembers' Group Life Insurance (FSGLI)

Family Servicemembers' Group Life Insurance (FSGLI) provides life insurance coverage for the spouse and dependent children of service members covered by full-time SGLI.

Am I Eligible For FSGLI?

You may be eligible for FSGLI if you are the spouse or dependent child of a service member who meets one of the following criteria:
- The service member is on active duty and covered by full-time SGLI.
- The service member is a member of the National Guard or Ready Reserve and covered by full-time SGLI.
- If you're married to someone covered by full-time SGLI, you are eligible for coverage, regardless of your own status (active duty, Reserve, Guard, retired, or civilian).

Who Is Covered Under FSGLI?
- The spouse of a service member covered by SGLI.
- Dependent children of a service member covered by SGLI.

How much coverage can I get with FSGLI?

- Spouses can receive coverage up to $100,000, but this cannot exceed the amount of the service member's SGLI coverage.
- Dependent children are automatically covered for $10,000, with no cost to the service member.

How do I get these benefits?

- For civilian spouses of service members: FSGLI coverage is automatic when the service member is signed up for full-time SGLI, and premiums are deducted from the service member's pay.
- For military spouses married on or after January 2, 2013: You must be signed up for FSGLI by your service member through the SGLI Online Enrollment System (SOES).

How much will my service member pay for spousal coverage?

The premiums for spousal coverage vary based on the age of the spouse. The premium increases with age and is deducted from the service member's pay. For example, if the spouse is under 35 years old and the coverage amount is $100,000, the premium will be $4.50 per month.

Can my servicemember make changes to their FSGLI coverage?

Yes, the service member can modify, reduce, or cancel spousal coverage using the SGLI Online Enrollment System (SOES).

How much will my service member pay for dependent coverage?

There is no cost for dependent coverage. Dependent children are automatically covered, and coverage continues until they are 18, or longer if they are full-time students or permanently disabled.

Can my service member extend coverage for our dependent child?

Yes, if the child is a full-time student between 18 and 22 years old or has a permanent disability, they may continue coverage under certain conditions.

How do I convert spousal FSGLI coverage to an individual insurance policy?

If your service member separates from the military, divorces you, or cancels the coverage, you can convert FSGLI coverage to a permanent individual life insurance policy within 120 days. This is only applicable if you meet the required conditions and you will be responsible for premium payments once the policy is converted.

Which forms are needed for claims or changes?

- **Report of Death of Family Member:** If a family member covered by FSGLI passes away, the service member needs to file this form (SGLV 8700).

- **Claim for Family Coverage Death Benefits:** To claim death benefits, this form (SGLV 8283A) must be filed.
- **Claim for Accelerated Benefits:** If the spouse is terminally ill, this form (SGLV 8284A) is needed for an advance on the insurance benefits.

Traumatic Injury Protection (TSGLI)

TSGLI, or Servicemembers' Group Life Insurance Traumatic Injury Protection, provides financial assistance to service members who sustain qualifying injuries during their military service. This coverage helps with the expenses associated with recovery and rehabilitation. If you've experienced a traumatic injury while serving, you may be eligible for TSGLI.

Recent Updates to TSGLI Benefits

As of April 14, 2023, VA broadened TSGLI benefits to cover additional types of care, including:
- Limb reconstruction surgeries
- Inpatient care at critical care and rehabilitation facilities, as well as skilled nursing facilities
- Transitional care to support your move from an inpatient facility back to home (referred to as a therapeutic pass)

If you're eligible for these expanded TSGLI benefits, you can now file a claim. If your previous claim was denied, you can submit a new one.

Am I Eligible For TSGLI?

You may qualify for TSGLI if you were covered by SGLI when you sustained a traumatic injury, and if you meet all of the following criteria:
- You experienced a scheduled loss that directly resulted from the traumatic injury.
- The injury occurred before midnight on the day you separated from the military.
- You experienced a scheduled loss within 2 years (730 days) of the traumatic injury.
- You survived for at least 7 full days after the injury (the 7-day period starts at the time of the injury and ends 168 full hours later).
- You were an active-duty service member, Reservist, National Guard member, on funeral-honors duty, or on 1-day muster duty.

Are any injuries excluded from TSGLI?

Yes, certain injuries do not qualify for TSGLI. Specifically, your injury must not meet any of the following criteria:
- The injury cannot be self-inflicted or result from an intentional attempt at self-harm.
- The injury cannot involve the use of an illegal drug or a controlled substance

that was taken without medical supervision.

- The injury cannot be the result of medical or surgical treatment for an illness or disease.
- The injury cannot occur while committing or attempting to commit a felony.
- The injury cannot be caused by a physical or mental illness or disease, except for cases related to wound infections, chemical/biological/radiological weapons, or the accidental ingestion of contaminated substances.

Can I get retroactive TSGLI for a past injury?

You may be eligible for retroactive TSGLI if you were injured between October 7, 2001, and November 30, 2005, and meet the qualifications listed above. This benefit applies regardless of where the injury occurred—on or off duty—and regardless of whether your SGLI coverage was active at the time of the injury.

Note: The previous requirement for injuries to be sustained during Operations Enduring or Iraqi Freedom (OEF or OIF) has been removed.

Who's covered?

Service members who are covered by SGLI.

What kind of life insurance benefits can I get through TSGLI?

Through TSGLI, you may receive between $25,000 and $100,000 in financial assistance to support your recovery from a traumatic injury.

How do I get these benefits?

If you are enrolled in full-time SGLI, you are automatically covered by TSGLI, even if the injury occurred while you were off duty. However, to receive payments—including retroactive benefits—you must file a claim. To do this, complete the Application for TSGLI Benefits (SGLV 8600) and submit it to the appropriate service branch by fax, email, or mail. The address for your service branch can be found on the form.

How do I appeal a decision if I'm denied benefits?

If your claim is denied, review the denial letter sent by your service branch. The letter will provide guidance on whether you should complete the TSGLI Appeal Request Form (SGLV 8600A) and include any deadlines for submitting your appeal. If instructed to do so, complete the form and submit it to your service branch.

How much will I pay for these benefits?

If you have SGLI coverage, your SGLI premium automatically includes a $1 monthly flat-rate charge for TSGLI, which is deducted from your base pay. This is the only cost associated with this benefit.

Service-Disabled Veterans Life Insurance (S-DVI)

Service-Disabled Veterans Life Insurance (S-DVI) offers affordable life insurance coverage for veterans with service-connected disabilities. However, as of December 31, 2022, new applications for S-DVI are no longer being accepted. If you're already enrolled in this program, you can continue to maintain your coverage. Continue reading for more information about S-DVI.

Am I eligible for life insurance through the VA as a veteran with a service-connected disability?

Yes. The VA introduced a new program called Veterans Affairs Life Insurance (VALife) for Veterans with service-connected disabilities. Applications for VALife opened on January 1, 2023.

Questions about your existing S-DVI policy

How much do my S-DVI premiums cost?

The cost of your premiums depends on several factors:
- Your age
- The amount of coverage you've selected
- The type of coverage plan you've chosen
- Whether you make monthly or annual payments

Can I get a waiver for my premiums?

Yes, in certain situations, you may be eligible for a premium waiver. The basic S-DVI policy offers a waiver for veterans who are totally disabled under specific conditions.

If you have supplemental S-DVI, you will still be required to pay premiums for this additional coverage, even if you qualify for a waiver on the basic S-DVI premiums.

Please note: Supplemental S-DVI also stopped accepting new applications as of December 31, 2022.

Can I switch from S-DVI to VALife?

Yes, you can. If you currently have S-DVI, you have the following two options:
1. You can apply for VALife now.
2. You can keep your S-DVI coverage as it is, with no action required on your part.

What you need to know about switching to VALife:
- If you apply for VALife by December 31, 2025, you can continue your S-DVI

coverage during the 2-year waiting period for VALife benefits. Your S-DVI policy (including those with premium waivers) will end when your full VALife coverage begins. During the waiting period, you will need to pay premiums for both policies.

- If you apply for VALife on or after January 1, 2026, your S-DVI (including policies with premium waivers) will end the day your VALife application is approved. During the 2-year waiting period, you will only need to pay premiums for VALife, but you will not have full coverage during that time.

Important note:

VALife does not offer premium waivers, so if you have a premium waiver for S-DVI, it will not carry over to your VALife policy.

Need more information?

If you have additional questions, you can contact the VA Life Insurance Center at 800-669-8477 (TTY: 711), Monday through Friday, from 8:30 a.m. to 6:00 p.m. ET.

They can assist you with inquiries regarding:
- VALife
- S-DVI
- Any other VA life insurance policies starting with V, J, RS, or W.

Veterans' Mortgage Life Insurance (VMLI)

Veterans' Mortgage Life Insurance (VMLI) provides mortgage protection for the families of veterans with serious service-connected disabilities who have made modifications to their homes to accommodate their needs.

Am I eligible for Veterans' Mortgage Life Insurance?

You may qualify for VMLI if you meet all of the following conditions:

- You have a severe disability that is service-connected or was worsened by your military service,
- You received a Specially Adapted Housing (SAH) grant to purchase, build, or modify your home (such as by installing ramps or widening doorways) to enhance your ability to live independently,
- You hold the title to the home,
- You have an active mortgage on the home,
- You are under the age of 70.

Who is covered?

This coverage is available to service members and veterans.

What kind of life insurance benefits can I get with VMLI?

With VMLI, you can receive up to $200,000 in mortgage protection, paid directly to the lender holding your mortgage.

Key details about VMLI:
- The benefits are paid directly to the bank or lender, not to a designated life insurance beneficiary.
- Your coverage will equal the remaining balance on your mortgage, with a maximum limit of $200,000.
- VMLI is a decreasing-term policy, meaning the coverage amount reduces as your mortgage balance decreases. If you pay off your mortgage, the VMLI coverage will end.
- VMLI does not have any loan or cash value and does not offer dividends.

How do I qualify for these benefits?

You must first apply for a Specially Adapted Housing (SAH) grant. If you are approved for the grant, your loan guaranty agent will help determine if you're eligible for VMLI. If you already have an SAH grant, reach out to your agent to inquire about VMLI.

Your agent will assist you in completing the Veterans' Mortgage Life Insurance Statement.

Important note: You must apply for VMLI before your 70th birthday.

How much will I pay for VMLI?

Your VMLI premium is based on several factors, including:
- Your age
- The current balance of your mortgage
- The remaining number of payments on your mortgage
- The amount of VMLI coverage you need

What happens if I move, refinance, or make changes to my mortgage?

To maintain your VMLI coverage, the home must remain your primary residence. If any of the following changes occur, you must inform VA of:
- Moving to a new residence
- Transferring your mortgage to a new lender
- Foreclosure or bankruptcy liquidation of the mortgage
- Refinancing your home with a new loan
- Selling the property

Please notify the Department of Veterans Affairs (VA) at:

Regional Office and Insurance Center
PO Box 7208 (VMLI)
Philadelphia, PA 19101

What to know if you refinance your home:

If you refinance your home after securing VMLI, your premium may increase if:
- You're older
- Your mortgage amount is higher
- Your loan term is longer
- You require more VMLI coverage

Miscellaneous Information About Government Life Insurance Policies

Power of Attorney is not acceptable for executing a change of beneficiary for government life insurance, even if certain state statutes allow it. Only a court-appointed guardian that is recognized by state statutes can execute a beneficiary designation. If the state statute does not give the guardian broad powers to authorize a beneficiary change, a specific court order is needed to effectuate a change.

Assignment of government life insurance is not allowed, for any reason, nor can ownership of a policy be transferred. Only the insured can exercise the rights and privileges inherent in the ownership of the policy.

Policy Loans are available on permanent plans of insurance. The policyholder can take up to 94% of the reserve value of the policy, less any indebtedness. The policy cannot be lapsed, and premiums must be paid or waived at least one year before a policy has a loan value. Changes in interest rates are made on October 1 of each year, if warranted. Rate changes are tied to the "ten-year constant maturities", U.S. Treasury securities index. A policyholder can apply for a loan by filing VA Form 29-1546, Application for Policy Loan.

The completed form can be faxed to (215) 381-3580, or mailed to:

Department of Veterans Affairs Regional Office and Insurance Center
PO Box 7327
Philadelphia, PA 19101

An Annual Insurance Policy Statement is mailed to the insured on the policy anniversary date of each policy. The statement provides the insured with information about his or her VA insurance. The statement should be reviewed for accuracy each year, and the VA should be contacted immediately if there are any discrepancies.

Totally Disabled or Terminally Ill Policyholders

If you have VA life insurance and become terminally ill or totally disabled, you may be eligible for certain benefit options. Your spouse might also be eligible for certain options if diagnosed with a terminal illness.

SGI Extension for Policyholders Who Become Disabled

You may be able to keep your SGLI coverage for up to two years after the date you leave the military if you're disabled when you leave. Both of the following have to be true:
- You're within 2 years of your separation date, and
- You're totally disabled or having certain conditions

Waiver of Premiums for Policyholders Who Become Totally Disabled

A waiver of premiums mean you don't have to pay your life insurance premiums. In most situations premiums can be waived up to one year before ethe receipt of a claim.

To get a waiver for your life insurance premiums, you'd have to meet all of these requirements:
- You have a mental or physical disability preventing you from being able to hold a job, and
- You're covered under Service-Disabled Veterans Life Insurance (S-DVI), and
- Your total disability happens before you're 65, but after the effective date of your life insurance policy, and
- Your total disability continues for at least 6 months in a row

There are exceptions to the conditions above, but if you think you could be entitled to a waiver of your premiums, apply as soon as you can, and the VA will determine if you qualify.

To apply, you should fill out and sign a Claim for Disability Insurance (VA Form 29-357) and mail it to the address listed on the form.

Accelerated Benefits for Terminally Ill Policyholders

Veterans and servicemembers who are eligible, as well as covered spouses of servicemembers can get accelerated benefits, meaning you can get up to 50% of the face value of your coverage in increments of $5,000 paid to you before death.

Both must be true:
- You have SGLI, Family SGLI or VGLI life insurance, and
- You or your covered spouse has a written statement from a doctor saying you have or your spouse has nine months or less to live.

Only the insured servicemember or veteran may apply for accelerated benefits. No one can apply on their behalf, and in the case of a terminally ill spouse, only the insured may apply.

If you're an SGLI or VGLI policyholder, you should fill out a Claim for Accelerated Benefits (SGLV 8284). If you're still on active duty or you're a Reservist, you need to turn the form into your service branch, because they have to fill out part of the form.

If you're a veteran, you should have your doctor fill out their portion of the form, and then send the completed form to:

The Prudential Insurance Company of America
PO Box 70173
Philadelphia, PA 19176-0173

If you're covered under Family SGLI, you should fill out a Claim for Accelerated Benefits (SGLV 8284A). You'll fill out one part, and your doctor will fill out another part of the application.

The VA pays the remaining amount of the face value of an insurance policy to your designated beneficiary or beneficiaries upon your death. In the situation with a terminally ill spouse, VA pays the rest of the insurance policy to you upon the death of your spouse.

CHAPTER 24

BURIAL AND MEMORIAL BENEFITS

VA burial benefits can help service members, veterans, and their family members plan and pay for a burial or memorial service in a VA national cemetery. Family members can also order memorial items to honor the service of a veteran.

Eligibility

Eligibility for burial in a VA national cemetery

Veterans, service members, and certain family members may be eligible for burial in a VA national cemetery. Find out whether you or someone you're planning a burial for qualifies for this benefit.

Who is eligible for burial in a VA national cemetery?

Veterans, service members, spouses, and dependents may be eligible for burial in a VA national cemetery, as well as other benefits, if they meet one of the following criteria.

One of these must apply:
- The individual qualifying for burial benefits is a veteran who did not receive a dishonorable discharge, or
- The individual qualifying for burial benefits is a service member who passed away while on active duty, active duty for training, or inactive duty for training, or
- The individual qualifying for burial benefits is the spouse or surviving spouse of a veteran (even if remarried after the veteran's death), or
- The individual qualifying for burial benefits is the minor child of a veteran (even if the veteran died before), or, in some cases, the unmarried adult dependent child of a veteran.

Eligibility information for specific groups

U.S. citizens who served in the Armed Forces of any government allied with the United States during wartime.

A U.S. citizen who served in the Armed Forces of a U.S. ally during a wartime period may be eligible if both of these conditions apply:

- The service member ended their active service honorably, through death or otherwise, and
- The service member was a U.S. citizen when they entered service and when they passed away.

Members of Reserve components or the Reserve Officers' Training Corps (ROTC)

National Guard and Reserve members

A National Guard or Reserve member may be eligible if any of these criteria are met:

- They met the minimum legal active-duty service requirements, were activated for full service, and did not receive a dishonorable discharge, or
- They were entitled to retirement pay at the time of their death, or would have been eligible for retirement pay if under 60 at the time of death, or
- They died while receiving medical treatment at the expense of the U.S. for an injury or illness from active-duty or training services under honorable conditions, or
- They were disabled or passed away from a disease or injury caused—or worsened—by their service during active duty for training, or
- They became disabled or passed away from an injury or certain cardiovascular conditions linked to their service during inactive-duty training.

Members of the ROTC

An ROTC member may qualify if:

- The officer passed away honorably while attending an authorized training camp or during an authorized cruise, or
- The officer passed away honorably while traveling to or from a training camp or cruise, or
- The officer passed away while hospitalized or receiving treatment for an injury or illness incurred during training or travel under honorable conditions.

Commissioned officers of the National Oceanic and Atmospheric Administration (NOAA)

A NOAA officer may qualify if any of the following are true:

- They served on full-time duty after July 29, 1945, or
- They served before July 29, 1945, in a hazardous area designated by the secretary of defense during wartime or a national emergency declared by the president, or

- They served in the Philippine Islands on December 7, 1941, and continued service until their death.

Commissioned officers of the Public Health Service (PHS)

A PHS officer may qualify if:
- They served on full-time duty after July 29, 1945, and their service involved active duty for training that led to a disability or death, or
- They performed full-time duty before July 29, 1945, during wartime, in detail with the Army, Navy, Air Force, Marine Corps, or Coast Guard, or
- They served in the military forces by presidential executive order, or
- They served on inactive-duty training and passed away due to an injury related to service.

World War II Merchant Mariners

A WWII Merchant Mariner may qualify if:
- They had oceangoing service during the armed conflict from December 7, 1941, to December 31, 1945, or
- They had oceangoing service during the armed conflict from December 7, 1941, to December 31, 1946, and passed away after November 11, 1998, or
- They served on blockships in support of Operation Mulberry during WWII.

To receive a DD214 documenting this service, applications can be mailed to:

Commandant (G-MVP-6)
United States Coast Guard
2100 2nd Street, SW
Washington, DC 20593

Philippine Armed Forces Veterans

A Philippine Armed Forces Veteran may qualify if:
- The veteran was a U.S. citizen or an alien lawfully residing in the U.S. at the time of death, and
- The veteran served before July 1, 1946, in the Philippine military (including recognized guerrilla forces) in service to the U.S. Armed Forces, and passed away after November 1, 2000, or
- The veteran enlisted between October 6, 1945, and June 30, 1947, with the consent of the Philippine government and passed away after December 16, 2003.

Hmong Individuals

Eligibility is based on two criteria for individuals who passed away on or after March 23, 2018, and resided in the U.S. at the time of death:

- They were naturalized under the Hmong Veterans' Naturalization Act of 2000, or
- They served honorably in a special guerilla unit or irregular forces in Laos in support of the Armed Forces between February 28, 1961, and May 7, 1975, and were living in the U.S. as a citizen or legal permanent resident at the time of their death.

Specific groups that aren't eligible

Certain family members

Family members who are not eligible include:
- A former spouse of a veteran whose marriage ended by annulment or divorce,
- Family members of a veteran convicted of subversive activities (unless the veteran receives a presidential pardon),
- Other family members who do not meet the eligibility requirements.

People who were drafted but never entered military service

If someone was ordered to report for induction but never entered military service, they are not eligible.

Veterans with certain discharges

Veterans are not eligible if:
- They separated from the Armed Forces under dishonorable conditions, or
- They have a service record that disqualifies them.

Veterans convicted of capital crimes

Veterans who have been convicted of a federal or state capital crime and sentenced to life imprisonment or the death penalty are not eligible. Veterans who have clear evidence of committing such crimes but could not be tried due to evading prosecution are also disqualified.

Veterans convicted of certain sex offenses

Veterans convicted of a Tier III sex offense and sentenced to life imprisonment are not eligible. These individuals are also disqualified from receiving a Presidential Memorial Certificate, burial flag, headstone, or marker.

Veterans convicted of subversive activities

Veterans convicted of subversive activities after September 1, 1959, are not eligible unless they have received a presidential pardon.

Burial In a Private Ceremony

Veterans buried in a private cemetery may qualify for the following benefits:
- Headstone or marker
- Medallion

Veterans buried in a private cemetery may also be eligible for the following memorial items:
- Burial flag
- Presidential Memorial Certificate

Note: Veterans buried in a private cemetery are not eligible for a plaque or urn.

Eligibility for burial or memorialization benefits

Is a spouse or dependent child buried in a private cemetery eligible for a headstone, marker, or medallion?

No. Spouses or dependent children buried in a private cemetery are not eligible for these benefits. Only an eligible veteran can receive a headstone, marker, or medallion for burial in a private cemetery.

Is a spouse or dependent child eligible for an inscription on the veteran's headstone or marker in a private cemetery?

Yes. If the spouse or dependent child is eligible for burial in a VA national cemetery (but is not buried there), an inscription can be made on the veteran's headstone or marker.

You'll need to apply for the inscription when you request the headstone or marker. The type of inscription will depend on when the veteran passed.

If the veteran died on or after October 1, 2019
- An eligible spouse or dependent child's name, birthdate, and death date can be inscribed on the veteran's headstone or marker.
- A term of endearment (such as "Loving Father") can be included if requested.

This inscription will appear on the back of an upright headstone or beneath the veteran's details on a flat marker.

If the veteran died before October 1, 2019
- An eligible spouse's name will be inscribed on the veteran's headstone or marker, under the words "Husband of," "Wife of," or "Spouse of." The spouse's birthdate and death date will not be inscribed.

- The inscription will appear beneath the veteran's information on either an upright headstone or flat marker.

In some cases, an eligible dependent child's name may be inscribed. You can apply for this type of inscription, and the request will be reviewed.

To apply for an inscription

Add the inscription information in block 18 of the Claim for Standard Government Headstone or Marker (VA Form 40-1330). Include documents that verify the spouse or dependent relationship, such as a marriage license or birth certificate.

If I'm planning in advance for my own burial in a private cemetery, how can I find out which benefits I'm eligible for?

You can complete a pre-need eligibility application to determine if you qualify for a VA headstone or marker.

Note: When a family member files a claim for a headstone or marker, they should include this note in block 27: "Decedent has a VA pre-need decision letter."

Private cemetery burial costs

How much does a burial in a private cemetery cost?

The cost varies. VA provides a headstone, marker, or medallion at no cost to you and your family. However, a private cemetery may charge for setting, placing, maintaining, or other services. It's recommended to inquire about these additional charges when planning a burial in a private cemetery.

Can VA help with the cost of a veteran's burial in a private cemetery?

Yes. If a veteran is eligible, VA may assist with some burial costs.

How do I request a headstone, marker, or medallion for a private cemetery burial?

Fill out a claim for burial or memorialization benefits.
- For a headstone, grave marker, or wall marker, submit the Claim for Standard Government Headstone or Marker (VA Form 40-1330).
- For a medallion to place on a privately purchased headstone or marker, submit the Claim for Government Medallion for Placement in a Private Cemetery (VA Form 40-1330M).

Note: If this is your second request or if you're requesting a replacement, explain this in block 27 of the form.

Make a copy of the veteran's DD214 or other discharge documents Make a copy of the veteran's DD214 or other discharge documents to submit with your claim. Do not send original documents, as they cannot be returned.

How to submit your claim and documents

You can submit your claim and supporting documents in the following ways:

- **Online**: Use the QuickSubmit tool through AccessVA.
- **By mail**: Send your claim and documents to:
  NCA FP Evidence Intake Center
  PO Box 5237
  Janesville, WI 53547
- **By fax**: Fax your claim to 800-455-7143.

If you need assistance, contact the VA at 800-697-6947, Monday through Friday, from 8:00 a.m. to 5:00 p.m. ET.

Important notes:
- Only the National Cemetery Administration can inscribe headstones or markers to ensure proper condition and consistency. Local contractors are not allowed to make inscriptions.

Additional information about burial in a private cemetery

What should I ask when preparing for a private cemetery burial?

When planning a private cemetery burial, consider asking the following questions:
- If the cemetery offers a free veterans' gravesite, will I be required to purchase an additional gravesite?
- What are the costs associated with buying an additional gravesite, if needed?
- Can I receive a written list of services my family and I will receive from the private cemetery during the burial?
- Will I get a written list of the necessary information and resources I must provide to the private cemetery for burial planning?
- Does the private cemetery have a trust fund to protect buyers?
- Are there any specific requirements for headstones or markers in the private cemetery?
- Do I need to purchase a marker base before ordering a VA headstone?
- Will I need to pay for setting, placing, or maintaining a VA headstone?
- Will I need to purchase a vault (also called a "grave liner") for the casket, and if so, what is the cost?

What should I do if I applied for a headstone, marker, or medallion for a veteran buried in a private cemetery, but the grave is still unmarked?

If the grave remains unmarked more than 30 days after submitting your claim, contact the VA at 800-697-6947 to verify they have received your claim. If it has been over 60 days and the grave is still unmarked, check with the cemetery, funeral home, or the party responsible for receiving the headstone, marker, or medallion. If they haven't received it, reach out to the VA at 800-697-6947.

Burial at Sea

Burial at sea is provided by the U.S. Navy. The National Cemetery Administration does not offer burial at sea services.

For more details, visit the Burial at Sea program on the MyNavy HR website.

If you need more information, you can call 833-330-6622. The Navy office is available 24/7.

Can I receive benefits for burial or memorialization for a veteran already buried at sea?

Yes, active-duty service members and veterans buried at sea may qualify for a headstone or marker.

Pre-Need Eligibility for Burial in a VA Cemetery

You can apply in advance to determine if you are eligible for burial in a VA national cemetery. This process, known as pre-need eligibility determination, can help simplify the burial planning process for your family members during a time of need.

Follow the steps below to apply.

Note: "Pre-need" refers to planning for your burial before the time of need. This form is for planning your burial in advance, not for immediate burial requests.

How to Prepare Before You Apply

Check if you qualify. You may be eligible if one of the following applies to you:
- You are a veteran who did not receive a dishonorable discharge when you separated from the military.
- You are the spouse or dependent child of a service member or veteran, even if the service member or veteran has passed away.
- In some cases, the adult dependent child of a service member or veteran (if unmarried).

Eligibility for burial in a VA national cemetery is based on your service history or the service history of the veteran or service member sponsoring your application for burial as a spouse, surviving spouse, or unmarried adult child.

Note: If a service member dies while on active duty, they are eligible for burial without a pre-need determination.

Select the VA National Cemetery Where You Prefer to Be Buried

Note: This application only applies to VA national cemeteries. If you are planning a burial in a VA grant-funded state, territory, or tribal veterans cemetery, you will need to contact the cemetery directly about their pre-need program. These cemeteries may have specific eligibility rules based on your location or residency.

Note: This application does not apply to Arlington National Cemetery or the United States Soldiers and Airmen's Home National Cemetery. To plan a burial at either of these cemeteries, you will need to contact Arlington National Cemetery directly.

Pre-need eligibility determination does not guarantee you will be buried in a specific VA national cemetery, as VA cemeteries do not accept reservations. However, your preferred cemetery will be taken into consideration when planning.

Documents and Information Needed for the Application

To apply, you will need the following:
- Your (or your sponsor's) Social Security number
- Date and place of birth
- Military status and service history (including dates of service, discharge status, and rank — typically found on the DD214 or other separation documents)
- Discharge papers (DD214 or other separation documents)

If you are applying as a spouse, surviving spouse, or unmarried adult child, you will also need to include your personal information, including your Social Security number.

If you are applying on behalf of someone else, you will need to provide documentation that shows you have the authority to apply for them, such as one of these forms:
- Appointment of Veterans Service Organization as Claimant's Representative (VA Form 21-22)
- Appointment of Individual as Claimant's Representative (VA Form 21-22a)

If you are applying for an unmarried adult child of a veteran or service member, you must provide supporting documents regarding the child's disability.

This includes:
- The date of the disability's onset
- A description of the disability (mental or physical)
- An explanation of how the child is dependent on the veteran
- The marital status of the child

How to Apply

You can apply online.

You can also apply by mail:
1. Fill out the Application for Pre-need Determination of Eligibility for Burial in a VA National Cemetery (VA Form 40-10007).
2. The applicant must sign the form. If the applicant is under 18, mentally unable to make decisions, or physically unable to sign, a spouse, parent, or court-appointed representative may sign the form on their behalf.
3. If signing on behalf of someone else, select box 33B and provide your details in blocks 34-37. Include supporting documents that show why the person cannot sign and your relationship to them.

Mail your completed application with supporting documents to:

NCA FP Evidence Intake Center
PO Box 5237
Janesville, WI 53547

Please only send copies of your DD214 and other supporting documents, as VA can't return the originals.

How to Apply by Fax

You can also fax your application to the National Cemetery Scheduling Office at 855-840-8299.

Need Assistance with Your Application?

For help with your application, call the toll-free hotline at 800-535-1117 (TTY: 711). VA is available Monday through Friday from 8:00 a.m. to 7:30 p.m. ET and Saturday from 9:00 a.m. to 5:30 p.m. ET.

You can also work with a trained professional known as an accredited representative to assist with your application for pre-need eligibility.

Note: These services are free. You should never pay anyone to help you fill out VA Form 40-10007 or submit your application.

What Happens After You Apply?

Once you submit your application, VA will notify you about the status and the estimated time for a decision. Due to a large number of pre-need eligibility applications, there may be delays in processing.

If you need more information or have questions about your application, call 800-535-1117 (TTY: 711). VA is there Monday through Friday from 8:00 a.m. to 7:30 p.m. ET and Saturday from 9:00 a.m. to 5:30 p.m. ET. Please wait to hear back about your application instead of submitting it again.

Veterans Burial Allowance and Transportation Benefits

Learn how to access burial allowances (often referred to as "veterans death benefits") to help cover the costs of burial, funeral, and transportation for a veteran.

Am I eligible for burial and funeral cost assistance for a veteran?

You may be eligible for a burial allowance if you are paying for the burial and funeral costs, and you will not be reimbursed by another organization, such as another government agency or the veteran's employer. You must meet these conditions:

One of the following relationships to the veteran must apply:
- Surviving spouse of the veteran (same-sex marriages are recognized),
- Surviving partner in a legal union (a formalized relationship recognized by the state),
- Surviving child of the veteran,
- Parent of the veteran,
- Executor or administrator of the veteran's estate, or
- A family member, friend, or representative from a funeral home, cemetery, or another organization.

In addition, the veteran must meet one of these conditions:
- The veteran died as a result of a service-connected disability,
- The veteran passed away while receiving care at a VA facility or one contracted by the VA,
- The veteran died while traveling at VA's expense for care,
- The veteran died with an active or reopened claim for VA compensation or pension, and would have been entitled to benefits before passing,
- The veteran died while receiving a VA pension or compensation,
- The veteran died while eligible for compensation or VA pension but opted for full military retirement or disability pay.

Burial Allowance Eligibility Exclusions

You cannot receive burial allowances for a veteran who died in one of these ways:
- While on active duty,

- While serving as a member of Congress,
- While serving a federal prison sentence.

Types of Burial Benefits You May Receive

If eligible, the following benefits may be available:
- VA burial allowance for burial and funeral costs,
- VA plot or interment allowance to cover the cost of the gravesite or burial,
- VA transportation reimbursement for moving the veteran's remains to their final resting place.

The VA covers burial for all legal burial methods, including cremation, burial at sea, or donation to a medical school.

Time Limit for Filing a Claim
- For non-service-connected deaths or unclaimed remains, claims must be filed within 2 years after the veteran's burial.
- For non-service-connected deaths while the veteran was receiving VA care, there is no time limit to file a claim.
- If the veteran's discharge status was upgraded after their death, claims must be filed within 2 years of the discharge status change.
- For service-connected deaths, there is no time limit for filing a claim.

Required Documents for the Application

You may need to submit the following documents:
- The veteran's death certificate, including the cause of death.
- An itemized receipt for transportation costs, if applicable.
- DD214 or other separation documents to verify military service.

If claiming burial benefits for a service-connected death, additional documents like medical records may be needed.

Submitting Medical Records

If you have access to the veteran's medical records, you can submit copies with your application or mail them separately after submission. If not, you may authorize the release of their records to the VA.
- For VA or federal health facility records, submit a statement using VA Form 21-4138.
- For non-VA facility records, you can either authorize the release online or fill out the necessary forms (VA Form 21-4142 and VA Form 21-4142a) to allow the VA to request the records on your behalf.

Do Surviving Spouses Need to File a Claim?

No, if you are the surviving spouse of the veteran, there is no need to file a claim for burial benefits, as long as you are listed as the veteran's spouse in their profile.

The VA will automatically pay a set amount to help with burial, plot, interment, or transportation costs when they receive notification of the veteran's death.

How to Apply for Burial Allowance and Transportation Benefits

You can apply either online or by mail:
- **Option 1: Apply Online**
  If you have previously started an application before May 23, 2024, some questions have been updated. You may need to provide additional information.

Apply for a veteran's burial allowance and transportation benefits online.
- **Option 2: Apply by Mail**
  Complete the Application for Burial Benefits (VA Form 21P-530EZ).

Mail the completed form and supporting documents to:

Department of Veterans Affairs
Pension Intake Center
PO Box 5365
Janesville, WI 53547-5365

For assistance, call 800-827-1000 (TTY: 711) Monday through Friday, from 8:00 a.m. to 9:00 p.m. ET. Alternatively, contact your VA regional office for further support.

Burial Allowance Amounts

Burial allowance amounts for a service-connected death

Status	Maximum Burial Allowance
If the veteran died on or after September 11, 2001	$2,000
If the veteran died before September 11, 2001	$1,500
If the veteran is buried in a VA national cemetery	VA may reimburse you for some or all of the costs of moving the veteran's remains

Burial allowance amounts for a non-service-connected death

Status	Maximum Burial Allowance
If the veteran died on or after October 1, 2024	$978 burial allowance and $978 for a plot
If the veteran died on or after October 1, 2023, but before October 1, 2024	$948 burial allowance and $948 for a plot
If the veteran died on or after January 5, 2023, but before October 1, 2023	$893 burial allowance and $893 for a plot
If the veteran died on or after October 1, 2022, but before January 5, 2023	$300 burial allowance and $893 for a plot
If the veteran died on or after October 1, 2021, but before October 1, 2022	$300 burial allowance and $828 for a plot
If the veteran died on or after October 1, 2020, but before October 1, 2021	$300 burial allowance and $807 for a plot
If the veteran died on or after October 1, 2019, but before October 1, 2020	$300 burial allowance and $796 for a plot
If the veteran died on or after October 1, 2018, but before October 1, 2019	$300 burial allowance and $780 for a plot
If the veteran died on or after October 1, 2017, but before October 1, 2018	$300 burial allowance and $762 for a plot
If the veteran died on or after October 1, 2016, but before October 1, 2017	$300 burial allowance and $749 for a plot
If the veteran died on or after October 1, 2015, but before October 1, 2016	$300 burial allowance and $747 for a plot
If the veteran died on or after October 1, 2014, but before October 1, 2015	$300 burial allowance and $745 for a plot
If the veteran died on or after October 1, 2013, but before October 1, 2014	$300 burial allowance and $734 for a plot

Note: If a veteran's remains aren't claimed, a burial allowance based on these rates may be provided to the person or organization responsible for the burial. If the deceased qualifies, VA may reimburse the costs of moving the veteran's remain to a VA national cemetery.

Burial allowance amounts for a non-service-connected death if the veteran was hospitalized by VA at the time of their death.

Status	Maximum Burial Allowance
If the veteran died on or after October 1, 2024	$978 burial allowance and $978 for a plot
If the veteran died on or after October 1, 2023, but before October 1, 2024	$948 burial allowance and $948 for a plot
If the veteran died on or after October	$893 burial allowance

1, 2022, but before October 1, 2023	and $893 for a plot
If the veteran died on or after October 1, 2021, but before October 1, 2022	$828 burial allowance and $828 for a plot
If the veteran died on or after October 1, 2020, but before October 1, 2021	$807 burial allowance and $807 for a plot
If the veteran died on or after October 1, 2019, but before October 1, 2020	$796 burial allowance and $796 for a plot
If the veteran died on or after October 1, 2018, but before October 1, 2019	$780 burial allowance and $780 for a plot
If the veteran died on or after October 1, 2017, but before October 1, 2018	$762 burial allowance and $762 for a plot
If the veteran died on or after October 1, 2016, but before October 1, 2017	$749 burial allowance and $749 for a plot
If the veteran died on or after October 1, 2015, but before October 1, 2016	$747 burial allowance and $747 for a plot
If the veteran died on or after October 1, 2014, but before October 1, 2015	$745 burial allowance and $745 for a plot
If the veteran died on or after October 1, 2013, but before October 1, 2014	$734 burial allowance and $734 for a plot

VA may also reimburse the costs of moving the veteran's remains if one of the following is true:

- The veteran was hospitalized or in a VA-contracted nursing home at the time of death, or
- The veteran died while traveling to VA-authorized care.

Headstone or Marker Allowance Amounts

Status	Maximum Headstone or Marker Allowance
If the veteran died on or after October 1, 2021	$231
If the veteran died on or after October 1, 2020, but before October 1, 2021	$231
If the veteran died on or after October 1, 2019, but before October 1, 2020	$236
If the veteran died on or after October 1, 2018, but before October 1, 2019	$290
If the veteran died on or after October 1, 2017, but before October 1, 2018	$195
If the veteran died on or after	$208

October 1, 2016, but before October 1, 2017	
If the veteran died on or after October 1, 2015, but before October 1, 2016	$218
If the veteran died on or after October 1, 2014, but before October 1, 2015	$199
If the veteran died on or after October 1, 2013, but before October 1, 2014	$205

Veterans Headstones, Markers, Medallions, Plaques, and Urns

Find out how to apply for benefits for burial or memorialization below.

Eligibility

For Veterans and Active-Duty Service Members to Get a Headstone, Marker, Plaque, or Urn

A veteran who didn't receive a dishonorable discharge or a service member who died while on active duty may be eligible for a headstone, marker, plaque, or urn if they meet these requirements.

At least one of the following must be true:

- The veteran or service member died on or after November 1, 1990, and their grave is currently marked with a privately purchased headstone, or
- The veteran or service member was buried in an unmarked grave, anywhere in the world.

Note: If the veteran or service member served before World War I, detailed documents (such as muster rolls or extracts from state files) may be required.

For veterans who served as enlisted personnel after September 7, 1980, or as officers after October 16, 1981, at least one of the following must also be true:

- The veteran served for a minimum of 24 months of continuous active duty, or
- The veteran died while serving on active duty.

Note: Hmong individuals who were living in the U.S. when they died are eligible if they were naturalized under the Hmong Veterans Naturalization Act of 2000 and died on or after March 23, 2018.

For Veterans and Active-Duty Service Members to Get a Medallion

Medallions are for eligible veterans and service members buried in a private cemetery marked with a privately purchased headstone or marker. VA may provide these types of medallions:
- Bronze
- Medal of Honor

Servicemembers who died while serving on active duty on or after April 6, 1917, are eligible for a medallion.

Veterans who didn't receive a dishonorable discharge may be eligible for a medallion if they meet the following requirements based on their service:
- Enlisted personnel who served before September 7, 1980, must have served for at least one day of active duty on or after April 6, 1917.
- Enlisted personnel who served after September 7, 1980, must have served for a minimum of 24 months of continuous active duty.
- Officers who served before October 16, 1981, must have served for at least one day of active duty on or after April 6, 1917.
- Officers who served after October 16, 1981, must have served for a minimum of 24 months of continuous active duty.

Note: A commissioned officer may be eligible for a medallion if they served in active Public Health Service on or after April 6, 1917.

For National Guard Members and Reservists

A National Guard member or Reservist may be eligible for a headstone, marker, medallion, plaque, or urn if they meet any of the following requirements based on their type of service. VA may provide these types of medallions:
- Bronze
- Medal of Honor

National Guard Members

At least one of the following must be true:
- The National Guard member was entitled to retirement pay at their time of death (or would have been entitled if they were over 60 years old), or
- The National Guard member served in federal status and for the period of time they were called to serve.

Reservists

At least one of the following must be true:
- The Reservist was entitled to retirement pay at their time of death (or would have been entitled if they were over 60 years old), or

- The Reservist was called to active duty for purposes other than training.

Note: National Guard members or Reservists who have only limited active-duty service for training aren't eligible in most cases, though they may be eligible in certain situations, such as if they died during or as a result of training.

For Spouses and Dependent Children

A spouse or dependent child buried in a national cemetery, state or tribal veterans cemetery, military post cemetery, or military base cemetery may be eligible for a headstone or marker. They may still be eligible even if they die before the veteran.

In most cases, a single gravesite and headstone are provided for all eligible family members. However, if two veterans are married and request separate gravesites and headstones, side-by-side gravesites with separate headstones can be provided.

Note: Spouses and dependent children buried in a private cemetery aren't eligible for a headstone or marker but may be eligible for an inscription on the veteran's headstone or marker.

Spouses and dependents aren't eligible for a medallion.

Can I Apply for Benefits for Burial or Memorialization?

You may apply for these benefits if you are representing the deceased veteran, service member, or family member in any of the following relationships or professional roles:
- A family member, or
- A personal representative (someone who officially represents the deceased), or
- A representative of an accredited Veterans Service Organization, or
- An employee of a state or local government whose official responsibilities include serving veterans, or
- Any person legally responsible for making arrangements for unclaimed remains or interment or memorialization details, or
- Any individual representing the deceased if the veteran's service ended before April 6, 1917.

You may also apply for a memorial headstone or marker if any of the following are true:
- The deceased's remains haven't been recovered or identified,
- The deceased's remains were buried at sea,
- The deceased's remains were donated to science, or
- The deceased's remains were cremated and scattered.

What Do I Need to Know About Applying for a Plaque or Urn?

Once a plaque or urn is chosen, the veteran is no longer eligible for burial in a VA national cemetery, and a government headstone, marker, or medallion won't be available for the veteran after the plaque or urn has been issued. The plaque or urn becomes your property once it is received.

How Do I Apply for Benefits for Burial or Memorialization?

You can apply for these benefits online, by mail, or by fax.

Fill Out an Application

For a headstone, grave marker, or wall marker, fill out the Claim for Standard Government Headstone or Marker (VA Form 40-1330).

For a medallion to be placed on a privately purchased headstone or marker, fill out the Claim for Government Medallion for Placement in a Private Cemetery (VA Form 40-1330M).

For a commemorative plaque or urn, fill out the Claim for Commemorative Urn or Plaque for Veterans' Cremains Not Interred (VA Form 40-1330UP).

Send the VA Your Application and Supporting Documents

You can send your application and documents in any of these ways:
- Online
  Submit your application and supporting documents online using the QuickSubmit tool through AccessVA.
- By Mail
  - Mail your application, along with a copy of the Veteran's DD214 or other discharge documents, to:
    - NCA FP Evidence Intake Center
      PO Box 5237
      Janesville, WI 53547
    - By Fax
      You can also fax your application to:
      800-455-7143

If you need help, please call 800-697-6947 (TTY: 711).

What Do I Need to Know About Burial in a Private Cemetery?

When planning for a burial in a private cemetery, note that:
- You don't need to pay for the headstone or marker itself, but you're responsible for the setting fee (placement cost). You must make arrangements for the placement.

- You can request a medallion to attach to a privately purchased headstone, marker, or niche cover in a private cemetery. Three sizes are available, and it comes with a kit for attachment.
- Additional costs, restrictions, and requirements may apply when planning a burial in a private cemetery.

If the Grave Remains Unmarked

If the grave remains unmarked for 60 days after you've applied for burial or memorialization benefits:

- After 60 days, contact the cemetery, funeral home, or other responsible party to confirm receipt of the headstone, marker, or medallion. If it hasn't been received, contact VA at 800-697-6947 (TTY: 711). They're available Monday through Friday, 8:00 a.m. to 5:00 p.m. ET.

Presidential Memorial Certificate

To qualify for a Presidential Memorial Certificate, the following conditions must be met:
1. The veteran or Reservist must be eligible for burial in a national cemetery.
2. The applicant must be the next of kin, family member, close friend, or an authorized representative of the veteran or Reservist.
3. Eligibility for burial in a national cemetery can be confirmed through the VA.

Receiving a Presidential Memorial Certificate Automatically or Through Application

If the veteran is buried in a national cemetery, the PMC will be automatically provided to the next of kin at the time of the burial. For veterans eligible for burial in a national cemetery but buried in a private cemetery, family members or close friends must apply for the PMC. Multiple applications for a PMC are allowed.

To expedite the process, include the veteran's military discharge documents and death certificate. Do not send original documents as they cannot be returned.

How to Apply for a Presidential Memorial Certificate

You can apply for a Presidential Memorial Certificate through five available methods:
- **Online:** Submit the application directly online.
- **By Mail:** Complete the *Presidential Memorial Certificate Request Form* (VA Form 40-0247) and send it, along with copies of the veteran's death certificate and DD214 (or other discharge documents), to:
NCA FP Evidence Intake Center
PO Box 5237
Janesville, WI 53547
- **Upload the Application**: Complete the *Presidential Memorial Certificate*

Request Form (VA Form 40-0247) and upload it with supporting documents using the QuickSubmit tool on AccessVA.

- **In Person**: You can submit the application at any VA regional office.
- **By Fax**: Complete the *Presidential Memorial Certificate Request Form* (VA Form 40-0247) and fax it, along with supporting documents, to 800-455-7143.

For assistance, contact the VA at 800-697-6947, Monday through Friday, from 8:00 a.m. to 5:00 p.m. ET.

Checking the Status of Your Application

If more than four months have passed since submitting your application for a Presidential Memorial Certificate and you have not received it, call 202-632-7300 to check the status. Do not submit a second application unless instructed by the VA.

Burial Flags to Honor Veterans and Reservists

The United States provides a flag to honor the military service of a veteran or Reservist by draping it over their casket or placing it with their urn.

Eligibility for a Burial Flag

You may be eligible for a burial flag if you are the next of kin or a close friend of the veteran or Reservist, and one of the following applies to their service:

- The veteran or Reservist served in wartime,
- The veteran or Reservist died while serving on active duty after May 27, 1941,
- The veteran or Reservist served after January 31, 1955,
- The veteran or Reservist served during peacetime, left military service before June 27, 1950, after completing at least one enlistment, or left due to a disability caused or aggravated by military service,
- The veteran or Reservist served in the Selected Reserves (in some cases), or served in the military forces of the Philippines while serving under the United States, and died on or after April 25, 1951.

For further clarification, call 800-827-1000, Monday through Friday, 8:00 a.m. to 9:00 p.m. ET.

How to Obtain a Burial Flag

To request a burial flag, complete the *Application for United States Flag for Burial Purposes* (VA Form 27-2008).

You can submit the completed application to:

- A funeral director
- A VA regional office

- A United States post office (call ahead to confirm availability)

For additional help, find your nearest VA regional office.

Caring for the Burial Flag

To ensure the flag remains in good condition, follow these guidelines:
- Avoid leaving the flag outside for extended periods to prevent weather damage.
- Display the flag carefully to avoid any damage.
- Do not attach words, symbols, or drawings to the flag.
- The flag should not be used to hold or carry anything.

For additional care instructions, refer to the last page of the *Application for United States Flag for Burial Purposes*, which also explains how the flag will be displayed and folded during the memorial service.

What to Do With a Flag You No Longer Wish to Keep

If the flag is in good condition, you may donate it to a national cemetery with an Avenue of Flags, where it will be flown on patriotic holidays.

If the flag is unserviceable (torn, faded, or damaged), you can give it to a Veterans Service Organization (VSO) for proper retirement.

Please do not send the flag back to the VA.

Replacing a Burial Flag

The VA does not replace flags that are lost, destroyed, or stolen. However, some veterans organizations may assist in obtaining a replacement.

Scheduling a Burial for a Veteran or Family Member

If you have a pre-need decision letter confirming eligibility, you or the funeral director can contact the National Cemetery Scheduling Office at 800-535-1117 (TTY: 711) to request a burial. The office is available Monday through Friday, 8:00 a.m. to 7:30 p.m. ET, and Saturday, 9:00 a.m. to 5:30 p.m. ET.

Keep in mind that the pre-need decision letter does not specify a particular cemetery or gravesite as these cannot be reserved in advance. In some cases, eligibility may need to be reviewed again at the time of death due to changes in laws or circumstances.

If you don't have a pre-need decision letter, you will need to choose a funeral director and follow these steps:
1. **Gather Information and Documents**: Collect the necessary documents to verify the deceased's eligibility for burial in a VA national cemetery. This

includes the veteran's DD214 or other discharge documents showing an honorable discharge. You may also need to provide additional documents to verify your relationship to the veteran or the status of any dependents. These may include a death certificate, medical records, divorce decrees, or other relevant documents. If you need assistance obtaining these documents, you can request help when you call. Discharge documents are not typically required if the veteran or dependent is already interred in a national cemetery.

2. **Provide Information About the Deceased:** You will need the following details about the deceased:
    o Full name, gender, date of birth, and Social Security or Military Service number (Veteran ID)
    o Relationship to the deceased
    o Marital status and date of death (including zip code and county at the time of death)

3. **Provide Information About the Next of Kin:** The next of kin (closest living relative) should provide:
    o Full name, relationship to the deceased, and Social Security number
    o Contact information (phone number, address)

4. **Additional Information**: In certain cases, additional information may be required, such as:
    o The surviving spouse's veteran or service member status
    o Information about any disabled children who may be buried in a national cemetery
    o Details of the spouse's burial in a VA cemetery if applicable

Decide on Burial Details

Specify the following:
- Preferred cemetery for burial
- Type of burial (casket or cremation)
- Memorial choice (headstone, grave marker, niche cover, or medallion)
- Any religious emblem or optional inscription
- Request burial honors or other military honors, such as a burial flag, a Presidential Memorial Certificate, or additional military honors beyond the basics

Contact the National Cemetery Scheduling Office

The funeral director can assist with these steps. They will send any discharge documents to the National Cemetery Scheduling Office by fax at 866-900-6417 or via email to NCA.Scheduling@va.gov. Call 800-535-1117 (TTY: 711) to confirm the burial application.

When Can I Schedule a Burial?

National cemeteries are open for burials Monday through Friday, with limited hours during federal holidays. To check availability, contact the National Cemetery Scheduling Office.

Contacting a National Cemetery Directly

You should contact a national cemetery in the following cases:
- Scheduling a burial for an active-duty service member
- Rescheduling or canceling a burial
- Changing previously provided information
- Requesting disinterment or relocation
- For specific information about cemetery policies

Financial Assistance for Burial Costs

If you are the surviving spouse or designated family member of a veteran, you may be eligible for financial assistance for burial and funeral costs.

Military Funeral Honors and Committal Services

Military memorial services at national cemeteries are conducted with the utmost dignity and respect.

Committal Service for a Veteran or Service Member

Upon arrival at the cemetery, a representative will meet with you to collect the necessary burial documents for the deceased.

The representative will then guide you and others present to the committal shelter, where the service will take place. The committal service, which typically lasts around 20 minutes, is held at this shelter, not at the gravesite. After the committal service, the burial will proceed.

Please note that viewing facilities are not available at national cemeteries, so the family must make arrangements for funeral services at another location.

Optional Elements of the Committal Service

The family can choose to have readings from a friend, family member, or clergy member during the committal service. Military funeral honors may also be requested and performed at the committal shelter. To arrange for these honors, the family can work with the funeral director, a Veterans Service Organization, or VA national cemetery staff.

Military funeral honors include:
- The playing of "Taps"
- A rifle detail
- Two uniformed service members who present the burial flag

If a headstone, marker, or medallion has been requested, it will be delivered within 60 days.

Paying Respects at a Committal Service

Family and friends can honor the deceased by:
- Bringing flowers to accompany the casket or urn as it is moved from the committal shelter to the gravesite
- Visiting the gravesite later in the day, after the ceremony has concluded (visits are not allowed immediately following the service)

Military Funerals at Arlington National Cemetery

Funerals at Arlington National Cemetery are managed by the Department of Defense. For more details about services at Arlington National Cemetery, visit their official website.

Bereavement Counseling

If you are the surviving spouse, child, or parent of a service member or veteran who has passed away, you may qualify for bereavement counseling through Vet Centers. Bereavement counseling, also known as grief counseling, offers emotional and psychological support for individuals dealing with the loss of a loved one.

Eligibility for Bereavement (Grief) Counseling

You may be eligible for bereavement counseling if you are the surviving spouse, child, or parent of someone who meets one of the following criteria:
- A service member who died while serving in the military
- A Reservist or National Guard member who died while on active duty
- A veteran who was receiving services at a Vet Center at the time of their death
- A veteran or service member who died by suicide

Benefits Available Through Bereavement Counseling

Bereavement counseling offers a range of free services, including:
- Outreach
- Counseling
- Referrals

Trained counselors and staff are available to help you navigate the emotional challenges following the death of a loved one. These services are available at community-based Vet Centers or other locations where you feel most comfortable. Telehealth options (phone or video appointments) are also available for added convenience.

How to Access Bereavement Counseling

To request bereavement counseling, you can reach out to your nearest Vet Center. Alternatively, you can call 877-927-8387 (TTY: 711) for assistance.

National Cemeteries

As part of the benefits available to veterans and their families, the Department of Veterans Affairs (VA) operates a network of national cemeteries across the country. These cemeteries provide a final resting place for veterans, their spouses, and dependent children, and are dedicated to honoring their service and sacrifices. Each cemetery is designed to offer a dignified and respectful environment, providing access to burial plots, headstones, and various memorial services.

This list of VA National Cemeteries will help you identify locations that may be available for burial or memorialization of a veteran or eligible family member. You can easily find your nearest VA National Cemetery by scanning the QR code below, which will direct you to a comprehensive list of all VA cemeteries across the United States.

How to Use the QR Code

Using the QR code is simple and fast. Follow these steps:
- Open the camera app on your smartphone or tablet.
- Point the camera at the QR code. Make sure the code is clearly visible in the screen's viewfinder.
- A notification will appear on your screen with a link. Tap the notification to open the link.
- The link will take you to the list of VA National Cemeteries, where you can find detailed information about locations, services, and eligibility.

cem.va.gov

Department of the Interior National Cemeteries

The Department of the Interior operates a number of national cemeteries that serve as a final resting place for veterans, their families, and other eligible individuals.

These cemeteries, managed by the National Park Service, are dedicated to honoring the service and sacrifice of those who have served our country. Each cemetery offers a peaceful and respectful environment, and many are located in historically significant areas.

This list of Department of the Interior National Cemeteries will guide you to locations that may be available for burial or memorialization. You can easily access the full list by scanning the QR code below, which will take you directly to the National Park Service's page with detailed information on these cemeteries.

Follow the same instructions for the National Cemeteries list on the previous page.

NPS.gov

CHAPTER 25

VET CENTERS

Vet Centers are local counseling facilities that offer a broad range of social and psychological services for eligible veterans, active-duty service members, National Guard and Reserve members, as well as their families. These centers provide professional counseling aimed at helping individuals successfully navigate the transition from military to civilian life, or cope with the effects of traumatic experiences, including military sexual trauma (MST).

Services include individual, group, marriage, and family counseling, along with referrals to other VA programs or community resources. The counselors and outreach staff, many of whom are veterans themselves, are equipped to provide support for issues such as grief, loss, trauma, and the challenges of reintegration after military service.

What Vet Centers Do (Readjustment Counseling)

Vet Centers are community-based counseling facilities offering a broad spectrum of social and psychological services to eligible veterans, active-duty service members (including National Guard and Reserve), and their families. These centers specialize in readjustment counseling to help individuals transition successfully from military to civilian life or cope with the aftermath of traumatic experiences, including military sexual trauma (MST).

Services include individual, group, marriage, and family counseling, along with referrals to additional VA or community services. Many of the counselors and outreach staff are veterans themselves, bringing both personal experience and professional expertise to address issues such as grief, loss, war trauma, and reintegration challenges.

Vet Center History

Established by Congress in 1979, Vet Centers were created in response to the significant challenges faced by Vietnam War veterans in adjusting to civilian life. These centers are part of the U.S. Department of Veterans Affairs and are community-based to better serve veterans in their local areas.

In 1991, in response to the Persian Gulf War, Congress expanded eligibility to include veterans from later conflicts, such as Lebanon, Grenada, Panama, the Persian Gulf, Somalia, and Kosovo/Bosnia.

In 1996, eligibility was further expanded to include World War II and Korean War veterans. The mission of Vet Centers is to offer a wide array of counseling, outreach, and referral services to assist eligible veterans in making a fulfilling transition from military service to civilian life. The eligibility was again extended in 2003 to veterans of Operation Enduring Freedom (OEF), Operation Iraqi Freedom (OIF), and other operations within the Global War on Terrorism (GWOT).

Additionally, family members of veterans from the aforementioned conflicts are also eligible for Vet Center services. In 2003, the VA Secretary authorized the centers to provide bereavement counseling services to the surviving parents, spouses, children, and siblings of service members who died while on active duty, including those who were federally activated from the Reserve and National Guard.

Vet Center Eligibility

Veterans and active-duty service members, including those in the National Guard and Reserve components, may be eligible for Vet Center services if they meet any of the following criteria:

- Have served in a combat theater or an area of hostility (see the full list below)
- Have experienced military sexual trauma (MST), regardless of gender or time in service
- Have provided mortuary services or direct emergency medical care to casualties of war while on active duty
- Have served as a member of an unmanned aerial vehicle (UAV) crew providing direct support to operations in a combat zone or area of hostility
- Were a Vietnam-era veteran who accessed care at a Vet Center prior to January 2, 2013
- Served on active duty in response to a national emergency or a major disaster declared by the president, or under state orders for a disaster or civil disorder
- Were part of the Coast Guard and participated in drug interdiction operations, regardless of location
- Are a current member of the Reserve Components assigned to a military command in a drilling status, who has a behavioral health condition or psychological trauma from military service that impacts their quality of life or adjustment to civilian life
- Are a veteran or service member using educational assistance benefits for schooling and experiencing readjustment counseling needs due to military service that affects their civilian life, ongoing military service, or educational settings

Family members of veterans and service members may also be eligible for services when their involvement helps support the goals of the veteran or service member.

Bereavement Services

In addition, family members are eligible for bereavement counseling if they fall under one of these categories:

- Family members of a veteran receiving Vet Center services at the time of their death
- Families of service members who died while on active duty
- Family members of veterans or service members who died by suicide

Helping Those Who May Not Meet Eligibility

If an individual is not eligible for Vet Center services, the staff will actively assist in finding other community resources that may be more appropriate for their needs.

The goal is to help, not turn away anyone in need, and VA will help connect you with the right support.

Combat Theater or Area of Hostility

Eligibility also extends to those who served in any of the following combat zones or areas of hostility:

- World War II (including American Merchant Marines)
- Korean War
- Vietnam War
- Lebanon
- Grenada
- Desert Storm
- Desert Shield
- Bosnia
- Kosovo
- Operations in the former Yugoslavia
- Global War on Terrorism
- Operation Enduring Freedom
- Operation Freedom's Sentinel
- Operation Iraqi Freedom
- Operation New Dawn

Services Offered at Vet Centers

Readjustment counseling encompasses a variety of psychosocial services designed to assist eligible veterans, service members, and their families in successfully transitioning from military to civilian life. These services include:

- Individual and group counseling for veterans, service members, and their families
- Family counseling to address military-related issues
- Bereavement counseling for families who have lost a loved one during active

duty
- Counseling and referral services for military sexual trauma (MST)
- Outreach and educational programs, including post-deployment health reassessments (PDHRA) and community events
- Substance abuse assessment and referral services
- Employment assessment and referral services
- Explanations and referrals for Veterans Benefits Administration (VBA) benefits
- Screening and referral for medical conditions such as traumatic brain injury (TBI) and depression

Do Vet Centers offer counseling for family members?

Yes, since 1979, family members of combat veterans and service members have been eligible to receive readjustment counseling services for military-related issues through Vet Centers.

Am I eligible for readjustment counseling at a Vet Center?

If you or a family member served in a combat zone and earned a military campaign ribbon (e.g., Vietnam, Southwest Asia, OEF, OIF), both you and your family are eligible for Vet Center services.

Where is counseling provided?

Readjustment counseling is available at community-based Vet Centers, which are conveniently located in neighborhoods near veterans, service members, and their families. These locations are separate from VA organizational sites to ensure confidentiality and reduce barriers to care. All Vet Center services are prepaid through military service.

Are Vet Centers open during non-traditional hours?

Yes, Vet Centers offer flexible appointment hours, including after normal business hours, to accommodate the schedules of veterans, servicemembers, and their families.

Bereavement Counseling Services

Bereavement counseling, often referred to as grief counseling, offers emotional and psychological support to individuals coping with the loss of a loved one. This type of counseling includes a wide range of services, such as outreach, individual counseling, and referrals, to help family members through their grief and transition.

Is Bereavement Counseling Available for Surviving Family Members?

Yes, the Department of Veterans Affairs (VA) provides bereavement counseling for family members of those who have died in military service. This includes family members of Reservists and National Guard members who died while on duty, as well as those who were receiving Vet Center services at the time of their death.

Additionally, family members of veterans and service members who die by suicide are eligible for these services.

Where Is Counseling Available?

VA's bereavement counseling services are offered at community-based Vet Centers located throughout the country, close to the families who need them. These services are provided at no cost to the families.

How Can You Access These Services?

Bereavement counseling is available through 300 Vet Centers nationwide, where services are confidential and free of charge.

Military Sexual Trauma Counseling

Military sexual trauma (MST) counseling provides support to those affected by sexual trauma during military service. Services may include individual or group counseling, marital and family therapy, referrals for benefits, assistance with community resources, and help with substance abuse issues. These services are designed to help individuals cope with the emotional impact of MST and regain confidence in daily life.

Am I Eligible for Military Sexual Trauma Counseling at Vet Centers?

Any veteran or service member, including members of the National Guard and Reserve, who has experienced sexual trauma while serving in the military, is eligible for MST counseling. These services are available regardless of gender or era of service.

Where Are Services Available?

MST counseling, along with assessments and referrals, is available at all Vet Center locations. Additionally, MST-related medical and mental health services can be accessed at your local VA Medical Center. To access these services, you can contact the Military Sexual Trauma Coordinator or your current VA healthcare provider.

Access the National Directory of VA Vet Centers

For your convenience, we've provided a quick and easy way to access the national directory of VA Vet Centers. By scanning the QR code below, you'll be able to instantly view a list of all VA Vet Centers across the country, making it easier to find the nearest center that can provide the services you need.

How to Use the QR Code
1.   Open the camera app on your smartphone or tablet.
2.   Point your device's camera at the QR code.
3.   A notification or link will pop up on your screen—tap the notification.
4.   The link will take you directly to the National Directory of VA Vet Centers.

This directory will help you locate a Vet Center nearby, where you can access counseling, support, and a variety of other services designed to assist Veterans and their families.

VA.gov

CHAPTER 26

DECISION REVIEWS AND APPEALS

Veterans and other claimants for VA benefits have the right to appeal decisions made by a VA regional office or medical center. The legacy VA appeals process changed and if you disagree with a VA decision dated on or after February 2019, you can choose from 3 decision review options to continue your case. If you disagree with the results of the initial option you choose, you can try another eligible option.

Appeals Modernization

The passage of the Veterans Appeals Improvement and Modernization Act of 2017 (Appeals Modernization Act), created a decision review process aimed at allowing VA to improve the delivery of benefits and services.

The process allows veterans to seek a faster resolution when they disagree with a VA decision.

If you received an initial claim after February 2019 and you disagree, you can choose one of three lanes to have your disagreement reviewed.

Supplemental Claim

You can file a Supplemental Claim to add new evidence relevant to your case or identity new evidence you want the VA to gather for you. A reviewer determines if the new evidence will change the decision.

Filing a Supplemental Claim for PACT Act-Related Conditions

If VA denied your claim in the past but now consider your condition presumptive, it encourages you to file a Supplemental Claim. The VA will review the claim again.

To file a Supplemental Claim, you have to add evidence that's new—not provided to the VA previously, and relevant to your case. You can file a Supplemental Claim anytime, but the VA recommends filing within a year from the date on your decision letter.

You can't file a Supplemental Claim if you have a contested claim.

New evidence means the VA didn't have it before the last decision. Relevant means it can prove or disprove something in your claim. You can submit this evidence yourself or ask the VA to get evidence for you. Evidence can include medical records from a VA medical center, from another federal health facility, or your private health care provider. VA won't accept a Supplemental Claim without new and relevant evidence.

To file a Supplemental Claim, fill out Decision Review Request: Supplemental Claim (VA Form 20-0995).

You can submit your application by mail or in person. If you're sending it by mail, send it to the VA regional office that matches the benefit type you selected on the form. For compensation, mail it to:

Department of Veterans Affairs Claims Intake Center
PO Box 4444
Janesville, WI 53547-4444

If you're submitting in person, you bring the completed form and supporting documents to a VA regional office.

If you get a Supplemental Claim decision you don't agree with, you can then request a Higher-Level review of the Supplemental Claim decision, or file for a Board Appeal. If you file for a Board Appeal, your case will be reviewed by a Veterans Law Judge. You also have the option to file another Supplemental Claim if you have additional evidence you'd like to submit for review.

Higher-Level Reviews

If you don't agree with a VA decision, you or your representative can request a new review to be done by a senior reviewer. The senior reviewer determines if there is an error or difference of opinion that would change the decision. You can't submit new evidence with a Higher-Level review.

You can request a Higher-Level Review of an initial claim or Supplement Claim decision. You have a year from the date on your decision letter to request a Higher-Level Review. You can't request a Higher-Level review after a previous Higher-Level Review or Board Appeal on the same claim. You can't request a Higher-Level review if you have a contested claim.

Informal Conferences

An informal conference is a call with the senior reviewer working on your case. If you choose to have an informal conference, the senior reviewer contacts you by phone to schedule a time to talk about your case. You or your representative during this time can discuss why you think the decision should change and identify evidence. If the senior reviewer doesn't get an answer when they call, they'll leave a voicemail. If they can't make contact after two attempts, they review and decide your case without talking to you.

If you request a Higher-Level review online, you can use the online form in step 3 to ask for an informal conference.

If you request a Higher-Level review by mail or in person, you can ask for an informal conference by marking the circle in item 16A on VA Form 20-0996.

You can only have one informal conference for every Higher-Level review.

If the reviewer finds an error, that might change the original decision. Then you'll get a new decision sent to you. If the reviewer finds the VA didn't help you get all the evidence needed for your claim, this is called a duty-to-assist error. To fix this error, the VA closes your Higher-Level review and opens a new Supplemental Claim. The VA will send a letter outlining the steps they're taking to fix the error. Then the VA will help you get missing evidence, and decide your case based on the new evidence.

If you get a Higher-Level Review decision you don't agree with, you can then file for a Board Appeal. When you file for a Board Appeal, your case will get reviewed by a Veterans Law Judge. You'll also have the option to file a Supplemental Claim if you have more evidence you want to submit for review.

Board Appeals

When you choose the Board Appeals option, you're appealing to a Veterans Law Judge at the Board of Veterans' Appeals in Washington D.C. A judge who's an expert in veterans law will review the case.

You can request a Board Appeal after an initial claim, Supplemental Claim or higher-Level Review decision. You can't request two Board Appeals in a row for the same claim. You have a year from the date on your decision letter to request a Board Appeal, unless you have a contest claim.

If you select a Board Appeal, you have three options.

Option 1: Request a Direct Review

When you choose the direct review option, a judge reviews your appeal based on evidence you already submitted. You can't submit new evidence, and you can't have a hearing. The direct review option takes an average of a year for the Board to complete.

Option 2: Submit New Evidence

If you choose this option, you submit new evidence for a Veterans Law Judge to review. You have to submit the evidence within 90 days of the date the VA receives your request for a Board Appeal. This option takes an average of 1 ½ years to complete.

Option 3: Request a Hearing

If you request a hearing with a Veterans Law Judge, you can add new and relevant evidence and submit it at the hearing or within 90 days after the hearing. Adding evidence is optional. You can speak to the Veterans Law Judge by a virtual hearing at home, a videoconference hearing at a VA location near your home, or an in-person hearing at the Board in D.C. where you have to pay your travel costs. It takes an average of two years for the Board to complete the hearing option.

You can request a Board appeal online, or by mail. To do it by mail, you fill out a Decision Review Request: Board of Appeal (Notice of Disagreement) (VA Form 10182). Send the completed form to:

Board of Veterans' Appeals PO Box 27063
Washington, D.C. 20038

You can also bring your completed form to a VA regional office.

If you don't agree with the Board's decision and you have new and relevant information supporting your case, you can file a Supplemental Claim. You also have the option to appeal to the U.S. Court of Appeals for Veterans Claims.

After You Request a Review

VA will mail you a decision packet when your review is complete, which will have details about the decision for your case.

While you wait, you don't need to do anything unless the VA asks for more information. Don't request another review if you haven't heard back. Instead contact VA.

You may be able to choose a different review option after submitting a form.

To switch after you submitted a Higher-Level Review or Supplemental Claim, both must be true:
- The VA hasn't decided your Supplemental Claim or Higher-Level review, and
- You're still within one year from the date on your original VA decision letter

To switch to a different review option, submit a new request for the option you want. Include a signed letter that indicates you want to withdraw your original decision review request.

To switch after you've already submitted a Board Appeal, all of the following must be true:
- You haven't submitted new evidence or had a hearing, and
- The Board hasn't decided your case, and
- You're still within one year from the date on your original VA decision letter

To switch to a Supplemental Claim or Higher-Level Review, submit a new request for the review option you want, and include a signed letter that says you want to withdraw your original Board Appeal request.

To switch to a different type of Board Appeal, all of the following must be true:
- You haven't submitted new evidence or had a hearing, and
- The Board hasn't decided your case, and
- You're still within one year from the date on your original VA decision letter or 60 days from your original Board Appeal request, whichever is later.

To switch to a different type of Board Appeal, submit a new Board Appeal request and choose the type you want. You won't have to withdraw your original request.

CHAPTER 27

VA REGIONAL OFFICES & BENEFITS OFFICES

The Department of Veterans Affairs (VA) operates a network of regional offices across the country, designed to help veterans and their families access essential services and benefits. Whether you're seeking information about VA benefits, filing a claim, or needing assistance with other inquiries, VA regional offices are dedicated to providing the support you need.

All VA Regional Offices are currently open, offering in-person services to veterans, while also continuing to provide services via phone and online for added convenience. These offices serve as local resources to help guide you through the VA's processes, with dedicated teams available to answer your questions and assist with claims.

Below, you'll find a QR code that links to the directory of VA Regional Offices, allowing you to quickly locate an office near you and access important details like hours of operation, services provided, and contact information for the regional office director.

How to Use the QR Code
1. Open the camera app on your smartphone or tablet.
2. Point your device's camera at the QR code.
3. A notification or link will appear—tap it.
4. You will be redirected to the VA Regional Office directory page where you can find the office closest to you and view the services they provide.

This directory will provide all the necessary details to connect you with the right resources and support in your area on **Benefits.va.gov.**

CHAPTER 28

STATE BENEFITS

Many states offer services and benefits to veterans in addition to those offered by the Department of Veterans' Affairs. To find out more about a particular state's programs, individuals should contact the following:

Alabama VA
100 North Union St.
Ste 850
Montgomery, AL 36104-3719
(334) 242-5077

Alaska VA
1201 N. Muldoon Rd.
Anchorage, AK 99504
(907) 257-4700

Arizona VA Services
3839 North Third St.
Phoenix, AZ 85012
(602) 255-3373

Arkansas VA
501 Woodlane St.
Ste 401 N
Little Rock, AR 72201
(501) 683-1787

California VA
1227 O Street, Suite 300
Sacramento, CA 95814
(800) 952-5626

Colorado VA
155 Van Gorden, Suite 210
Lakewood, CO 80228
(303) 914-5832

Connecticut VA
287 West Street
Rocky Hill, CT 06067
(860) 616-3652

Delaware VA Robbins Building
802 Silverlake Blvd, Suite 100
Dover, DE 19904
(302) 739-2792
(800) 344-9900 (in-state only)

Florida VA
Mary Grizzle Building,
Room 311-K
11351 Ulmerton Road
Largo, FL 33778
(727) 319-7440

Georgia VA
2 MLK Jr Dr. SE
Atlanta, GA 30334
(404) 656-2300

Hawaii VA Mailing Address:
459 Patterson Road
E-Wing, Room 1-A103
Honolulu, HI 96819-1522
Location:
Tripler Army Med Center (Ward Road) VAMROC,
E-Wing, Room 1-A103
Honolulu, HI 96819
(808) 433-0420

Idaho VA
351 Collins Road
Boise, ID 83702
(208) 708-1301

Illinois VA
833 South Spring St.
Springfield, IL 62704
(217) 782-6641

Indiana VA
777 North Meridian St. Ste 300
Indianapolis, IN 46204-2738
(317) 232-3910

Iowa Commission of Veterans'
Affairs
7105 N.W. 70th Avenue
Camp Dodge - Building 3663
Johnston, IA 50131-1824
(515) 252-4698

Kansas Commission on
Veterans' Affairs
Jayhawk Towers Suite 1004
700 S.W. Jackson Street
Topeka, KS 66603-3714
(785) 296-3976

Kentucky VA
1111B Louisville Road
Building Frankfort, KY 40601
(502) 564-9203

Louisiana VA
602 N. Fifth St.
Baton Rouge, LA 70802
(225) 219-5000

Maine Bureau of Veterans'
Services
117 State House Station
Augusta, ME 04333
(207) 287-7020

Maryland VA
16 Francis St. 4th Floor
Annapolis, MD 21401
(410) 260-3838

Massachusetts Department of
Veterans' Services
600 Washington Street, 7th Floor
Boston, MA 02111
(617) 210-5480

Michigan VA
3423 N. Martin Luther King Jr.
Blvd, Bldg 32
Lansing, MI 48906
(800) 642-4838

Minnesota VA
State Veterans Service Building
20 West 12th Street, Rm. 206
St. Paul, MN 55155-2079
(651) 296-2562

Mississippi State Veterans'
Affairs Board
34660 North St. Ste 200
Jackson, MS 39202
(601) 576-4850

Missouri Veterans' Commission
205 Jefferson Street
12th Floor Jefferson Building
Jefferson City, MO 65102
(573) 751-3779

Montana Veterans' Affairs
Division 1956 Mt. Majo St.
PO Box 4789
Fort Harrison, MT 59636
(406) 324-3742

Nebraska VA
301 Centennial Mall South, 4th
Floor
P.O. Box 95083
Lincoln, NE 68509-5083
(402) 471-2458

Nevada Commission for
Veterans' Affairs
6630 McCarran Blvd.
Bldg C, Ste. 204
Reno, NV 89509
(775) 688-1653

New Hampshire Office of
Veterans' Service
1 Minuteman Way
Concord, NH 03301
(603) 225-1200

New Jersey VA
101 Eggert Crossing Road
Lawrenceville, NJ 08648
(609) 530-6892

New Mexico Department of
Veterans' Services
407 Galisteo St. Rm. 134
Santa Fe, NM 87501
(505) 218-3125

New York Division of Veterans'
Affairs
2 Empire State Plaza 17th Floor
Albany, NY 12223-1551
(518) 474-6114

North Carolina Division of
Veterans' Affairs
413 N. Salisbury Street
Raleigh, NC 27603
(844) 624-8387

North Dakota VA
4201 38th St S # 104
Fargo, ND 58104
(701) 239-7165

Ohio Governor's Office of
Veterans' Affairs
77 South High Street
Columbus, OH 43215
(614) 644-0898

Oklahoma VA
2312 NE 36th St.
Oklahoma City, OK 73111
(405) 523-4000

Oregon VA
700 Summer St. NE
Salem, OR 97301
(503) 373-2373

Pennsylvania VA
Fort Indiantown Gap
Building S-O-47
Annville, PA 17003-5002
(717) 861-8910

Rhode Island Office of Veterans'
Affairs
500 Jefferson Blvd.
Warwick, RI 02886
(401) 921-2119

South Carolina Department of
Veterans' Affairs
1800 St. Julian Place, Ste. 305
Columbia, SC 29204
(803) 734-0200

South Dakota Division of
Veterans' Affairs
425 East Capitol Avenue
Pierre, SD 57501
(605) 773-3269

Tennessee VA
312 Rosa Parks Ave.
Nashville, TN 37243-1010
(615) 741-2345

Texas Veterans' Commission
1700 Congress Ave.
Austin, TX 78701
(512) 463-6564

Utah Division of Veterans' Affairs
550 Foothill Blvd, Ste. 105
Salt Lake City, UT 84113
(801) 326-2372

Vermont State Veterans' Affairs
118 State Street
Montpelier, VT 05602
(802) 828-3379

Virginia VA
James Monroe Building
101 North 14th St., 17th Floor
Richmond, VA 23219
(804) 786-0286

Washington VA
1102 Quince St. SE,
PO Box 41150
Olympia, WA 98504-1150
(800) 562-2308

West Virginia Division of
Veterans' Affairs
300 Technology Dr., Ste. 201
South Charleston, WV 25309
(304) 746-4497

Wisconsin VA
201 West Washington Avenue
Madison, WI 53703
(800) 947-8387

Wyoming Veterans' Affairs
Commission
2135 Rimrock Rd., PO Box 7843
Madison, Wi 53707
(800) 947-8387

American Samoa Veterans'
Affairs
P.O. Box 982942
Pago Pago,
American Samoa 96799
(001) 684-633-4206

Guam Veterans' Affairs Office
Mailing
172 S. Marine Corps Dr.
Asan, GU 96910
(671) 475-8388

Puerto Rico Public Advocate for
Veterans' Affairs
2 Avenida Juan Ponce de Leon
San Juan, PR 00917
(787) 758-5760

Government of the Virgin Islands
Division of Veterans' Affairs
1013 Estate Richmond
Christiansted St. Croix VI
00820-4349
(340) 727-8389

CHAPTER 29

RECORDS

Military service records are important documents that detail a service member's time in the armed forces. These records, including your DD Form 214 (Report of Separation), are stored at the National Archives and Records Administration (NARA) and serve as an official record for veterans who have been discharged from the U.S. Army, Navy, Air Force, Marine Corps, and Coast Guard.

For recently separated veterans, their service records can be found online via the VA eBenefits portal. However, veterans and their next of kin can also obtain free copies of their DD214 and other military service records through multiple avenues, including the following:

- eVetRecs system: Use this online tool to submit a request.
- Mail or Fax: Complete a Standard Form SF-180 and send it by mail or fax to the appropriate location.

Types of Military Service Records Available

Military personnel records may contain a range of information about a service member's military career, including:
- Enlistment details
- Duty stations and assignments
- Training, qualifications, and performance
- Awards, medals, and decorations
- Disciplinary actions
- Insurance and emergency contact information
- Administrative remarks
- Separation and discharge details (including DD Form 214 or equivalent)

Please note that detailed battle participation or engagement information is not typically included in these records.

Health Records and Personnel Files

While Official Military Personnel Files (OMPF) often include both personnel and health records, this practice was discontinued in 1992 by the military branches. For health-related service records, please refer to Military Medical and Health Records.

Archival Records and Availability

Military records are stored at the National Personnel Records Center (NPRC) and are typically available for veterans who are discharged, retired, or deceased. Records are usually transferred to NPRC within six months after these events occur. However, records of those still in the active or inactive reserves or National Guard are not held at the NPRC.

Important: As part of an agreement between NARA and the Department of Defense, military personnel files become permanent records 62 years after a service member's separation. This ensures that the records are accessible for public research after a certain period.

Access to Archival Records

Once military service records reach 62 years old, they are classified as archival records and are made available to the public. These records can be accessed online or by request for a fee.

Persons of Exceptional Prominence (PEP) Records

Some records of historically significant individuals, such as presidents, military leaders, and public figures, are opened to the public earlier. These "Persons of Exceptional Prominence" (PEP) records can be requested after 10 years following the individual's death.

DD Form 214 and Other Discharge Forms

The DD Form 214 is the most widely used document to verify military service and determine eligibility for various veteran benefits. This form typically includes information such as:
- Date and place of entry into active duty
- Service member's rank and job specialty
- Decorations, medals, badges, and campaign awards
- Total creditable service
- Separation information (e.g., type of separation, reason, eligibility for reenlistment)

Before 1950, similar forms were used for discharge documentation.

How to Request Your Military Service Records

You can request your records through several methods, including online requests, mailing a completed SF-180 form, or contacting the NPRC directly. For more detailed instructions on how to request records, visit the official website for Military Records Requests: Standard Form SF-180.

If you need help or have any questions, consider using the MyVA411 line or check the status of your request online.

Correcting Military Service Records

Under the Department of Defense Instruction (DODI) 1336.01, which mandates the electronic creation and transmission of DD Form 215, the National Archives and Records Administration (NARA) no longer handles the creation of DD Form 215 for corrections to DD Form 214.

If your military record is classified as archival (i.e., if you were discharged, retired, or passed away in service more than 62 years ago), you must request corrections through the review board for your specific service branch. Instructions on the process for these corrections are provided below.

For records that are not archival, you must directly contact the personnel command of your respective service branch (e.g., Navy Personnel Command, Army Human Resources Command) to request the correction. Refer to the table below for the relevant contact addresses for each branch.

If you are seeking a change to your character of service (e.g., upgrading a dishonorable discharge to honorable), you will need to apply to your service branch's review board.

Important: Do not submit these requests to the National Archives. Use the specific contact addresses provided for your branch of service.

Corrections to Military Service Records:
- **Military Service Record Corrections**: Submit DD Form 149, *Application for Correction of Military Records*, to the relevant service branch. This form can be downloaded online or obtained from veterans' organizations or VA offices.
- **Discharge Status Review**: Submit DD Form 293, *Application for the Review of Discharge or Dismissal from the Armed Forces*, to the relevant service branch for review of your discharge status.
- **Correction of Military Records**: The Secretary of the relevant military department, through the appropriate board for correction of military records, has the authority to make changes to military records to correct errors or remove injustices. The board may review cases involving discharge actions, including those from courts-martial.

To ensure a request is considered, the veteran or their representative typically must file the application within three years of discovering the error or injustice. However, if it is in the interest of justice, the board may waive this time limit. Applicants must provide sufficient evidence to justify the correction, such as signed statements from witnesses or supporting documentation.
- **Review of Discharges**: Each military branch maintains a discharge review board that can modify or change discharges or dismissals not resulting from a general courts-martial. The board does not have authority over medical discharges. Survivors, next of kin, or legal representatives of deceased or incompetent veterans may also request a review. Discharges made more than 15 years ago require petitioning the service's Board for Correction of

Military Records with DD Form 149.

- **Discharge Review Eligibility**: If a discharge was due to a continuous period of unauthorized absence lasting more than 180 days, the individual is generally ineligible for VA benefits, unless the VA determines there were compelling circumstances. The boards for correction of military records may also address these cases.

Veterans with disabilities incurred during service may still qualify for benefits regardless of their separation or discharge status. Veterans separated under other than honorable conditions can apply for recharacterization of their discharge if they submit the appeal within 15 years of their discharge date.

For more detailed information, contact the discharge review board for your specific service branch using DoD Form 293.

Veterans' Medical and Health Records

Military service records, including medical and health records, are typically stored at the National Personnel Records Center (NPRC). These records, known as Official Military Personnel Files (OMPFs), contain information on an individual's military service history, including personnel data. In many cases, these files also include health records; however, the process for storing medical records changed in the 1990s.

Historically, health records, including outpatient, dental, and mental health treatment records, were stored alongside personnel records at the NPRC. These health records documented the medical care veterans received while in service, such as physical exams, routine doctor visits, lab tests, and non-hospital treatments. Clinical records, which refer to inpatient (hospitalization) records, were typically kept separate and handled differently.

From the 1990s onward, military services stopped transferring medical records to the NPRC. Instead, they began sending health records to the Department of Veterans Affairs (VA) for processing.

Here's how the storage of military health records has evolved over time:

Branch	Status	Date	Record Location
Army	Discharged, retired, or separated from any component	10/16/1992 to 12/31/2013	Department of VA, Records Management Center
		on or after 01/01/2014	AMEDD Record Processing Center
Navy	Discharged, retired, or separated from	01/31/1994 to 12/31/2013	Department of VA, Records Management

			Center
		on or after 01/01/2014	BUMED Navy Medicine Records Activity
Air Force	Discharged, retired, or separated from any component	05/01/1994 to 12/31/2013	Department of VA, Records Management Center
		on or after 01/01/2014	AF STR Processing Center
Marine Corps	Discharged, retired, or separated from any component	05/01/1994 to 12/31/2013	Department of VA, Records Management Center
		on or after 01/01/2014	BUMED Navy Medicine Records Activity
Coast Guard	Discharged, retired, or separated from Active Duty	04/01/1998 to 09/30/2014	Department of VA, Records Management Center
	Reservists with 90 days active duty for training	on or after 10/01/2014	USCG HSWL SC Medical Administration

Filing a Claim for Medical Benefits

If you are filing a medical claim with the Department of Veterans Affairs (VA), you do not need to request your military health records from the NPRC. Once your claim is filed, the VA will retrieve the original health records directly from the NPRC. It's important to note that many health records were already transferred to the VA before the 1973 fire, which affected many records stored at the NPRC.

Veterans who have filed a medical claim should contact the VA to check whether their health records are already on file. You can reach the VA toll-free at 1-800-827-1000, which will connect you to the nearest VA office for further assistance.

Requesting Your Military Service Records (Including DD214)

If you need a copy of your DD214 or other military service records, you can request them from the National Archives. These records can provide important information about your military career, including your discharge status, assignments, awards, and more.

Types of Information You Can Access

When you request your military service records, you may receive the following information:

- Character of discharge (from your DD214 or other separation documents)
- Duty stations and assignments
- Medals and decorations (awards)
- Qualifications, licenses, and certificates

How to Request Your Records from the National Archives

There are several ways to request your military records:

Option 1: Request Online

You can easily request your records through the National Archives' eVetRecs tool. Simply go to the eVetRecs website and select "Make a new request." You will receive an email confirmation once your request has been received.

Option 2: Request via Mail or Fax

Fill out the "Request Pertaining to Military Records" form (Standard Form 180) and send it by mail or fax to the appropriate address listed on the last page of the form. Get Standard Form 180 to Download

Other Options for Obtaining Records

- **For DOD Records**: If you were discharged after certain dates, you can request your records directly from the Department of Defense through the milConnect website.
- **For Marines (1998-present) and Coast Guard (2008-present)**: Contact your personnel command directly for records.

How to Request Someone Else's Military Records

If you're a family member planning a veteran's burial, you don't need to request the veteran's military service records yourself. The National Cemetery Scheduling Office will try to locate the records needed to determine burial eligibility. However, if you are the next of kin of a veteran who has passed, you can request their military records online, by mail, or by fax.

Important Documents for Family Members Requesting Records

To request records for a deceased veteran, you will need to provide one of the following documents:

- The veteran's death certificate or another public record of death
- A letter from a funeral home

If you are not the next of kin, you may still be able to request records depending on the discharge date. Records older than 62 years are public, while newer records require the next of kin's authorization for full access.

How to Check the Status of Your Request

Once your request has been submitted, you can check its status. You may check online or call the NPRC customer service line at 314-801-0800 (be aware that this is a long-distance call for most customers).

Note: Please allow sufficient time for processing before inquiring about your request status.

Cost of Records

Requests for records are generally free for veterans, next of kin, and authorized representatives unless the records are considered "archival" (i.e., over 62 years old). In those cases, a fee may apply:

- Routine OMPFs (5 pages or fewer): $25 flat fee
- Routine OMPFs (6 pages or more): $70 flat fee
- Exceptional Prominence (PEP) OMPF: $0.80 per page (minimum $20)

Additional Information
- You can also access military service records by contacting state or county veterans agencies or hiring an independent researcher.

Alternative Methods to Obtain Military Service Records

If you are unable to access your military service records online through the usual channels, there are several other methods you can use to request them. Here are a few options for obtaining your records:

1. eBenefits Portal (For Recent Veterans)

Recent veterans may be able to access their military service records through the joint Department of Veterans Affairs and Department of Defense eBenefits Portal. This is an easy way to obtain your DD214 and other important records.

2. Write a Letter to Request Records

If you cannot access or use the standard forms for requesting your records, you may send a letter to request military service records. Your letter should include all necessary details to help locate your records. For full information on how to write a request, refer to the guidelines for **Military Records Requests: Standard Form SF-180**.

3. Contact State or County Veterans Agencies

Some states, counties, and municipalities maintain copies of certain military service records. If you're a veteran, you can contact your local state or county veterans' agency to inquire about available records.

Note: Be cautious about third-party services that offer to obtain your DD214 for a fee. These services are often offered as a paid service, but the same records can be accessed for free through official government channels.

4. What Are Federal vs. Archival Records?

Records are considered "archival" if they are over 62 years old. When military records reach this age, they are made available to the public and can be requested for a fee. Non-archival records, typically those from more recent service members, are usually accessible without a fee to the veteran or next of kin. Archival Records can be ordered for a fee:

5. Alternate Record Sources (For Damaged Records)

If your military records were damaged, such as those lost in the 1973 fire at the National Personnel Records Center (NPRC), the NPRC may attempt to reconstruct certain service data using alternate sources. These sources are helpful in documenting military service and may include:

- **Personnel-Related Data**: Final pay vouchers, service number indexes, enlistment ledgers, and more.
- **Medical-Related Data**: Records from the U.S. Army Surgeon General's Office, which include medical treatment details for Army personnel from 1942-1945 and 1950-1954.

If your records were part of the 1973 fire loss, you may need to fill out additional forms (such as **NA Form 13075** or **NA Form 13055**) to assist in reconstructing the data.

6. Public Access to Archival Records

Once a service member's records are 62 years old, they become available to the public. These records can be requested through the National Archives for a fee. These documents include a variety of military service information, such as service dates, character of discharge, and specific military assignments.

7. Requesting Records for Next of Kin

If you are the next of kin (surviving spouse, child, or parent) of a deceased veteran, you may request military service records. You will need to provide proof of death (such as a death certificate or funeral home letter). If the service member was discharged more than 62 years ago, their records are now open to the public and can be requested by anyone.

For records of service members discharged less than 62 years ago, the request will need to be submitted with written authorization from the next of kin.

Contact Information:

For more details or to submit your request, you can mail or fax your request to the NPRC using the following contact details:

- **NPRC Mailing Address**:
  National Personnel Records Center
  Military Personnel Records
  1 Archives Drive
  St. Louis, MO 63138
- **NPRC FAX Number**: 314-801-9195
- **NPRC Phone Number**: 314-801-0800

If you need assistance or have further questions about your records, you can reach the NPRC directly or contact your state or county veterans agency for support.

Veterans' Service Officer (VSO) Information

Veterans Service Officers (VSOs) play a crucial role in helping military veterans, retirees, and their families access the records and benefits they are entitled to. This guide is designed to assist VSOs in obtaining necessary information from the National Personnel Records Center (NPRC) and understanding the process of requesting military service records.

General Information

Military personnel records become "archival" 62 years after discharge, retirement, or death in service. Once records reach this age, they are generally available to the public for a fee. However, requests for federal benefits (such as VA home loans) are typically processed free of charge. State-level requests, such as for veteran license plates, may require a fee. For more information, refer to the section on "Official Military Personnel Files (OMPF)" and archival holdings.

It's important to note that the NPRC, which stores non-archival records, is separate from the National Archives at St. Louis, which holds archival records once they become public. Both institutions are housed in the same building, which can be confusing.

The **DD Form 214** (or equivalent separation document) is essential for accessing many veteran benefits. This document has been used for separations/retirements since 1950, replacing earlier forms like the WD AGO 53-55. The NPRC processes separation documents more quickly than other records, so it's best to request only the specific records needed to avoid unnecessary delays.

Be Specific When Requesting Records

When submitting requests, be as specific as possible. For example, if you need medical records for a specific treatment, say:
"I need my inpatient medical record from May 1968, at Womack Army Hospital, Fort Bragg, NC, for knee surgery."

Avoid vague requests like, "Send me medical stuff," as this will result in delays.

Preferred Request Methods

- **eVetRecs**: This online tool is the preferred method for submitting requests, as it allows for electronic signatures and provides a tracking number for your request.
- **Standard Form 180**: If eVetRecs is not an option, you can fill out the SF-180, sign it, and fax or mail it to the NPRC.

If you assist someone with submitting their request, consider helping them complete the eVetRecs form online in your office or provide them with the SF-180 form for submission.

NPRC's Record Holdings

The NPRC holds records for military personnel who are no longer active, including those discharged, retired, or deceased. Records for personnel still in reserves or the National Guard are not stored at the NPRC.

Separation and Retirement Dates

When requesting records, it's important to know the correct separation, retirement, or discharge date. Many veterans mistakenly refer to their release from active duty (REFRAD) date instead of their official separation date. For example, a veteran might say they were discharged in 1993, but they were likely released from active duty in 1993 and transferred to the inactive reserve, with their separation actually occurring in 1998. Understanding the correct dates can affect where the records are stored.

Accessing Medical Records

For veterans filing medical benefit claims, there's no need to request their medical records from NPRC. After the claim is submitted, the VA will directly obtain the necessary records from the NPRC. If veterans have previously filed claims, it's best to contact the VA to confirm if their records are already available.

Requesting Burial Benefits

For veterans, retirees, and their next of kin seeking burial or death benefits, the National Cemetery Scheduling Office is the primary point of contact. This office will verify service through the NPRC when requesting burial in a National Cemetery.
If the veteran is not being interred at a National Cemetery, a request for a Separation Document (DD Form 214) should be submitted directly to the NPRC. In urgent cases, such as for an upcoming funeral, the request should indicate its urgency and be submitted to NPRC's Customer Service team.

Records Reconstruction

In cases where records were lost or destroyed—such as in the 1973 fire at NPRC—

alternative sources may be used to reconstruct the service history. This process can take additional time, but the NPRC will do its best to locate and reconstruct service records using available data.

By understanding the procedures for requesting and correcting military service records, VSOs can more effectively assist veterans and their families in obtaining the necessary documentation for benefits and services. For specific requests or assistance, contacting the appropriate service department directly or using eVetRecs is highly recommended.

Locations of Service Records

ARMY (includes Army Air Corps and Army Air Forces)

Status	Time Frame	Personnel Record Location	Health Record Location
Enlisted	1789 to November 1, 1912	NARA, Washington DC	N/A
Officer	1789 to July 1, 1917	NARA, Washington DC	N/A
Enlisted	November 1, 1912, to October 15, 1992	National Personnel Records Center	Note: Many records were destroyed by the 1973 Fire
Officer	July 1, 1917, to October 15, 1992	National Personnel Records Center	Note: Many records were destroyed by the 1973 Fire
All Personnel	October 16, 1992, to September 30, 2002	National Personnel Records Center	Department of Veterans Affairs
All Personnel	Discharged, deceased or retired on or after October 1, 2002, to December 31, 2013	U.S. Army Human Resources Command	Department of Veterans Affairs
All Personnel	Discharged, deceased or	U.S. Army Human	AMEDD Record

	retired on or after January 1, 2014	Resources Command	Processing Center
All Active Duty	All	U.S. Army Human Resources Command	
All National Guard	All	The Adjutant General (of the appropriate state, DC, or Puerto Rico)	

AIR FORCE

Status	Time Frame	Personnel Record Location	Health Record Location
Officer and Enlisted – Discharged, deceased, or retired **(Last Name HUBBARD through Z)** **(See General Officer Below)**	September 25, 1947 – December 31, 1963 **Note:** Some records may have been destroyed by the 1973 Fire	National Personnel Records Center	
Officer and Enlisted – Discharged, deceased, or retired **(Last Name A thru HUBBARD)** **(See General Officer Below)**	September 25, 1947 – December 31, 1963	National Personnel Records Center	
Officer and Enlisted – Discharged, deceased, or retired	January 1,1964 to April 30, 1994	National Personnel Records Center	

(See General Officer Below)			
Officer and Enlisted – Discharged, deceased, or retired **(See General Officer Below)**	May 1, 1994 to October 1, 2004	National Personnel Records Center	Department of Veterans Affairs
Officer and Enlisted – Discharged, deceased, or retired **(See General Officer Below)**	October 2, 2004 to December 31, 2013	Air Force Personnel Center HQ AFPC/DPSSRP **Note:** records are stored electronically at ARMS but requests are serviced by: National Personnel Records Center	Department of Veterans Affairs
Officer and Enlisted – Discharged, deceased, or retired **(See General Officer Below)**	January 1, 2014, to Present	Air Force Personnel Center HQ AFPC/DPSSRP **Note:** records are stored electronically at ARMS but requests are serviced by: National Personnel Records Center	AF STR Processing Center
Current Active Duty – officer and enlisted (including National Guard on Active Duty) and TDRL	All	Air Force Personnel Center HQ AFPC/DPSSRP	

General Officers retired with pay **(Note: If deceased see "Officer and Enlisted" status blocks above.)**	All	Air Force Personnel Center HQ AFPC/DPSSRP	
Current Reserve, including retired reserve in nonpay status **(Note: If retired but drawing retirement pay, normally age 60, see "Officer and Enlisted" status blocks above.)**	All	Air Reserve Personnel Center Buckley AFB	
Current National Guard Officers (not on active duty) or National Guard released from active duty	All	Air Reserve Personnel Center Buckley AFB	
Current National Guard Enlisted, not on active duty	All	The Adjutant General (of the appropriate state, DC, or Puerto Rico)	

NAVY

Status	Time Frame	Personnel Record Location	Health Record Location
Officer – Discharged, deceased, or retired	Before January 1, 1903	Archives I Reference Service Branch, Washington, DC	
Enlisted – Discharged, deceased, or retired	Before January 1, 1886	Archives I Reference Service Branch, Washington, DC	
Officer – Discharged, deceased, or retired	January 1, 1903, to December 31, 1963	National Personnel Records Center	National Personnel Records Cent
Enlisted –	January 1,	National Personnel	National

Discharged, deceased, or retired	1886, to December 31, 1963	Records Center	Personnel Records Center
Officer and Enlisted – Discharged, deceased, or retired	January 31, 1994, to December 31, 1994	National Personnel Records Center	Department of Veterans Affairs
Officer and Enlisted – Discharged, deceased, or retired	January 1, 1995, to December 31, 2013	National Personnel Records Center	Department of Veterans Affairs
Officer and Enlisted – Discharged, deceased, or retired	January 1, 2014 – Present	National Personnel Records Center	BUMED Navy Medicine Records Activity
Current Active Duty, Reserve, and TDRL	All	Navy Personnel Command	

MARINE CORPS

Status	Time Frame	Personnel Record Location	Health Record Location
Officer and Enlisted – Discharged, deceased, or retired	January 1, 1964, to April 30, 1994	National Personnel Records Center	N/A
Officer and Enlisted – Discharged, deceased, or retired	May 1, 1994 to January 1, 1999	National Personnel Records Center	Department of Veterans Affairs
Officer and Enlisted – Discharged, deceased, or retired	January 1, 1999 to December 31, 2013	U.S. Marine Corps, Manpower Management Records & Performance Branch (MMRP)	Department of Veterans Affairs
Officer and Enlisted – Discharged, deceased, or retired	January 1, 2014 to Present	U.S. Marine Corps, Manpower Management Records & Performance Branch (MMRP)	BUMED Navy Medicine Records Activity
Individual Ready Reserve or Fleet Marine Corps Reserve	All	Marine Forces Reserve	
Current Active Duty, Officer and	All	U.S. Marine Corps, Manpower	

Enlisted, Selected Marine Corps Reserve and TDRL		Management Records & Performance Branch (MMRP)	

COAST GUARD (Including Revenue Cutter Service, Life-Saving Service, and Lighthouse Service)

Status	Time Frame	Personnel Record Location	Health Record Location
All – Discharged, deceased, or retired	January 1, 1898 to March 31, 1998	National Personnel Records Center	N/A
All – Discharged, deceased, or retired	April 1, 1998 to September 30, 2014	National Personnel Records Center	Department Veterans Affairs
All – Discharged, deceased, or retired	October 1, 2014 - Present	National Personnel Records Center	USCG HSV SC Medica Administrat
Current Active Duty, Reserve, or TDRL	All	USCG Personnel Command	

VOLUNTEERS

Status	Time Frame	Record Locatic
All Personnel	Military service performed during an emergency, 1775 to 1902	NARA, Washingt DC

CONFEDERATE STATES

Status	Time Frame	Record Location
All Personnel	1861 to 1865	NARA, Washington DC

PENSION CLAIM FILES

Status	Time Frame	Record Location
All Personnel	Claims for pensions based on Federal military service, 1775 to 1916	NARA, Washington DC

OUNTY LAND WARRANT APPLICATION FILES

Status	Time Frame	Record Location
All Personnel	Claims based on wartime service, 1775 to 1855	NARA, Washington DC

ELECTIVE SERVICE

Holdings	Record Location
WWI Selective Service Records	Order copies of WWI Draft Registration Cards online
WWII - Vietnam Era Selective Service Records*	National Archives at St. Louis
After January 1, 1960	Selective Service System

lease Note: Men born from March 29, 1957 - December 31, 1959, were not quired to register with Selective Service because the registration program was spended when they would have reached age 18.

Military Awards and Decorations

ne National Personnel Records Center (NPRC) does not issue service medals; this handled by the specific military service departments. Requests for the issuance or placement of military service medals, decorations, and awards should be directed the branch of service where the veteran served. However, for Air Force and Army rsonnel (see exceptions), the NPRC can verify the awards a veteran is entitled to d forward the request to the appropriate service department for medal issuance. se the addresses provided below for your requests.

ow Do I Request Military Awards and Decorations?

- **For the Veteran**: Generally, military services will process replacement medal requests for the veteran at no cost. This includes requests by family members with the signed authorization of the veteran.
- **For the Next-of-Kin (NOK)**: The process (and cost) for replacement medals differs between service branches and depends on who is making the request, especially if the record involved is archival. [Click here for details.]
- **For the General Public**: If the service member separated from military service 62 years ago or more, the public can purchase a copy of the veteran's Official Military Personnel File (OMPF) to determine their awards and obtain medals from a commercial source. If the service member separated less than 62 years ago, the public may request information via the Freedom of Information Act (FOIA). See Access to OMPFs by the General Public for more information.

Army
- **Where to Write for Medals**:
National Personnel Records Center
1 Archives Drive

St. Louis, MO 63138

- **Where Medals are Mailed From**:
  U.S. Army TACOM
  Clothing and Heraldry (PSID)
  P.O. Box 57997
  Philadelphia, PA 19111-7997
- **For Issues or Appeals**:
  U.S. Army Human Resources Command
  Soldier Program and Services Division - Awards and Decorations Branch
  ATTN: AHRC-PDP-A
  1600 Spearhead Division Avenue, Dept 480
  Fort Knox, KY 40122-5408

Air Force (includes Army Air Corps and Army Air Forces)

- **Where to Write for Medals**:
  National Personnel Records Center
  1 Archives Drive
  St. Louis, MO 63138
- **Where Medals Are Mailed From** (Active Duty & Reserve Veterans):
  Headquarters Air Force Personnel Center
  HQ AFPC/DP1SP
  550 C Street West, Suite 12
  Randolph AFB, TX 78150-4714
- **For Issues or Appeals** (Reserve & Air Guard Veterans):
  Air Reserve Personnel Center
  HQ ARPC/DPTARA
  18420 E Silver Creek Ave Bldg 390 MS 68
  Buckley AFB, CO 80011

Navy

- **Where to Write for Medals**:
  National Personnel Record Center
  1 Archives Drive
  St. Louis, MO 63138
- **Where Medals are Mailed From**:
  Navy Personnel Command
  PERS 312
  5751 Honor Drive
  Building 769 Room 158
  Millington, TN 38055-3120
- **For Issues or Appeals**:
  Department of the Navy
  Chief of Naval Operations (DNS-35)
  2000 Navy Pentagon
  Washington, DC 20350-2000

Marine Corps
- **Where to Write for Medals**:
  National Personnel Record Center
  1 Archives Drive
  St. Louis, MO 63138
- **Where Medals are Mailed From**:
  Navy Personnel Command
  PERS 312
  5751 Honor Drive
  Building 769 Room 158
  Millington, TN 38055-3120
- **For Issues or Appeals**:
  Commandant of the Marine Corps
  Military Awards Branch (MMMA)
  2008 Elliot Road
  Quantico, VA 22134

Coast Guard
- **Where to Write for Medals & Where Medals Are Mailed From**:
  Coast Guard Personnel Service Center
  4200 Wilson Blvd, Suite 900 (PSC-PSD-MA)
  Stop 7200
  Arlington, VA 20598-7200
- **For Issues or Appeals**:
  Commandant U.S. Coast Guard
  Medals and Awards Branch (PMP-4)
  Washington, DC 20593-0001

Important Information for the Next-of-Kin (NOK):
- **Who is the NOK?**
  - For the Air Force, Navy, Marine Corps, & Coast Guard: The NOK is defined as the un-remarried widow/widower, son, daughter, father, mother, brother, or sister.
  - For the Army: The NOK is the surviving spouse, eldest child, father or mother, eldest sibling, or eldest grandchild.

How Archival or Non-Archival Records Affect Requests for Medals:
- The OMPF is used to verify the awards a veteran may be entitled to. These records become "archival" 62 years after the service member's separation from the military.
- **Archival records** are open to the public and can be requested by NOK without cost.
- **Non-archival records** are maintained under the Federal Records Center program and are subject to access restrictions.

Cold War Recognition Certificate:
- The Cold War Recognition Certificate was approved for all military members and qualified federal personnel who served during the Cold War era from

September 2, 1945, to December 26, 1991.

- **NPRC** provides copies of DD-214s (or equivalents) or SF-50s to authorized requesters. For more information, refer to the Cold War Certificate Program - HRC Homepage.

Note: The 1973 Fire at the NPRC destroyed or damaged a significant portion of records from Army and Air Force personnel discharged between 1912 and 1964. Alternate record sources may be used to reconstruct service data in such cases, but this may result in longer processing times.

Download VA Benefit Letters

To access certain benefits, veterans may need proof of their status. You can easily download your VA Benefit Summary Letter (also referred to as a VA award letter) and other related documents online.

Sign In with a Verified Account

To download your VA benefit letters, you'll need to sign in with an identity-verified account via one of the VA's account providers. This verification helps protect your personal information and prevents fraudulent activity.

If you don't have a verified account yet, you can create a **Login.gov** or **ID.me** account.

Types of VA Letters Available for Download

Once signed in, you'll be able to download various VA letters that provide details on your benefits and service history.

How to Download a VA Letter

Before downloading, you'll be prompted to review your address on file. This address will appear on your letter. If it's incorrect, you can update it, but the letter will still be valid even if the address is outdated.

Note: You'll need the latest version of Adobe Acrobat Reader to view and download your VA letters. It's available for free.

What If the Letter I Need Isn't Available Through This Tool?

Currently, you can only download the VA letters listed after signing in.

What If I Experience Issues Downloading My Letter?

If you encounter any problems, please contact the **MyVA411** information line at 800-698-2411 (TTY: 711) for assistance.

Veteran ID Cards

Veterans have several options for identification cards that can be used to verify their status and access benefits. You only need one of these cards to prove you're a Veteran.

Here's an overview of the different types of VA ID cards and other Veteran ID options.

Department of Defense Identification Card

A Department of Defense (DoD) Identification Card serves as proof of military status and grants access to services at military installations. This card also allows you to receive discounts at many stores, businesses, and restaurants that offer veterans discounts. If you already have a DoD Identification Card, there's no need to request another photo ID to claim your veteran status or to receive discounts.

You may be eligible for a DoD ID card if one of the following applies to you:
- You're retired from the military
- You're currently on active duty
- You're part of the National Guard, Reserves, Selected Reserves, or Inactive Ready Reserve

Note: Depending on your status, the DoD will issue either a Common Access Card (CAC) or a Uniformed Services ID Card (USID). You will need to either be a sponsor or have one to receive either of these cards.

How to Apply for a DoD Identification Card

To apply, you must complete the Application for Identification Card/DEERS Enrollment (DD Form 1172-2).

After completing the form, submit it to a Real-Time Automated Personnel Identification System (RAPIDS) office for processing.

Veteran Health Identification Card

The Veteran Health Identification Card (VHIC) is provided once you're enrolled in VA health care. It serves as identification for checking into VA appointments and can also be used for discounts at participating stores, businesses, and restaurants. If you have a VHIC, you won't need any additional photo ID cards to prove you're a veteran or access those discounts.

How to Get a Veteran Health Identification Card

To receive a VHIC, you must be enrolled in VA health care. If you're not already enrolled, you can apply online now.

If you're already enrolled in VA health care, you can request your VHIC online or at your nearest VA medical center.

Veteran ID Card

The Veteran ID Card (VIC) is a digital photo ID that helps you claim discounts at various retailers, businesses, and restaurants. This card eliminates the need to carry your military discharge papers or share sensitive personal information to access these discounts. Having a VIC means you don't need another photo ID to prove you're a veteran.

Eligibility for a Veteran ID Card

You may be eligible for a VIC if you meet both of these requirements:
- You served on active duty, in the Reserves, or in the National Guard (including the Coast Guard)
- You received an honorable or general discharge (under honorable conditions)

If you received an other-than-honorable, bad conduct, or dishonorable discharge, you're not eligible for a VIC. If your discharge status is uncharacterized or unknown, your eligibility will need to be verified before approval.

Note: As of September 2022, all new VICs are digital. If you already have a physical Veteran ID Card, you can continue to use it for discounts.

Veteran's Designation on a State-Issued Driver's License or ID

All 50 states and Puerto Rico offer a veteran designation on state-issued driver's licenses or IDs. The type of designation may vary from state to state, but in most cases, it will allow you to access veterans' discounts at participating stores, businesses, and restaurants.

How to Get a Veteran's Designation on Your State-Issued ID

Most states require a copy of your discharge papers (DD214 or other separation documents) to apply for the veteran's designation. Some states may request additional documentation.

Please check with your state's Department of Motor Vehicles for details on what documents are required to apply for a veteran's designation in your state.

Get Your VA Medical Records Online

The VA offers online tools for managing, reviewing, printing, saving, downloading and sharing your VA medical records and personal health information.

Use VA Blue Button to Manage Your Records Online

To get started, you'll need to sign in with a verified account to protect your personal health information and prevent fraud. If you don't have an account, you can create one with Login.gov, ID.me, or another provider. If you're unsure if your account is verified, you can sign in here and verify your identity.

Once signed in, you can do the following:

- **Download Your VA Blue Button Report**: This report includes details from your VA medical records, personal health records, and, in some cases, your military service records.
- **Download a Health Summary**: View key health data such as allergies, medications, and lab results.
- **Build Your Personal Health Record**: Add information such as medical history, emergency contacts, and medications.
- **Track Vital Signs, Diet, and Exercise**: Use the online journals to track health and fitness.
- **Share Your Health Data**: Securely share personal health information with your VA health care team.

Who Can Manage VA Medical Records Online?

To use all the features of VA Blue Button, these conditions must apply:
- You must be enrolled in VA health care.
- You must be registered as a patient at a VA health facility.
- You need a verified account through Login.gov, ID.me, Premium DS Logon, or My HealtheVet.

How to Access Your Medical Records

Once signed in, go to your welcome page dashboard and select Health Records. You'll be directed to a page where you can access:
- Your VA Blue Button report
- Your VA health summary
- Your VA medical images and reports

Add Information to Your Health Record

You can also add information to your personal health record. Go to the main menu and select Track Health to enter:
- Vital signs
- Health history
- Health goals
- Food and exercise data

Get Notifications for Medical Reports

You can receive email notifications when medical images and reports are available. Sign up on the My HealtheVet website and ensure "VA medical images and report available notification" is enabled in your settings.

Can't Access All Medical Records?

If you can't access certain records, you can request a full copy from your VA health facility or the Department of Defense, depending on where you received care.

Security and Privacy

The VA uses secure systems to protect your personal health information. If you download or print your records, be responsible for protecting that data.

Sharing Your Health Information

The Veterans Health Information Exchange (VHIE) allows the VA to share your health information securely with participating providers, including those in the Department of Defense. You can opt out at any time if you don't want your information shared.

CHAPTER 30

CORRECTION OF RECORDS BY CORRECTION BOARDS

Note: Supporting documents aren't needed to submit an initial claim under the Camp Lejeune Justice Act of 2022. The Navy Judge Advocate may request records from claimants at a later date, but not as part of the initial claim filing.

Retirees may feel that their records need correcting or amending for any number of reasons. Correction boards consider formal applications for corrections of military records. Each service department has a permanent Board for Correction of Military (Naval) records, composed of civilians, to act on applications for correction of records.

In order to justify the correction of a military record, the applicant must prove to a Corrections Board that the alleged entry or omission in the record was in error or unjust. This board considers all applications and makes recommendations to the appropriate branch Secretary.

An application for correction of record must be filed within three years after discovering the error or injustice. If filed after the three-year deadline, the applicant must include in the application reasons the board should find it in the interest of justice to accept the late application. Evidence may include affidavits or signed testimony executed under oath, and a brief of arguments supporting the application. All evidence not already included in one's record must be submitted. The responsibility for securing new evidence rests with the applicant.

To justify any correction, it is necessary to show to the satisfaction of the board that the alleged entry or omission in the records was in error or unjust. Applications should include all available evidence, such as signed statements of witnesses or a brief of arguments supporting the requested correction. Application is made with DD Form 149, available at VA offices, from veterans' organizations or from the internet. Each of the military services maintains a discharge review board with authority to change, correct or modify discharges or dismissals that are not issued by a sentence of a general courts-martial. The board has no authority to address medical discharges.

The veteran or, if the veteran is deceased or incompetent, the surviving spouse, next of kin or legal representative may apply for a review of discharge by writing to the military department concerned, using DoD Form 293. This form may be obtained at a VA regional office, from veterans' organizations or from the Internet. However, if the discharge was more than 15 years ago, a veteran must petition the appropriate service Board for Correction of Military Records using DoD Form 149, which is discussed in the "Correction of Military Records" section of this booklet. A discharge review is conducted by a review of an applicant's record and, if requested, by a hearing before the board.

Discharges awarded as a result of a continuous period of unauthorized absence in excess of 180 days make persons ineligible for VA benefits regardless of action taken by discharge review boards unless VA determines there were compelling circumstances for the absence. Boards for the correction of military records also may consider such cases.

Veterans with disabilities incurred or aggravated during active military service may qualify for medical or related benefits regardless of separation and characterization of service. Veterans separated administratively under other than honorable conditions may request that their discharge be reviewed for possible recharacterization, provided they file their appeal within 15 years of the date of separation. Questions regarding the review of a discharge should be addressed to the appropriate discharge review board at the address listed on DoD Form293.

Jurisdiction

Correction boards are empowered to deal with all matters relating to error or injustice in official records. The boards cannot act until all other administrative avenues of relief have been exhausted. Discharges by sentence of Special Court-Martial and administrative discharges cannot be considered by correction boards unless:
- Application to the appropriate Discharge Review Board has been denied and rehearing is barred; or
- Application cannot be made to the Discharge Review Board because the time limit has expired.

Application

DD Form 149, Application for Correction of Military or Naval record, must be used to apply for the correction of military records. It should be submitted, along with supporting evidence, to one of the review boards listed below:

Army

Army Review Boards Agency (ARBA)
ATTN: Client Information and Quality Assurance 251
18th Street South, Suite 385
Arlington, VA 22202

Navy & Marine Corps

Board for Correction of Naval Records
701 S. Courthouse Road
Bldg 12, Suite 1001
Arlington, VA 22204-2490
(703) 604-6884

Coast Guard

DHS Office of the General Counsel
Board for Correction of Military Records
245 Murray Lane, Stop 0485
Washington, DC 20528
(202) 447-4099

Air Force

Board for Correction of Air Force Records
SAF/MRBR
550-C Street West, Suite 40
Randolph AFB, TX 78150-4742

Decisions

In the absence of new and material evidence the decision of a correction board, as approved or modified by the Secretary of the Service Department, is final. Adverse decisions are subject to judicial review in a U.S. District Court. Decisions of the Boards for Correction of Military or Naval Records must be made available for public inspection. Copies of the decisional documents will be provided on request.

CHAPTER 31

DISCHARGE REVIEW

Discharge Review Boards

Each branch of service has discharge review boards to review the discharge or dismissal of former service members. (The Navy Board considers Marine Corps cases.)

Online Tool for Discharge Upgrade Process

The Department of Defense (DoD), through a joint program with the VA, has launched a new web-based tool that provides customized guidance to veterans who want to upgrade or change the conditions of their military discharge.

By answering questions, veterans can receive information on the specific armed services board to contact, the forms to fill out, special guidance applicable to their case, where to send their application, and helpful tips for appealing their discharge.

The military has estimated that tens of thousands of veterans with less than honorable discharges are especially likely to have unjust discharges deserving of upgrades. These are veterans who were discharged due to incidents relating to post-traumatic stress disorder, traumatic brain injury or sexual orientation. Fragmented and confusing information has historically deterred veterans from obtaining crucial information and — in many cases — necessary benefits.

The discharge upgrade tool is available at https://www.vets.gov/discharge-upgrade-instructions.

Consideration for Veterans' Discharge Upgrade Requests

The Defense Department released guidance in 2017 to clarify the liberal consideration given to veterans who request upgrades of their discharge saying they had mental health conditions or were victims of sexual assault or sexual harassment.

The new guidance clarifies that the liberal consideration policy includes conditions resulting from post-traumatic stress disorder, traumatic brain injury, sexual assault or sexual harassment. The policy is meant to ease the burden on veterans and give them a reasonable opportunity to establish the extenuating circumstances of their discharge.

Under new guidance, the following are some of the key things involved in discharge relief:

- Evidence may come from sources other than a veteran's service record and may include records from the DoD Sexual Assault Prevention and Response Program (DD Form 2910, Victim Reporting Preference Statement), and/or DD Form 2911 (DoD Sexual Assault Forensic SAFE Report), law enforcement authorities, rape crisis centers, mental health counseling centers, hospitals, physicians, pregnancy tests, tests for sexually transmitted diseases, and statements from family members, friends, roommates, co-workers, fellow servicemembers, or clergy.
- Evidence may also include changes in behavior, requests for transfer to another military duty assignment, deterioration in performance, inability of the individual to conform their behavior to the expectations of a military environment, substance abuse, periods of depression, panic attacks or anxiety without an identifiable cause, unexplained economic or social behavior changes, relationship issues or sexual dysfunction.
- Evidence of misconduct, including any misconduct underlying a veteran's discharge may be evidence of a mental health condition, including PTSD, TBI or of behavior consistent with experiencing sexual assault or sexual harassment.
- The veteran's testimony alone, written or oral, may establish the existence of a condition or experience, that the condition or experience existing during or was aggravated by military service, and that the condition or experience causes or mitigates the discharge.
- Absent clear evidence to the contrary, a diagnosis from a licensed psychiatrist or psychologist is evidence the veteran had a condition that could excuse or mitigate the discharge.
- Evidence that may reasonably support more than one diagnosis should be liberally considered as supporting a diagnosis, where applicable, that could excuse or mitigate the discharge.
- A veteran asserting a mental health condition without a corresponding diagnosis of such condition from a licensed psychiatrist or psychologist will receive liberal consideration of evidence that may support the evidence of such a condition.
- Review Boards are not required to find that a crime of sexual assault or an incident of sexual harassment occurred in order to grant liberal consideration to a veteran that the experience happened during military service, was aggravated by military service, or that it excuses or mitigates the discharge.

Authority

Discharge review boards can be based on the official records and such other evidence as may be presented, upgrade a discharge or change the reason and authority for discharge. Discharge review boards cannot grant disability retirement, revoke a discharge, reinstate any person in the service, recall any person to active duty, act on requests for re-enlistment code changes or review a discharge issued by sentence of a general court-martial. Discharge review boards have no authority to address medical discharges.

Discharges awarded as a result of a continuous period of unauthorized absence in excess of 180 days make persons ineligible for VA benefits regardless of action taken by discharge review boards, unless VA determines there were compelling circumstances for the absence. Boards for the correction of military records also may consider such cases.

Application

DD Form 293, "Application for Review of Discharge or Dismissal from the Armed Forces of the United States," is used to apply for review of discharge. (If more than 15 years have passed since discharge, DD Form 149 should be used.) The individual or, if legal proof of death is provided, the surviving spouse, next-of-kin or legal representative can apply. If the individual is mentally incompetent, the spouse, next-of-kin, or legal representative can sign the application, but must provide legal proof of incompetence. The instruction for completing DD Form 293 must be read and complied with.

Time Limitation

Initial application to a discharge review board must be made within 15 years after the date of discharge.

Personal Appearance

A personal appearance before the Discharge Review Board is a legal right. A minimum 30-day notice of the scheduled hearing date is given unless the applicant waives the advance notice in writing. Reasonable postponements can be arranged if circumstances preclude appearance on the scheduled date.

All expenses of appearing before the board must be paid by the applicant. If no postponement of a scheduled hearing date is requested and the applicant does not appear on the date scheduled, the right to a personal hearing is forfeited and the case will be considered on the evidence of record.

Hearings

Discharge review boards conduct hearings at various locations in the U.S. Information concerning hearing locations and availability of counsel can be obtained by writing to the appropriate board at the address shown on DD Form 293. Those addresses are listed at the end of this chapter.

Published Uniform Standards for Discharge Review

A review of discharge is conducted to determine if an individual was properly and equitably discharged. Each case is considered on its own merits. A discharge is considered to have been proper unless the discharge review determines:

- That there is an error of fact, law, procedures, or discretion which prejudiced the rights of the individual, or
- That there has been a change of policy which requires a change of discharge

A discharge is considered to have been equitable unless the discharge review determines:

- That the policies and procedures under which the individual was discharged are materially different from current policies and procedures and that the individual probably would have received a better discharge if the current policies and procedures had been in effect at the time of discharge; or
- That the discharge was inconsistent with the standards of discipline; or
- That the overall evidence before the review board warrants a change of discharge. In arriving at this determination, the discharge review board will consider the quality and the length of the service performed, the individual's physical and mental capability to serve satisfactorily, abuses of authority which may have contributed to the character of the discharge issued and documented discriminatory acts against the individual.

An authenticated decisional document is prepared, and a copy provided to each applicant and council. A copy of each decisional document, with identifying details of the applicant and other persons deleted to protect personal privacy, must be made available for public inspection and copying. These are located in a reading room in the Pentagon, Washington, DC. To provide access to the documents by persons outside the Washington, D.C. area, the documents have been indexed. The index includes case number of each case; the date, authority and reason for, and character if the discharge, and the issues addressed in the statement of findings, conclusions and reasons.

Interested parties may contact the DVARO or the State veterans Agency for the location of an index. A copy of the index will be made available at the sites of traveling board hearings during the period the board is present. An individual can go through the index and identify cases in which the circumstances leading to discharge are similar to those in the individual's case. A copy of these case decisional documents can be requested by writing to:

DA Military Review Boards Agency
ATTN: SFBA (Reading Room) Room 1E520
The Pentagon Washington, D.C. 20310

Examination of decisional documents may help to identify the kind of evidence that was used in the case and may indicate why relief was granted or denied. Decisional documents do not set precedence - each case is considered on its own merits.

Reconsideration

An application that has been denied can be reopened if:

- The applicant submits newly discovered evidence that was not available at the time of the original consideration.

- The applicant did not request a personal hearing in the original application and now desires to appear before the board. If the applicant fails to appear at the hearings, the case will be closed with no further action.
- The applicant was not represented by counsel in the original consideration and now desires counsel and the application for reconsideration is submitted within 15 years following the date of discharge.
- Changes in policy, law or regulations have occurred or federal court orders have been issued which substantially enhances the rights of the applicant.

Service Department Discharge Review Board Addresses Army Discharge

Review Board
Attention: SFMR-RBB
251 18th St. South Suite 385
Arlington, VA 22202-4508

Navy & USMC
Secretary of the Navy Council of Review Boards
720 Kennon St. SE Suite 309
Washington, DC 20374

Air Force
Air Force Military Personnel Center
Attention: DP-MDOA1
Randolph AFB, TX 78150-6001

Coast Guard
DHS Office of the General Counsel Board for Correction of Military Records
Mailstop # 485
245 Murray Lane
Washington, DC 20528

CHAPTER 32

PENAL AND FORFEITURE PROVISIONS

The first section of this chapter outlines basic information for veterans with questions concerning the effect of incarceration on VA benefits. The later sections of this chapter provide detailed information regarding misappropriation by fiduciaries, fraudulent acceptance of payments, forfeiture for fraud, forfeiture for treason, and forfeiture for subversive activities.

Basic Information

VA benefits are restricted if a veteran, surviving spouse, child, or dependent parent is convicted of a felony and imprisoned for more than 60 days. VA may still pay certain benefits, however, the amount paid depends on the type of benefit and reason for imprisonment. Following is information about the benefits most commonly affected by imprisonment.

Please note that overpayments due to failure to notify VA of a veteran's incarceration results in the loss of all financial benefits until the overpayment is recovered.

VA Disability Compensation

VA disability compensation payments are reduced if a veteran is convicted of a felony and imprisoned for more than 60 days. Veterans rated 20 percent, or more are limited to the 10 percent disability rate. For a veteran whose disability rating is 10 percent, the payment is reduced by one-half. Once a veteran is released from prison, compensation payments may be reinstated based upon the severity of the service-connected disability(ies) at that time.

The disability compensation paid to a veteran incarcerated because of a felony is limited to the 10% disability rate, beginning with the 61st day of imprisonment. For a surviving spouse, child, dependent parent of veteran whose disability rating is 10%, payment is at the 5% rate. This means that if a veteran was receiving $188 or more prior to incarceration, the new payment amount will be $98. If a veteran was receiving $98 before incarceration, the new payment amount will be $49.

If a veteran resides in a halfway house, participates in a work release program, or is on parole, compensation payments will not be reduced.

The amount of any increased compensation awarded to an incarcerated veteran that results from other than a statutory rate increase may be subject to reduction due to incarceration.

VA Disability Pension

VA will stop a veteran's pension payments beginning on the 61stday of imprisonment for conviction of either a felony or misdemeanor. Payments may be resumed upon release from prison if the veteran meets VA eligibility requirements.

VA Medical Care

While incarcerated veterans do not forfeit their eligibility for medical care, current regulations restrict VA from providing hospital and outpatient care to an incarcerated veteran who is an inmate in an institution of another government agency when that agency has a duty to give the care or services.

However, VA may provide care once the veteran has been unconditionally released from the penal institution. Veterans interested in applying for enrollment into the VA health care system should contact the nearest VA health care facility upon their release.

Educational Assistance / Subsistence Allowance

Beneficiaries incarcerated for other than a felony can receive full monthly benefits, if otherwise entitled. Convicted felons residing in halfway houses (also known as "residential re-entry centers") or participating in work-release programs also can receive full monthly benefits. Claimants incarcerated for a felony conviction can be paid only the costs of tuition, fees, and necessary books, equipment, and supplies.

VA cannot make payments for tuition, fees, books, equipment, or supplies if another Federal State, or local program pays these costs in full.

If another government program pays only a part of the cost of tuition, fees, books, equipment, or supplies, VA can authorize the incarcerated claimant payment for the remaining part of the costs.

Clothing Allowance

In the case of a veteran who is incarcerated in a Federal, State, or local penal institution for a period in excess of 60 days and who is furnished clothing without charge by the institution, the amount of any annual clothing allowance payable to the veteran shall be reduced by an amount equal to 1/365 of the amount of the allowance otherwise payable under that section for each day on which the veteran was so incarcerated during the 12-month period preceding the date on which payment of the allowance would be due.

Payments to Dependents

VA may be able to take part of the amount that the incarcerated veteran is not receiving and pay it to his or her dependents, if they can show need. Interested dependents should contact the nearest VA regional office for details on how to apply. They will be asked to provide income information as part of the application process.

VA will inform a veteran whose benefits are subject to reduction of the right of the veteran's dependents to an apportionment while the veteran is incarcerated, and the conditions under which payments to the veteran may be resumed upon release from incarceration.

VA will also notify the dependents of their right to an apportionment if the VA is aware of their existence and can obtain their addresses.

No apportionment may be made to or on behalf of any person who is incarcerated in a Federal, State, or local penal institution for conviction of a felony.

An apportionment of an incarcerated veteran's VA benefits is not granted automatically to the veteran's dependents. The dependent(s) must file a claim for an apportionment.

Restoration of Benefits

When a veteran is released from prison, his or her compensation or pension benefits may be restored. Depending on the type of disability, the VA may schedule a medical examination to see if the veteran's disability has improved or worsened.

Misappropriation by Fiduciaries

Whoever, being a guardian, curator, conservator, committee, or person legally vested with the responsibility or care of a claimant or a claimant's estate, or any other person having charge and custody in a fiduciary capacity of money heretofore or hereafter paid under any of the laws administered by the VA for the benefit of any minor, incompetent, or other beneficiary, shall lend, borrow, pledge, hypothecate, use, or exchange for other funds or property, except as authorized by law, or embezzle or in any manner misappropriate any such money or property derived wherefrom in whole or in part, and coming into such fiduciary's control in any matter whatever in the execution of such fiduciary's trust, or under color of such fiduciary's office or service as such fiduciary, shall be fined in accordance with Title 18, or imprisoned not more than 5 years, or both.

Any willful neglect or refusal to make and file proper accountings or reports concerning such money or property as required by law shall be taken to be sufficient evidence prima facie of such embezzlement or misappropriation.

Fraudulent Acceptance of Payments

Any person entitled to monetary benefits under any of the laws administered by the VA whose right to payment ceases upon the happening of any contingency who thereafter fraudulently accepts any such payment, shall be fined in accordance with Title 18, or imprisoned not more than one year, or both.

Whoever obtains or receives any money or check under any of the laws administered by the VA without being entitled to it, and with intent to defraud the United States or any beneficiary of the United States, shall be fined in accordance with Title 18, or imprisoned not more than one year, or both.

Forfeiture for Fraud

Whoever knowingly makes or causes to be made or conspires, combines, aids, or assists in, agrees to, arranges for, or in any way procures the making or presentation of a false or fraudulent affidavit, declaration, certificate, statement voucher, or paper, concerning any claim for benefits under any of the laws administered by the VA (except laws pertaining to insurance benefits) shall forfeit all rights, claims, and benefits under all laws administered by the VA (except laws pertaining to insurance benefits).

Whenever a veteran entitled to disability compensation has forfeited the right to such compensation under this chapter, the compensation payable but for the forfeiture shall thereafter be paid to the veteran's spouse, children, and parents Payments made to a spouse, children, and parents under the preceding sentence shall not exceed the amounts payable to each if the veteran had died from service-connected disability. No spouse, child, or parent who participated in the fraud for which forfeiture was imposed shall receive any payment by reason of this subsection. Any apportionment award under this subsection may not be made in any case after September 1, 1959.

Forfeiture of benefits by a veteran shall not prohibit payment of the burial allowance, death compensation, dependency and indemnity compensation, or death pension in the event of the veteran's death.

After September 1, 1959, no forfeiture of benefits may be imposed under the rules outlined in this chapter upon any individual who was a resident of, or domiciled in a State at the time the act or acts occurred on account of which benefits would, but not for this subsection, be forfeited unless such individual ceases to be a resident of, or domiciled in, a State before the expiration of the period during which criminal prosecution could be instituted. The paragraph shall not apply with respect to:
- Any forfeiture occurring before September 1, 1959; or
- An act or acts that occurred in the Philippine Islands before July 4, 1946.

The VA is authorized and directed to review all cases in which, because of a false or fraudulent affidavit, declaration, certificate, statement, voucher, or paper, a forfeiture of gratuitous benefits under laws administered by the VA was imposed pursuant to this section or prior provisions of the law, on or before September 1

1959. In any such case in which the VA determines that the forfeiture would not have been imposed under the provisions of this section in effect after September 1, 1959, the VA shall remit the forfeiture, effective June 30, 1972.

Benefits to which the individual concerned becomes eligible by virtue of any such remission may be awarded, upon application for, and the effective date of any award of compensation, dependency and indemnity compensation, or pension made in such a case shall be fixed in accordance with the facts found, but shall not be earlier than the effective date of the Act or administrative issue. In no event shall such award or increase be retroactive for more than one year from the date of application, or the date of administrative determination of entitlement, whichever is earlier.

Forfeiture for Treason

Any person shown by evidence satisfactory to the VA to be guilty of mutiny, treason, sabotage, or rendering assistance to an enemy of the United States or its allies shall forfeit all accrued or future gratuitous benefits under laws administered by the VA.

The VA, in its discretion, may apportion and pay any part of benefits forfeited under the preceding paragraph to the dependents of the person forfeiting such benefits. No dependent of any person shall receive benefits by reason of this subsection in excess of the amount to which the dependent would be entitled if such person were dead.

In the case of any forfeiture under this chapter, there shall be no authority after September 1, 1959, to:
- Make an apportionment award pursuant to the preceding paragraph; or
- Make an award to any person of gratuitous benefits based on any period of military, naval, or air service commencing before the date of commission of the offense.

Forfeiture for Subversive Activities

An individual who is convicted after September 1, 1959, of any offense listed below shall, from and after the date of commission of such offense, have no right to gratuitous benefits (including the right to burial in a national cemetery) under laws administered by the VA based on periods of military, naval, or air service commencing before the date of commission of such offense, and no other person shall be entitled to such benefits on account of such individual. After receipt of notice of the return of an indictment for such an offense, the VA shall suspend payment of such gratuitous benefits pending disposition of the criminal proceedings. If any individual whose rights to benefits has been terminated pursuant to this section, is granted a pardon of the offense by the President of the United States, the right to such benefits shall be restored as of the date of such pardon.

The offenses referred to in the previous paragraph are:

Sections 894, 904 and 906 of Title 10 (articles 94, 104, and 106 of the Uniform Code of Military Justice).

Sections 792, 793, 794, 798, 2381, 2382, 2383, 2384, 2385, 2387, 2388, 2389, 2390, and chapter 105
of Title 18.

Sections 222, 223, 224, 225 and 226 of the Atomic Energy Act of 1954 (42 U.S.C 2272, 2273, 2274,
2275, and 2276).

Section 4 of the Internal Security Act of 1950 (50 U.S.C. 783).

The Secretary of Defense, the Secretary of Transportation, or the Attorney General, as appropriate, shall notify the VA in each case in which an individual is convicted of an offense mentioned in this chapter.

CHAPTER 33

APPLICATION AND CHARACTER OF DISCHARGE

Applying for Benefits and Your Character of Discharge

Generally, in order to receive VA benefits and services, the veteran's character of discharge or service must be under other than dishonorable conditions (e.g., honorable, under honorable conditions, general). However, individuals receiving undesirable, bad conduct, and other types of dishonorable discharges may qualify for VA benefits depending on a determination made by VA.

Basic eligibility for Department of Veterans Affairs (VA) benefits depends upon the type of military service performed, the duration of the service, and the character of discharge or separation. VA looks at the "character of discharge" to determine whether a person meets the basic eligibility requirements for receipt of VA benefits under title 38 of the United States Code.

Any discharge under honorable conditions satisfies the character of discharge requirement for basic eligibility for VA benefits. Certain types of discharges, along with the circumstances surrounding those discharges, bar an individual from basic eligibility for VA benefits. Other types of discharges require VA to make a character of discharge determination in order to assess basic eligibility for VA benefits.

Under the law (38 U.S.C. § 5303), a release or discharge for any of the following reasons constitutes a statutory bar to benefits, unless it is determined that the Servicemember was insane at the time he/she committed the offense that resulted in the discharge:
- Sentence of a general court-martial
- Being a conscientious objector who refused to perform military duty, wear the uniform, or otherwise comply with lawful orders of competent military authority
- Desertion
- Absence without official leave (AWOL) for a continuous period of 180 days or more, without compelling circumstances to warrant such prolonged unauthorized absence (as determined by VA)

- Requesting release from service as an alien during a period of hostilities or This means that if an individual is discharged for any of the above reasons, the law prohibits VA from providing any benefits
- Resignation by an officer for the good of the service

VA reviews military service records, including facts and circumstances surrounding the incident(s) leading to the discharge. VA also considers the following when making its determination:
- Any mitigating or extenuating circumstances presented by the claimant
- Any supporting evidence provided by third parties who were familiar with the circumstances surrounding the incident(s) in question
- Length of service
- Performance and accomplishments during service
- Nature of the infraction(s), and
- Character of service preceding the incident(s) resulting in the discharge.

VA considers whether an individual was insane when determining whether a statutory bar to benefits exists. When no statutory bar to benefits exists, the impact of disabilities may be considered during the analysis of any mitigating or extenuating circumstances that may have contributed to the discharge.

Specific Benefit Program Character of Discharge Requirements

Compensation Benefits

To receive VA compensation benefits and services, the veteran's character of discharge or service must be under other tan dishonorable conditions (e.g. honorable, under honorable conditions, general).

Education Benefits

To receive VA education benefits and services through the Montgomery GI Bill program or Post- 9/11 GI Bill program, the veteran's character of discharge or service must be honorable.

To receive VA education benefits and services through any other VA educational benefits program, including the Survivors' and Dependents' Educational Assistance (DEA) program, the veteran's character of discharge or service must be under other than dishonorable conditions (e.g., honorable, under honorable conditions, general).

Home Loan Benefits

To receive VA home loan benefits and services, the veteran's character of discharge or service must be under other than dishonorable conditions (e.g. honorable, under honorable conditions, general).

Insurance Benefits

Generally, there is no character of discharge bar to benefits to Veterans' Group Life Insurance. However, for Service-Disabled Veterans Insurance and Veterans' Mortgage Life Insurance benefits, the veteran's character of discharge must be other than dishonorable.

Pension Benefits

To receive VA pension benefits and services, the veteran's character of discharge or service must be under other than dishonorable conditions (e.g., honorable, under honorable conditions, general).

Review of Discharge from Military Service

Each of the military services maintains a discharge review board with authority to change, correct or modify discharges or dismissals not issued by a sentence of a general court- martial. The board has no authority to address medical discharges.

The veteran or, if the veteran is deceased or incompetent, the surviving spouse, next of kin or legal representative, may apply for a review of discharge by writing to the military department concerned, using DD Form 293, "Application for the Review of Discharge from the Armed Forces of the United States." This form may be obtained at a VA regional office, or from Veterans organizations.

However, if the discharge was more than 15 years ago, a veteran must petition the appropriate Service's Board for Correction of Military Records using DD Form 149, "Application for Correction of Military Records Under the Provisions of Title 10, U.S. Code, Section 1552." A discharge review is conducted by a review of an applicant's record and, if requested, by a hearing before the board.

Discharge Related to Mental Health Conditions, Sexual Assault, or Sexual Harassment

In December 2016, the Department announced a renewed effort to ensure that veterans are aware of the opportunity to have discharges and military records reviewed. Following a review, it was determined that clarifications were needed regarding mental health conditions, sexual assault and sexual harassment. New guidance was issued.

Clarifying Guidance to Military Discharge Review Boards and Boards for Correction Requests by Veterans for Modification of Their Discharge Due to Mental Health Conditions, Traumatic Brain Injury, Sexual Assault or Sexual Harassment

Requests for discharge relief usually involve four questions, which include:
- Did the veteran have a condition or experience that may excuse or mitigate the discharge?
- Did that condition exist/experience occur during military service?

- Does that condition or experience actually excuse or mitigate the discharge?
- Does that condition or experience outweigh the discharge?

Liberal consideration will be given to veterans for petitioning for discharge relief when the application for relief is based in whole or in part on matters relating to mental health conditions including PTSD, TBI, sexual assault or sexual harassment.

Evidence may come from sources other than a veteran's service record and may include records from the DoD Sexual Assault Prevention and Response Program (DD Form 2910, Victim Reporting Preference Statement) and/or DD Form 2911 DoD Sexual Assault Forensic Examination (SAFE) Report, law enforcement authorities, rape crisis centers, mental health and counseling centers, hospitals, physicians, pregnancy tests, tests for sexually transmitted diseases and statements from family members, friends, roommates, co-workers, and fellow servicemembers or clergy.

Evidence may also include changes in behavior, requests for transfer to another military assignment, deterioration in work performance, inability of the individual to conform their behavior to expectations of a military environment, substance abuse, episodes of depression or panic attacks, anxiety without an identifiable cause, unexplained economic or social behavior changes, relationship issues, or sexual dysfunction.

Evidence of misconduct, including any misconduct underlying a veteran's discharge may be evidence of a mental health condition, including PTSD, TBI or behavior consistent with experience sexual assault or sexual harassment.

The veteran's testimony alone, oral or written, may establish the existence of a condition or experience, that the condition or experience existed during or was aggravated by military service, and that the condition or experience excuses or mitigates the discharge.

The Department of Defense today announced a renewed effort to ensure veterans are aware of the opportunity to have their discharges and military records reviewed Through enhanced public outreach, engagement with Veterans Service Organizations (VSOs), Military Service Organizations (MSOs), and other outside groups, as well as direct outreach to individual veterans, the department encourages all veterans who believe they have experienced an error or injustice to request relief from their service's Board for Correction of Military/Naval Records (BCM/NR) or Discharge Review Board (DRB).

Additionally, all veterans, VSOs, MSOs, and other interested organizations are invited to offer feedback on their experiences with the BCM/NR or DRB processes including how the policies and processes can be improved.

In the past few years, the department has issued guidance for consideration of post-traumatic stress disorder (PTSD), as well as the repealed "Don't Ask, Don't

Tell" and its predecessor policies. Additionally, supplemental guidance for separations involving victims of sexual assault is currently being considered.

The department is reviewing and consolidating all of the related policies to reinforce the department's commitment to ensuring fair and equitable review of separations for all veterans. Whether the discharge or other correction is the result of PTSD, sexual orientation, sexual assault, or some other consideration, the department is committed to rectifying errors or injustices and treating all veterans with dignity and respect.

To request an upgrade or correction:

Veterans who desire a correction to their service record or who believe their discharge was unjust, erroneous, or warrants an upgrade, are encouraged to apply for review.

For discharge upgrades, if the discharge was less than 15 years ago, the veteran should complete DD Form 293 and send it to their service's DRB (the address is on the form). For discharges over 15 years ago, the veteran should complete the DD Form 149 and send it to their service's BCM/NR (the address is on the form).

For corrections of records other than discharges, veterans should complete the DD Form 149 and submit their request to their service's BCM/NR (the address is on the form).

Key information to include in requests:

There are three keys to successful applications for upgrade or correction. First, it is very important to explain why the veteran's discharge or other record was unjust or erroneous—for example, how it is connected to, or resulted from unjust policies, a physical or mental health condition related to military service, or some other explainable or justifiable circumstance.

Second, it is important to provide support, where applicable, for key facts. If a veteran has a relevant medical diagnosis, for example, it would be very helpful to include medical records that reflect that diagnosis. Third, it is helpful, but not always required, to submit copies of the veteran's applicable service records. The more information provided, the better the boards can understand the circumstances of the discharge.

BCM/NRs are also authorized to grant relief on the basis of clemency. Veterans who believe their post-service conduct and contributions to society support an upgrade or correction should describe their post-service activity and provide any appropriate letters or other documentation of support.

Personnel records for veterans who served after 1997 should be accessible online and are usually retrievable within hours of a request through the Defense Personnel Records Information Retrieval System (DPRIS). Those who served prior to 1997 or for whom electronic records are not available from DPRIS, can request their records from the National Personnel Records Center (NPRC).

Frequently Asked Questions

The following are answers to some of the common questions people have about discharge upgrades.

Can I Get Benefits Without a Discharge Upgrade?

Even with a less than honorable discharge, you might be able to access some VA benefits throughout the Character of Discharge review process. When you apply for VA benefits, the VA will review your record to determine if your service was honorable for VA purposes. The review can take up to a year. You provide the VA with documents supporting your case, similar to what you'd send with an application to upgrade your discharge as evidence.

VA recommends finding someone to advocate on your behalf, such as a Veterans Service Organization (VSO) or lawyer.

You can ask for a VA character of discharge review while at the same time applying for a discharge upgrade from the Department of Defense (DoD) or the Coast Guard.

If you need mental health services related to PTSD or other mental health problems linked to your service including conditions related to an experience of military sexual trauma, you might qualify for VA benefits immediately, even without a VA Character of Discharge review or a discharge upgrade.

What I Already Applied for An Upgrade or Correction and Was Denied?

If your previous upgrade application was denied, you can apply again but may have to follow a different process. You're most likely to be successful in applying again if your application is significantly different from when you last applied. For example you may have evidence not available to you when you last applied, or the DoD might have issued new rules about discharges. DoD changed the rules for discharges related to PTSD, TBI and mental health in 2014, military sexual harassment and assault in 2017, and sexual orientation in 2011.

What If I Have Discharges for More Than One Period of Service?

If the Department of Defense or Coast Guard determined you served honorably in one period of service, you may use that honorable characterization to establish eligibility for VA benefits, even if later on you received a less than honorable discharge. You earned your benefits during the period when you served honorably, and make sure you specifically mention your period of honorable service when you apply for VA benefits. The only exception is for service-connected disability benefits. You're only eligible if you suffered disabilities during your period of honorable discharge. You can't use an honorable discharge from one period of service to establish eligibility for a service-connected disability from a different period of service.

CHAPTER 34

ACCREDITED REPRESENTATIVES

The Department of Veterans Affairs accredits three types of representatives. These are Veterans Service Organization (VSO) representatives, attorneys and agents.

This is to ensure claimants have access to responsible, qualified representation or VA benefit claims. VA-accredited representatives must have good moral character and be capable of providing competent representation. The VA's Office of General Counsel (OGC) is responsible for making those determinations through its accreditation process. The accreditation process differs depending on the type of accreditation being sought. An accredited VSO representative is someone who's been recommended by a VSO for accreditation, recognized by VA to assist or benefit claims.

The VSO has certified to VA that the representative possesses good character and is fit to represent veterans and their families as an employee or member of their organization. An attorney is someone who is a member in good standing of at least one State bar. When an attorney applies for VA accreditation, VA typically presumes that the attorney possesses the good character and fitness necessary to represent Veterans and their family members based on the attorney's state license to practice law. An accredited claims agent is someone who is not an attorney but who has undergone a character review by OGC and has passed a written examination about VA law and procedures.

What An Accredited Representative Does

VA-accredited representative can help you understand and apply for any VA benefits you may be entitled to including compensation, education, Veteran readiness and employment, home loans, life insurance, pension, health care, and burial benefits. A VA-accredited representative may also help you request further review of, or appeal, an adverse VA decision regarding benefits. The VA's Office of General Counsel is responsible for making these determinations through its accreditation process. The accreditation process varies depending on which type of accreditation is being sought. An accredited VSO is someone who's been recommended for accreditation by a VSO recognized by VA to help assist with VA benefit claims.

The VSO has certified to VA that the representative possesses good character and is fit to represent veterans and their families as an employee of their organization or member. An attorney is someone in good standing of at least one State bar. When an attorney applies for VA accreditation, VA presumes the attorney has good character and the necessary fitness needed to represent veterans and their family members based on the attorney's state license to practice law. An accredited claims agent is someone who's not an attorney but went through a character review by OGC and has passed a written exam on VA law and procedures.

The VA Office of General Counsel keeps a list of VA-recognized organizations and VA-accredited organizations who have authorization to help in the preparation, presentation and prosecution of VA benefit claims.

The Role of an Accredited Representative

Most of the representation provided to claimants on initial benefit claims is performed by VA- recognized VSOs and their accredited representatives. A VSO can help with gathering needed evidence and submitting a Fully Developed Claim. VSOs can correspond with VA on behalf of you about your claim. VSOs always provide representation free of charge for VA claims.

Many VSOs also sponsor programs like providing transportation to and from medical appointments at VA facilities.

Accredited Attorneys and Claims Agents

VA-accredited attorneys and claims agents will do most of their representation after VA issues an initial decision on a claimant's claim. This is when attorneys and claims agents can charge fees for representation. During this stage of the process of adjudication, an attorney or claims agent might help you further develop the evidence to support your claim. They can also help you create persuasive and legal arguments to submit to VA, and help you navigate the VA appeals process.

Fee for Service

VA-recognized VSOs and their representatives always provide their services on benefit claims for free. Unlike a VSO, a VA-accredit attorney or agent can charge a fee for their representation in appealing or requesting an additional review of an adverse VA decision.

Only a VA-accredited attorney or claims agent can charge a fee for assisting in a claim for VA benefits, and only after VA issues an initial decision on the claim, and they have complied with the power-of-attorney and the fee agreement requirements.

How to Challenge a Fee

If you were charged a fee and you believe it was unreasonable or too high, you can file a motion to challenge it. The Office of General Counsel (OGC) of the

Department of Veterans Affairs will review the fee agreement if you file a motion with the office.

There is no requirement to use any particular format or writing style when writing a motion. It can be as simple as a letter you write to OGC.

However, OGC won't review the fee agreement unless your motion meets all of these requirements:

- Your motion must be in writing. A telephone call won't satisfy the requirement.
- Your motion has to include your full name and your VA file number.
- Your motion must state the reason or reasons why the fee called for in the agreement is unreasonable.
- You have to attach your motion to any evidence you want OGC to consider.

You need to serve a copy of your motion on the attorney or claims agent involved in the matter by mailing or delivering it to them.

To begin the OGC review of your fee agreement, you must mail a motion and proof of service to:
Department of Veterans Affairs
Office of General Counsel (022D)
810 Vermont Ave. NW Washington, DC 20420

Proof of service is a statement by the person who sent or delivered the motion that includes the date and manner of service, the name of the person served, and the address of the place of delivery.

You have 120 days from the date of the final VA action, which in most instances is 120 days from the date of the fee eligibility decision to file a motion for review of a fee agreement. That means that a motion meeting all requirements including proof of service, must be filed at the above address, before the 120-day time limit expires.

After you file a motion, the involved attorney or claims agent may file a response to your motion with OGC within 30 days from the date on which you serve them with your motion. They are required to serve you with a copy of their response.

You then have 15 days from the date you're served with a response to file a reply with OGC. You also have to serve the attorney or claims agent with a copy of your reply.

Fifteen days after the date the attorney or claims agent response or 30 days after you serve the attorney or claims agent if they don't respond, OGC will close the record in the proceedings and no further evidence will be accepted.

The General Counsel will issue the final decision, which is appealable to the Board of Veterans Appeals.

How to Find a Representative

VA Office of General Counsel maintains a list of VA-recognized organizations and VA-accredited individuals that are authorized to assist in the preparation, presentation and prosecution of VA benefit claims. This is available online.

You can also find a VSO office in your regional benefit office.

If you want to appoint a VA-recognized VSO to represent you or manage your current representative, you can do so online using eBenefits. You should speak to your VSO first before submitting an online request.

You can also appoint a VA-recognized VSO by completing VA Form 21-22, Appointment of Veterans Service Organization as Claimant's Representative.

You can appoint an attorney, claims agent or a specific, individual VSO representative to represent you by completing VA Form 21-22a, Appointment of Individual as Claimant's Representative.

You can then mail the completed form to:

Department of Veterans Affairs Claims Intake Center
PO Box 444
Janesville, WI 53547-444

You can discharge your attorney, claims agent or VSO representative at any time and for any reason by informing VA of your request in writing. You can also replace your representative with a new representative by filing a new VA Form 21-22, Appointment of Veterans Service Organization as Claimant's Representative or VA Form 21-22a, Appointment of Individual as Claimant's Representative.

If you believe your VA-accredited representative acted unethically or violated the law, you can file a complaint with the VA's Office of General Counsel.

CHAPTER 35

ACCRUED BENEFITS

When you file a claim for Veterans Pension, Survivors Pension, VA DIC or accrued benefits, VA reviews all available evidence to determine eligibility. Accrued benefits are benefits that are due but not paid prior to a beneficiary's death. Examples include:

- A claim or appeal for a recurring benefit that was pending at the time of death, but all evidence needed for a favorable decision was in VA's possession.
- A claim for a recurring benefit had been allowed, but the beneficiary died before award.

At the time of death, one or more benefit checks weren't deposited or negotiated.

Eligibility

VA pays accrued benefits based on the claimant's relationship to the deceased beneficiary. If there is no eligible living person, VA pays accrued benefits based on reimbursement.

Accrued benefits are paid to the first living person listed below:

Relationship to the Deceased Veteran	Accrued Benefit
Surviving spouse	Full amount to surviving spouse
Dependent children, including those between the ages of 18 and 23 who are attending school and those who are found helpless	Equal shares among children
Parents (both)	Equal shares if parents are dependent at the time of veteran's death
Sole surviving parent	Full amount to surviving parent, if dependent at the time of veteran's death

If the death is that of a surviving spouse, the accrued benefit is payable to the veteran's children. However, accrued Dependent's Educational Assistance (DEA) is payable only as reimbursement on the expenses of last sickness and burial.

If the death is of a child, the accrued benefit is payable to the surviving children of the veteran. They must be entitled to death, compensation, dependency and indemnity compensation or death pension, with two exceptions:

- If the deceased child was entitled to an apportioned share of the surviving spouse's award, the accrued benefit is payable only as reimbursement. It can reimburse expenses of the deceased child's last sickness or burial.
- If the deceased child was in receipt of death pension, compensation or DIC, a remaining child who has elected DEA benefits is only entitled to the unpaid benefits due prior to the commencement of DEA benefits.

The line of succession for accrued benefits is set by law. If a preferred beneficiary doesn't file or prosecute a claim, payment isn't permitted to the person with equal or lower preference. This applies to a waiver of right to payment as well.

Reimbursement

If there isn't an entitled living person based on relationship, VA may reimburse the person who paid for or is responsible for the last illness and burial. If payments were made from the estate of the deceased beneficiary, the executor or administrator of the estate should file the claim. The amount payable as reimbursement is limited to the actual expenses paid and it's limited to the accrued benefits available.

Substitution

Substitution allows a person eligible for accrued benefits to substitute a deceased beneficiary on a pending claim or appeal. The substitute claimant may submit evidence in support of the pending claim, or appeal for potential accrued benefits.

Applying for Accrued Benefits

The forms that you may need to complete to file for accrued benefits include:

- VA Form 21P-601, Application for Accrued Amounts Due a Deceased Beneficiary
- VA Form 21P-534EZ, Application for Dependency and Indemnity Compensation, Death Pension and Accrued Benefits
- VA Form 21P-535, Application for Dependency and Indemnity Compensation by Parent(s) including Accrued Benefits and Death Compensation When Applicable
- VA Form 21P-0847, Request for Substitution of Claimant Upon Death Claimant

VA must receive an accrued benefits claim within one year of the beneficiary's death and/or the date of notification to the beneficiary.

VA has to receive a substitution claim within one year of the original claimant's death. If the substitute dies, the next substitute has one year from the original substitute's death to file a claim.

Evidence

The evidence must show that both of the following are true:
- The VA owed the deceased claimant payments based on existing ratings, decisions or evidence that the VA had when the claimant died, but the VA didn't make the payments before the death of the claimant, and
- You're the surviving spouse, child or dependent parent of the deceased veteran

You will need to submit the veteran's DD214 or other separation documents and a copy of the veteran's death certificate showing cause of death. You can also give the VA permission to gather both.

If a representative of the beneficiary's estate has been assigned, the VA needs a certified copy of the letters of administration or letters testamentary with the signature and seal of the appointing court.

If you're submitting a reimbursement claim for the veteran's last illness and burial expenses, VA needs a copy of all billing and account statements for services and supplies connected to the expenses. The billing or account statement should be submitted on the regular billhead of the creditor. The statement needs to show:
- The dates, nature and costs of services or supplies provided
- The name of the deceased veteran who paid for the services or supplies
- Proof the expenses have already been paid, and if so, who made those payments

CHAPTER 36

SURVIVOR AND DEPENDENT COMPENSATION (DIC)

If you're the surviving spouse, child or parent of a service member who died in the line of duty, or a veteran who died from a service-related injury or illness, you may be able to get a tax-free monetary benefit. The benefit is called VA Dependency and Indemnity Compensation or VA DIC.

Information for Survivors with PACT Act-Related Claims:

If you think you're eligible for VA DIC under the PACT Act, you can submit a new claim. If the VA denied your claim in the past, and it thinks you may be eligible now, they may try to contact you. They may be able to reevaluate your claim, but you don't have to wait for them to contact you before you reapply.

If you're a surviving family member of a veteran, you may be eligible for these benefits:

- A monthly VA DIC payment if you're the surviving spouse, dependent child or parent of a veteran who died from a service-connected disability.
- A one-time accrued benefits payment if you're the surviving spouse, dependent child or dependent parent of a veteran who the VA owed unpaid benefits at the time of their death.
- A survivor's pension if you're the surviving spouse or child of a veteran with wartime service

Definitions

Veteran: in this chapter, the term includes a person who died in the active military, naval, or air service.

Social Security Increase: in this chapter, the term means the percentage by which benefit amounts payable under Title II of the Social Security Act (42 U.S.C. 401 et seq.) are increased for any fiscal year because of a determination under section 215(i) of such Act (42 U.S.C. 415(i)).

Permanently Housebound: for the purposes of this chapter, the requirement of "permanently housebound" will be considered to have been met when the individual is substantially confined to such individual's house (ward or clinical areas, if institutionalized) or immediate premises due to a disability or disabilities which it is reasonably certain will remain throughout such individual's lifetime.

Eligibility

Surviving Spouse

You may be eligible for VA benefits or compensation as a surviving spouse if you meet one of these requirements:

- You live with the veteran or service member without a break until their death, or
- If you're separated, you weren't at fault for the separation

One of the following must also be true:

- You married the veteran or service member within 15 years of their discharge from the period of military service during which the qualifying illness or injury started or got worse, or
- You were married to the veteran or service member for at least 1 year, or
- You had a child with the veteran or servicemember

If you're remarried, you can continue to receive compensation if one of the following is true:

- You remarried on or after December 16, 2003, and you were 57 years of age or older at the time you remarried, or
- You remarried on or after January 5, 2021, and you were 55 years of age or older at the time you remarried

You'll need to provide evidence with your claim to show one of these descriptions is true for the veteran or servicemember. Evidence may include documents like medical test results, military service records and doctor's reports.

- The servicemember died while on active duty, active duty for training, or inactive duty or training, or
- The veteran died from a service-connected illness or injury, or
- The veteran didn't die from a service-connected illness or injury but was eligible to receive VA compensation for a service-connected disability rated as totally disabling for a certain period of time

If the veteran's eligibility was due to a rating of totally disabling, they must have had this rating:

- For at least 10 years before their death, or
- Since their release from active duty and for at least 5 years immediately before their death, or
- For at least 1 year before their death if they were a former prisoner of war who died after September 30, 1999

Note: Totally disabling means the veteran's injury made it impossible for them to work.

As a Surviving Child

You may be eligible for benefits or compensation if all of the following are true as a surviving child:
- You aren't married, and
- You aren't included on the surviving spouse's compensation, and
- You're under the age of 18 or under the age of 23 if attending school.

Note: If you were adopted out of the veteran's or servicemember's family but meet the other criteria for eligibility you would still quality for compensation.

You'll need to provide evidence with your claim. You'll have to provide evidence showing that at least one of the following is true:
- The servicemember died while on active duty, active duty for training or inactive duty training, or
- The veteran died from a service-connected illness or injury, or
- The veteran didn't die from a service-connected illness or injury but was eligible to receive VA compensation for a service-connected disability that was rated as totally disabling for a certain period of time.

If the veteran's eligibility was due to a service-connected disability rated as totally disabling, they must have had this rating:
- For at least 10 years before their death, or
- Since their release from active duty and for at least 5 years immediately before their death, or
- For at least 1 year before their death if they were a former prisoner of war who died after September 30, 1999.

Note: Totally disabling means the veteran's injuries make it impossible for them to work.

As a Surviving Parent

You may be eligible for VA benefits or compensation if you meet these requirements.

Both of these must be true:
- You're the biological, adoptive or foster parent of the veteran or service member, and
- Your income is below a certain amount

Note: The VA defines a foster parent as someone who served in the role of a parent to the veteran or servicemember before their last entry into active service.

You'll have to provide evidence to show that certain descriptions are true for the veteran or service member. You'll have to provide evidence showing at least one

of these is true:
- The servicemember died from an injury or illness while on active duty or in the line of duty while on active duty for training, or
- The servicemember died from an injury or certain illnesses in the line of duty while on inactive training, or
- The veteran died from a service-connected illness or injury.

Applying for Compensation

If you're the surviving spouse or child of a service member who died on active duty a military casualty assistance officer will help you complete an Application for DIC Death Pension, and/or Accrued Benefits by a Surviving Spouse or Child (VA Form 21P-534a). The officer then helps you mail the form to the correct VA regional office.

If you're the surviving spouse of a child or veteran, you fill out an Application for DIC, Death Pension, and/or Accrued Benefits (VA Form 21P-534EZ).

If you're a surviving parent, you fill out an Application for Dependency and Indemnity Compensation by Parents (VA Form 21P-535).

You can work with an accredited representative to apply for this benefit, or you can use the QuickSubmit tool, available through AccessVA. This allows you to upload your form online. You can also go to a VA regional office and get help from an employee, or mail your form to this address:

Department of Veterans Affairs Pension Intake Center
PO Box 5365
Janesville, WI 53547-5365

You might want to submit an intent to file form before applying for DIC benefits. This can give you time to gather evidence, and avoid a later start date, which is known as an effective date. If you notify the VA of your intent to file, you might be eligible to receive retroactive payments.

Amount of DIC Payments to Surviving Spouses

Surviving spouses of veterans who died after January 1, 1993, receive a basic monthly rate of $1,653.07 (effective December 1, 2024)

Surviving spouses entitled to DIC based on the veteran's death before January 1, 1993, receive the greater of:
- The basic monthly rate of **$1,653.07**
- An amount based on the veteran's pay grade. (See following sections for Pay Grade tables and Determination of Pay Grade.)

There are additional DIC payments for dependent children. (Refer to the following charts.)

Additional Allowances for Surviving Spouses

Add **$351.02** to the basic monthly rate if, at the time of the veteran's death, the veteran was in receipt of or entitled to receive compensation for a service-connected disability rated totally disabling (including a rating based on individual unemployability) for a continuous period of at least eight years immediately preceding death, AND the surviving spouse was married to the veteran for those same eight years.

Add **$409.53** per child to the basic monthly rate for each dependent child under age 18. If the surviving spouse is entitled to Aid & Attendance, add **$409.53** to the basic monthly rate. If the surviving spouse is Permanently Housebound, add **$191.85** to the basic monthly rate.

Enlisted Veteran Pay Grades E-1 to E-9

Monthly Payment Rates
Effective December 1, 2024

Veteran's Pay Grade	Monthly Payment (in U.S. $)
E-1, E-2, E-3, E-4, E-5, E-6	1,653.07
E-7	1,710.20
E-8	1,805.47
E-9 regular	1,883.00
E-9 special capacity Veteran served as: • Sergeant Major of the Army or Marine Corps, or • Senior enlisted adviser of the Navy, or • Chief Master Sergeant of the Air Force, or • Master Chief Petty Officer of the Coast Guard	2,032.67

Added or Increased Amounts
If this description is true...

Description	Adjusted Payment (in U.S. $)
The veteran had a pay grade of E-1 to E-7, a VA disability rating of totally disabling, and spouse was married to the veteran for at least 8 years	Add $351.02
The veteran had a pay grade of E-8 or E-9, a VA disability rating of totally disabling, and the spouse was married to the veteran for at least 8 years	Increase payment to $2,004.09
You have 1 or more children under 18	Add $409.53 per child

Warrant Officer Pay Grades W-1 to W-4

Monthly Payment Rates

Veteran's Pay Grade	Monthly Payment (in U.S. $)
W-1	1,745.61
W-2	1,814.98
W-3	1,868.03
W-4	1,976.88

Added or Increased Amounts
If this description is true...

Description	Adjusted Payment (in U.S. $)
The veteran had a VA disability rating of totally disabling and the spouse was married to the veteran for at least 8 years	Increase payment to $2,004.09
You have 1 or more children under 18	Add $409.53 per child

Officer Pay Grades O-1 to O-10
Monthly Payment Rates

Veteran's Pay Grade	Monthly Payment (in U.S. $)
O-1	1,745.61
O-2	1,805.47
O-3	1,929.24
O-4	2,044.89
O-5	2,250.36
O-6	2,537.44
O-7	2,738.36
O-8	3,008.18
O-9	3,217.69
O-10 regular	3,529.26
O-10 special capacity (Veteran served as: Chairman of the Joint Chiefs of Staff, or Chief of Saff of the Army or Air Force, or Chief of Naval Operations, or Commandant of the Marine Corps	3,787.77

Added or Increased Amounts

If this description is true...

Description	Adjusted Payment (in U.S. $)
The veteran had a pay grade of O-1 to O-3, a VA service-connected disability rating of totally disabling, and spouse was married to the veteran for at least 8 years	Increase payment to $2,004.09
You have 1 or more children under 18	Add $409.53 per child

Determination of Pay Grade

With respect to a veteran who died in the active military, naval, or air service, such veteran's pay grade shall be determined as of the date of such veteran's death, or as of the date of promotion after death, while in a missing status.

With respect to a veteran who did not die in the active military, naval, or air service, such veteran's pay grade shall be determined as of:

- The time of such veteran's last discharge or release from active duty under conditions other than dishonorable; or
- The time of such veteran's discharge or release from any period of active duty for training or inactive duty training, if such veteran's death results from a service-connected disability incurred during such period, and if such veteran was not thereafter discharged or released under conditions other than dishonorable from active duty.
- If a veteran has satisfactorily served on active duty for a period of six months or more in a pay grade higher than that specified in the previous paragraphs of this section, and any subsequent discharge or release from active duty was under conditions other than dishonorable, the higher pay grade shall be used if it will result in greater monthly payments to such veteran's surviving spouse under this chapter. The determination as to whether an individual has served satisfactorily for the required period in a higher pay grade shall be made by the Secretary of the department in which such higher pay grade was held.

DIC Payments to Children

Surviving, Unmarried Adult Child of a Veteran, When the Veteran's Surviving Spouse is Also Eligible for DIC

VA will make this monthly payment to you separately as the adult surviving child in addition to the eligible surviving spouse's compensation.

Monthly Payment Rates
Effective December 1, 2024

Child Status	Monthly Payment (in U.S. $)
Child between 18 and 23 who's in a qualified school program	346.95
Helpless child over 18 (An adult child who became permanently unable to support themselves before age 18)	697.96

Whenever there is no surviving spouse of a deceased veteran entitled to DIC, DIC shall be paid in equal shares to the children of the deceased veteran at the following monthly rates (effective December 1, 2024):

Number of Veteran's Eligible Children	Monthly Rate for Each Child (in U.S. $)	Total Monthly Payment (in U.S. $)
1	697.96	697.96
2	502.04	1,004.07
3	436.74	1,310.23
4	389.80	1,559.21
5	361.64	1,808.19
6	342.86	2,057.17
7	329.45	2,306.15
8	319.39	2,555.13
9	311.57	2,804.11

Added amounts:
- For each additional eligible child in a family of 10 or more children, add $248.98.
- For each helpless child over 18, add $409.53 to your monthly rate above. This will be your total monthly payment. For example, if there are 2 eligible surviving children, and one of them is a helpless child, the rate for that child would be $911.57($502.04 + $409.53).

DIC Payments for Parents

DIC Rates If Only 1 Parent Is Alive

These rates apply if you qualify for VA Dependency and Indemnity Compensation (DIC) as a surviving parent and both of the following conditions are true:

1. You are the only surviving parent of the veteran.
2. You are either not remarried or you are remarried and living with your spouse.

Note: Your yearly income refers to the total amount you earn during a full calendar year (January 1 to December 31). This includes all income sources such as wages, salary, earnings from investments, rental properties, gifts, income from dependents living in your home, and certain retirement benefits. If you are remarried and living with your spouse, your spouse's income is also considered.

DIC Rates for Surviving Parent (If Only One Parent is Alive)
Effective December 1, 2024

$1,900 to $4,100

Yearly Income Limit (in U.S. $)	Beginning Monthly Rate (in U.S. $)	Yearly Income Limit (in U.S. $)	Beginning Monthly Rate (in U.S. $)	Yearly Income Limit (in U.S. $)	Beginning Monthly Rate (in U.S. $)
$800	$819	$2,000	$723	$3,000	$643
$900	$811	$2,100	$715	$3,100	$635
$1,000	$803	$2,200	$707	$3,200	$627
$1,100	$795	$2,300	$699	$3,300	$619
$1,200	$787	$2,400	$691	$3,400	$611
$1,300	$779	$2,500	$683	$3,500	$603
$1,400	$771	$2,600	$675	$3,600	$595
$1,500	$763	$2,700	$667	$3,700	$587
$1,600	$755	$2,800	$659	$3,800	$579
$1,700	$747	$2,900	$651	$3,900	$571
$1,800	$739	$3,000	$643	$4,000	$563
$1,900	$731	$3,100	$635	$4,100	$555

$4,200 to $7,100

Yearly Income Limit (in U.S. $)	Beginning Monthly Rate (in U.S. $)	Yearly Income Limit (in U.S. $)	Beginning Monthly Rate (in U.S. $)	Yearly Income Limit (in U.S. $)	Beginning Monthly Rate (in U.S. $)
$4,200	$547	$5,200	$467	$6,200	$387
$4,300	$539	$5,300	$459	$6,300	$379
$4,400	$531	$5,400	$451	$6,400	$371
$4,500	$523	$5,500	$443	$6,500	$363

$4,600	$515	$5,600	$435	$6,600	$355
$4,700	$507	$5,700	$427	$6,700	$347
$4,800	$499	$5,800	$419	$6,800	$339
$4,900	$491	$5,900	$411	$6,900	$331
$5,000	$483	$6,000	$403	$7,000	$323
$5,100	$475	$6,100	$395	$7,100	$315

$7,200 to $10,100

Yearly Income Limit (in U.S. $)	Beginning Monthly Rate (in U.S. $)	Yearly Income Limit (in U.S. $)	Beginning Monthly Rate (in U.S. $)	Yearly Income Limit (in U.S. $)	Beginning Monthly Rate (in U.S. $)
$7,200	$307	$8,200	$227	$9,200	$147
$7,300	$299	$8,300	$219	$9,300	$139
$7,400	$291	$8,400	$211	$9,400	$131
$7,500	$283	$8,500	$203	$9,500	$123
$7,600	$275	$8,600	$195	$9,600	$115
$7,700	$267	$8,700	$187	$9,700	$107
$7,800	$259	$8,800	$179	$9,800	$99
$7,900	$251	$8,900	$171	$9,900	$91
$8,000	$243	$9,000	$163	$10,000	$83
$8,100	$235	$9,100	$155	$10,100	$75

$10,200 and above

Yearly Income Limit (in U.S. $)	Beginning Monthly Rate (in U.S. $)	Yearly Income Limit (in U.S. $)	Beginning Monthly Rate (in U.S. $)	Yearly Income Limit (in U.S.$)	Beginning Monthly Rate (in U.S. $)
$10,200	$67	$10,500	$43	$10,800	$19
$10,300	$59	$10,600	$35	$10,900	$11
$10,400	$51	$10,700	$27	$10,974	$5.08
If living with spouse: $10,975 to $25,936	$5	If not living with spouse: $10,975 to $19,295	$5		

DIC Rates If Both Parents Are Alive

If the eligible parent does not live with a spouse

These rates apply if you are eligible for VA DIC as a surviving parent and both of the following conditions are true:
1. Both you and the other surviving parent of the veteran are alive.
2. You are not living with the other surviving parent of the veteran or with a current spouse.

Note: Your yearly income is defined as the total amount of money you earn during one calendar year (January 1 to December 31). This includes all income sources such as wages, salary, investment income, rental income, gifts, income from dependents living in your home, and certain retirement payments. If you are remarried and living with your spouse, your spouse's income is also included in the calculation.

$8000 to $4,300

Yearly Income Limit (in U.S. $)	Beginning Monthly Rate (in U.S. $)	Yearly Income Limit (in U.S. $)	Beginning Monthly Rate (in U.S. $)	Yearly Income Limit (in U.S. $)	Beginning Monthly Rate (in U.S. $)
$800	$594	$2,000	$498	$3,200	$402
$900	$586	$2,100	$490	$3,300	$394
$1,000	$578	$2,200	$482	$3,400	$386
$1,100	$570	$2,300	$474	$3,500	$378
$1,200	$562	$2,400	$466	$3,600	$370
$1,300	$554	$2,500	$458	$3,700	$362
$1,400	$546	$2,600	$450	$3,800	$354
$1,500	$538	$2,700	$442	$3,900	$346
$1,600	$530	$2,800	$434	$4,000	$338
$1,700	$522	$2,900	$426	$4,100	$330
$1,800	$514	$3,000	$418	$4,200	$322
$1,900	$506	$3,100	$410	$4,300	$314

$4,400 to $7,300

Yearly Income Limit (in U.S. $)	Beginning Monthly Rate (in U.S. $)	Yearly Income Limit (in U.S. $)	Beginning Monthly Rate (in U.S. $)	Yearly Income Limit (in U.S. $)	Beginning Monthly Rate (in U.S. $)
$4,400	$306	$5,400	$226	$6,400	$146
$4,500	$298	$5,500	$218	$6,500	$138
$4,600	$290	$5,600	$210	$6,600	$130
$4,700	$282	$5,700	$202	$6,700	$122
$4,800	$274	$5,800	$194	$6,800	$114
$4,900	$266	$5,900	$186	$6,900	$106
$5,000	$258	$6,000	$178	$7,000	$98
$5,100	$250	$6,100	$170	$7,100	$90
$5,200	$242	$6200	$162	$7,200	$82
$5,300	$234	$6,300	$154	$7,300	$74

$7,400 and above

Yearly Income Limit (in U.S. $)	Beginning Monthly Rate (in U.S. $)	Yearly Income Limit (in U.S. $)	Beginning Monthly Rate (in U.S. $)	Yearly Income Limit (in U.S. $)	Beginning Monthly Rate (in U.S. $)
$7,400	$66	$7,600	$50	$8,000	$18
$7,500	$58	$7,700	$42	$8,100	$10
$7,600	$50	$7,800	$34	$8,162	$5.04
$7,700	$42	$7,900	$26	$8,163 to $19,295	$5
$7,800	$34	$8,000	$18		
$7,900	$26	$8,100	$10		

If the eligible parent lives with the Veteran's other parent or a current spouse

These rates apply to you if you are eligible for VA DIC as a surviving parent and both of the following conditions are met:
1. Both you and the veteran's other surviving parent are alive.
2. You are living with the veteran's other surviving parent or a current spouse

Note: Your yearly income refers to the total amount you earn during one calendar year (from January 1 to December 31). This includes income from all sources, such as wages, salary, investment income, rental income, gifts, income from dependents living in your home, and certain retirement payments. If you are remarried and living with your spouse, your spouse's income will also be included.

$1,000 to $3,900

Yearly Income Limit (in U.S. $)	Beginning Monthly Rate (in U.S. $)	Yearly Income Limit (in U.S. $)	Beginning Monthly Rate (in U.S. $)	Yearly Income Limit (in U.S. $)	Beginning Monthly Rate (in U.S. $)
$1,000	$560	$2,000	$480	$3,000	$400
$1,100	$552	$2,100	$472	$3,100	$392
$1,200	$544	$2,200	$464	$3,200	$384
$1,300	$536	$2,300	$456	$3,300	$376
$1,400	$528	$2,400	$448	$3,400	$368
$1,500	$520	$2,500	$440	$3,500	$360
$1,600	$512	$2,600	$432	$3,600	$352
$1,700	$504	$2,700	$424	$3,700	$344
$1,800	$496	$2,800	$416	$3,800	$336
$1,900	$488	$2,900	$408	$3,900	$328

$4,000 and above

Yearly Income Limit (in U.S. $)	Beginning Monthly Rate (in U.S. $)	Yearly Income Limit (in U.S. $)	Beginning Monthly Rate (in U.S. $)	Yearly Income Limit (in U.S. $)	Beginning Monthly Rate (in U.S. $)
$4,000	$320	$5,000	$240	$6,000	$160
$4,100	$312	$5,100	$232	$6,100	$152
$4,200	$304	$5,200	$224	$6,200	$144
$4,300	$296	$5,300	$216	$6,300	$136
$4,400	$288	$5,400	$208	$6,400	$128
$4,500	$280	$5,500	$200	$6,500	$120
$4,600	$272	$5,600	$192	$6,600	$112
$4,700	$264	$5,700	$184	$6,700	$104
$4,800	$256	$5,800	$176	$6,800	$96
$4,900	$248	$5,900	$168	$6,900	$88
$7,000	$80	$7,100	$72	$7,200	$64
$7,300	$56	$7,400	$48	$7,500	$40
$7,600	$32	$7,700	$24	$7,800	$16
$7,900	$8	$7,937	$5.04	$7,938 to $25,936	$5

Miscellaneous Information Regarding Income Limitations for Parents

The VA may require, as a condition of granting or continuing DIC to a parent that such parent, other than one who has attained 72 years of age and has been paid DIC during two consecutive calendar years, file for a calendar year with the VA, a report showing the total income which such parent expects to receive in that year, and the total income which such parent received in the preceding year. The parent or parents shall notify the VA whenever there is a material change in annual income.

In determining income under this section, all payments of any kind, or from any source shall be included except:
- Payments of a death gratuity.
- Donations from public or private relief or welfare organizations.
- Payments under this chapter (DIC), Chapter 11 of Title 38, United States Code (Disability Compensation), and Chapter 15 of Title 38, United States Code (Non- Service-Connected Disability/Death Pension);
- Payments under policies of servicemembers group life insurance, United States Government life insurance, or national service life insurance, and payments of servicemen's indemnity.
- 10% of the number of payments to an individual under public or private retirement, annuity, endowment, or similar plans or programs.

Amounts equal to amounts paid by a parent of a deceased veteran for:
- A deceased spouse's just debts.
- The expenses of the spouse's last illness, to the extent such expenses are not reimbursed under Chapter 51 of Title 38 of the United States Code.

- The expenses of the spouse's burial to the extent that such expenses are not reimbursed under Chapter 23 or Chapter 51 of Title 38 of the United States Code.
- Reimbursements of any kind for any casualty loss (as defined in regulations which the VA shall prescribe), but the amount excluded under this clause may not exceed the greater of the fair market value or the reasonable replacement value of the property involved at the time immediately preceding the loss.

Amounts equal to amounts paid by a parent of a deceased veteran for:
- The expenses of the veteran's last illness, and expenses of such veteran's burial, to the extent that such expenses are not reimbursed under Chapter 23 of Title 38 of the United States Code.
- Profit realized from the disposition of real or personal property other than during business.
- Payments received for discharge of jury duty or obligatory civic duties.
- Payments of annuities elected under Subchapter I of Chapter 73 of Title 10.

Where a fraction of a dollar is involved, annual income shall be fixed at the next lower dollar. The VA may provide by regulation for the exclusion from income under this section of amounts paid by a parent for unusual medical expenses.

CHAPTER 37

SURVIVOR BENEFITS: SURVIVOR BENEFIT PLAN (SBP) & SSIA

Survivor Benefit Plan Overview

The Survivor Benefit Plan (SBP) lets retirees make sure after their death there's a continuous lifetime annuity for their dependents. The annuity is based on a percentage of retired paid and is called SBP. The annuity is paid to an eligible beneficiary, and it pays eligible survivors an inflation-adjusted monthly income.

A military retiree pays premiums for SBP coverage when they retire. Premiums are paid from gross retired pay and don't count as income. There are less tax and out-of-pocket costs for SBP as a result. The premiums are partially funded by the government.

The costs of operating the program are taken on by the government, so the average premiums are usually significantly below what it would cost to get a conventional insurance policy. SBP can be a good option for most retirees, but government contributions are based on assumptions in average cases and may not apply to all cases.

The maximum SBP annuity for a spouse is based on 55% of the member's retired pay. If the member retires under REDUX, it's the pay the member would have received under the high- three retirement system. A smaller amount may be chosen.

Eligible children can also be SBP beneficiaries, alone or added to spouse coverage. If children are added to spouse coverage, the children receive benefits only if the spouse dies or otherwise isn't eligible to receive the annuity. Children equally divide a benefit that is 55% of the member's elected base amount.

Child coverage is somewhat inexpensive because children only get benefits while they are considered eligible dependents.

Coverage is also available for a former spouse, or if the retiree has no spouse or children, for an insurable interest, like a parent or business partner.

SBP and Estate Planning

Retired pay can be an asset. It stops when a retiree dies, but no one will know when that might be, so SBP can be a source of protection, similar to life insurance. There are differences in SBP premiums and benefits compared to insurance plans.

Like life insurance, SBP protects survivors against a loss of financial security when a retired member dies. It also protects survivors against the potential of outliving the benefit.

SBP also protects against the risk of inflation through Cost-of-Living Adjustments or COLAs. SBP alone is not a complete estate plan, but it can be an important part of a larger plan.

Eligible Beneficiaries

When you apply for retirement, you may have been asked to complete a Data for Payment of Retired Personnel Form. On that form, you would choose a beneficiary. The types you can choose from are detailed below.

Spouse Only

The most common election for a retiree to make is for only his or her spouse to be covered based on full retired pay. Cost is calculated at a maximum of 6.5% of the elected level of coverage.

If you have an eligible spouse and you choose anything less than full coverage, the spouse's notarized signature must be obtained for the election to be valid.

Spouse coverage is designed to provide a lifetime monthly income for your surviving spouse after you diet.

The SBP annuity is determined by the base amount you elect. The base may range from a minimum of $300 up to a maximum of full retired pay. The annuity is 55% of the base amount. The base amount and the payments to the surviving spouse will generally increase at the same time and by the same percentage that COLAs are made to retired pay.

Your surviving spouse may remarry after age 55 and continue to receive SBP payments for life. If your surviving spouse remarries before age 55, SBP payments will stop. Payments may resume if the marriage later ends due to death or divorce

Former Spouse

SBP allows election of coverage for former spouses. Costs and benefits under this option are identical to those for spouse coverage.

When former spouse coverage is elected, the current spouse must be informed. Only one SBP election may be made. If there is more than one former spouse, the member must specify who will receive coverage.

Former spouse and children coverage may also be elected. The children covered are the eligible children from the marriage of the member to the covered former spouse. The children will only receive payments if the former spouse remarries before age 55 or dies. Eligible children will divide 55% of the covered retired pay in equal shares.

Child Only

This option pays SBP to your child regardless of your marital status. Your children will get the SBP until they turn 18 or age 22, if a full-time, unmarried student. Children mentally or physically incapable of self-support remain eligible, while unmarried, for as long as the incapacitation exists.

Disabled Dependent

You can contribute your SBP payments to a Special Needs Trust (SNT) to allow a disabled dependent to continue receiving federal disability payments.

A SNT is a trust designated for beneficiaries who are disabled, either physically or mentally. It is written so the beneficiary can enjoy the use of property that is held in the trust for their benefit. At the same time, it allows the beneficiary to receive essential needs-based government benefits.

CSB/Redux Cost and Benefits

CSB/REDUX is the only retirement system that includes a re-adjustment to its retired pay amount. At age 62, retired pay is recomputed to what it would have been under High-36. Also, at age 62, a one-time COLA adjustment is made that applies the cumulative effects of High-36 COLA (CPI) to the new retirement base. Afterwards, future COLAs are again set to CPI minus 1%.

Special Survivor Indemnity Allowance (SSIA)

Surviving family members of some veterans are entitled to the Dependency and Indemnity Compensation (DIC) benefit from VA. The benefit is for survivors of those who died on active duty or were severely disabled. Military retirees can elect to provide a monthly income for their family members if they die first, which is known as the Survivor Benefit Plan.

Federal regulators made the decision that a survivor receiving both of these payments is essentially receiving two federal incomes from the same source, which is illegal. To prevent this from happening, Congress created the Special Survivor Indemnity Allowance (SSIA). The goal of the program was to help survivors continue receiving a portion of that money.

For a number of years, the DoD withheld the amount of the DIC payment from a survivor's SBT check. In 2020, a law created the SSIA, which was previously a temporary program. Now, the SSIA is phased in through 2021 and 2022 and by 2023 there won't be an SBP/DIC offset anymore.

For 2022, affected survivors received the full DIC amount from the VA each month. DFAS will pay the SBP payment with 1/3 of the DIC payment deducted from it, as well as an SSIA payment up to $346 a month.

Would You Like Additional Copies Of
<u>What Every Veteran Should Know</u>?

Simply tear out this form, and:
Phone 309-757-7760 or Fax 309-278-5304
Mail To: VETERANS INFORMATION SERVICE
P.O. Box 111
East Moline, IL 61244-0111

ORDER ONLINE AT: www.vetsinfoservice.com

☐   Yes! Send me _____ copies of *"What Every Veteran Should Know"*, at $30.00 each (shipping & handling included). I request the _____ (specify: <u>current already released 2025,</u> or <u>pre-reserve 2026</u>) edition. New annual books are published every March 1st.

☐   Yes! I would like to subscribe to *"What Every Veteran Should Know"* monthly supplement (an 8-page newsletter which keeps your book up-to-date), and receive _____ copies of all 12 monthly issues (1 year) for $38.00 per subscription (shipping & handling included).

☐   Yes! I want to save money, and receive both the book and the monthly supplement. I would like _____ sets, at $65 per set (shipping & handling included).

Name   Current Customer ID?

Address

City / State / Zip Code

Telephone Number   E-mail Address

Amount Enclosed   Daytime Phone # (including area code)

Method of Payment:

☐ Check   ☐ Visa   ☐ MasterCard   ☐ Money Order

Credit Card #   3-digit CVV   Expiration Date
(Month/Year)

Signature

Thank you for your order!
If you have any questions, feel free to contact us at
(309) 757-7760
www.vetsinfoservice.com - Email: help@vetsinfoservice.com

Would You Like Additional Copies Of
What Every Veteran Should Know?

Simply tear out this form, and:
Phone 309-757-7760 or Fax 309-278-5304
Mail To: VETERANS INFORMATION SERVICE
P.O. Box 111
East Moline, IL 61244-0111

ORDER ONLINE AT: www.vetsinfoservice.com

☐ Yes! Send me _____ copies of *"What Every Veteran Should Know"*, at $30.00 each (shipping & handling included). I request the _____ (specify: <u>current already released 2025,</u> or <u>pre-reserve 2026</u>) edition. New annual books are published every March 1st.

☐ Yes! I would like to subscribe to *"What Every Veteran Should Know"* monthly supplement (an 8-page newsletter which keeps your book up-to-date), and receive _____ copies of all 12 monthly issues (1 year) for $38.00 per subscription (shipping & handling included).

☐ Yes! I want to save money, and receive both the book and the monthly supplement. I would like _____ sets, at $65 per set (shipping & handling included).

Name   Current Customer ID?

Address

City / State / Zip Code

Telephone Number   E-mail Address

Amount Enclosed   Daytime Phone # (including area code)

Method of Payment:

☐ Check   ☐ Visa   ☐ MasterCarc   ☐ Money Orde

Credit Card #   3-digit CVV   Expiration Date
(Month/Year)

Signature
Thank you for your order!
If you have any questions, feel free to contact us at
(309) 757-7760
www.vetsinfoservice.com - Email: help@vetsinfoservice.com

Would You Like Additional Copies Of
<u>What Every Veteran Should Know</u>?

Simply tear out this form, and:
Phone 309-757-7760 or Fax 309-278-5304
Mail To: VETERANS INFORMATION SERVICE
P.O. Box 111
East Moline, IL 61244-0111

ORDER ONLINE AT: www.vetsinfoservice.com

☐ Yes! Send me _____ copies of *"What Every Veteran Should Know"*, at $30.00 each (shipping & handling included). I request the _____ (specify: <u>current already released 2025,</u> or <u>pre-reserve 2026</u>) edition. New annual books are published every March 1st.

☐ Yes! I would like to subscribe to *"What Every Veteran Should Know"* monthly supplement (an 8-page newsletter which keeps your book up-to-date), and receive _____ copies of all 12 monthly issues (1 year) for $38.00 per subscription (shipping & handling included).

☐ Yes! I want to save money, and receive both the book and the monthly supplement. I would like _____ sets, at $65 per set (shipping & handling included).

Name   Current Customer ID?

Address

City / State / Zip Code

Telephone Number   E-mail Address

Amount Enclosed   Daytime Phone   (including area code)

Method of Payment:

☐ Check   ☐ Visa   ☐ MasterCard   ☐ Money Order

Credit Card #   3-digit CVV   Expiration Date
(Month/Year)

Signature

Thank you for your order!
If you have any questions, feel free to contact us at
(309) 757-7760
www.vetsinfoservice.com - Email: help@vetsinfoservice.com

Would You Like Additional Copies Of
<u>What Every Veteran Should Know</u>?

Simply tear out this form, and:
Phone 309-757-7760 or Fax 309-278-5304
Mail To: VETERANS INFORMATION SERVICE
P.O. Box 111
East Moline, IL 61244-0111

ORDER ONLINE AT: www.vetsinfoservice.com

☐   Yes! Send me _____ copies of *"What Every Veteran Should Know"*, at $30.00 each (shipping & handling included). I request the _____ (specify: <u>current already released 2025,</u> or <u>pre-reserve 2026</u>) edition. New annual books are published every March 1st.

☐   Yes! I would like to subscribe to *"What Every Veteran Should Know"* monthly supplement (an 8-page newsletter which keeps your book up-to-date), and receive _____ copies of all 12 monthly issues (1 year) for $38.00 per subscription (shipping & handling included).

☐   Yes! I want to save money, and receive both the book and the monthly supplement. I would like _____ sets, at $65 per set (shipping & handling included).

_____

Name   Current Customer ID?

_____

Address

_____

City / State / Zip Code

_____

Telephone Number   E-mail Address

_____

Amount Enclosed   Daytime Phone # (including area code)

Method of Payment:

☐ Check   ☐ Visa   ☐ MasterCarc   ☐ Money Orde

_____

Credit Card #   3-digit CVV   Expiration Date
(Month/Year)

_____

Signature

Thank you for your order!
If you have any questions, feel free to contact us at
(309) 757-7760
www.vetsinfoservice.com - Email: help@vetsinfoservice.com